Fieldwork in South Asia

Fieldwork in South Asia

MEMORIES, MOMENTS, AND EXPERIENCES

Edited by

Sarit K. Chaudhuri
Sucheta Sen Chaudhuri

First published in 2014 by

SAGE Publications India Pvt Ltd
B1/I-1 Mohan Cooperative Industrial Area
Mathura Road, New Delhi 110 044, India
www.sagepub.in

SAGE Publications Inc
2455 Teller Road
Thousand Oaks, California 91320, USA

SAGE Publications Ltd
1 Oliver's Yard, 55 City Road
London EC1Y 1SP, United Kingdom

SAGE Publications Asia-Pacific Pte Ltd
3 Church Street
#10-04 Samsung Hub
Singapore 049483

Published by Vivek Mehra for SAGE Publications India Pvt Ltd, typeset in 10/12 pts Adobe Garamond Pro by Diligent Typesetter, Delhi and printed at Saurabh Printers Pvt Ltd, New Delhi.

Library of Congress Cataloging-in-Publication Data

Fieldwork in South Asia : memories, moments, and experiences / edited by Sarit K. Chaudhuri and Sucheta Sen Chaudhuri.
    pages cm
  Includes bibliographical references and index.
    1. Ethnology—Fieldwork—South Asia. 2. Ethnologists—South Asia—Anecdotes. 3. Anthropologists—South Asia—Anecdotes. 4. Historians—South Asia—Anecdotes. 5. South Asia—Social life and customs. I. Chaudhuri, S. K. (Sarit Kumar) II. Chaudhuri, Sucheta Sen, 1963–
GN635.S57F48   306.0954—dc23   2014   2014022713

ISBN: 978-81-321-1742-1 (HB)

The SAGE Team: Supriya Das, Vandana Gupta, Nand Kumar Jha, and Dally Verghese

This book is dedicated to
Prof. A.C. Bhagabati,
Prof. T. Mibang, and
Prof. T.B. Subba
whose works and interactions have always inspired us.

Thank you for choosing a SAGE product! If you have any comment, observation or feedback, I would like to personally hear from you. Please write to me at contactceo@sagepub.in

—Vivek Mehra, Managing Director and CEO,
SAGE Publications India Pvt Ltd, New Delhi

Bulk Sales

SAGE India offers special discounts for purchase of books in bulk. We also make available special imprints and excerpts from our books on demand.

For orders and enquiries, write to us at

Marketing Department
SAGE Publications India Pvt Ltd
B1/I-1, Mohan Cooperative Industrial Area
Mathura Road, Post Bag 7
New Delhi 110044, India
E-mail us at marketing@sagepub.in

Get to know more about SAGE, be invited to SAGE events, get on our mailing list. Write today to marketing@sagepub.in

This book is also available as an e-book.

Contents

List of Abbreviations

AAA	American Anthropological Association
ADC	Additional Deputy Commissioner
ASI	Anthropological Survey of India
ATM	Automatic Teller Machine
BLCC	Bunyad Literacy Community Council
BSPP	Burma Socialist Party Programme
CIA	Central Intelligence Agency
CGI	Corrugated Galvanized Iron
CNN	Cable News Network
DUDA	Department of Underdeveloped Areas
ESRC	Economic and Social Research Council
FCC	Facilitator of Community Conservation
GB	Gaun Burrah
GP	Gram Panchayat
GPS	Global Positioning System
GT	Grand Trunk
Head GB	Village Headman
IAY	Indira Awaas Yojna
ICSSR	Indian Council of Social Science Research
IFAD	International Fund for Agricultural Development
IIT/D	Indian Institute of Technology, Delhi
IIT/K	Indian Institute of Technology, Kanpur
IIT/KH	Indian Institute of Technology, Kharagpur
ILO	International Labour Organization
ILP	Inner Line Permit
IRP	Indian Reserve Police
IT	Information Technology

KIA	Kachin Independence Army
KIO	Kachin Independence Organization
Marxist CPM	Communist Party of India
MCAM	Master Craftsmen's Association of Mithila
MGNREGS	Mahatma Gandhi National Rural Employment Guarantee Scheme
MLA	Member of Legislative Asssemby
NAP	Nagaland Armed Police
NEFA	North Eastern Frontier Agency
NEHU	North-Eastern Hill University
NEPED	Nagaland Environment Protection and Economic Development
NGO	Non-governmental Organization
NNC	Naga National Council
NREGS	National Rural Employment Guarantee Scheme
NSCN	National Socialist Council of Nagaland
NST	Nagaland State Transport
PLA	Participatory Learning Analysis
PRA	Participatory Rural Assessment
PTG	Primitive Tribal Group
PWD	Public Works Department
RAP	Restricted Area Permit
RRA	Rapid Rural Appraisal
RTI	Right to Information Act
SCCI	Sialkot Chamber of Commerce and Industry
SDO	subdivisional officer
SDPT	Sialkot Dry Port Trust
SLORC	State Law and Order Restoration Council
SOAS	School of Oriental and African Studies
TMC	Trinamul Congress
TMO	Telegraphic Money Order
UN	United Nations
UNDP	United Nations Development Programme
UNICEF	United Nations Children's Fund
UTCs	Umang Taleemi Centres

Foreword

This book of essays is a timely reminder of the importance and multi-faceted depth and variety of anthropological fieldwork. Each essay evokes the experience of immersion in 'other cultures', physically and intellectually, through heart, mind, and spirit.

Taken together, they emphasize the ethnographic relationship, and act as a counterpoise to the tendency, still strong in South Asian Anthropology, to 'objectify' the people and cultures that form our subjects of study, in the colonial-era mode of hierarchical knowledge.

Modern anthropologists increasingly understand that 'objective' knowledge—in as much as this can be achieved—depends on subjective forms of knowledge, meaning an understanding of the wider social structure, including the ethnographer's place in this, and therefore also a high degree of self-knowledge.

Knowledge about other cultures emerges through relationships. This means that understanding one's own relationships is vital, in a context where even the most traditional, marginalized culture exists now in a very wide, local, and globalized social structure of external relationships carrying influence and power.

So this is, above all, a book about relationships—multi-layered relationships among people encountered in the field, the ethnographic relationship itself, with all its personal raw edges, as well as relationship with the land and even non-human realms (e.g., in Anungla Aier's and Ben Campbell's essays).

Good listening is a prerequisite for productive fieldwork. In Mandy Sadan's words, about her time among Kachins in north Burma,

> I soon learned that asking questions only resulted in receiving answers; in contrast, listening, rather than speaking, following rather than leading, led to questions, answers, discussions, and lines of thought that could not be anticipated, opening up areas of knowledge and learning that were much more vital and penetrating.

One way of understanding the emergence of post-colonial, self-reflexive anthropology is a journey towards 'objects of study' becoming subjects, able to articulate multiple viewpoints through the medium of and alongside the work of an anthropologist.

The richness and variety of viewpoints displayed in the following pages is hard to exaggerate, including several authors who emphasize the difference between doing fieldwork in a foreign country and doing it in one's own—which can be just as foreign an experience—witness Ali Khan's sensitivity to the intrusiveness of anthropological questioning in rural/industrial Pakistan, with emphasis on 'maintaining naiveté' and deconstructing the rhetoric of foreign aid and government policy.

Almost every essay touches on uncomfortable questions of unequal power, violence—most disturbingly in Debojyoti Das' personal experience of armed attack in remotest Nagaland, and even of 'the invention of tradition'—for example, Ellen Bal among Garos and A.C. Sinha on the sad shadow of ethnic cleansing in Bhutan.

But each essay also contains precious insight into the positive aspects of human societies in South Asia that many people look to anthropology for confirmation of—for example, the exceptional warmth in the accounts of Garo fieldwork by both Robbins Burling and Erik de Maaker, and the continuities in the midst of globalizing change, or Campbell's emphasis from among the Tamang in Nepal of 'the value that non-anthropologists can derive from ethnographic knowledge', especially in rethinking human relationships with land and food.

Content-wise there is a welcome emphasis here on India's north-east, along with bordering areas of Bangladesh and Burma/Myanmar, with two pieces on the Nagas, three on the Garos—in Bangladesh and Meghalaya—and one each in Bhutan, among the Riang tribe in Tripura, and among Kachins in North Burma. Other essays take us on fascinating journeys into Nepal, Sri Lanka, Pakistan, the Nicobar Islands, Ladakh, West Bengal in political transition, Harijan Madhubani painters in Bihar, and a Department of Anthropology in Kolkata, ending with a deep-delving dialogue between Ganesh Devy and Daniel Rycroft questioning Adivasi field-studies and identity.

The editors' emphasis on vast differences in social constructions of reality, along with shifting ethnographic conventions, sets the scene in the opening essay, while Arjun Guneratne reminds us how anthropology is often characterized as 'the art of making the strange familiar and the familiar strange'.

But what if we have accepted too readily the marginalized place anthropologists tend to accept for themselves? Actually, in terms of what the ethnographic relationship has taught other professions, and how anthropology has helped reveal different cultures to each other, if not to themselves, our discipline has had a major influence on how people think. But not yet nearly as much as it could!

When one of my main teachers, J.P.S. Uberoi, asked once in a memorable lecture in London—Why do anthropologists still tend to study mainly marginal groups and people with much less power than themselves? Why don't they study groups of equal, or even superior social status?—this prised open a major set of possibilities, which has inspired my work ever since—a potentiality for anthropology to play a much larger role in analysing the power structures and systems of values and beliefs that characterize modern mainstream societies, from an independent position that maintains an overview of the vast differences and possibilities of human societies.

What we understand about a society we live in for fieldwork may make us an 'expert' in that culture—however limited we may know our expertise to be! But actually, potentially, we learn even more from the people we relate with there about our own culture, and if we can tap into this, and into marginalized cultures' knowledge about mainstream society—often from very bitter experience of how it has treated them—anthropology can give the world what many people look to it for: insight into how to deconstruct corrupt power structures and demonstrate community that works.

The marginalized groups whose realities are opened to view here show many ways of being, sharing, relating, economizing, ... that the world's policy-makers would do well if they start to listen to; and anthropologists should not be shy of seeking fresh ways to help people open their minds to possibilities outside today's perennial media-feed, suggesting that gentler, more harmonious ways of being human actually do exist, in plenty.

Felix Padel
Eminent anthropologist and activist who studied in Oxford and
Delhi School of Economics and also remained
affiliated to University of Sussex, UK

Preface

Our first anthropological fieldwork exposure was among the Totos of North Bengal, a small tribe located in a single village (called Totopara) on the bordering area between Bengal and Bhutan. Almost three decades back, our revered teacher, Hirendra Nath Chakrabarty, took the whole batch of undergraduate students of the University of Calcutta to that village. And later we came to know that late B.K. Roy Burman developed his concept of 'bridge and buffer communities' based on his doctoral research among the Totos who are today categorized as Primitive Tribal Group (PTG) as per the constitutional provision of the Government of India. Later on as postgraduate students of the Department of Anthropology of the same university, we had chances to work among the Konda Reddis and Savaras of Andhra Pradesh under the guidance of late P.K. Bhowmick. Both the teachers actually tried to teach us how to do fieldwork among the communities which were far away from our own physical location and some of whose languages were even unknown to us. Both our teachers taught us the art and craft of understanding 'other culture' but in two different ways. In contemporary methodological vocabulary all these attempts may be bracketed as looking for 'exotic culture' or 'other culture' given the remoteness of the habitat of those tribes or even contested constitutional tag of PTG attached to all these three tribes though for us it was a sincere effort to understand the diversity of the tribal world, which also contributed to the growth of human civilization.

What is important in this brief retrospection is that every time we went to work or tried to engage with the communities on different researchable issues, we found that we need to move beyond the textual boundaries which a typical or even advanced methodological textbook usually prescribes. Every fieldwork generates new set of contextual questions and surfaces new challenges which we need to negotiate based on our experiential wisdom making fieldwork more a collective engagement with people and places.

Beginners need to take care of methodological books but the moment one likes to grow as a professional or plans to undertake research, one has to look for the texts which emerged out of the actual field experiences as those writings can only open up new vistas to understand complexity of the issues involved in every fieldwork to locate the self or the other.

In later course, being teachers in the university system, we encouraged students/researchers of different levels to introduce more with experience of eminent scholars and made them aware about the new waves of critiques related to poetics and politics of ethnographic representation. So we found students and research scholars were highly benefitted by reading such writings of M.N. Srinivas, T.N. Madan, T.N. Pandey, late B.K. Roy Burman, P.K. Mishra, Surajit Sinha, Yogesh Atal, Edward Jay, Baidyanath Saraswati, Meenakshi Thapan, Vinay Srivastava, Kirin Narayan, and many more eminent scholars who largely shared their dense field memories and experiences in the context of India.

This has actually fuelled in us an idea of a book which will not be confined to the field narratives from India rather it would encompass a wider region called South Asia by bringing many diverse experiences of scholars together. Fortunately, we have got the chance to discuss this idea with many scholars from India and abroad and immediately received huge insights and even instant offer to extend support in the form of contributing essays. We prepared a concept note and circulated the same to many possible and potential contributors whom we knew personally or were introduced by others. This process we had initiated almost three years back with a plan that this volume may see the light of the day by the end of 2011 or beginning of 2012. In the process we missed some eminent anthropologists who were preoccupied with responsibilities but each of them appreciated our attempt. Most of such messages are still in our mailbox sent by scholars such as Ralph Nicholas, William Sax, Philippe Ramirez, Nadim Omar, Fabrizio Ferrari, Chas Mckhann, Bernard Bate, Ashley South, Sumit Jain, and late Anjan Ghosh. We are greatly indebted to T.B. Subba who introduced us to Arjun Guneratne and Ben Campbell, having long experience of working in Sri Lanka and Nepal. We are grateful to University Florence Press for giving permission to reprint Guneratne's revised essay originally published in the book *The Anthropologist and the Native: Essays for Gananath Obeyesekere*, which was edited by H.L. Seneviratne in 2009. When we approached Robbins Burling (whom we address as Rob) to republish his essay on Return to Rengsanggri, he immediately agreed and it was again T.B. Subba, the then editor of North-Eastern Hill University, *Journal of Social Sciences and Humanities*, who gave us immediate permission for the same.

We wanted to ensure that this volume contains a blend of well-known senior scholars and upcoming younger scholars who have made a significant landmark in their own ways. Naturally, along with persons, such as Robbins Burling, Arjun Guneratne, Bell Campbell, A.C. Sinha, Vijoy Sahay, G. Devy, Daniel Rycroft, Ellen Bal, Ali Khan, Erik de Maaker, and Gautam Bera, we have essays written by Mandy Sadan, Bhaskar Chakrabarti, Arnab Das, Debojyoti Das, Anungla Aier, Suman Nath, Neel Rekha, and Abeer Gupta. We must disclose the fact that Abeer became part of our academic venture very recently. His presentation in a recent international seminar on transborder communities and culture in Asia was highly impressive and incidentally we were looking for someone who could share experience of working among the people of Leh and Ladakh as the reviewer suggested. He gracefully accepted our offer to contribute an essay. Finally when we sent the Author's Approval Form of SAGE to all our writers, we received a mail from Saiful Islam of University of Dhaka that because of prolonged delay he had published his paper in a journal. We are fully sympathetic to his necessity as a young scholar. But that was the only essay on Bangladesh and hardly 15 days remained with us to deliver the final manuscript to the commissioning person of SAGE. Thankfully it was Ellen Bal of University of Amsterdam who came to our rescue with a valuable essay within the scheduled time frame on the Garos of Bangladesh for which she is known all over the academic world by sacrificing her academic break from her extremely tight schedule. Special thanks to our friend Ala Uddin, an Anthropologist at the University of Chittagong, who took special initiative so that we could have another valuable essay on the Mundas of Bangladesh by a scholar from University of Dhaka but because of space constraints we could not incorporate the same. For similar reason we missed Rycroft's second valuable essay.

We like to place it in records that eventually, finalization of our manuscript got delayed because of an unprecedented incident in our academic institution but we would like to gratefully acknowledge all our contributors who stood with us and showed great patience to ensure that like modern ethnography, production of a book with scholars of such diverse nation-states has to be a collective engagement threaded with mutual trust and commitment.

We must thank Sugata Ghosh, Rekha Natarajan, Sutapa Ghosh, Supriya Das, Vandana Gupta and other members (Radhika Haswani and Guneet Kaur) of SAGE Publications who tried to ensure that this book must see the light of the day. We have greatly benefitted from the comments of both internal and external reviewers on the basis of which we had to rework and focus on writing Introduction as well as reframing essays in the book. We could not cover all regions of India due to space constraints. However, we would like to deeply acknowledge the help extended by our friend, Debarshi Nath of Tezpur University for close reading of the Introduction chapter; Ratna Tayeng, and L.P. Munia—doctoral scholars of the Department of Anthropology, Rajiv Gandhi University, for helping us in finalizing documentation sections of various essays and Glossary. Special thanks to our friends as well as former and present colleagues of Rajiv Gandhi University, such as J.L. Dawar, Deepak Singh, P.K. Kuri, Vandana Upadhyay, Asima Ranjan Parhi, M. Hussain, Bodhisattava Kar, Arup Jyoti Saikia, and Vibha Joshi, for their help and inspiring words. Finally, we fondly like to place in record the name of our son, Purab Riddhi, who always took keen interest in all our academic engagements.

Hope this book will gain wide attention among the scholars who value the strength of insights which field-based researchers can generate to understand the diverse realities of society and culture located within and across the region called South Asia.

Sarit K. Chaudhuri
Sucheta Sen Chaudhuri

Introduction: Evolving Concerns of Fieldwork

Sarit K. Chaudhuri and Sucheta Sen Chaudhuri

Ethnographic fieldwork is not an idea that hatched overnight.

W.H. Auden (1988: 14)

Fieldwork constitutes the core of modern anthropology. It involves distinctive methods and techniques, sustained involvement with people of own or other cultures. Dense understandings about different conceptual frames as well as intricacies of multiple social realities are prerequisite necessities in this divine empirical endeavour. Clifford (1988a: 2) writes:

> Fieldwork is one answer—some say the best—to the question of how the understanding of others, close or distant, is achieved. Fieldwork usually means living with and living like those who are studied. In its broadest, most conventional sense, fieldwork demands the full-time involvement of a researcher over a lengthy period of time (typically unspecified) and consists mostly of ongoing interaction with the human targets of study of their home ground … Fieldworkers represent themselves as 'marginal natives' (Freilich, 1970) or 'professional strangers' (Agar, 1980) who, as 'self-reliant loners' (Lofland, 1974) or 'self-denying emissaries' (Boon, 1982) bring forth a cultural account, an ethnography, from the social setting studied.

In one of the well-referred book concerning warning and advice of doing fieldwork, Wax (1971/1985: 363) concludes, '[F]ieldwork is as much a social phenomenon (involving reciprocity, complex role playing, the invention and obeying of rules, mutual assistance, and play) as it is an individual phenomenon (involving observation, recording, testing, analysing, defining, theorizing and model building).'

He (1971/1985: 363) further categorically reiterates, '[G]ood fieldwork is not something performed by an isolated intellectual or researcher but something created by all the people in that social situation being studied.' An attempt to reconfigure the field (Caputo, 2000: 19–31) for late 20th century anthropology brings us closer to the ideas of redefining the notion of field which goes beyond the idea of a site of research involving physical displacement or a geographically distant place to have an encounter with the 'exotic other' as argued by many (Gupta and Ferguson, 1992, 1997). There are a large number of scholars who tried to deal with the questions and issues associated with the very emergence of fieldwork tradition in anthropology and its essential linkages with the notion of culture that remained as the cornerstone in the ethnographic journey. This enterprise ('open-air' ethnography) also evolved through the critical inputs of the scholars who tried to enrich our complex understandings on human societies beyond the geographical and historical locations.

Auden (1988: 25) argued,

> To produce an ethnography requires decisions about what to tell and how to tell it. Ethnographies are written with particular audiences in mind and reflect the presumptions carried by authors regarding the attitude, expectations and background of their intended readers.

But what about the experience of an ethnographer and how that shapes an ethnographic journey leading to an end product, are also equally significant issues to understand both the texts and the contexts of the ongoing human journey. However, such discourses are comparatively less focused reflecting the memories or the moments in retrospective frames that are bound to create an enormous space for critical engagements.

Any sincere practitioner of the discipline is aptly aware of the contested domains that precisely surfaced with the publication of the book *Writing Culture* by Clifford and Marcus in 1986. Marcus (2012: 430–431) himself wrote:

> After the 1990s writing culture debates that put in play a paradigm of critique for anthropological research—from, say, the early to mid-1990s onwards—anthropology in the United States had then to rethink itself, as did a number of other disciplines, in relation to the perception of reality of macro social changes that went under the rubric of globalisation. As a discipline, it had to work through knowledge economies, global projects of political economy, assemblages, or circulations to find its way to both its traditional and new subjects at the ethnographic scale (face-to-face, everyday) in which

it is committed to work. This task was more than just recontextualising or re-narrating the scenes or locations where ethnography could be done. It meant literally moving in scapes or flows, reinventing the new ones.

According to Thapan (1998: 3),

Clifford and Marcus were representative of a 'new wave' in anthropology which sought to change the direction of anthropology from an objectivist discipline, grounded in a tradition of observation and thick description, to one which sought to allow more space to the polyphony of voices and partial truths that emerged from a collective and shared understanding of social reality.

Examining Byron's (1992) and Fabian's (1990) notion of 'other' and process of 'othering' in anthropology she (1998: 8) lamented,

[T]he process of othering however indicates a movement from a there to here, from a then to and this movement implies a presence. It is this presence that needs to be restored to the discourse of anthropology so that we are no longer engaged in representing the other through interpretation or by giving voice but rather in allowing the others to be present.

However, *Writing Culture* has paved the way for another volume, *After Writing Culture* (James and Hockey, 1997) as well as plethora of publications questioning the construction of ethnographic texts or identifying the crisis of ethnographic representation, blaming falsely for 'exoticising' or 'romanticising' the 'other' or looking for space leading to multivocality and host of many other issues. There are scholars who tried to trace the contested path of ethnographic research (Berreman, 2004; Obeyeesekere, 2004; Pool, 1991; Ranjan, 2011).

However, we still strongly believe that in the ultimate analysis none of these issues or dilemmas can reduce the actual necessities of fieldwork within 'own' or 'other' cultures though all the criticisms have redefined or relocated its contextual ties for understanding intrinsic multiplicities of human existence. Contemporary anthropology cannot be sustained with the comfort zones of libraries, archives, or even by fancy fieldwork. And these lessons we have learned from the history of our discipline. Within such a backdrop, we like to relocate our self and other within our anthropological journey—a journey which has a profound significance in terms of learning the craft of the trade, identifying relevant techniques, finding ways for immersion into a culture(s) or locating contested voices, and finally unfolding deeper understanding of cultures or social world. And precisely for this, the tradition of doing fieldwork has been embraced by many other social science disciplines including history to have an access to people's own voices which hardly found any space within the conventional disciplinary frames.

We used the word 'memory' in the very title of the volume not from a psychological perspective which is predominantly focused on short-term memory, rather we are concerned with the growing scholarship in the disciplines of social sciences projecting memory as a social phenomenon which is intrinsic to the construction of collective identities as well as the individual's sense of self (Waterson and Kian-Woon, 2012a: 17). The existing studies of memory as a social phenomenon show that it is also embedded with multiple tensions and oppositions between the individual and the societal, the popular and the official, dominant and suppressed narratives (Waterson and Kian-Woon, 2012b: 1–13). And by moments we wanted to focus on temporal and contextual specificities of variegated field locations as experienced by the fieldworkers themselves through their various forms of discourse with the 'self' and the 'other'.

We do not intend to recreate a typical methodological text for guiding researchers or students, rather we are much more concerned to listen and learn from the memories and significant moments of fieldwork done by eminent South-Asian anthropologists, or sociologists and even historians, having strong groundings in fieldwork tradition and dealing with emergent as well as contemporary issues of both anthropological/sociological and historical importance. We hope these contributions will lead us towards a deeper understanding of emerging concerns of fieldworks located in various field sites of Southeast Asia without making any effort towards finding normative rules for the whole region.

A few valuable publications on this theme are traceable, initiated by Srinivas et al. (1979), Beteille and Madan (1975) followed by a few others (Sinha, 1978; Srivastava, 2004) but none of these works are threaded within a South-Asian frame which may have an immense value for exploring lineage of anthropological traditions, probable challenges, limits as well as possibilities of varied field experiences in the wider context of social science in general. Such retrospection may also add new dimensions to our existing body of knowledge by relocating the strength of contemporary fieldwork tradition which is not yet delinked from the past but is obviously trying to evolve giving space to new strategies and methodological concerns. We tried to ensure that contributors would deal with any specific field experience or they can narrate or can compare multiple field realities to drive a point or would initiate dialogue to deal with multiple issues discussed earlier. We wanted to create a space where a fieldworker may even simply share his/her memorable moments of fieldwork without much bothering about various issues or contested domains in an explicit way. In the process a reader will have an option to locate or relocate the ethnographic or other forms of texts in the context of growing methodological contours and dilemmas in the social science generally based on empirical understandings. So it may not be a frozen text rather may melt before the eyes of an engaged reader bringing new meanings to field experiences. We strongly feel that the way eminent as well as emerging scholars from different regions have extended their valuable contributions dealing with the wide range of critical issues, this volume may be perceived as a reader, not only dealing with various intricate aspects or concerns of fieldwork tradition or even research techniques but also relocating critical voices of contemporary anthropological or sociological understandings embedded within South-Asian experience.

It may be mentioned here that many scholars believe that in spite of South Asia being a metaphor for the linguistic, cultural, and religious diversity, there is hardly consensus on how many countries actually constitute this region and this is precisely due to existing complexities of geopolitics overtly or covertly ingrained within the region. According to Mittal and Thursby (2006: 3), 'Although more or less neutral term, the edges of the region it designates remain ambiguous. In scholarly works, Myanmar is sometimes considered to be a South Asian country, while at the other terms the former British province is classified as part of Southeast Asia.' In the present volume we have incorporated contributions covering all South-Asian nation-states though Maldives remained untouched as we could not locate scholars to join our academic endeavour.

This book has two broad divisions. Section I consists of essays which are focused on countries, such as Bangladesh, Bhutan, Burma, Pakistan, Nepal, and Srilanka, whereas Section II contains essays reflecting studies from different regions of India. Due to paucity of textual space we could not cover every region of India and similarly, for rest of the nation-states of South Asia, we could only devote a single essay each. Given the nature of existing ethno-cultural diversity in each of the South-Asian nation-states, no single book can be a representative one encompassing such huge socio-political canvas. But we tried to weave through selectively the diverse as well as unique aspects of society and culture through the ethnographic lens to capture the latent or manifested essence of South Asia across the ethnic divide. In the following pages we have tried to capture the essence of each essay in the context previously discoursed.

Two decades ago, Ellen Bal set out to deconstruct essentializing imaginaries of tribe and to prevent the history of the Garos of Bangladesh 'from becoming distorted memory'. Her close scrutiny of (colonial) history revealed how these pejorative notions were part and parcel of the processes of marginalization and exclusion, but also have become instrumental in Garo 'struggles for space'. In this essay, Ellen reflects on her experiences as a historian/anthropologist amongst the Garos. This essay is as much about her reflections on her position amongst the Garos, and her engagement, their 'cause'. In fact, Ellen's long-term connection to the Garos has allowed her to uncover myriad inconsistencies between 'private' experiences and reflections, and 'public' representations. In fact, Garos seem to have more to gain from the persistence of the tribal category than from her careful reconstruction of their (discriminatory) past and present experiences as a minority in Bangladesh. In the final part of the essay she raises the question as to how to position herself in this field of 'tribal' or indigenous issues and she argues that the concept of 'trickster' (van Meijl, 2005) allows to invest in her friendships with Garos and to engage with their cause, but also creates the space for critical analysis of the complex processes of ethnicization and the political struggles taking place, and to assess whether the seemingly successful strategies may indeed lead to structural empowerment, or whether they cause new forms of dependency, divide, marginalization, and structural injustice.

In the next essay, Khan takes the reader on a journey to the field site known as Sialkot before analysing some of the advantages and disadvantages of undertaking ethnographic fieldwork at home. The essay then goes on to discuss graphically how the structure of organizations and the characteristics of individuals that the fieldworker may associate within the field can affect the quality of information gathered in the field. This essay gives a situational analysis of child labour, the working children in Sialkot's sports industry of northern Pakistan and the issues that influence anthropological fieldworker's position. It gives a full account of the author's experiences, who works in a non-governmental organization for the upliftment of child labour. The first part of the essay deals with regional history, economy, religion, and the people's day-to-day life. The second part of the essay deals with the author's position of being a part of an organization and its practical problems as he experiences in the fieldwork. It also gives a comparative analysis of the Bunyad organizational culture and the International Labour Organization (ILO) organizational culture and their developmental discourse as well as the plight of their imbalanced power relations with their subject and the rhetoric tension that exists between the two organizations.

Sinha answers some fundamental questions in relation to his choice of research sites in the Himalayan region, which precisely is Sikkim and Bhutan, and in the process he tells us how Vidyarthi was instrumental in subscribing tothe idea of doing research in Bhutan during his initial days as a Masters student of anthropology. His valuable biographical note can be taken as a fantastic liaison with the anthropologist or sociologist or any field researcher on how to devise alternative creative ideas in order to unearth research data where the state or its machinery may not be so kind to extend necessary help which ideally should have been extended to a researcher. So he had to look for multiple trips to Bhutan rather than a long-term stay in the country because their bureaucracy did not co-operate at all. His narrative brings certain segments of the society facing the dictum of state policy—fundamental issues of research strategy going beyond the prescription of standard textbooks. This will be of immense help to many young researchers who like to take up challenges of anthropological or sociological research in similar contexts. He has clarified that ultimately one needs to continuously evolve his/her field strategy through creative engagement with self and other, and only that can assure a meaningful journey towards the end product of a research. Taking his case studies or encounters during fieldwork in the Himalayan kingdom, he created a space for critical rethinking to understand the conformity and conflicts in the course of nation building process.

Mandy Sadan made a unique effort to write on the fieldwork history bringing in sharp focus the nature of transition she witnessed during her prolong stay in Burma. In fact, she narrates a crucial phase of transition where she was engaged in doing research among the people of Kachin group initiated in 1997. It is a well-known fact that during 1964–1988 Burma remained as one of the most closed countries of the world. However, in 1996 the declaration of the 'Visit to Myanmar' led a confused transitional state of affair affecting the life of the people in variegated ways. And with the closure of university, large body of youth got engaged in computer training courses leading to the expansion of printed public sphere. The resultant outcome of such new ventures was the grand celebration of *manua* festival symbolizing consolidation of Kachin identity. According to Sadan, this had created a space for her research project that would revitalize knowledge of traditional Kachin cultural practices. She shares her academic interest for which she was able to deal with Colonel Green's most noteworthy achievements which contributed a lot for the historical representation of the Nung region located in north of Putao in non-administered territory. She narrated her role as facilitator in the context of Kachin nationalism with an objective of enhancing the data on the UK collection through digitalization programme. Through her fieldwork experience, she explained the process on behalf of local committee to develop new meaning of traditional modes and models of non-Christian past and social memory in contemporary society.

The point Ben Campbell makes is to highlight the difference that long-term fieldwork makes in our understanding processes of change in Himalayan societies. It is not simply to talk about fieldwork as a practice of enquiry using various techniques of information gathering. Rather, the relational webs that fieldwork requires and gives impetus to build in cumulative strength as wholly unforeseen events move participants in the field of enquiry in a parallel movement to core theoretical concerns in the social sciences—in this case productionist, environmental, and globalized understandings of social relations. There are three phases to Campbell's fieldwork, and they have built relationally, politically, and technologically inresponsive trajectories.

Arjun Guneratne provides us fascinating comparative ideas on the intricacies as well as ethical discourse in fieldwork based on his three different field sites, which are Nepal and two different locations in Srilanka itself. This personal narrative clearly indicates the complexities of village life. Moreover, it teaches us how an anthropologist's association with one faction may place him in an uncomfortable situation, which makes his work not only difficult but also challenging. It alerts us to the fact that in field situation villagers may also remain equally inquisitive about the state or the country an anthropologist/field researcher belongs to. He also clearly explains anthropologist's role as a cultural broker who mediates between his own milieu and that of the culture he is describing.

Robbins Burling narrates an insightful experience of anthropological restudies concerning a tribal village of North-east India. In fact, Robbins Burling first travelled to the Garo hills in 1954 and lived among the Garos of Rengsanggri village for two years and this generated his well-acclaimed book on the village, which is considered as a classic in the context of anthropological tradition of village studies. Later, he got an opportunity to revisit the village in 1996—after 42 years of his first visit. This essay reflects his embeddedness among the Garo villagers and how successfully he remained ingrained in the people's memory, even after four decades without any communication they still recognised him. So Burling vividly narrates the very apparent and distinctly visible change which came along with modern education, upgradation of productive technology, healthcare, and obviously with massive Baptization leaving a few old Garo individuals, though the concept of household as an eternal principle for organizing village life has survived. The whole narrative brings back into focus the strength of long-term anthropological fieldwork and underscores the power of anthropological restudies to comprehend the nature of continuity and change not merely by statistics rather by immersing into a culture.

Erik de Maaker focused on fieldwork that he had done between 1999 and 2001 in the Garo Hills of eastern Meghalaya (India). He tried to explore how he, in the course of this PhD research, has related to the people concerned. He described how relationships emerged and developed, and how people reacted to his involvement with their lives. He concludes by arguing that although his research did not have the intention to expose the village concerned, it did certainly contribute to it being put on the map as a 'traditional' village. As far as he can judge, this seems to have worked out positively for the villagers. It has made people more aware of the importance that is being attributed by an outside world to their cultural practices, and ensures that they receive a positive kind of attention from state organizations and the like.

de Maaker categorically stated that over the last two decades of the previous century, anthropology has moved away from the kind of fields that it used to cherish before. Where previously anthropological research was typically linked to a single field site, now a multi-site approach has become the standard (Marcus, 1995). This provided better possibilities for comparison of the data collected, enabling a better and broader understanding of the topic being studied. Nevertheless, there are certain research topics that continue to benefit from (predominantly) the research based on a single site. The fieldwork that he has conducted on death-related practices required close engagement with a limited number of people. Not only because of the level of 'trust' and 'rapport' required for the fieldwork but also since the research demanded that he took the multiple dimensions of the relationships maintained by the people concerned into account. To achieve this, he had to meet them in various roles—in relation to their land, as traders, as kinsmen, or when acting in accordance with their religious responsibilities. This could be achieved best by interacting with a single set of people over a prolonged period.

Debojyoti Das narrated his experience at the perilous field site in Nagaland, one of the well-known states in India's northeastern borderland. His whole discourse pivoted around some fundamental questions, such as, how anthropologists cope with the ethical issues that emerged out of collecting field data from chaotic and dangerous situations. In his own words:

> [D]oing fieldwork in politically disturbed fields means negotiating and surviving from dangers that often come without warning. Anthropological

ethics committee in the UK as elsewhere is unenthusiastic on setting practical guidelines that could defend the interest of anthropologists doing fieldwork.

He narrates that the conventional ethical requirements in anthropology do not speak of the researcher's safety, security, and well-being in violent environments. Anthropologist's well-being is often taken for granted as 'common sense knowledge' in violent field sites. His 14-month fieldwork among the Nagas and the critical hostage situation which he had to negotiate with has generated a very valuable understanding which may be useful for the anthropologists who are dealing with similar violent field situations. This can be best expressed in his own words,

> Ethnographers thus working in dangerous fields are pressed with the challenge of innovating new strategies for the preservation of their well-being while at the same continuing to identify and explain the unique social interrelation that arise amidst crisis and strife.

In his 14 months stay in Nagaland he engaged with the problems and steered his way through at times adopting alternative routes that were quite unconventional and dared to experiment with new methods of data collection quite unconventional in ethnographic research. He concludes that the end result has been a reflective memory that perhaps is a humble exercise towards understanding the dangers in fieldwork.

Anungla Aier textualizes an interesting narrative, the context of a small Naga tribe. The Khiamneungan is one of the largest yet lesser known of the Naga tribes. They occupy the eastern most flank of the Indo-Myanmar border. More than half of the Khiamneungan villages lie across the border in Myanmar. In Nagaland, they are located in Tuensang district under the Noklak sub-division. Among the tribes of Nagaland, it is one tribe about whom there exists very limited literature. During the last one and half year, the author has been working on oral traditions and folklore of the Naga tribes of Nagaland. During the fieldwork, one of the features of Khiamneungan oral tradition that stood out was the tradition of having specific 'Knowledge Keepers/Story Tellers' of the clans. The essay is a recollection of searching for those Story Tellers and takes the reader through the journey of travelling to four of the Khiamneungan villages. It presents how the past events such as migration stories; origin myths, and such oral traditions are kept under the custody of the 'Knowledge keepers' and how such stories are narrated among the Khiamneungan tribe.

Gautam Bera deciphers his structuralist persuasion in Chapter 11 discovering the symbolism connected with human culture and the ideational system inherent in the social organization. Functional character of myths and beliefs associated with mortuary practices of the Riang is the context of the present study. Author met the Riang of Tripura on his repetitive field visits spanning more than a decade. In this essay, Bera specifically wanted to locate the nature of paradigm shift that is manifested through ritual performances and here the author specifically tries to locate the nature of changes that happen in routinized performance. His brief ethnographic note on the Riang unfolds the pattern of social structure based on kinship rules and regulations of non-state societies. According to him, the creation myths and related beliefs as well as practices as regulatory mechanism of social institution controlled human habits and behaviour that further associated with material culture.

In Chapter 12, Arnab hinges on the experiences of individual fieldworkers engaged with the organizations of fieldwork practices in a university of India. The university has been premier in establishing anthropology as a department in India and is peopled by individuals of similar urban cultural milieu. For nearly 20 years the author himself has been in the roles of student, researcher, teacher, colleague, and supervisor of research at the Department of Anthropology in the said university. Within the range of positions of 'going native' on sharing the variation and changes in anthropological fieldworks in the post-colonial backdrop, this articulation endeavours to voice both themselves and the organizations of practices constructing the fieldworks and reflecting them back into the same. Not withstanding the reflexive agenda of anthropology, the contexts of working on/with/for fieldworkers and fieldworks help strategizing different discourses (e.g., narrative, interpretive, dialogic, and critical) in embodying the ethnographic account. Based principally on retrospective and prospective dimensions of the experience of the author and other fieldworkers, especially of the young trainee students and researchers, his essay emphasizes certain critical issues, such as (1) the organizations of fieldwork practices, (2) the areas and issues of fieldwork, (3) the experiences of the methods, stages, other associates, and accessories of fieldwork, (4) post-fieldwork experiences, and finally (5) the emergent ways of making sense of fieldwork.

Suman and Bhaskar's essay deals with nuances of everyday politics in rural West Bengal. Taking conceptual cues from Geertz, Ortner, and other scholars, they argued that thick political narratives may enhance an ethnographer's understanding of micro social dynamics embedded within emerging political processes. They intend to explore the local level of political processes to understand the certain basic facts, such as nature of political polarization, rural people's actual participation in local governance, and the growing deep divide among the leaders and common mass. They choose one village Panchayat bordering with Orissa in the backdrop of historic political transition that has taken place leading to the rise of Trinamool Chhatra Parishad (TMCP) for running state craft. They collected large number of oral narratives from two distinctive sets of people; one who were the old settlers and later are the recent settlers in the study area. These oral narratives bring into focus various crucial and contested issues, such as immigration politics, role of political leaders as middlemen, collection of fund for individual accumulation as well as for growth of party funds, neglecting actual grievances of rural mass, failures of CPM party machinery to discipline its own cadres, etc., which contributed to the political transition in West Bengal by closing the 34 years political dominance by the left front under the leadership of CPM. This essay reveals that an ethnographer has to invent or mould his methodological strategies which include choosing of actual field sites and finding key actors rather than moving with preconceived ideas or frames and in the process one can locate the notion of multivocality in the construction of ethnographic text even by using pseudonyms.

Neel Rekha's essay is a memoir of fieldwork in Madhubani among Mithila painting artists between 1999 and 2004. Mithila painting, more popularly known as Madhubani painting, has acquired immense popularity in the past few decades. This essay describes how her ethnographic fieldwork aimed at locating the history of Mithila paintings and comprehending how the mechanism of assertion of identity of upper caste women painters, ultimately led to the discovery of Harijan Mithila paintings—a hitherto unknown aspect of Maithil culture and tradition. The methodologies evolved during fieldwork and continuous interactions with Mithila artists not only helped her trace the history of evolution of Harijan Mithila painting but also locate contested voices in Maithil history. Recalling her interactions with noted artists, such as Jamuna Devi, Shanti Devi, Chano Devi, Roudi Paswan, and Uttam Paswan, she demonstrated how their attempts to evolve a distinctive tradition of their own led to the rediscovery of their rich cultural history. The overall purpose of the essay is to demonstrate the importance of ethnographic fieldwork in historical studies.

Vijoy Sahay brings into light his third field trip in 1974 among the Nicobories, located in Nancowrie Island and narrates succinctly the history of Rani-hood, which was invented during the days of Isolone—a title actually given by the Tehsildar and then passed over from one generation to another. Then, he gives an account how their progeny accumulated enormous landed property and in the process created discontentment among the local population. In 2002, he revisited the same island and came to know how new interpretation of Queenhood is texted and became deeply shocked listening to the death of his key informant. He displayed why observation is considered one of the prime techniques by narrating rituals and celebration of the rite-de-passage of Rani Laxmi's daughter. He also narrated his deadly encounter in the sea while he was rowing a canoe during his trip to Enunga village. His nickname given by the Cowrians, people with whom he worked, symbolized his ability to penetrate and understand the society for which anthropologists are known throughout the world. By bringing everyday encounter graphically within the narratives, he actually helped us to understand that one need to negotiate constantly with the difficult field situation rather than moving with preconceived notions generated by textbooks dealing with fieldwork methods.

Keeping the contested methodological space in view, Abeer narrates his field journey which gradually evolved over time and he tries to address the issues related to subjectivity in anthropology. He also attempts to speak about the self and other through narrative discourse in a manner which lends to a profession that is deeply embedded in building insights and intuition by sharing his own field space spread over Jammu, Kashmir, and Ladakh—a melting pot of culture as well as a linguistic nightmare where he stayed for three years. Drawing from his own field experience linked with his research in material culture as well as others, engaged with issues concerning various places and people of the region, Abeer tries to construct what entails continuing to do visual anthropological fieldwork against all odds which come in between.

The last essay contains a dialogue between Daniel Rycroft and Ganesh Devy on various critical issues concerning indigenous studies and fieldwork in the context of India. Daniel's initiation into the research on Adivasi and their Hindu linkages was established through the understanding of aesthetic sensibilities of the Patkars of Bengal and Jharkhand. Gradually, he became interested in subaltern studies through the work of Ranajit Guha which helped him look at the whole question of insurgency in the context of an agrarian anti-colonial society. This has ultimately culminated into a book entitled *Representing Rebellion: Visual Aspects of Counter-insurgency in Colonial India* (2006) through which he entered into the contested domain of 'Adivasi', 'Tribe', question of 'Indigeneity' as well as 'Adivasi self rule' in the context of India taking his queue from research in eastern India. In response to Devy's question, Daniel has raised very fundamental issues relating to the convergence of subaltern studies and indigenous studies. This dialogue leads to an interesting turn throwing light on Devy's cognition on Indigeneity, Schedule Caste Buddhism interphase. This dialogue is not explicitly based on field experience but it reveals how dialogue can lead to a 'thick description' of expanding knowledge base. At the same time can it be a method of critically engaged anthropological journeying to understand identity issues or even the expansion of 'Red Corridor' in Adivasi dominant forested areas across the inter-states border of India. It includes narratives that emerged out of sustained field experience as well as understanding and leads us to rethink certain covert or overt perceptions relating to indigenous people or Adivasis, 'enframing Adivasi culture' in the context of emerging political–economic compulsions of our nation-state in the era of economic reforms and globalization. This dialogue has also surfaced a critical thinking on the post-colonial tribal policies, bringing Gandhi's idea of Swaraj and Elwin's inspirational engagement with the Adivasis and also the plight of the Adivasis in the context of ongoing Maoist movements. These are becoming a central question to the Indian state while dealing with issues such as development, displacement, and ownership of huge natural resources.

Considering the complexities of the issues in South Asia, emerging concerns of fieldwork and the space available within this volume, we tried to be selective giving comparatively more space to different regions of India. Nevertheless, we tried to accommodate a wide range of experiences across the political and cultural boundaries of nation-states. This collective effort of editors and essay contributors ultimately converge a fundamental idea, that is, in spite of contested ideas embedded in ethnographic journey or limitations in construction of ethnographic text which new waves of thinking tried to underscore in post-writing culture phase, within anthropology or even within the larger frame of social science itself, an alternative paradigm is yet to evolve in an exclusive way to comprehend multilayered discourse concerning human social realities rather than going back to the people for understanding 'self' or 'other'.

All total 17 chapters of this book reveal this evolving reality in the context of the disciplines such as anthropology or sociology in specific and field-based social science disciplines in general. This book may also open up relevant future discourse related to limits and possibilities of ethnographic enterprise, relocating politics and poetics of experientially driven ethnographies or on similar host of issues taking each of the South-Asian nation-states as case studies keeping in view the historical growth of research in these countries, as well as the large number of scholars from within and outside the region are engaged with. However, there cannot be any denial of the fact that ethnographic conventions are historically situated and also change over time as Clifford commented (1988b: 6). And this volume collectively carries forward this fundamental methodological premise for understanding human journey.

References

Auden, W.H. 1988. In Pursuit of Culture. In J.V. Maanem (ed.), *Tales of the Field: On Writing Ethnography*, pp. 13–44. Chicago, Illinois: The University of Chicago Press.

Berreman, G.D. 2004. Ethnography: Method and Product. In V.K. Srivastava (ed.), *Methodology and Fieldwork*, pp. 157–190. New Delhi: Oxford University Press.

Beteille, A. and T.N. Madan. 1975. *Encounter and Experience: Personal Account of Fieldwork*. Delhi: Vikas Publishing House.

Byron, R.F. 1992. Ethnography and Biography: On the Understanding of Culture. *Ethnos*, 57(3–4): 169–182.

Caputo, V. 2000. At 'Home' and 'Away' Reconfiguring the Field for Late Twentieth-century Anthropology. In V. Amit (ed.), *Constructing the Field: Ethnographic Fieldwork in the Contemporary World*, pp. 19–31. London: Routledge.

Clifford, J. 1988a. Fieldwork, Culture and Ethnography. In J.V. Maanem (ed.), *Tales of the Field: On Writing Ethnography*, pp. 1–12. Chicago, Illinois: University of Chicago Press.

———. 1988b. *The Predicament of Culture: Twentieth century Ethnography, Literature and Art*. Cambridge: Harvard University Press.

Clifford, J. and G.E. Marcus. 1986. *Writing Culture: The Poetics and Politics of Ethnography*. Berkeley, California: University of California Press.

Fabian, J. 1990. Presence and Representation: The Other and Anthropological Writing. *Critical Inquiry,*16: 753–772.

Gupta, A. and J. Ferguson. (eds). 1992. Beyond 'Culture': Place Identity and Politics of Difference. *Cultural Anthropology*, 7(1): 6–23.

———. 1997. *Anthropological Locations: Boundaries and Grounds of a Field Science*. Berkley, California: University of California Press.

James, A. and J.L. Hockey. 1997. *After Writing Culture: Epistemology and Praxis in Contemporary Anthropology*. London: Routledge.

Marcus, G.E. 1995. Ethnography in/of the world System: The Emergence of Multi-Sited Ethnography. *Annual Review of Anthropology*, 24:95–117.

———. 2012. The Legacies of Writing Culture and the Near Future of Ethnographic Form: A Sketch. *Cultural Anthropology*, 27(3): 427–455.

Mittal, S. and G. Thursby. (ed.) 2006. *Religions of South Asia: An Introduction*. London: Routledge.

Obeyeesekere, G. 2004. The First Intersubjectivity: The Anthropologist and the Native. In V.K. Srivastava (ed.), *Methodology and Fieldwork*, pp. 85–93. New Delhi: Oxford University Press.

Pool, R. 1991. Postmodern Ethnography? *Critique of Anthropology*, 11(4): 309–331.

Ranjan, G. 2011. Ethnography of Development: Challenges and Promise. *The NEHU Journal*, IX(2 July): 49–62.

Rycroft, Daniel. 2006. *Representing Rebellion: Visual Aspects of Counter-insurgency in Colonial India.* New Delhi: Oxford University Press India.

Sinha, S. (ed.) 1978. *Field Studies on the People of India.* Calcutta: Indian Anthropological Society.

Srinivas, M.N., A.M. Shah, and E.A. Ramaswamy. 1979. *Fieldworker and the Field: Problems and Challenges of Sociological Investigation.* New Delhi: Oxford University Press.

Srivastava, V.K. (ed.) 2004. *Methodology and Fieldwork.* New Delhi: Oxford University Press.

Thapan, M. (ed.). 1998. *Anthropological Journeys: Reflections on Fieldwork.* New Delhi: Orient Blackswan.

van Meijl, Toon. 2005. The Critical Ethnographer as Trickster. *Anthropological Forum,* 15(3): 235–245.

Waterson, R. and K. Kian-Woon. (eds). 2012a. *Introduction in Contestations of Memory in Southeast Asia.* Singapore: NUS Press.

Waterson, R. and K. Kian-Woon. 2012b. The Work of Memory and the Unfinished Past: Deepening and Widening the Study of Memory in Southeast Asia. In R. Waterson and K. Kian-Woon (eds), *Contestations of Memory in Southeast Asia,* pp. 17–50. Singapore: NUS Press.

Wax, Rosalie H. 1971/1985. *Doing Fieldwork: Warnings and Advice.* London: University of Chicago Press.

SECTION I

Experience of South Asian Nations

1

A Historian/Anthropologist and
the Garos of Banglade...

Experience of
South Asian
Nations

1

A Historian/Anthropologist amongst the Garos of Bangladesh

Ellen Bal

Introduction

Upon return to the city, after a period of field research, my research partner Suborno would occasionally be questioned by his Garo friends in Dhaka about our findings. 'Did she notice these bad things?' they would ask him when he shared our observations with them. And next, they would instruct him to only show me the positive sides of their community. They seemed more worried about my observations as an outsider, than about the problems that were prevailing amongst Garos.

In November 1993, I travelled to Bangladesh for a one-month preliminary field trip, to prepare my one-year field research amongst the Garos of Bangladesh, scheduled from March 1994 to March 1995. These Garos of Bangladesh have long been known as a 'tribe', whose members are generally imagined and represented as uncultivated, undeveloped, and naive, without much of a history, living isolated from sophisticated mainstream society. Such 'tribalist'[1] imaginations rarely make much sense when we study people who fall into this category. Yet, remarkably the body of these ideas, perspectives, and ensuing policies has stayed similar after British colonial rule had come to an end.

As a historian/anthropologist-to-be, I set out to reconstruct the history of ethnic identification amongst this small and fairly unknown so-called tribe in Bangladesh. Ever since my study of modern Indian history in New Delhi a few years earlier, I had both been fascinated and irritated by the tribalist representation of a wide range of ethnic and cultural minorities of the subcontinent, generally bracketed together under the labels tribe, Scheduled Tribe, or Adivasi. Even though the commissioner for Scheduled Castes and Tribes had admitted in the early 1950s that no uniform test to classify the 'Scheduled Tribes' had been developed, he also felt that three features indeed were common to all tribal people: (1) their tribal origin, (2) their primitive way of life and habitation in remote and not easily accessible areas, and (3) their general backwardness in all respects (Report of the Commissioner for SC & ST, 1952: 11).[2]

This tautological nature of such a depiction heightened my sense of unease and irritation with tribalist discourse. Fellow students in New Delhi from the 'tribal' North-east India, and who were generally referred to as chinkys in a derogatory manner by others because of their different looks, had never struck me as backward, primitive, or odd in any way. It also intrigued me that a good number of historians were engaging in intense debates about the role of colonialism in (the articulation of) caste identities (e.g., Inden, 1990, and later Bayly, 1999), but generally stayed away from debates about existing notions of distinct isolated 'tribes' in South Asia, and their often tense and problematic relations with 'non-tribal' others.

And so I became a woman with a mission; just like those historians critiquing essentialized notions of caste, I set out to unravel the idea of 'the primitive tribe' and was going to (re-)write their history of becoming distinct and marginalized. The Garos of Bangladesh were to be my case study. I was aware that I could not free myself from my subjectivity and value commitment, and that I was dealing with highly complex and fairly sparse material. My reconstruction of the past would not be Garo history *wie es eigentlich gewesen* (how it really was). However, I was adamant in my attempt, on the basis of meticulous research of a variety of sources, to deconstruct dominant notions of 'tribes' as 'people without history' and to prevent their history 'from becoming distorted memory' (Iggers, 2010: 32).

In this essay, I will reflect on my experiences as a historian—who has gradually also developed into an anthropologist—and on some of the main findings that emerged from the study. I will also show how my interlocutors themselves have embraced essentializing categorizations and notions of tribe in public domain, in order to carve out space in a 'minority-unfriendly' context. Lastly, I want to raise an issue that has been bothering me increasingly since I completed the study here discussed. My long-term engagement with Garos in Bangladesh has allowed me to uncover myriad inconsistencies between Garo 'private' experiences and reflections, and 'public' (re-)presentations. Yet, what do we do, as anthropologists/historians, when we discover that our research subjects have less to gain from our careful reconstructions of their pasts, no matter how distorted these are, than from the persistence of essentializing categories that better serve their political/emancipative agendas.

The essay is as much about my observations of Garos, as it is about my reflections on my position amongst them and my engagement with 'their cause'. I make no sharp distinction between any of the aforementioned concepts such as tribe, 'indigenous people' or Adivasi, although I realize that their historical trajectories and objectives differ widely. In terms of connotations, however, they show remarkable similarities in many ways. Indigenous people are as much imagined as 'undeveloped', isolated, helpless, naïve, and 'jungly' as tribes previously were.

Field Research amongst the Garos of Bangladesh

I completed my dissertation in 2000. Seven years later a revised version of my study was published (Bal, 2007). Although this essay is primarily based on that research project, it addresses a number of changes in Bangladesh that have occurred since the completion of my research. For example, after a slow start in the 1990s, the notion of Indigenous People has become widely popular and influential amongst Bangladeshi 'tribes', donors, NGOs, and 'progressive' strands of civil society since the turn of the millennium. In many public domains and media, 'indigenous people' (or its Bengali equivalent 'Adivasi') has slowly begun to replace older designations such as tribe, *upojati* (sub-nation) or *pahari* (hill people). Today, it seems that the notion of 'indigenous people', whether it is useful as an analytical concept or not, is there to stay for much longer (Cf. Karlsson, 2003).

Unlike the Bengali anthropologist Kibriaul Khaleque (1985), who conducted ethnographic research amongst the Garos of Modhupur in the late 1970s and 1980s, I generally encountered hospitality and friendship. While Khaleque was treated with a lot of suspicion and was not allowed to stay in one of the Garo villages, for me 'getting access' was fairly easy and uncomplicated. Clearly the complex history of othering and discrimination in Bangladesh had come to mark day-to-day relationships between Bengalis and Garos, and infested many of them with a deep-rooted sense of distrust and even hatred vis-à-vis each other. Being a young and female foreigner from Europe, which also came with all kinds of disadvantages (such as not knowing the local languages), placed me outside these problematic relationships.

My first contact was a Catholic Garo nun in Dhaka. The Salesian Sisters of Monipuri Para were ready to accommodate me for a couple of days, before handing me over to a local Garo family. The family emptied out one of their three small rooms and let me live with them for the remaining three weeks of my stay. In this small house, infested with mosquitoes and with the visible signs of a recent flood still marking the walls of their home, I made my first Garo friends. Naive and inexperienced as I was, I presumed I was staying with a relatively poor family and I felt uncomfortable taking so much of their limited space. It was only after my return to Bangladesh a few months later, that I discovered they belonged to one of the most successful and richest Garo families in Bangladesh. They owned a two-storey concrete building, one of the very few at the time, in one of the Garo border villages, and possessed plenty of land. My research associate Suborno and I later came to jokingly refer to this enormous house as our holiday resort. We would occasionally spend a day or two there, take a refreshing dip in the sizeable pond, enjoy some *chu* (Garo rice beer) on the roof, while watching the star-lit sky and pondering over past and present experiences of being Garo in Bangladesh (among other things) with members of the household. Clearly, not all Garos were equally poor and marginalized.

Reconstructing a History of Othering and Exclusion

My study of Garo ethnicity provided detailed insights into historical processes of labelling, categorization, identification, and (violent) othering. The scarcity of written sources rendered oral history and life narratives imperative to my research. Garo recollections of their personal experiences made it painfully clear that their recent past (and that of other Bangladeshi minorities for that matter) was one marked by 'othering' and exclusion (van Schendel and Bal, 1998). Elsewhere, I analyse these processes in detail (Bal, 2007). Close scrutiny of the available historical bits and pieces, combined with in-depth interviews, revealed how during the last two centuries the subsequent states of British India, East Pakistan, and Bangladesh took (intentional) steps to (partially) exclude and at times even evict 'tribal' minorities from their states. These processes of marginalization in turn became imperative in the ethnicization of Garos.

In *A Recent History of Bangladesh* (2009), Willem van Schendel points at the paradoxical relation between two dominant and competing models for national identification in East Pakistan/Bangladesh: the Muslim and the Bengali identity. Muslim identity stood at the basis of independent Pakistan and different from Hindu-dominated India. The Bengali identity gained momentum in the struggle against West Pakistani domination. Garos and many other Bangladeshis do not adhere to these competing identifications. These Bangladeshis, roughly constituting one per cent of the total population, are neither Muslim nor Bengali. They have always remained excluded from mainstream society to some extent.

One extreme example would be their flight from East Pakistan in 1964. Within a time span of a few weeks, thousands of Garos fled across the border into India, while the government of Pakistan (knowingly) failed to protect them against the mass influx of local Muslim settlers and Bengali Muslim refugees from Assam. Their flight was not merely a result of this sudden immigration of thousands of land-hungry settlers (supported by local police and the East Pakistan Rifles), but also caused by persistent feelings of fundamental insecurity in Pakistan amongst these Garos. While many Garos referred to these 1964 events as conscious attempts of the Pakistan government to chase them out of the country, our interlocutors also pointed to that year as a turning point. It was then, one of our informants told us, that Garos put aside their differences and realized they were one and the same people (Bal, 2007: 178–184).

Private Experiences and Public Representations of Garo-ness

To an outsider, the Garos of Bangladesh easily come across as a close-knit, harmonious, and peaceful community. In view of their efforts to keep up this image, this is not surprising. Such a strategy is by no means exceptional for minority communities. Subject to discrimination and exclusion, members of minority communities tend to magnify differences between themselves and others and under-communicate internal discord to maintain a positive image to the outside world (Cf. Eriksen, 2002: 29–30). Social identities and self-perceptions are never constructed in a void. People derive their identity in comparison with others and so it is impossible to study self-defining processes in isolation from other communities or groups (e.g., Tajfel, 1981). Tribalist discourse was not merely a result of colonial research projects but as much a response to the self-image, scientific background, and administrative needs of the various colonial observers themselves. In a similar vein, Garos often figure as 'the ultimate other' in processes of Bengali identity making and vice versa.

For the purpose of this essay, it is important to point out that many 'typical Garo qualities' that were asserted in public conformed to tribalist imagery. Garos often articulated their 'tribal character' to articulate their distinct identity. Hence, while 'tribalist discourse' is inherently essentializing, its purpose and relevance can be highly dynamic. The example of Suborno's anxious friends in the introduction already illustrated that the image that Garos wished to convey to outsiders (non-Garos) did not necessarily correspond with their own experiences and self-perceptions. In fact, his friends seemed less worried about internal discord and problems than about me observing those. However, my insider/outsider position allowed me to observe the paradoxical relations between self-perceptions and experiences and public representations. At a certain moment, my own position was such that I could peep behind the curtains, although, of course, not always, not everywhere, and not with everyone. Relationships of mutual trust were developed and my network of Garo friends, acquaintances, and 'relatives' slowly expanded. Suborno's anxious friends started to accept me and confide in me.

On numerous occasions, Garos would emphasize their innocent and honest character, their intimate connections to nature, their 'tribal culture' and traditions, and their harmonious and truthful character. I found it particularly interesting, but in a way also unsettling, that these dominant self-understandings and expressions were not formed independently of 'outside' or etic perceptions of Garos. On the contrary, tribalist discourse, which seemed inherently essentializing and pejorative to me, clearly served as a guideline for public expressions of Garo-ness. Particularly three distinct images of Garo-ness stood out. Albeit by no means mutually exclusive, each one seemed grounded in a different strategy. The discourse of 'modernity' presented a picture of people who had outgrown their primitive tribal image and had developed into modern citizens. The discourse of Garo 'pride and victimhood' on the other hand stressed the tribal character of the Garos, repeated a number of typical Garo characteristics and blamed external developments, institutions, and organizations for losing that tribal identity. The 'people-of-nature' discourse built on the notion that Garos (tribes/indigenous people) are intimately linked with their natural environment and will ultimately disappear if 'nature disappears'. In this way, it made a strong appeal to organizations who are supportive of indigenous rights.

The first English issue of the *Mandi-rang-ni Chiti* (Garo newsletter) reflected the urgent need felt amongst young urban Garos to work on the image of the Garos in Bangladesh:

> It is somehow in order to introduce ourselves as a people, on behalf of all who work in Dhaka that we have decided to publish this letter in English twice a year. Ignorance, at its best, creates nothing (at its worst, we know how harmful it can be), knowledge, on the other hand, opens up many possibilities. We will be pleased to come into contact with you on a regular basis and share with [sic] our culture and thoughts. (Paraka, 1996)

This particular Garo newsletter was published in order to introduce the Garos to expatriates in Dhaka, who employ a good number of Garos in their homes as housemaids, cooks, gardeners, drivers, or guards. The newsletter asserted that 'The Garos used to be known as head-hunters, and were the fear of British and Bengalis alike. Now they have learned modern ways and have to a large extent become literate.' Perhaps a primitive and fearful people once, as it was argued, they have now become educated. They have adapted to modern society and have adopted modern lifestyles. In other words, Garos are no longer the primitive people they once were. On the last page, Paraka, the organization behind the publication of the newsletter, was introduced. Here, it was also emphasized that Garos have developed into an internationally oriented community, well-adjusted to modern life, while preserving their distinct identity:

> The centre [Paraka] is run mainly by young people, these being the ones who most keenly feel the threats and opportunities of modern society. The Garos have moved from a close-knit, simple village society, complete with its own laws and customs, to the modern international society within less than a hundred years. Like so many other peoples in Asia, they had not participated in the development which led up to our present-day society— they were swept into it and have had to take it all in their stride to be able to survive.

In sum, the representation confronts the negative tribal image by relegating it to the past. Once a primitive tribe, Garos have outgrown that backward position and have become successful, literate, and modern citizens of Bangladesh.

Memories and experiences of victimhood provide one of the pillars of Garo ethnicity. Garos stressed their position as victims of historical and contemporary injustice, pointing at the Bengali Muslims and the post-colonial state as their main enemies and the cause of their problems, and referring to the 'autonomous' position they once supposedly had. They presented themselves as victims, emphasized their image as helpless and naive, and called upon others to protect them and to grant them special rights. Two aspects of Garo victimhood stood out: (1) as a (Christian) tribal or indigenous minority they are victims of (Muslim) Bengali repressions and post-colonial state policies; (2) as 'tribals' or Adivasis, they are inextricably linked to nature and their very existence depends on being with nature; with the disappearance of forests, Garos will vanish too.

The following article in *Chiring*, a magazine distributed by the Dhaka branch of the Bangladesh Garo Student Organization (Bagachas), also emphasized the helplessness of Garos:

> There is a saying that, if a child does not cry, even its mother does not want to give it the breast, so the child cries in order to get mother's breast. But the sorrows of the forest dwellers are confined to the forest. The silent crying of their hearts cannot be heard by the civilized people who live in the cities. But the most regrettable thing is that in this modern age of civilisation there are some people who live in inaccessible hilly villages and there is nobody to bother about them. ¼ The cunning infiltrators have beguiled them of their forests, have driven them out, and taken forcible possession of their lands, those forest dwellers today, homeless and landless, move from one place to another in search of forest and safety for life. They are so helpless, having to live like foreigners in their own land.

The article alludes to many aspects of tribalist discourse: it compares forest dwellers with helpless infants, who have to cry in order to be nurtured. Their powerlessness rendered them homeless and landless, and they are dependent on the help of other, civilized people.

The notion that Garos are intimately connected to nature was also central in a documentary entitled *Mandi* (1994). At one point, the documentary stages a local Garo leader who strongly argues that Garos are 'children of the forest'. He contends that the forest provides them with more than material resources and argues that Garos have always been inextricably bound up with the forest; without the forest they cannot survive. It is true that many Garos of the Modhupur forest have suffered from state policies and other developments that caused the loss of land and the eviction of many peasants (e.g., Timm, 1991). These Garos, however, form a minority amongst the Garos of Bangladesh.[3] An interesting response to the film was given by a Garo student from the border area. This part of Bangladesh, where most Garos are engaged in wet-rice cultivation, is as scarcely forested as most of the country. The documentary startled this student. She never knew that Garos could not survive without forests. Her village was not situated in a forested area and her parents had never lived in a forest either, but were doing pretty well. Here, the metaphor of Garos as 'children of the forest' even caught a Garo student by surprise.

Garos in the 21st Century

One of my Garo friends from the old days has made it to the upper ranks of indigenous leadership. He has become a public figure in Bangladesh, is frequently invited for public lectures by foreign donor organizations, and attends international meetings on indigenous issues in Bangkok, Geneva, or New York. My friendship with him allows me to get a better insight into identity politics in Bangladesh. When I visit Dhaka, we have long discussions about current developments and the future of indigenous people in the country. Once, after he showed me a short film on Garos that he had produced, I jokingly accused him of 'inventing tradition'. He responded with a smile and said he liked the term. 'Indigenous people' have gained relevance in Bangladesh. Donors have included their issues and provide huge funds for indigenous rights projects. Unlike in the 1990s or before then, when tribes were merely considered exotic and certainly not a subject for serious historical research, many Bangladeshi (Bengali) academics have now specialized in indigenous issues and present themselves as expert on minority issues in their country.

One morning, I had an interview with a number of young staff members in my friend's small NGO. Most of them were Garo, two of them Chakma. We also talked about the photographs used for decorating one of the office walls. These portrayed a festive celebration of *wangala* (originally a Garo harvest festival) in a way I had not seen before. With the disappearance of the traditional *sangsarek* religion, *sangsarek* rituals had lost much of their relevance and appeal for the Garos. Only in the 1990s, the Christian churches had revived its celebration in 'a Christian way', in order to bring Garos from different denominational backgrounds together, and to emphasize their distinct Garo cultural and religious (read: Christian) identity.

The photographs in the office, however, showed no overt signs of Christianity. I saw young women dressed in beautiful, recently designed Garo costumes, cheering at the launch of a hot air balloon (a newly introduced element clearly inspired by Buddhist festivities). Some of the women wore a collection of jewellery, which were, as I later learned, collected by my friend during his trips to Thailand, India, Philippines, etc. Expats from Dhaka (representatives from the European Commission and European embassy) cheerfully participated in dances and rituals, wearing curious hats and colourful 'tribal' make-up, besides their habitual cameras. Yet, when I commented teasingly that these snapshots presented a wonderful example of the invention of tradition, one of the young staff members became upset and sternly reacted that I was looking at true Garo traditional culture. Missionaries had spoilt *wangala*, but their boss (my friend) had reintroduced original Garo culture. I then realized how quickly the recent introduction of indigenous people's discourse (with an emphasis on 'authentic' indigenous culture) has also influenced emic notions of Garo identity, culture, and history. This young girl needed no exploration of 19th and 20th century history 'as it had been' but an assertion of Garo culture as truly indigenous (Bal, 2010).

Engaged Anthropologist: Trickster or Traitor?

Two decades ago, I set out to deconstruct essentializing imaginaries of tribe and to prevent Garo history 'from becoming distorted memory'. Close scrutiny of (colonial) history demonstrated how these pejorative notions were part and parcel of processes of marginalization and exclusion, but also have become instrumental in Garo 'struggles for space'. I have observed how Garos themselves embrace notions of 'tribal identity' and culture, in order to tap into newly introduced discourses on indigenous people's rights. Some of the 'recently invented traditions' to assert their distinct 'tribal identity' have in fact become part of Garo culture.

How to position oneself in this field of 'tribal' or indigenous issues and interests? This question has become increasingly pertinent since my first encounters with Garos. If my interlocutors have more to gain from reconstructing tribalist categories than from a careful reconstruction of (discriminatory) past and present processes, what should be my role as an engaged anthropologist/historian? van Meijl (2005) used the notion of trickster as a metaphor for the critical ethnographer who adopts multiple identities 'to reconcile the irreconcilable demands that are essential to ethnography'. In his perspective, anthropologists who sympathize with the political agendas of their research subjects may take a role as advocates and mediators, but also step back and reflect on the construction of indigenous strategies and agendas. Positioning myself as a trickster allows me to invest in my friendships with Garos, and to engage with their cause and that of other Bangladeshi minorities, but it also creates the space for critical analysis of the complex processes of ethnicization and the political struggles taking place, and to assess whether the seemingly successful strategies, which Garos have embraced, lead to structural empowerment, or whether they cause new forms of dependency, divide, marginalization, and structural injustice. 'The anthropologist who engages in politics and scholarship is not a traitor, but rather a trickster, someone who embodies different roles in different contexts and combines both in what I would label critical ethnography' (van Meijl, 2005: 241).

Notes

1. 'Tribalist discourse' refers to the way in which (South Asian) tribes have been depicted—as if they share a number of 'essentially tribal characteristics' that are fundamentally different from, even opposite to, 'civilized' society. It shows a striking similarity with Orientalist representations of people from the Orient (as described by Edward Said, in van Schendel, 1992).
2. After the Partition in 1947, the Indian government developed special policies for so-called backward tribes (Scheduled Tribes). In post-colonial Pakistan and Bangladesh no similar policies vis-à-vis marginalized minorities were developed.
3. By the end of the 1990s, I estimated that of the 80,000–100,000 Garos in Bangladesh, approximately 14,000 were living in Modhupur (Bal, 2007: 11).

References

Bal, Ellen. 2007. *They Ask If We Eat Frogs: Garo Ethnicity in Bangladesh*. Singapore: ISEAS.

———. 2010. Taking Root in Bangladesh: States, Minorities and Discourses on Citizenship. In Erik de Maaker and Markus Schleiter (eds), *IIAS Newsletter. Special Issue 'Indigenous India'* (Special Issue No. 53), pp. 24–25.

Bayly, Susan. 1999. *Caste, Society and Politics in India from the Eighteenth Century to the Modern Age*. The New Cambridge History of India: IV, Vol. 3. Cambridge: Cambridge University Press.

Eriksen, Thomas Hylland. 2002. *Ethnicity and Nationalism: Anthropological Perspective* (2nd edition). London: Pluto Press.

Iggers, Georg G. 2010. The Role of Professional Historical Scholarship in the Creation and Distortion of Memory. *Chinese Studies in History*, 43(3): 32–44.

Inden, Ronald. 1990. *Imagining India*. Oxford: Basil Blackwell.

Karlsson, Bengt G. 2003. Anthropology and the 'Indigenous Slot': Claims to and Debates about Indigenous Peoples' Status in India. *Critique of Anthropology*, 23: 403–423.

Khaleque, Kibriaul. 1985. My fieldwork Experiences in a Garo Village of Bangladesh. In Anwarullah Chowdhury (ed.), *Pains and Pleasures of Fieldwork*, pp. 207–223. Dhaka: National Institute of Local Government.

Mandi. 1994. 28 minutes. Directed by Ashfaque Munir. Produced by SEHD.

Paraka. 1996. *Mandi-rang-ni Chiti* (Easter Issue), p. 1.

Report of the Commissioner for SC & ST. 1952. Volume 1. New Delhi, p. 11.

Said, Edward W. 1995. *Orientalism*. London: Penguin Books.

Tajfel, Henry. 1981. *Human Groups and Social Categories: Studies in Social Psychology*. Cambridge: Cambridge University Press.

Timm, R.W. 1991. *The Adivasis of Bangladesh*. London: Minority Rights Group.

van Meijl, Toon. 2005. The Critical Ethnographer as Trickster. *Anthropological Forum*, 15(3): 235–245.

van Schendel, Willem. 1992. The Invention of the 'Jummas': State Formation and Ethnicity in Southeastern Bangladesh. *Modern Asian Studies*, 26(1): 95–128.

———. 2009. *A History of Bangladesh*. New York: Cambridge University Press.

van Schendel, Willem and Ellen Bal. 1998. Name Ki Ache? In Willem van Schendel and Ellen Bal (eds), *Banglar Bahujati: Bangali Anyanya Jatir Prasanga*, pp. 9–24. Calcutta: International Centre for Bengal Studies.

2

Power and Authority in the Field

Ali Khan

The Field Site

Having spent the best part of a month in the capital city of Islamabad organizing my stay in the field I was ready to proceed to the field-work site. Located in the north-east of Pakistan's most populous province, Punjab, Sialkot is approximately 220 km from Islamabad. The drive was estimated between four and six hours depending on traffic. My intention was to get there before sunset and as a result I departed early in the morning. Driving becomes considerably more difficult as dusk falls. There are few overhead lights and the glare of headlights from oncoming traffic blinds the driver, making night-time driving hazardous. To compound difficulties not only had I never been to Sialkot but a pit stop at a mechanic's on the way extended to almost six hours and it was not until 4:00 pm that I was able to resume my journey.

Sialkot is not situated en route the new eight-lane motorway that connects Islamabad and the provincial capital, Lahore. Instead, it is reached by driving along the famous Grand Trunk (GT) Road described by Kipling in his book *Kim* as being 'such a river of life as exists nowhere else in the world'. A less romanticized account is given by Sir Malcolm Darling (1934: 72), a senior British officer in the Indian Civil Service, 'The road was pleasanter in the days of Kim, and though untarred, it could not have been dustier, for as lorry met lorry, both were forced on to the nearby earthy tracks on either side and the air became thick as London fog.'

The road is now tarred but apart from a massive increase in traffic nothing much has changed including the dustiness and the habit of larger vehicles forcing others off the road. Within an hour of leaving Islamabad, I had passed the town of Gujar Khan from where I was to learn later, that a *biraderi* (patrilineage) of *lohars* (blacksmiths) had migrated to Sialkot over a hundred years ago. They settled in Sialkot in a village called Kotli Loharan (literally 'abode of the blacksmiths') and distinguished themselves during British times for excellence in damascened work. Later their skill formed the basis of Sialkot's surgical manufacturing goods industry and spread to a number of other villages, which again took the inspiration for their names from the occupation of their inhabitants, notably Talwaran Mughlan (Sword of the Mughals) and Talwaran Rajputan (Sword of the Rajputs). Towns on either side of the GT Road have grown rapidly due to their proximity to the main commercial transport artery. On entering a new town, the road on both sides becomes surrounded by colourful local bazaars selling fruits, vegetables, chicken, meat, and locally made handicrafts. Roadside restaurants known as *khokhas*, particularly popular with truckers, sell a variety of freshly made dishes—usually a *daal* (lentils), a couple of vegetarian dishes and a meat dish. To complete the menu, there is an excessively sweet, milky tea. In winter, trade is further bolstered by the sale of hot *samosas* and *gajar ka halva* (a dessert made of carrots and cream). In summer, locally made ice-cream called *kulfi* makes a welcome appearance. The villages dotted round the town of Gujar Khan form the rural hinterland of the district. Many villagers work in the town but prefer to live in their villages commuting to town every morning. There is a reluctance to move from ancestral family lands, which are seen as providing men with their identity. For women, because marriage is patrilocal, the attachment to land is not as strong. But the 'roots of men' should not be severed with the land from where they have come. Even those who migrate tend to return to their ancestral villages or, in the event of those migrating to countries as far as the United Kingdom, at least maintain the 'myth of return'. As a result, all those who have land tend to retain small agricultural fields in the villages. Wage work in the urban areas complements any income received from agricultural work. Punjabis of all the ethnic groups in Pakistan are said to show the closest attachment to their *zameen* (land). A history of settlement in this fertile land has led to this long standing relationship so much so that the land is often seen and referred to as *maa*—the 'mother'. If the Pathan from the Frontier province is seen as the indomitable warrior, the Muhajir[1] as the urbane professional, the overwhelming image of the Punjabi is that of the 'son of the soil'.

The pattern of concentrated urban commercial activity around the main road with the more rural, residential base at a distance surrounding the urban core is repeated for other towns along the GT Road. Apart from the bazaars lining the roadside, the most common sights are the numerous automobile workshops catering to many breakdowns that occur on the road. Almost all the mechanics are taught entirely 'on the job', many having learned their skill as part of an apprenticeship that sees boys starting work from as early an age as eight. At that point, the boys known as *shagirds* (apprentices) usually carry out simple chores—filling tyres with air, fetching tea for the ustaad (expert), and cleaning the cars once they have been repaired. Apart from lunch the 'apprentices' will rarely receive any further benefits and will unlikely be paid more than ₹20–30 per day (US$0.25–0.35). In time, the young worker will increasingly be given more complex tasks to tackle. In two to three years of his training the apprentice will start earning a monthly salary and his aim, like those before him, will be to reach the rank of master mechanic. The cycle then repeats itself with a new generation of ustaads and *shagirds*. For many parents and their children this may not represent an ideal career but it allows the children the 'luxury' of two meals a day and in a country where schools have failed to attract or retain large numbers of students, it is often viewed as the best alternative. This 'traditional' form of 'education' or socialization, as anthropologists have termed it, involves learning by 'observing' and 'doing'. Football stitching follows a similar pattern as will be examined in the subsequent essays. While I was not entering what the American journalist Jonathan Silvers (1996) had described as a land populated and run by children, it was a land where children participated more openly in the sphere of work rather than being excluded from the work place as in the West.

Summer had not yet come to an end but the sun was beginning to set earlier, so by dusk I was only halfway to Sialkot passing through the towns of Jhelum, Lalamusa, and Kharian. Jhelum is famous for being the place where Alexander the Great defeated Porus. Later Jhelum, like Kharian, became a British cantonment town and still retains its old military character with army academies, barracks, life-sized model tanks, and other armaments all part of the town's monuments. Lalamusa has the slightly less flattering distinction of being the centre of 'fake' merchandise—toys, batteries, and electrical items—are all made in Lalamusa but with a bit of imagination in the labelling process—they are effectively made in the United States. I had heard stories of how manufacturers in Lalamusa label their goods 'made in lalam USA'—the lalam written in very small print and the USA being bold but have to admit to not believing these accounts until

I purchased a set of batteries at the town. Needless to say they were 'Made in Ialam USA'. After a short tea break, I was off again, my speed slowing considerably as night fell.

Punjab's Industrial Belt

Leaving Kharian behind and passing through numerous smaller towns, I entered the city of Gujarat—one of the main industrial cities in Punjab's north-eastern industrial belt. Gujarat has made a reputation for itself as a producer of furniture and electric fans—both the ceiling and tabletop variety. Crossing over the river Chenab—one of the five rivers that run through Punjab,[2] the GT Road carries on towards Gujranwala and on to the provincial capital, Lahore, which, with a population of five million, is Pakistan's second largest city and its cultural and historical centre. Gujranwala borders Sialkot district on the west and south-west and has become a hub of industrial activity in ceramics; iron safes; and copper, brass, and aluminium utensils.

Both Gujarat and Gujranwala, unlike Sialkot, have developed medium- and large-scale industry. Sialkot's industry has remained focused on small-scale industrial units based almost entirely on local Sialkoti entrepreneurs who emerged from the ranks of artisan to become the industrialists of today.[3] In contrast, Punjab's other industrial areas have their economic development fuelled by Muslim industrialists who migrated from India during Partition. Very few settled in Sialkot,[4] the primary reason being the district's proximity to the disputed border with India. The second reason given is that Lahore, Gujranwala, and Faisalabad, Punjab's other large industrial centres, had already developed their small- and medium-scale industry and this provided entrepreneurs more opportunity to start up economic activity. In addition, migrating entrepreneurs were usually 'compensated' for loss of livelihood resulting from migration by being given businesses left behind by Sikhs and Hindus who moved to India. Sialkot, in contrast, was the centre of cottage industry and this meant fewer opportunities for outsiders. Despite the departure of the Sikh and Hindu entrepreneurial class, the majority of workers remained behind continuing to work at home or in small groups. As a result there were not many 'establishments' that remained unoccupied.

The minimal change in the composition of Sialkot's population meant that industry continued to be based on the indigenous artisan class. This was a unique feature of industry in Sialkot and it led to a strong feeling of local ownership of those industries and skills associated with them. The ingenuity of the Sialkoti craftsmen, their mastery of specialist skills, and their spirit of enterprise is deeply ingrained in the minds of Sialkotis and is reflected in the many tales of the 'legendary' craftsmen of Sialkot. For example, it was a common retort by respondents during my field interviews that all the cutlery and surgical goods made in Sialkot had 'made in England' stamped on them but were in fact crafted by Sialkot's blacksmiths. On more than one occasion I was told the legend of the worker from Kotli Loharan who built a steam engine on his own, only to have his hands cut off by the British for fear that their own industry could face competition from the extraordinarily skilled blacksmiths of Kotli Loharan. There are also many stories of the legendary *mochi* (cobbler) who when asked to repair a football by an English priest, not only repaired it but also made several new ones from leather left over from his work with leather saddles. The sports industry in Sialkot is said to have its genesis here. The skill of the Sialkoti craftsmen has become a part of the folklore surrounding the success of the industry in Sialkot indicating the importance of the historical dimension of craftsmanship in Sialkot.

To reach Sialkot, one must part ways with the GT Road having crossed the river Chenab. A smaller road veers off the Gujranwala bound GT Road towards Wazirabad and finally Sialkot. Wazirabad itself has a long history in medium- and small-scale manufacturing producing quality cutlery and crockery.

The 45 km to Sialkot city, via Wazirabad, would take another hour. The 'detour' represents an important turn. Northern Punjab's industrial belt consisting of Gujarat, Gujranwala, and Lahore is all serviced by the GT Road and their location along this main artery is an important advantage that Sialkot lacks. Again the proximity to the Indian border is a factor. The plains of Sialkot slope down from the uplands of the Himalayas and its north-eastern border is shared with the disputed territory of Kashmir. On a clear day one can see the Himalayan peaks and the Indian military watchtowers. During the 1965 war, the village of Chawinda (No. 115) in Sialkot was apparently the site for the largest tank battle since the Second World War. As the Indian army advanced into the district they were held back by Pakistani soldiers allegedly tying bombs to themselves and crawling under Indian tanks. Even today the villages along the border are prone to shelling as Indian and Pakistani troops exchange fire. As a consequence of its sensitive location there has been little government investment or support, making the success of its industry all the more celebrated.

Sialkot

There was considerably less traffic on the Wazirabad–Sialkot road but the road had deteriorated alarmingly from the chaotic but relatively well-maintained GT Road. Darkness had fallen by the time I passed a police checkpoint sign that signalled entry into Sialkot district—it did not need to—every 100 m or so there were signs pointing off the road towards 'Stitching Centres'. The influence of football stitching was immediately evident. Since the 1970s Sialkot has risen to become the hub of world's football manufacturing industry producing, by the early 1990s, three out of four footballs manufactured worldwide. About 15 km further, I read a signboard for Sambrial Dry Port. This is the depot from where all Sialkot's manufactured items are exported.

At the dry port, five or six massive trucks marked SDPT (Sialkot Dry Port Trust) were parked on the roadside. On one side a building marked Duty Free Shop was visible and on the other side the port itself. From the little hole I could see through the locked gates, crates of packed material lay ready for onward loading. Sambrial falls in the Daska tehsil[5] of Sialkot district. There are two further tehsils making up the district—Sialkot tehsil and Pasrur tehsil. Sialkot tehsil (population 1.2 million) is the most populous and urbanized, followed by Daska (population 860,611) and Pasrur (population 611,871). Altogether the district's population stands at just over 2.7 million.[6] Daska's larger towns, like Sambrial and Begowala Jhamut, are situated along the main road which travels on to Sialkot city. The surrounding villages in the tehsil are connected to this main road via unmetalled tracks. These approach roads often become impassable during the monsoon season (July–September), making contact with the villages difficult. The agricultural lands of Daska are amongst the most fertile regions and the installation of tube wells to exploit the subsoil water led not only to increase in the production of seasonal crops but also to the start of a cottage industry in the manufacture of diesel engines and accessories. Sialkot district, along with its tradition in cottage industries, is also renowned for the production of the famed basmati variety of rice.

Leaving Sambrial I was suddenly struck by a foul, acrid smell. My headlights caught pools of fluorescent red liquid on either side of the road. In the background was what looked like a large factory and on closer inspection it turned out to be a leather manufacturing plant. Sialkot has a long history of making leather products starting with saddles made in colonial times. Recently, the industry has grown rapidly and manufactured items including sports goods, leather jackets, gloves, and motorcycle apparel. But the enlargement in production has meant a subsequent increase in the toxic waste produced during the tanning process. Recent studies on leather tanning factories in another part of Punjab (Kasur) have revealed high levels of cancer and Hepatitis B amongst workers and local inhabitants. I was later informed that Sialkot was also suffering similarly and that a recent United Nations report had stated that within five years every person in Sialkot city would be affected by waste from the tanneries. There is a plan to move the tanneries away from the city to a separate site where a proper filtration and waste unit can be set up, but until that is implemented tannery waste is a serious concern.

Sialkot city is barely 5 km from this spot but luckily the toxic smell was no longer evident. On entering Sialkot city, there was some semblance of lighting and life. One major road, which appeared to pass through the heart of the city, was being re-laid. The drive to Sialkot after the turn-off from the GT Road had been dark and isolated throughout. Most villages were at some distance from the road and small towns like Sambrial had long since closed up for the night. Sialkot city was still awake at 10:00 pm. A few tea stalls and roadside restaurants were serving people but I had been told that Sialkot was a city that worked hard during the day and closed up soon after nightfall. Much of this was a reflection of the fact that many of the labourers working in the city come from the surrounding villages swelling the city's population of 400,000 to considerably more during the day. Having commuted early in the morning, most workers return home at the end of the day. Coming into Sialkot may be time consuming and relatively expensive in terms of daily transport costs but the city provides a wider range of employment than the rural areas, particularly in times when rice and wheat crops are not being sown. Although living in the city is more expensive than in the villages where food and accommodation in particular are cheaper. There is also the desire to own and maintain the family land.

Ten minutes later I stumbled onto the field residence of an NGO with whom I had arranged accommodation. I reached Sialkot in one piece—the birthplace of two of Pakistan's most famous poets: the revolutionary Faiz Ahmed Faiz and the Cambridge educated philosopher-poet, Muhammad Iqbal, who in 1930 envisioned the concept of Pakistan as a separate nation-state for the Muslims of the subcontinent. Today, Iqbal's old house, located in the bustling centre of Sialkot city, has been transformed into a modest museum and library. In the following days, the curator at Iqbal Manzil, Rana Naeem would hold me hostage while relating tales of the early history of Sialkot. Over a succession of lunches, usually consisting of *pullao* (rice and meat) taken away from a nearby restaurant, Naeem would pull out books, documents, and gazetteers to help piece together a picture of early Sialkot.

> Sialkot is an ancient city and district. There have been people settled here for centuries—and there were, till Independence, many religions represented here. The Sikhs have always seen Sialkot as a holy place and every year they come from across the world to pay homage at the temple of Guru Baba Nanak—the founder of their religion. There are also several shrines of Sufis (Muslim saints), the most well known being the mosque and shrine of Imam Sahib. It is one of the oldest strongholds of the Muslim religion and is held in great reverence throughout Punjab. But the earliest accounts of Sialkot appear in the ancient Hindu religious epics, the Mahabharata and the Ramayana, during which the city is described as flourishing until floods left the entire area under water and uninhabited for a thousand years. Sialkot was rediscovered by a Hindu warrior of Kshatriya tribe and rose to become their political and military centre until Alexander the Great laid siege to it and subsequently razed it to the ground.[7] After that, the city's next resurgence came under the Mauryan Emperor, Ashoka,[8] during whose reign the city became a centre of Buddhist learning. Following further upheavals and invasions, notably by the Huns and the Central Asian invader, Mahmud Ghaznavi, Sialkot's fortunes continued to ebb and flow, until the onset of the Mughal Empire.[9] The stability that followed allowed the city to rebuild. Then Sialkot started becoming a famous industrial centre.

Rana Naeem talked endlessly, thrilled at having found someone interested in his 'home town', and whom he could impress with his knowledge. As he appeared to have few occasions to flaunt his expertise he ensured that my lunches with him lasted late into the afternoons. He somewhat reluctantly photocopied material for me, provided me several important contacts in Sialkot, and invited me back on numerous occasions. I found later that his reluctance to photocopy material was based on the fact that most of his 'inside' accounts of Sialkot were gleaned from the material he photocopied for me. Nevertheless, it did mean that 'his' information was generally backed up by historical accounts of the region.[10]

Back in my bedroom, as I stared out of my curtainless window, the monsoon air was still warm and moist but a ceiling fan made it less oppressive. In winter it would get much colder—dropping to almost zero degrees in a few months—and there would be thick fog that envelopes this part of Punjab for two to three weeks. Just outside the house I could see the local railway station. Every morning a crowded train would stop here bringing daily-wage commuters to the numerous industrial workshops that have been part of the Sialkot's history for so long and which are still dotted around the city today. I would find that Sialkot city was the focal point of football industry but the industry's structure had meant that the work areas had pushed their way 'out' into the surrounding villages. Unlike the commuters streaming into Sialkot city, my fieldwork would take me in the opposite direction—to the outlying villages that provide labour for football stitching.

Fieldwork

Besides introducing the field site, this essay deals with how the background and structure of organizations involved in a developmental project to eradicate child labour from the football stitching industry influenced the nature of the information they gathered. It, therefore, makes sense that prior to an examination of those organizations, a similar analysis is undertaken to show how the background of the author may have affected the overall research including fieldwork. It also allows for the introduction of Bunyad, the NGO involved in the project and through whose assistance I undertook fieldwork in Sialkot.

My family belongs to a section of society that can be described as the westernized, urban-based intelligentsia—part of the elite but not part of the landowning political ruling class. I, like my parents and siblings, was educated abroad and when in Pakistan lived only in the capital city of Islamabad, which remains the area least 'representative' of Pakistan. The city was designated as the capital of Pakistan in 1958 mainly to offset the economic importance of Karachi. In 1966, the first building of the new capital was occupied and since then Islamabad has come to be dominated by diplomats and federal government officials. Accordingly, in order to cater to these national and international elite, the facilities—schools, hospitals, parks, and electricity supply—are of a much higher standard than in any other part of Pakistan. My upbringing in and outside Pakistan was a 'privileged' and elite one. As a result, we spoke English at home and hardly ever wore traditional dress. It was only during a three-year research-based position with the World Bank in Islamabad that took me to the rural areas of Pakistan where I became aware of a larger world outside the confines of the capital. It was during this exposure to a world that had not existed for me previously that the interest in research on a related field first emerged.

My decision to undertake research on child labour was cemented through my association with Shaheen Atiq-ur-Rehman. Shaheen is a second cousin of my mother and I have personally known her for several years. In the early 1990s, Shaheen formed an NGO by the name Bunyad. Child labour was one of the areas that Shaheen's NGO focused on. During my stint at the World Bank I visited several of Bunyad's projects and was deeply impressed by Shaheen's commitment towards the less 'privileged' sections of society. When I informed her of my desire to start a PhD she suggested that I consider research on a new project that was being prepared—the Sialkot football stitching project. The decision to examine this particular project, then, was made for two reasons—first, a personal interest in child labour and second, on a more practical level, my access to Bunyad and their child labour project via Shaheen. I was aware that child labour was a sensitive topic and eliciting information on it would be problematic without an entry point. Bunyad gave me that entry point allowing me to grab the opportunity to tap into information that had not yet been fully explored. Shaheen informed me:

> You come and look at every aspect of the project. My boys will help you in everything and we need all the help that we can get. I can arrange for your stay in Sialkot. Come for a year if you like though I have so much to show you that you will have enough information for a PhD in two months.

Shaheen had made the field accessible to me, not simply through Bunyad, which had opened 140 non-formal schools for child stitchers in Sialkot and was the organization closely involved at the 'grassroots' with football stitchers, but also through her extensive contacts with international agencies and more importantly with an array of people in Sialkot—from industrialists to football stitchers. My association with Bunyad and with Shaheen was invaluable, both in the initial entry into the villages where I undertook fieldwork and subsequently when I would search for more of the 'insider' accounts from informants. As soon as I was introduced as 'Madam's nephew', people became warm towards me. Furthermore, the fact that I myself came from a high status, widely respected family[11] that had roots with the movement to secure Pakistan as a separate homeland for Muslims of India[12] was a further advantage in the field. Many of those I interacted with in the field were aware of these important family connections and as Razavi (1992: 155), who undertook fieldwork at home in Iran, has pointed out, 'being identified with a highly respected local family allays initial distrust'. The association with Bunyad literally opened up the field for me not only in terms of football stitchers but also in terms of examining the development organizations involved in the wider process. Without this backing, I doubt if I would have been able to get access to, for example, Qayyum, the owner of the independent home factory, or to Iftikhar Shah, the contractor responsible for keeping strangers like myself out of the stitching centre he was in charge of. I also doubt that I would have received the same co-operation from the adult stitchers who became my informants or the football manufacturers I interviewed. Furthermore, I had the advantage of a 'free hand' in terms of my investigation of Bunyad and the way that the NGO itself worked as well as its interaction with 'partner' organizations.

Having gained an enviable level of access, I soon found that many preconceived ideas that were part of my own upbringing were to be challenged. I began my research taking for granted that all child work was abhorrent and damaging for children, that education represented the only antidote to child labour and that the two were mutually exclusive activities. Moreover, I shared the belief that parents behaved 'irrationally' by having large families and then sending their children to work rather than school. In addition, there has been little anthropological study done in Sialkot. The recent initiatives against child labour have meant a proliferation of rapid assessment surveys, short-term studies, and situation analyses. However, these writings have tended to remain within international development agency and NGO circles. More accessible were a number of journalistic pieces. With little other direct information available, my earliest impressions of Sialkot were dominated by these media representation of Sialkot and it was this which formed the basis of my planned methodology. Two of the most influential articles specifically concerning child labour in Sialkot's sports industry (Schanberg, 1996; Silvers, 1996) were typical of early writings on child labour in Pakistan.

> In recent months, Western journalists had been threatened and assaulted for reporting on child labour in this still feudal society, particularly in those industries where legions of small children toil for 60 cents a day to make products for export to the US and other developed countries.

Silver's article had similarly mentioned an attack on a Norwegian trade union delegation as they visited a sports factory. The delegation's guide and cameraman were apparently severely beaten by armed men believed to be working for the sports factory being inspected. In addition to these reports was the violent death of Iqbal Masih, the child labourer turned human rights activist. Whether or not the accounts were correct, my most immediate concerns regarding fieldwork were linked to the element of danger that had been highlighted by Silvers and Schanberg and by the murder of Iqbal Masih.

Apart from my own uneasiness, the second issue influencing fieldwork methodology was a direct outcome of the way the discourse on child labour in Sialkot developed through media reporting and subsequent pressure on Sialkot over the involvement of children in its export industries. The growing resentment ensuing from what was locally seen as the imposition of an external reality leading to interference in Sialkot's affairs left target informants suspicious and occasionally hostile to outsiders. Business had been adversely affected and this had negative repercussions on both local industrialists and stitchers. Foreign media had in many local eyes, sensationalized events to create undue hysteria against Sialkot's world famous sports goods industry. More practically, all this attention was affecting the livelihood of workers. In such an environment, suspicion and mistrust of outsiders was running high. Earlier studies on child labour had noted that workers and villagers had been reluctant to reveal information about working children. A survey carried out in Sialkot by Save the Children (1997) reported that villagers had been told by subcontractors not to talk about working children to researchers, and many workers feared the loss of jobs and livelihoods. It was this environment that I faced on arrival in Sialkot and it was these conditions that dictated the method of subsequent fieldwork.

Organizational Ideology

Pottier (1993: 7) points out that project ethnography must focus on the internal functioning of development organizations themselves, 'in particular on their ideologies; the modes adopted for decision making and the practice of personnel recruitment'. In this second part of the essay I will attempt to show how the different ideologies, internal hierarchies, training techniques, and office cultures of two of the main organizations involved in the project to prevent children from stitching footballs influenced not only the nature of the information they collected but also the discourse on child labour in Sialkot and the subsequent implementation of the programme. On the one hand, it led to a more harmonious and positive relationship which benefitted my own fieldwork; on the other, it discouraged the receptivity, patience, open mindedness, and respect for the opinions of others that active participation demands, leading eventually to a marginalization of the target 'beneficiaries'. The stitcher's views became no more than legitimizing inputs. A deconstruction of the rhetoric of policy reveals the self-interest and power relations that underpin and dictate the direction that the emerging discourse on child labour took. Ultimately, the power of one organization over the other led to a 'discourse coalition', which again was based on a representation of reality that had more to do with the organization's own survival than with the reality of football stitchers. In Sialkot, the organizational structure of the international organization, the information gathered, and the analysis of this information were all geared towards the survival of the organization and maintaining the imposed representation of reality rather than challenging it.

In the given environment, it was essential that a considerable effort be made towards establishing trust on both the sides. Without trust I would not have the confidence to ask the sensitive questions I needed to. Similarly, without trust my respondents would, at best, pay lip service to my queries leaving me with access to only surface-level information. In this crucial period of building trust I was helped immeasurably by my association with Bunyad.

Bunyad

Bunyad means 'foundation' in Urdu and refers to the NGO's aim of providing the skills that it believes form the basis of society. Bunyad, or to give its full name, Bunyad Literacy Community Council (BLCC) was founded in 1994 and its remit centres on the provision of non-formal education to families in low-income areas of Pakistan. Special emphasis is given to female education. BLCC is based in Lahore but has field offices all over Punjab.

The NGO was founded by Shaheen Atiq-ur-Rehman, its charismatic and dedicated vice-chairperson. Her father was governor of Punjab and a widely respected figure. However, despite her elite background, Shaheen has always been unique in her ability to relate to the 'poor' and today her reputation in Punjab is second to none. I am reminded of the occasion, when one of Bunyad's projects was chosen as a 'model' to be shown to the then World Bank president James Wolfensohn. I was accompanying Shaheen on the trip to the site when we were informed that the World Bank 'reconnaissance' team that were to pre-test the site were running late and may have had to abandon the proposed visit. The only way for the group to beat the clock would be to use the still unopened section of the motorway between Islamabad and Lahore. When we approached the barrier, the World Bank team swaggered out of their shiny white Land Cruiser. From our less impressive jeep we saw the motorway police refuse point blank the request to use the motorway. Shaheen, known less for her patience or diplomacy and more for her brutal honesty and frankness, stormed out from behind the wheel, mouthing the choicest Punjabi expletives to herself, 'We have to be in Lahore in 45 minutes. I will take responsibility for these people.' On seeing her, the policeman and his officer immediately stated in unison 'Madam, if you are taking them to Lahore it must be important. Please go ahead.' With a salute the police sent us on our way.

Prior to turning to NGO activities, Shaheen had served as a minister for Social Welfare in the provincial Punjab Government. As someone who knows her can testify, Shaheen distinguished herself during her stint as a minister as one of the only government officials accessible to the public. Unlike many of her counterparts who chose to remain ensconced in their 'ivory towers', Shaheen in her element visited the people she 'served'. A boisterous, no nonsense, battle tank, she thrived on 'getting her own hands dirty', tirelessly visiting the villages and projects that her ministry was responsible for. When her stint as a minister ended, Shaheen proceeded to set up Bunyad as a way of continuing the work she started in her role as a minister. Her efforts towards the alleviation of poverty in Pakistan have been recognized internationally and Shaheen has received honours from a number of United Nations agencies. However, her most overt recognition comes from the low-income groups who frequently air their admiration for the sincerity of her attempts to assist them. She remains committed to working closely with these groups in Pakistan and has consistently rejected offers to take up international assignments.

Hailey (2001) citing evidence from research in the development and growth of South Asian NGOs points out that several of the most successful NGOs in South Asia had inspirational leaders. Like Shaheen Atiq-ur-Rehman, these leaders had a strong commitment to social justice and helping the rural poor. They had a clear vision of how they would contribute to local development, which underpinned all their work and interaction with local communities. Hailey mentions Shoaib Sultan Khan, who pioneered participatory development initiatives for the Aga Khan Rural Support Programme in northern Pakistan from 1982. Even before Shoaib Sultan Khan, Akhter Hameed Khan, seen as the 'father' of development in Pakistan, had successfully instituted 'self-help' projects in the urban slums of Karachi (Khan, 1996). Like Shaheen, both Akhter Hameed Khan and Shoaib Sultan Khan were inspirational leaders who ran their NGOs in a highly personalized manner. All these three inspirational leaders were able to develop strong personal loyalties among both the local villagers and their own staff, and 'there seems to be a sense of awe and reverence in the way that staff members and local people refer to them' (Hailey, 2001: 92). They also had the ability to empathize with a wide range of people, and to listen to their needs in an appropriate manner. Respect, empathy, and the strong stamp of their leaders characterized the work of these NGOs, including Bunyad. Without these exceptional leaders at the helm of their affairs, these NGOs are unlikely to have made the impact that they did.

However, while Shaheen is internationally known and has contacts with organizations like United Nations and World Bank, her relationship with their country headquarters is often not so smooth. This is partly an outcome of what Shaheen sees as an overly bureaucratic nature of the organizations with which she often interacts on a day-to-day basis and those organizations' reactions to what they see as Bunyad's haphazard and unconventional approach.

Bunyad's work ethic undoubtedly revolves around the domineering personality of its founder. But her urgency and desire to cover as many low-income communities as quickly as possible is often at odds with the rules, regulations, and reporting procedures that organizations such as the World Bank require to be strictly followed. The clash, then, is between formal organization systems that conform, at least in theory, to many of the elements described by Weber (1947) in his description of bureaucracies and more informal organizations that lack these 'Weberian' characteristics. We shall examine these in more detail in the following section.

Each room in Bunyad's headquarters is occupied by three or four staff members and there is constant chatter and movement between these rooms. Files are piled up in one corner, textbooks and school supplies to be sent to the field in another. The office appears chaotic but vibrant and in this unique manner Bunyad has established itself as Pakistan's largest NGO in the field of education, currently undertaking 5,000 villages in different districts of Punjab. Shaheen has a small office from where she oversees policy and deals with the NGO's public relations. Staff members pop in and out to ask 'Madam' a host of questions. Just before I left for the field when I visited the office I overheard:

> Madam, Malik Nazir rang from Sialkot to say that the International Labour Organization is planning a field visit to our weakest non-formal school.
> Tell him that he should ask the International Labour Organization man—Dilawar—to ring me here. If Dilawar tries any hanky panky with us, I'll have his balls cut off. He has been trying to have us removed from the project for months now.

The bearer of the message made an amused retreat from the office. Staff were used to their 'boss' employing 'strong' language. But it summed up

Shaheen and her relationship with her staff members. She is, all at once, a protective elder sister, a guide, and a mentor. I was, however, about to hear more of the tension between Bunyad and the International Labour Organization (ILO) when I reached Sialkot.

The staff at the Bunyad headquarters is young and consists of almost an equal number of men and women, many of whom are college graduates from the Department of Social Work at University of Punjab. The university increasingly caters to the middle and lower classes. The elite have long since abandoned national institutions and prefer to send their children abroad for education. Most of the staff members are paid a starting salary ranging between ₹3,000 and 7,000 (US$35–80) a month—barely enough to make ends meet. But in most cases the recent graduates/staff members are subsidized by parents in terms of housing and meals, and therefore see their stint in Bunyad as a valuable starting point in an organization with a good reputation. Several of the staff members are keen to spend some time working in rural areas to gain the 'field' experience that their course did not include. There is also the attraction of working with Shaheen Atiq-ur-Rehman who brings the same informality of interaction to the office that characterizes her relationship with the communities that Bunyad works with. This rapport is an important hallmark of Shaheen's relationship with her fellow staff members and with Bunyad's partner organizations. It is, therefore, also central to Bunyad's ideology and work ethic. Bunyad, as an organization, exuded a young, energetic, and informal approach. There was little instituted hierarchy within the organization though everyone was aware of who was in charge. This philosophy would also define the outlook, approach to work, and charter for action for Bunyad's field staff in Sialkot.

Fieldwork and Fieldworkers

My introduction to Bunyad's field office staff in Sialkot marked my initiation to fieldwork. Bunyad had agreed to rent me a single room in their field residence. The residence was located in Uggokki, a semiurban locality on the outskirts of Sialkot city. The house consisted of four bedrooms. The two double bedrooms were occupied by two staff members each. The single rooms, including the one allocated to me, were of single occupancy. The only furniture present was the *charpai*s (simple string beds) and a dining table with two wooden benches. I decided to do without a *charpai* preferring instead to put my mattress on the floor. An overhead fan provided relief from the mosquitoes but not the heat, which in summer reached up to 40°C. In winter, a single rod heater was the only source of warmth. There was hot water in summer courtesy of the water tank on the roof being 'naturally' heated by the fierce summer sun. In winter there was only cold water and the staff joked that when hot water was required there was only cold water and when cold water was required there was only hot!

My housemates at the Bunyad residence, especially Mohammed Aslam, Malik Nazir, Danish Reza, and Abdul Razzaq became, over the duration of my fieldwork, not only important informants and key 'gatekeepers' but also close friends. These four were involved in Bunyad's programme to 'rehabilitate' child stitchers. Effectively, my new 'colleagues' became research assistants, and rapidly familiarized me with Sialkot by providing vital contextual information about the villages, local culture, and subtleties of language. Furthermore, they acted as 'ambassadors at large, introducing fieldworkers to the local community and discretely explaining the presence to people who might be too shy or suspicious to ask directly (Devereux and Hoddinott, 1992: 26)'.

So it was usually the experienced Aslam, the meticulous Razzaq, or the maverick Danish, who introduced me to a new group of villagers by saying,

This is Ali bhai [brother]. He has come all the way from England to spend a year with us in Sialkot to learn about how these recent initiatives against child labour have affected all of us in Sialkot.

Bunyad has been working in Sialkot since late 1997 following the signing of the Atlanta Agreement in February 1997. The Agreement was drawn up in Atlanta, United States, by the Sialkot Chamber of Commerce and Industry (SCCI), which consists of a group of local industrialists, the ILO, the United Nations Children's Fund (UNICEF) and 'Save the Children'— United Kingdom. All the partners were assigned different roles with the central aim of the Agreement being the progressive withdrawal of children working in football manufacturing. The ILO had to monitor the entire programme to ensure that children were being phased out of the production process and were being placed in non-formal schools. The ILO contracted Bunyad as the NGO responsible for the provision of non-formal schools. Of the other partners, UNICEF worked on strengthening the government education system, 'Save the Children' was given charge of gathering community level information in an effort to gauge the effect of the instituted programme on communities, and the SCCI was responsible for persuading manufacturers to join the programme.

Bunyad's remit involved setting up 140 free, non-formal education schools in those villages which were identified as having the highest concentration of child stitchers. The schools—in keeping with development discourses' stress on being an elevating, 'redemptive' process—were known as Umang Taleemi Centres (UTCs)—Schools of Hope. Bunyad conducted its field operations through five field councillors, three of whom were also my housemates. Two further councillors were locally based and lived in their own houses in Sialkot. Each councillor was assigned a certain number of schools and was responsible for ensuring that the schools under his remit functioned smoothly through ensuring regular supplies of teaching materials and closely monitoring staff and student attendance. Problems were reported to the councillors, to be forwarded to the field Project Manager, who was responsible for co-ordinating field activities (see Figure 2.1).

Within my first week in the field I realized that one of my most basic assumptions concerning fieldwork methodology needed to be adjusted. Sialkot city would not be the focus of my activities. The football industry was based in the city but by the 1970s had decentralized to the surrounding villages. A further realization hit me when I spent an hour on the back of a motorbike travelling to one of the most far-flung villages in the district. Sialkot district measures 3,016 km^2 and some villages lay more than 35 km from the city centre and are accessible only by motorbike. This research was not going to follow traditional South-Asian village anthropology that used intensive village-based studies as their focus (e.g., Eglar, 1960; Kessinger, 1974). Instead I travelled from one end of the district to the other. My 'research community' was bound only by the proviso that there were children stitching footballs in a particular place thereby making the fieldwork process-based, rather than place-based. The process in this case was stitching footballs and it was Sialkoti stitching rather than a particular location that formed the unit of my analysis.

As football stitching had spread to include almost all of Sialkot's approximately 1,500 villages, I decided to concentrate on those villages where Bunyad had identified concentrations of stitchers, and had accordingly established non-formal schools, as my focal locations. These villages were spread evenly through Sialkot's three tehsils—Pasrur, Daska, and Sialkot. In the course of fieldwork I also managed to visit a number of villages where schools had not been established. This provided additional and often contrasting information to that gathered from the sample villages. However, the majority of the information gathering was focused in villages where existing contacts had been built up primarily through the NGOs setting up of

Figure 2.1:
Bunyad field office structure

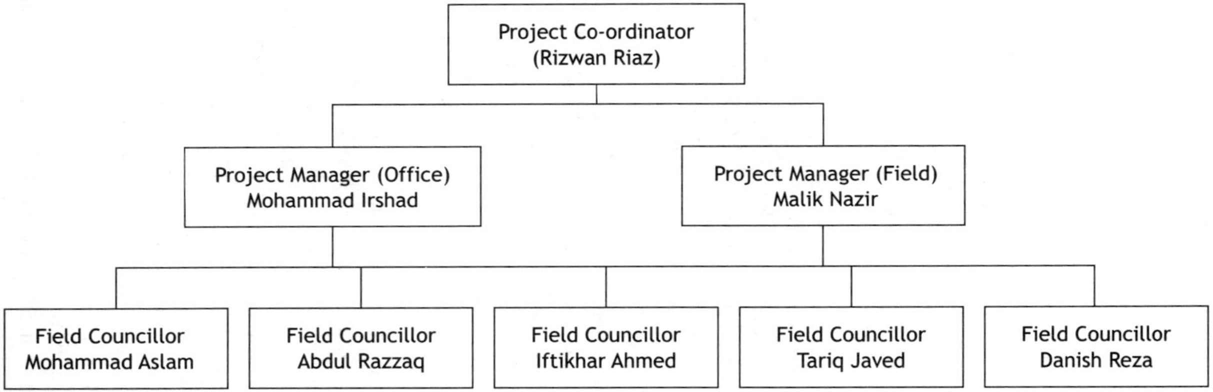

Source: Author.

schools. From the core group of child stitchers placed in non-formal schools I traced linkages to their parents as well as looser ties to other members of the village. The schools also provided links to children who had dropped out. This was an important group as some children had found alternate work and interviewing them provided vital information on the decision making process of those children who chose to work rather than stay in school. Once respondents were identified and entries were gained, the effort left was to gather information from children and parents as well as those who were more directly involved in the business aspect of the industry, primarily the subcontractors and the industrialists.

Malik Nazir, Abdul Razzaq, Danish Reza, and Mohammed Aslam all had spent the best part of two years of their lives working closely with communities throughout Sialkot in an attempt to popularize Bunyad's schools. Nazir was the most educated with a Masters degree in Social Work from Punjab University and had been given the position of the field project manager. The remaining three were field councillors. Razzaq and Danish had completed their college education, while Aslam's association with school had finished at the end of primary school. Malik Nazir spoke some English. Razzaq and Danish spoke less, Aslam not at all. They spoke to each other in Punjabi but were also fluent in Urdu. All came from modest backgrounds and from families based in rural Punjab rather than larger cities. The two locally based councillors—Iftikhar and Tariq—were of similar backgrounds and both, like Aslam, spoke no English and had only a primary level education. Nevertheless, there was a strong camaraderie between the staff and no evident hierarchy within the group. Even Malik Nazir, the team leader, rarely if ever, overtly displayed his authority over the others. Decisions were made collectively and on the basis of joint discussion. Each team member's opinion was elicited and considered even if it was not always implemented. The fact that four of the six team members worked and lived together meant that there was an even closer 'bonding'. Furthermore, all of the staff was approximately of the same age—between 25 and 32. The only exception, and the one staff member who failed to gel with the rest of the group in the field office, was Muhammad Irshad. Irshad, or Irshad Sahab[13] as he was known to one and all, was around 50 and was a local Sialkoti who had served in the army at a junior level. Irshad was the office project manager and was responsible for compiling accounts, distributing salaries, and filing financial reports. He brought all his military meticulousness to the office and would spend all day examining what time the team members arrived at the office and what time they left. He was strictly a 'desk man' as compared to the field-based councillors and the field project manager. Irshad was also acutely conscious of what he perceived was his status as the man in-charge of the office. As such, he expected that a certain respect and deference be paid to him—for his seniority as an officer as well as his seniority in age. On most occasions the field staff acquiesced, although it was usually done tongue and cheek, in a kind of mock and overly deferential manner. Irshad was often the target of much mischief courtesy the councillors and Malik Nazir. 'Irshad Sahab your hair is looking excellent today. I hope I have such hair when I reach your age' was the usual comment of the day when Irshad arrived with freshly dyed hair. Never quite sure whether it was a genuine compliment or not Irshad ended up taking offence on some days and ignoring it altogether on others. But Irshad aside, the Bunyad staff members worked well together as a team. They were hardworking, honest, and took pride in their work. However, one point that struck me about the arrangement of the field team and which I asked Shaheen about, was the team's all-male composition, especially as much of the work involved dealing with women and children. Furthermore, staff at Bunyad's headquarters in Lahore was equally divided between male and female employees. The answer was characteristically frank and practical.

> I can't send girls out into the field in Sialkot. We have only one residence in Sialkot. These men have never lived with unrelated women in the same house. I will end up having to deal with affairs and unwanted pregnancies. It's too much of a risk and would jeopardise the entire programme.

For me, the initial meeting with the fieldworkers came as an unexpected culture shock. Coming from a 'privileged' background, doing fieldwork 'at home' was not quite what I had expected. I felt as out of place here as I believe I would have been had I decided to undertake fieldwork outside Pakistan. It was an encounter that also brought home my own upbringing as part of the elite—completely divorced from the everyday life of the majority of the population.

But once we had moved beyond the initial awkwardness, the 'adjustment' period was short. The fact that I spoke Urdu as they did, and that Punjabi and Urdu are mutually understandable meant that communication began immediately and I soon found that there was more in common between the fieldworkers and myself than I had first assumed, starting with a love of cricket. It is often said about Pakistan, that the only two things that bind the country together are Islam and cricket. So, the early morning live television telecasts from Sydney at 4:00 am and 7:00 am from Perth[14] were important 'bonding' sessions. Dinners were also always communal events and after a day in the field, socializing was usually limited to spending time together. As a result, within a month, I found that I was getting benefitted from some of the advantages of working at home including developing surprisingly close relationships with informants and 'research associates'. This was strongly influenced by our cultural affinity. There was also a store of knowledge I had acquired over the years simply from 'being Pakistani'. In addition to the importance of understanding and speaking the language, this store of knowledge meant that it was easier to pick up on subtleties—to understand people not only by the words that they used but also by their tone of voice, the way they reacted to certain subjects, and by their body language and gestures.

My 'acceptance' by the fieldworkers and subsequently through them as part of a familiar local institution, by villagers involved in football stitching, was also assisted by the fact that I had to spend a year doing fieldwork. Many of my informants, starting with my four 'research assistants', seemed almost flattered that I was spending a year in Sialkot away from the 'luxuries' of England in order to learn about their project and way of life. Secondly, my (not premeditated) strategy of, to use Spradley's term, 'maintaining naiveté'—the skill of being a novice—was also useful. In this, I was perhaps helped, like Gans (1982: 57) by 'what seems to be an honest face, a visible earnestness about wanting to do research, and a quiet demeanour that perhaps tells people that I will not be a threat to them'. In the environment of mistrust that was prevalent in Sialkot at the time of fieldwork and in order to discover the hidden principles of another way of life (Spradley, 1979: 4), the role of novice assisted in reducing the 'threat' factor and facilitated frank discussions with informants.

Therefore, one of the key components of my fieldwork strategy revolved around stating clearly my need to understand from the point of view of the football stitchers what they felt about the external imposition of a programme that directly targets their way of life. I felt this was the best approach to encourage respondents to see this as an opportunity for them to talk and for me to listen and learn. Often this meant spending hours 'held hostage', as in the case of Rana Naeem, giving an informant the chance to express his views on a range of subjects. Admittedly, there were occasions where we talked more about Shahid Afridi's batting and less on the effects of the decline in football stitching work. But on other occasions I was told about the continued involvement of children in the industry despite the programme. This series of unstructured interviews, described by Spradley (1979) as a series of friendly conversations into which the researcher slowly introduces new elements to assist informants to respond as informants, became an invaluable source of field data.

Thus the specific environment of mistrust in Sialkot, meant that my methodology was adjusted to ensure that engendering trust, was the foundation of any information. However, this proviso did impose certain restrictions on fieldwork.

At the outset, the fact that I was dealing with a large and dispersed population meant that trust building had to be negotiated on an almost daily basis. Furthermore, and related to research ethics, throughout fieldwork, I felt the intrusiveness of anthropological examination weighing heavily on my mind. Encroaching on another's way of life involves the encroached giving up part of their space and risking losing control of how they are represented. I was acutely aware that in Sialkot informants went out of their way to volunteer information to me. Some of this information was sensitive and divulging it may have had repercussions for them. In addition, I had little or nothing to offer them in return. In this situation I felt, even as a token gesture towards the integrity of the researcher–informant relationship, that I would abandon all use of cameras and dictaphones. This had a beneficial effect on my interviews in which the informants felt more comfortable without the intrusiveness of cameras or tape recorders. Moreover, the awkwardness of asking for a photograph or if a conversation could be taped was then bypassed. This was important not so much because of my discomfort at asking for photographs or taping conversations but because I felt that having volunteered so much information already, asking for more in the form of photographs or taped conversations would be going beyond my own limits as a researcher. Yet, on the few early occasions when I did ask whether I could take a photograph there were no refusals—only a slight hesitation. Nevertheless, I felt that this was overly exploitative of my informants and would have a negative impact on the quality of information volunteered. In fact in an effort to promote as relaxed an atmosphere as possible during the interviews I also abandoned the use of note taking during informal conversations with informants. Instead I would write up conversations on return to my room following a day in the field.

It is also worth pointing out that interviewing children requires different approaches to those involving adults. However, when I had undertaken some pre-fieldwork research on methodologies for interviewing children (James and Prout, 1998; James et al., 1998; Toren, 1993) in the field I relied largely on my general approach of reducing the 'threat' factor of the researcher. Winning the trust of child informants is crucial to gaining genuine information from them. In this, I found that my position as a young fieldworker helped me to reduce the distance between adult researcher and child informant. Furthermore, regular participation with children in events such as school plays, singing contests, sports events, and traditional games and perhaps, best of all, invitations to judge cookery contests at schools was extremely beneficial in enhancing my rapport with both children and community members.

However, the biggest influence on the manner I was able to gather information from the field came from my association with Bunyad and through the positive relationship that the NGO's fieldworkers had developed with child stitchers and their families. I believe and aim to show in the following pages, that this rapport between the two groups could be attributed to the ideology of the NGO, the social background of the fieldworkers, and their resulting attitudes towards the 'community'.

Informal and Anti-Bureaucratic—The Bunyad Organizational Ideology

On the one hand it could be argued that Bunyad promoted an unprofessional approach that led to ad-hocism and haphazardness in policy. But as Nicholson (1994: 75) points out in her examination of the fit between bureaucracies and indigenous systems in Papua New Guinea, there are demonstrable benefits in confusion and uncertainly, particularly in the room it gives managers to manoeuvre. In Bunyad, employees usually got positions through being recommended by fellow staff members. There was no structured recruitment drive and interviews if they were held, tended to be brief and informal. The Bunyad workers were committed, if anything, to anti-bureaucratic and egalitarian forms of organization. As such they exhibited the reverse of Weber's description of formal bureaucracy: there was no system of 'graded authority'; very little in the way of 'expert training', a rather fluid attitude towards rules, and a minimum number of written documents of the sort Weber had in mind in his analysis of bureaucracies. On the other hand, with low salaries being offered, it was likely that only those with some commitment to Bunyad's aims or those who saw it as part of a career in social work would be interested in taking up a position. Field positions were demanding and required dedication and hard work. It was rare for Bunyad's fieldworkers to return home before 6:00 pm having started at 8:00 am. Anyone finding this routine difficult did not remain with the organization long. My four research assistants had been with Bunyad for over two years and while they undoubtedly found the pay insufficient, they saw this as a trade-off for working in a line of work that provided a high degree of 'job satisfaction'.

For Aslam, as I suspect for the others, there was the added incentive of working for Madam Shaheen to whom he was completely devoted. These individuals were not highly educated. They were not trained in methods of 'community participation' or 'mobilization'. Nor did they have any knowledge of the various participatory techniques that are hallmark of current Western models of NGOs. This finding is consistent with Hailey's (2001) conclusion that participatory technologies such as Rapid Rural Appraisal (RRA), Participatory Rural Assessment (PRA), and Participatory Learning Analysis (PLA), and their associated tools and techniques may be of less consequence than the development literature suggests. Instead there appears to be a much greater reliance on personal engagement in order to shape decisions, operational issues, and programme design.

> In reviewing evidence from South-Asian NGOs it has been striking how important informal, personal interaction has been ... staff appear to have engaged with, and listened to, the communities with whom they work in an unstructured, informal manner. This highly personalized interaction has clearly shaped their programmes, and created a bond of trust between key staff and the communities with whom they work. (Hailey, 2001: 88–89)

Bunyad's work strategy was based on these principles and contrasts markedly with what Hailey (2001: 89) dubs the 'tyrannical' and 'formulaic' nature of participative technologies of organizations, such as Bunyad's funding agency, the ILO. Furthermore, the way that Bunyad developed this relationship is indicative of the attitudes that Bunyad's staff held towards those they were working with. But this close relationship did not emerge overnight. It required considerable effort as Aslam explained to me:

> At the start of the project we hadn't received any funding from the ILO. As a result we did not have motorcycles to go round the villages. I used to walk from village to village trying to persuade parents to send their children to school. We went from door to door in every village. We called group meetings and spoke to village elders. Initially they were extremely hostile towards us because they felt we were responsible for the decline in stitching work. But slowly the schools started attracting students and people realized that we were genuinely trying to minimize the effects of a decline in stitching work. Now after two years, I know nearly all the people in the thirty villages that I cover. They have come to accept us because week after week, rain or shine, they see us bringing books for schools, supporting the teachers and they see their children receiving some basic education.

The NGO staff invested considerable time, emotion, and energy building up relationships of trust and shared understanding between themselves and local people. The relationship between Bunyad and the villagers they worked with was founded on regular contact, personal ties, shared beliefs, and mutual dialogue. Bunyad's dedication and commitment lay at the root of their enviable rapport with the villagers.

The councillors rarely conveyed an air of superiority or power over the villagers with whom they worked. Neither was there an environment of reprimand nor of punishment. If children did not attend school, efforts were made to find out why this was so. But whatever course of action was taken was done in consultation with the parents and the children concerned. The only group who were regularly pushed to maintain a basic standard were the teachers. As Mohammed Aslam pointed out, the councillors had to visit villages where schools had been established on an almost daily basis. This regular contact meant certain accountability to the villagers and the development of a relationship—implying give and take on both the sides. A relationship also implies that both sides have a degree of understanding and empathy with one another other. There is a feeling of participation with rather than separation from.

The attitude of the NGO workers and their backgrounds allowed a distrustful group of 'beneficiaries' to accept and trust them as individuals who were sincere in their attempts at guiding and mentoring them. It helped that Bunyad's fieldworkers came from rural backgrounds and were familiar with the way of life in villages. All of them had also grown up doing some work in their childhood and were unfamiliar with the Western construct of childhood. As a result there was no immediate internalized rejection of child work as a breach of an inviolable right. But more important was the absence of a patronizing attitude that views indigenous processes and knowledge as inferior and unworthy of serious analysis. In its place was an openness to understand the point of view of the 'beneficiaries', which was clearly helped by the fact that their views were not overly different from those of the fieldworkers. This promoted mutual understanding between the groups. Furthermore, it was a relationship that once established was nurtured through the daily interactions that the councillors had with the children and wider social networks as well as through their organization of and participation in the frequent functions for students, teachers, and villagers.

Shaheen Atiq-ur-Rehman attended as many of these functions as she could, not only to keep staff morale high but also to try and raise the status, within the village, of the school teachers whom she saw as critical for the success of the schools. Apart from the larger functions there were smaller, day-to-day events that councillors would make a point to participate in.

Power and Authority—the ILO Organizational Ideology

The influence of the 'Bunyad ideology' and the attitudes of its staff members become apparent when contrasted with the ideology and approach of Bunyad's funding agency, the ILO. In contrast to Bunyad, the ILO is the archetypal formal organization with a bureaucratic organizational structure revolving around 'job descriptions, the hierarchy of decision making, goals, rules, and policies' (Wright, 1994: 17). Weber argued that bureaucracies achieve rational efficiency through well-defined formal structures. Each bureaucracy administers its official duties through an explicit hierarchical system. Specified roles and statuses divide work into delimited spheres of professional competence. Theoretically, bureaucracies are independent of personalities, their leaders' and members' lives do not intrude in the work environment. Candidates are appointed on the basis of their technical qualifications and their work roles are defined by a consistent set of abstract rules. Being a bureaucrat is a career, and promotion occurs in a regularized manner (Britan and Cohen, 1980: 10–11). The contrast with Bunyad's organization is apparent and it is not surprising that the differing structures have produced different approaches.

The ILO was created in 1919, at the end of the First World War. It thereby preceded the formation of the United Nations by almost three decades. Over the decades, the ILO has developed a long standing bureaucracy and as Britan and Cohen (1980: 19) point out, agencies with entrenched bureaucracies, such as the United Nations, 'often develop their own cultural orientations, goals, rituals, language, and norms'. Most studies on formal organizations have tended to concentrate on how individuals affect the organization and less on how organizations affect the individual. But being in a bureaucracy engenders certain patterns of behaviour, cultural norms, and sets of shared, learned, and transmitted behaviours. It is the function of the organization to pass on and reinforce this shared culture of its staff members so that this culture and ideology have a pervasive influence on the staff they surround.

The ILOs Pakistan headquarters are in the capital city, Islamabad. An imposing, newly constructed, three storey complex stands in one of Islamabad's most enviable locations. In the car park outside are numerous vehicles emblazoned with the ILO logo. A few of the shiniest and largest ones have drivers tending to them. The entrance to the building is guarded by security officials and entry without an appointment is not possible. Inside, the building is centrally air conditioned and finished in marble. The language of the workplace is English and the male staff is almost exclusively dressed in English style trousers and shirts rather than the traditional *salwar kameez*.[15] Women in Pakistan, regardless of background, will most commonly wear *salwar kameez*, though the styles and materials of these depend on affordability. Senior staff members have spacious single offices to themselves and there are several large conference rooms all furnished with specially imported furniture. The most senior posts are reserved for the foreign 'experts' transferred to Pakistan as part of the 'technical assistance' that international organizations provide to the host countries. These experts form part of the diplomatic corps in the country—a group that lives in the country but is neither bound by its laws nor is dependent on local facilities. Many foreign missions offer such a range of facilities for their staff that there is little need or incentive for them to come into contact with the host population. Staffs have access to separate hospitals, separate shops selling imported items, and separate schools, none of which are open to the general public, allowing these diplomats to live in a world within a world. Just beneath the foreign experts are the senior local staffs. But as George and Sabelli (1994: 113) point out in their critique of the World Bank, 95 per cent of Bank staff members from developing countries received all or part of their education in the developed world and will tend to be drawn from the elite groups that were discussed in the first essay. Similarly, at the ILO, recruitment procedures are strict and highly competitive, with university level qualifications from a foreign university being particularly valuable. What we have in international organizations then is a professional group representing the 'crème de la crème' all coming from similar educational and class backgrounds (George and Sabelli, 1994: 102):

> Put in the same place several hundred people who have been trained in the same schools to think in the same way, recruit them precisely because they have excelled in this training, provide them further with high salaries and many benefits, give them power to impose their doctrines on hundreds of thousands of (by definition) ignorant people and you are unlikely to produce a climate of humility and tolerance.

The transnational elite—comprising of people with particular backgrounds and beliefs that may or may not be shared by large segments of the outside society (Britan and Cohen, 1980: 9)—therefore are able to dominate policy, and their propensity of viewing local populations and their values as separate and inferior to their own is constantly reinforced by the social milieu of the international organization and the attitudes of those occupying the key positions.

Invariably, senior staff, sitting regally in the back seat, will be driven to work by uniformed drivers and be referred to by the secretaries and drivers as 'Sir' or 'Sahab'. At the end of the day they return to their colonial style houses to be waited on by a team of domestic servants. The feeling of superiority is further reinforced by the associative power of the ILO as a foreign based, international organization with 'foreign experts' working for the development of the country. Included in its identity is this elevated status and most importantly its position as a donor. The most frequently cited constraint to the formation of an authentic partnership—with partner organizations or with communities—is the control of the money. The position as a donor immediately produces an imbalance in power relations. Knowledge on the part of the staff members that they are employed by an internationally renowned organization that is empowered to make or withhold eagerly desired loans is not conducive to humility. The ILO is a symbol of power and authority and by association with it, staff members assume these characteristics. As Lukes (1973: 15 in Wright and Shore, 1997: 9) points out, 'once internalized these norms influence them to think, feel and act in certain ways'. The organization's identity is used to enhance and even replace the individual's identity. Even the drivers of the ILO vehicles feel it their right to use their position of authority. Therefore, the occasions when drivers of diplomatic cars break traffic rules and then shout out, *Yeh gari UN ki hai* (This is a UN car) implying that the same rules do not apply for international organizations and their personnel.

But while staff is happy enough to take on the organization's identity and will sometimes forcefully parade the ILO's ideology as part of their job, outside the 'confines of work', these values are often conveniently forgotten. For example, it was not uncommon to find UN personnel buying hand knotted carpets by the dozen in Islamabad's markets. Yet invariably, these very people denounce child labour in their daily meetings and reports. Similarly, senior local staff sometimes have young children working as 'domestic' help in their homes. In Washington, World Bank staff is reportedly amongst the worst offenders of labour laws through their treatment of personal domestic staff. It is a separation between the ideology of the organization that is to be followed as part of the job and life outside work, which is not bound by the need to adhere to the same values.

The ILO field office in Sialkot is less impressive than the country headquarters, but only comparatively. The same identification with the organization remains in place. The feeling of superiority from the international status of the ILO is, if anything, even stronger in a small city like Sialkot where the exposure to similar organizations is less than in the capital. This approach is highlighted in the attitude of ILO staff towards both their local NGO partner in the project and the targets of the project. Bunyad's 'junior' status in the partnership is based on the NGO's position as a recipient of funding from the ILO. The power unequivocally lies with the donor agency. At a physical level, the difference between the two organizations is immediately apparent and reflected in the location and size of the respective field offices. Bunyad's Sialkot office consists of a single room and attached bathroom, located on the roof of the ILO building. Two desks, a few chairs, and a cupboard are the sum of the furniture. There is a computer but their request for a telephone line has been pending for several months, so calls have to be received downstairs in the ILO office. There is no air conditioning and the ceiling fan has almost no effect when the searing summer sun roasts the roof. In contrast, the ILO office downstairs is equipped with air conditioning in every room, an array of telephone lines, Internet facilities, and wall-to-wall carpeting. A kitchen provides a canteen for staff members. Outside, the driveway is occupied by two ILO Land Cruisers—one for the Programme Manager Mr Zaheer Dilawar and the foreign technical expert, Mr Jacques Pols and the other to be used by the ILOs female monitors for visiting designated stitching centres. In contrast to the *salwar kameez* worn by Bunyad councillors, the male ILO staff wore trousers and shirts, and often preferred to speak to me in English rather than in Punjabi or Urdu. Only the lowest paid members—the cook and the cleaner—spoke in Punjabi and wore *salwar kameez*.

The difference in 'power' between the two organizations was based upon a number of factors, the most important being the international/ local organization distinction and the fact that the ILO was funding Bunyad. Without continued ILO support, Bunyad would not be a part of the project. This asymmetry was not only reflected and reinforced by the physical environment of the two organizations but also translated into the arrogant attitude that most ILO staff members had towards not only their Bunyad counterparts but also the 'project beneficiaries' with whom they were working. I believe that this attitude had a major impact on the way that the programme was administered and on the nature and quality of information gathered by the ILO personnel. It also led to a divergence in the approach towards what was professed to be a common cause-promoting the best interests of the children.

In fact, ILO staff members rarely felt it necessary to take the advice of the Bunyad field councillors. The general attitude being that the less educated, unprofessional, and largely rural-based staff of a local organization would be unlikely to add anything of importance that the far more educated and competent ILO staff working for a foreign organization had not already covered. The only occasions that the Project Manager Malik Nazir was summoned downstairs by the ILO project manager was to demand that some particular information be gathered by Bunyad for an ILO report or to complain about the quality of Bunyad's output. This same attitude of superiority spilled over into the ILO's relationship with the project beneficiaries in Sialkot.

Many Sialkotis resented the 'loss of control' of their own affairs, seeing it as unwarranted intervention by foreigners unfamiliar with Sialkot's social fabric. As 'not an outsider' (by virtue of being identified with Bunyad) and a fellow Pakistani, I was expected to better understand the problems faced by local 'communities'. This feeling of inclusiveness was strong in Sialkot, mainly as a result of the child labour eradication programme being seen as a foreign intervention—an effort funded and designed abroad and implemented and monitored largely through an international organization. As a result, the distinction between the 'foreign interventionist' group and the 'national' local group was strong and well-defined—strong enough, in fact, to exclude those local Pakistanis who worked with foreign organizations and were therefore associated with them. As a reflection of this distinction, villagers addressed the Bunyad field councillors as Aslam *bhai* (brother) or Razzaq *bhai* whereas ILO monitors were addressed with the far more distant *sahab* (sir). The ILO monitors as well as senior staff come with the paraphernalia of an international organization and this constantly reminds the hosts of the power and resources of the organization, thereby immediately differentiating them from the project's beneficiaries. The ILO identity and the internalizing of this identity by ILO staff members were sufficient to deprive them of their 'insider' status. You could therefore be Pakistani and even Sialkoti and still be an outsider. In fact, local Pakistanis who worked with international organizations were often resented. Furthermore, the hierarchical nature of the relationship between the groups meant that communication between them became not a two-way conversation but a matter of the more powerful group—the one considered to have expert knowledge—giving information to the less powerful group.

In this environment, along with the field councillors, I was party to much of the 'hidden transcript' that manifested itself in the form of bitterness against foreign intervention and the ILO. Villagers talked of the ILO and its monitors with disdain complaining that they would come in their big cars, with their *gora* (white) bosses to make sure that children were not working. 'We tell them what they want to hear and get rid of them quickly. They are happy with that. All they do is fill out forms and take them back to their offices', said Nazir Ahmed, the stitcher who had earlier complained bitterly about the reduction in footballs reaching homes. The subcontractors of the various stitching centres are even more dismissive of the ILO monitors. From time to time (once every six weeks is the current lap time according to the ILO) the ILO's monitors check designated units to ensure that no children[16] are working in the facility. It is an issue that rankles the subcontractors and stitchers alike, not necessarily because they believe that children should be allowed to work but because of the feeling that they are constantly under surveillance. A number of subcontractors I spoke to chafed at what they perceived was the arrogant and officious attitude of the ILO monitors. Again, the surveillance nature of their work made them ideal candidates for resentment. The result was that they were seen simply as interferers bent upon causing problems. They rarely brought good news but could often be the bearers of reprimands and sanctions. 'These ILO monitors come once every two months, ask us whether any children have been working at the unit and then they disappear for the next two months,' smirked one of my subcontractor informants with a degree of contempt. 'Even if there were any children, the whole village knows when they arrive and word gets round quickly.' Thus, it is not only development officials who ascribe ignorance to locals. The reverse also occurs.

During my stay in the field, an added point of tension developed between Bunyad and the ILO. It was also an example of how the rhetoric of policy and the official discourse masked the interplay of interests of individuals and organizations and how these dynamics adversely affected the impact of the project on target populations. Bureaucratic disputes dictated how the programme was administered so that it was often these tussles rather than responses to the needs of the people that determined programme implementation.

Conflict and Resolution

In late 1999, the first stage of the project was coming to a close. This meant that the ILO would evaluate Bunyad's progress before deciding to renew their contract. Effectively, Bunyad was on 'probation' pending an end of year report. As rumour began to spread that some members at the ILO field office were 'against' Bunyad (see Shaheen Atiq-ur-Rehman's quote earlier in the essay) and would try and engineer the NGO's exit, communication between the two organizations became increasingly fraught. Behind the scenes a struggle developed between the ILO and Bunyad field offices. Zaheer Dilawar, Head of the ILO office in Sialkot, had felt slighted that his authority had been undermined when Shaheen Atiq-ur-Rehman complained directly to ILO Headquarters in Geneva of his arrogant attitude towards Bunyad staff.

As relations deteriorated communication began to break down further. At one point, in a desperate attempt to open an informal channel of communication, I was requested to see Mr Pols, ILO Sialkot's Dutch technical advisor, on the pretext of him asking about my research. This was also an opportunity for me to wear my 'other' hat—that of the 'outsider'. I was not a Bunyad staff member but was familiar with their work and staff. As a result of this ambiguous status I was able to position myself as a mediator with the international organization—someone who could represent Bunyad's views but who could present them in the language of the outsiders. I could also, through my good rapport with Shaheen, ensure that the concerns that the international organizations had were passed on to her directly. In fact, in time I became a channel of information not only for the international organizations but also for villagers and even the NGO fieldworkers.

On this occasion, Pols indicated that Bunyad had become extremely defensive in its attitude—a response to the fact that by this stage every move on the part of the ILO was seen as a conspiracy to throw Bunyad out of the project. There was some truth to both sides. Zaheer Dilawar appeared to have taken the issue personally and was bent upon showing that Bunyad was unable to implement the project successfully. Bunyad on the other hand felt that the random choice of their non-formal schools for evaluation was anything but random. The trading of 'misinformation' generated through the increasingly adversarial relationship between the two field offices became part of the statistics on child labour. The ILO version stressed that the poor standard of Bunyad's schools meant that children were either not enrolling in them or were dropping out and rejoining the labour force. Bunyad insisted that the ILO used as a model only the very weakest schools that had been established. Apart from the spread of misinformation there was a complete breakdown in the sharing of information—a tactic whose effects I felt first hand. Prior to this breakdown in communication, ILO had been quite open with information that I requested, none of which was sensitive or confidential. Then one day I requested a list of stitching units monitored by the ILO in Sialkot. I had previously brought up the subject and had been told that I could photocopy the relevant maps. Furthermore, a map of the centres was pasted up in their lobby displaying the lack of confidentiality concerning the requested information. Normally, Abid, the staff member in charge of data input, would pull out a file and photocopy the relevant document. This time he stated that I would have to ask Dilawar Sahab. I duly knocked on Dilawar's door and went in only to be told that the requested information was highly confidential. Far from working together as a partnership, the organizations were actively trying to place hurdles in each other's path. Any semblance of partnership—of working together towards a common goal—was overshadowed by the bureaucratic bickering that increasingly shaped the discourse of child stitchers in Sialkot.

The result was a suspension in funding and delays in the distribution of salaries for Bunyad's field officers and teachers in the schools. For the last two months of my fieldwork the field staff worked without wages and with no indication that the project would continue. The uncertainty spilled over to the implementation of the project. Delays in salaries of teachers caused community members to speculate that the non-formal schools were to be closed down. Supplies to the schools were also disrupted and student achievement suffered. Furthermore, football stitchers complained that children had firstly been stopped from working and now the schools set up were also going to be shut down leaving families and children with no options. It was Bunyad that lost face in the villages where they worked.

Bunyad's end of year report was to be prepared by the Sialkot project's Programme Co-ordinator—Mr Rizwan Riaz—a Lahore-based 'consultant'. Unfortunately, Riaz had made a minimal contribution to Bunyad's project to the point that he decided not to be based at his field office in Sialkot except for the occasional day visit from Lahore. Riaz's initial suspicion of me quickly gave way to saccharine coated flattery of my research when he discovered my relationship with Shaheen. His appointment had been a gamble by Shaheen. She had hoped that Riaz—who in his previous career had been a television personality, primarily on account of his baritone voice and silky smooth on-screen demeanour—could use the same suave charm and smooth talking to put across Bunyad's point of view in a form that would be viewed favourably by the funding organization. Riaz was meant to keep the ILO 'sweet'. Unfortunately, the gamble failed as even his obsequious charm failed to compensate for the neglect of all his other responsibilities. On a salary of ₹40,000, over 10 times that of the field councillors, and speaking impeccable English, he also demanded that his superior authority and status be recognized and respected. His attitude towards his staff was patronizing and he clearly regarded their input to be of little value. There was nothing that he could be taught by the field staff. Riaz was only concerned when he was asked to prepare the final report. On this occasion it was even more critical as it was on the basis of this report that the decision on extending funding would be made. In the event of the 'emergency', Riaz was driven down to Sialkot for the day and firmly informed his team that the required information had to be gathered in two weeks. The one dissenting voice, from Danish, requesting that at least three weeks would be needed to undertake the said task, was brutally silenced. Danish was humiliated for implying that he was not willing to work hard when required and for having dared to challenge the authority of the programme co-ordinator. There was no further dissent. It was a familiar pattern. Data was demanded either by Bunyad Headquarters or by the ILO in an unrealistic time scale and the field councillors were forced to collect the information or admit to not working hard enough. The result was inaccurate data with field councillors either deputing data collection to teachers in their schools or then filling out forms with no opportunity of verifying or clarifying information. This usually resulted in the inflated attendance of children at school and an 'exemplary' decline in the number of children stitching footballs. The purpose appeared not to be focused on gauging the situation in the field but on stating that a particular survey had been undertaken and the results tabulated. The exercise of data collection became more important than the data itself. It could be argued that the programme was task and growth-oriented rather than responsive to the needs of the 'beneficiaries'. On this occasion, the field councillors, having been informed of the importance of the exercise, worked long hours to ensure that the survey was completed on time. The outcome, though, was the same as when data was collected by teachers.

When Riaz had the data tabulated and analysed, the picture that emerged pointed to weaknesses in the programme design and implementation. As a result, the figures were manipulated to show that Bunyad's schools were exemplary and that the incidence of working children had declined dramatically. Any notion of highlighting the real situation and including, for example, reports of the resentment by football stitchers towards the imposed project—primarily due to the decline in income following a fall in home-based stitching—was discarded from fear that it would provide 'elements' in the ILO ammunition to remove Bunyad from the project. As a result, either the information collected was inaccurate or even when it was accurate it was manipulated to cater to the interests of the organizations involved in the project. The project's survival depended on maintaining or creating sufficient ignorance about what was happening locally. As Gardner and Lewis point out (1996: 73),

> only statements which are useful to the development institutions concerned are therefore included in their reports; radical or pessimistic analysis are banished. The discourse is thus dynamically interrelated with development practice, affecting the actual design and implementation of projects.

Therefore, dominant interests were able, through concealing parts of the social reality, even that generated by their own research methodologies, to manipulate the reality of others. Whereas for a while a struggle had emerged between the agendas of the ILO and Bunyad field offices, this struggle was ultimately replaced by a 'discourse coalition' (Hajer, 1995). Both the organizations were engaged in managing their own survival as well as trying to carry out the tasks assigned to them and as van Ufford (1993: 138, in Weber [1947]) points out these two aspects are often incompatible. The campaign to denigrate each other was therefore set aside in favour of the unproblematic continuation of the programme as a whole. It was the result of a political and discursive struggle that ultimately resulted in the production of a unified document. The Bunyad figures were manipulated to show the success of the project—the number of children in schools showed an increase and correspondingly those involved in football stitching declined dramatically. Each project (Moore, 1996, in Werbner, 1999: 132–133) 'generates its own micro-politics over personnel, benefits, techniques and objectives, and often over the very existence of the project'.

The requirements of the various development institutions ensured that the current reality, reinforced by Bunyad and the ILO, is one of children in schools, free from labour and its harmful effects. This representation is the outcome of the power relations of those driving developmental programmes and as Escobar (1991: 674) points out, development institutions are part and parcel of how the world is put together so as to ensure a certain process of ruling. The outcome suited both Bunyad and the ILO as two of the agencies involved in the implementation of the programme. Funding for Bunyad continued for a further year. However, the ILO displayed and reinforced its own authority by contracting another NGO to 'share' the task of social protection along with Bunyad. The football stitchers in the midst of this struggle become Foucault's objectified persons, 'the objectified person is seen but he does not see, he is the object of information, never a subject of communication' (1977: 200). The stitchers are the objects of information to be acted upon bureaucratically but who are not involved in the shaping of the information on them. They do not have the power (as conceived by Lukes, 1974) to set agendas or manipulate conceptions of interest. The fact that this group lacks the power to make itself heard also means that there is very little knowledge about the way football stitchers, including children, view their own situation. They may be represented by dominant discourses based not on shared lives, problems, and experiences but on external observations that are often mediated by a Western episteme and historicity.

This essay has discussed the way that the characteristics of individuals (including the fieldworker) and organizations that the fieldworker may interact within the field can affect the quality of information that is gathered in the field. It also analyses how the developmental discourse affects the information that is presented to a wider public and how this ultimately becomes the 'reality' that defines the field area.

Notes

1. Muslim migrants who moved to Pakistan from parts of present day India.
2. The word Punjab means 'five rivers' and refers to the rivers that flow through the province—the Ravi, the Beas, the Sutlej, the Chenab, and the Jhelum.
3. For an account of this see *Culture, Class, and Development in Pakistan*, Weiss (1991).
4. Sialkot received the lowest percentage of refugee workers at only 21 per cent compared to an average of 49 per cent for Punjab. Faisalabad 70 per cent, Gujranwala 50 per cent, Multan 50 per cent, and Lahore 43 per cent were dominated by migrants (Government of Pakistan, 1970: 2–3).
5. Tehsil is the smallest administrative unit of a district. Two or more tehsils constitute a District and three or more districts form a Division. Sialkot comprises three tehsils—Sialkot tehsil, Daska tehsil, and Pasrur tehsil. I will attempt to clarify the usage of 'Sialkot' by referring separately to Sialkot city, Sialkot tehsil, and Sialkot district. Where 'Sialkot' is used on its own, it will refer to the entire district of Sialkot.
6. Figures from District Census Report of Sialkot 1998, Government of Pakistan.
7. In 326 BC according to Ahmed Nabi Khan (1964).
8. 273–237 BC.
9. 1527–1701 AD.
10. There is in fact very little in terms of specific recent historical accounts of Sialkot. Most accounts were written in the Colonial period though there are some accounts that go back as far as the time of Alexander the Great.
11. My grandmother abdicated her position as heir apparent to the Indian princely state of Bhopal to emigrate to Pakistan during Independence and was Pakistan's second female Ambassador. My father was Pakistan's Foreign Secretary and also served as High Commissioner to the United Kingdom and Ambassador to France and Jordan.
12. My great grandfather, as ruler of the second largest Muslim state in India, worked closely with the founder of Pakistan, Mohammed Ali Jinnah during the negotiations for the independence of Pakistan.
13. Sahab is a term of respect equating roughly to 'Sir'.

14. Pakistan was touring Australia at the time.
15. Traditional dress of tunic and baggy trousers.
16. The ILO defined children in the football stitching project as those in the age range 5–14 years. For the purpose of this thesis I shall use the same age range (5–14 years) when referring to children.

References

Britan, G.M. and R. Cohen. 1980. *Hierarchy and Society: Anthropological Perspectives on Bureaucracy.* Philadelphia, Pennsylvania: Institute for the Study of Human Issues.

Darling, M. 1934. *Wisdom and Waste.* Oxford: Oxford University Press.

Devereux, S. and J. Hoddinott (eds). 1992. *Fieldwork in Developing Countries.* Loughborough: Harvester Wheatsheaf.

Eglar, Z.S. 1960. *A Punjabi Village in Pakistan.* New York: Columbia University Press.

Escobar, A. 1991. Anthropology and the Development Encounter. *American Ethnologist,* 18(4): 658–682.

Foucault, M. 1977. *Discipline and Punish.* Harmondsworth: Penguin.

Gans, H.J. 1982. The Participant Observer as a Human Being: Observations on the Personal Aspects of Fieldwork. In Robert G. Burgess (ed.), *Field Research: A Sourcebook and Field Manual*, pp. 53–62. London: Allen and Unwin.

Gardner, K. and D. Lewis. 1996. *Anthropology, Development and the Post Modern Challenge.* London: Pluto Press.

George, S. and F. Sabelli. 1994. *Faith and Credit: the World Bank's Secular Empire.* London: Penguin.

Government of Pakistan. 1970. *Pakistan Census.* Islamabad: Statistics Division, Government of Pakistan.

———. 1998. *District Census Report of Sialkot Population.* Islamabad: 2000 Census Organisation, Statistics Division, Government of Pakistan.

Hailey, J. 2001. Beyond the Formulaic: Process and Practice in South-Asian NGOs. In Bill Cooke and Uma Kothari (eds), *Participation: The New Tyranny?* pp. 88–102. New York: Zed Books.

Hajer, M. 1995. *The Politics of Environmental Discourse: Ecological Modernization and Policy Process.* Oxford: Clarendon.

James, A. and A. Prout. 1998. A New Paradigm for the Sociology of Childhood? In A. James and A. Prout (eds), *Constructing and Reconstructing Childhood.* Basingstoke: The Falmer Press.

James, A., C. Jenks, and A. Prout. 1998. *Theorising Childhood.* Cambridge: Polity Press.

Kessinger, T.G. 1974. *Vilyatpur, 1848–1968: Social and Economic Change in a North Indian Village.* Berkeley, California: University of California.

Khan, A.N. 1964. *Sialkot: An Ancient City of Pakistan*. Lahore: The Punjabi Abadi Academy.

———. 1996 *Orangi Pilot Project: Reminiscences and Reflections*. Karachi: Oxford University Press.

Lukes, S. 1974. *Power: A Radical View*. Basingstoke: Macmillan.

Nicholson, T. 1994. Institution Building: Examining the Fit between Bureaucracies and Indigenous Systems. In Susan Wright (ed.), *Anthropology of Organizations*, pp. 68–95. London: Routledge.

Pottier, J. 1993. Introduction: Development in Practice: Assessing Social Science Perspectives. In Johan Pottier (ed.), *Practicing Development: The Social Sciences Perspective*, pp. 1–13. New York: Routledge.

Razavi, S. 1992. Fieldwork in a Familiar Setting: The Role of Politics at the National, Community and Household Levels. In Stephen Devereux and John Hoddinott (eds), *Fieldwork in Developing Countries*, pp. 152–163. Loughborough: Harvester Wheatsheaf.

Schanberg, S.H. 1996. Six Cents an Hour. *Life Magazine*, The Time Inc. Magazine Company, USA.

Silvers, J. 1996. *Child Labour in Pakistan*. The Atlantic Monthly, 1 February.

Spradley, J.P. 1979. *The Ethnographic Interview*. New York: Holt, Rinehart and Winston.

Toren, C. 1993. Making History: The Significance of Childhood Cognition for a Comparative Anthropology of Mind, Royal Anthropological Institute. *Man*, 28(3): 461–478.

van Ufford, P.Q. 1993. Knowledge and Ignorance in the Practice of Development Policy. In M. Hobart (ed), *An Anthropological Critique of Development*, pp. 117–135. London: Routledge.

Weber, M. 1947. *The Theory of Social and Economic Organisation*. New York: The Free Press.

Weiss, A.M. 1991. *Culture, Class and Development in Pakistan*. Boulder, Colarado: Westview Press.

Werbner, R. 1999. The Reach of the Postcolonial State: Development, Empowerment/Disempowerment and Technocracy. In Angela Cheater (ed.), *The Anthropology of Power*. London: Routledge.

Wright, S. (ed.). 1994. *Anthropology of Organizations*. London: Routledge.

Wright, S. and C. Shore (eds). 1997. *The Anthropology of Policy*. London: Routledge.

3

Story of My Research in Bhutan

A.C. Sinha

The story of my research is bound to be biographical and for that I may not have to be apologetic. In fact, it may answer a number of questions, which I had been asked by fellow academics and readers of my books on Bhutan. To begin with, I have been asked what made me interested in study on Sikkim, Bhutan, Nepalese, and Himalayas at large. I have a very long answer to this simple question and that is what I propose to do over here. Moreover, I shall be dealing with my academic preparation before launching the field study, the type of data I could collect and the research output I managed to publish. I acknowledge the role played by the elements of 'chance' in my case. I was born in a peasant family in a village in the Gangetic plains, state of Bihar, India. Naturally, I had seen neither a hill/ mountain, nor a jungle, nor a tribesman till I came to Ranchi, in Chota Nagpur plateau in South Bihar, at the age of 16 in 1958 for enrolling myself for college education. Furthermore, there was no tradition of higher education in my family prior to myself, rather I was the first graduate, Masters degree holder, and PhD, all rolled into one in my village. Naturally, question of guidance from anybody did not arise in my case. If anybody is to be remotely held responsible for my inquisitiveness and academic inclination, it was my extremely religious and mentally alert grandfather. It so happened that there was a tradition in my family that prior to retiring to bed after dinner; the children of the joint family had to massage the aching bones of the grandfather and listen to his religious, mythical, and historical stories. Some of the stories would be didactic, in which he would invariably ask for the morals of the stories.

I had developed an interest in reading literary fiction quite early in my school days and I would avoid mathematics. However, I was good in geography and history in my school days. I would fancy myself to be a well-read and widely travelled person. But I was acutely aware of the family financial problems, especially after abolition of zamindari (a system of fief, in which over-lords grant rent-free holdings to local notables) in 1956. So, I would imagine myself to secure a job of a librarian so that I could read all the books in the library or be a geographer so that I could travel to distant places and discover new areas. When I joined college, I offered literature, geography, and economics as my subjects. Apart from the first two subjects, I offered sociology as one of the subjects in my bachelor classes. The course in sociology in Patna University had a paper on social anthropology, which was taught by Dr Moinuddin Raz, who dwelt on various theories of culture among others. He also informed his students that anthropologists travelled to distant places to study primitive communities. Perhaps, unconsciously my interests began to shift to anthropology. Next year, I travelled to Ranchi and got myself enrolled in a Masters degree course in anthropology, in which there were 32 students. It was an extremely active department in Ranchi University, where apart from MA previous, there was an equal number of MA final year students, a number of research students, and the research staff working on research projects. The department had developed a tradition of weekly seminars, held on Thursdays in which the Head of the Department, Dr Lalita Prasad Vidyarthi, the president of the session, used to encourage the students to give seminar and take part in the discussion. He would identify the potential qualities of individual students and encourage them to take pride in anthropological researches, as he would emphasize that it was only the anthropologists who do fieldwork among the primitive people.

Inspiration for Research in the Eastern Himalayas

Prof. Vidyarthi decided to take MA (Previous) students on an educational excursion tour to Assam, Nagaland, Manipur, NEFA, and Sikkim in February–March 1964 and I was one of them. It was a team of about a dozen of animist, Christian, Hindu, Muslim boys and girls, in which every student was assigned some or the other work for smooth travel during the period of excursion. While travelling to a place/community or stopping somewhere during the journey, the students were to study hurriedly whatever literature was available on the place/community. Similarly, travelling by any means of transport or visiting a community/place of interest, one had to observe the environment, people, economy, life-style, behaviour and write them in the diary every day. The diaries would be presented to Dr Vidyarthi every evening prior to dinner and he would read them and comment on and discuss the entries one by one in the following days. He would himself open up, what he had observed at times and ask some of us to comment on and initiate us in the process of observation, making relevant notes, and initiation of discussion on some or the other issues. There were occasions when out of exhaustion or sheer mischief, we did not present the promised daily completed diaries, he would ignore it for a day or so, but there were occasions when he went on 'a mock hunger strike' in the absence of the diaries. Among others, we took part in the cremation of our host in Shillong, anthropologist Verrier Elwin in February 1964, and then visited Gallongs in Siang district, NEFA. At the last leg of our excursion, while at Gangtok in Sikkim, I wrote in my diary that except Geofre Gorer's (1938) *Living in a Lepcha Village*, there was not much study made on Sikkim. Prompt came the comment: 'Why can't you take up the challenge to fill the gaps?' And the die was cast on that day, perhaps on 12 or 13 March 1964, I promised him in the presence of fellow students to undertake the study of Sikkim without realizing the implications of it at that time. It appears that every anthropologist is some sort of a romantic creature, as he/she falls in a lifelong love affair with the community under study and he starts referring to it as my tribe/my village/my community. The samehappened with me even prior to initiating my field study on Sikkim, as I was reminded of my promise to my teacher, Dr Vidyarthi. And my love affair with Sikkim continued even after four and a half decades of those eventful days of 1964.

I landed myself with a job of lecturer in social anthropology at Gujarat Vidyapeeth, Ahmedabad (an institute of national importance started by Mohandas K. Gandhi in 1920 as a system of education parallel to the existing English system in western India, far away from Sikkim). For two years, I did nothing about the research, but I had not forgotten my promise. Prof. Vidyarthi chanced to visit Ahmedabad in October 1967 and we discussed the possibilities of getting me registered for a PhD degree on a topic related to Sikkim, but it did appear to be improbable at the time. Fed up with arrogant Gandhian idealism at the Vidyapeeth, I quit the job and got myself a fellowship for doing PhD in sociology at Indian Institute of Technology, Kanpur (IIT/K) in January 1968. Once I completed my coursework, I was assigned as a candidate to be supervised by Dr Ali Ashraf, a political sociologist, who had done a study of the 'City Government of Calcutta' earlier. I went on an exploratory visit to Sikkim before I drew my research proposal for the approval of the Research Committee of the Humanities and Social Sciences. I made a presentation to the Committee and after that my supervisor told me: 'I neither know anthropology, nor Sikkim. You are a mature person; you should be smart enough to guard your interests. You go ahead and do your research, but keep me posted with. You will always have my support.' And I did get his utmost support, as I was his first PhD student and he found funds for my costly eight months long field study in those trying days of financial crisis. The extent of his confidence in my work may be gauged by the fact that he had chosen Leo E. Rose, editor Asian Survey and S.C. Dube, Director, Indian Institute of Advanced Study, Simla, among my thesis examiners, who did recommend award of the proposed degree on the thesis: 'Elite in Sikkim: A Study in Political Development'.

Exploration of Fieldwork in Bhutan

Among the courses required to be completed as preparatory to writing the dissertation was a course on 'Community Power Structure'. Among its list of literature was Floyd Hunters' work with the same title and Robert E. Dahl's *Who Governs?* both the works were based on field study. While Hunters' was based on his intensive field study through anthropological technique of reputational method of the American city of Atlanta, Dahl's study was a product of his field data through positional method from New Haven. These studies inspired me and I toyed with the idea of making a comparative study of power structure in the capital cities of the two Himalayan kingdom of Sikkim and Bhutan, Gangtok and Thimphu, by combining both the above field methods of data collection. Fired with the zeal of a novice enthusiast, I visited Gangtok in February/March 1969, a town of about 7,000 inhabitants, an ideal site for manageable fieldwork. Thus, I wrote in my second book on Bhutan:

> Having drawn a tentative research plan, I began corresponding to relevant contacts. It took me no time to learn that none of the two kingdoms had centres of higher education, newspapers, radio stations, and other means of communication in the contemporary sense. No doubt, their capital 'towns' were connected with the wheeled transport immediately in past, but the interior areas—mostly forested and snow-capped hills and mountains—remained in splendid isolation. These were under the charge of the most oriental, despotic

rulers, whose whims and eccentricities were legends. Naturally, the persons in authority, whom my letters were addressed to, acknowledged none of my numerous letters. (Sinha, 2001: 9–10)

Enthused with the zeal of a discoverer, I undertook a travel to Thimphu at the same time of my exploratory visit to Gangtok with all types of difficulties, which I ignored as if I was a pioneer. Once I reached there, I found that the capital town of the Druk Gyalpo (the King of Bhutan) was being built at that time. It was a surprise to discover that the capital was in fact in making and there was nothing like a town. There was the Dzong (fort, from where administration is run) by the river, where the king and his government functioned; there was only one street in 'the town' on which there were some shops with local consumer goods; there were labourers all around erecting some or the other buildings; there were paddy fields hovering all around the Himalayan heights; it was something like a construction camp with building materials scattered around the dusty half built structures. I found my first night free accommodation in the only Indian type sweetmeat shop, which was unbearably filthy and uncomfortable, but it was free of cost, provided I could have dinner of *aloo-puri*s, of course on payment. As if I had a choice to make, there was no other accommodation whatsoever to boot. The next day, I went to visit the Dzong in the best of my dress and ran into Bakhu (now it is known as simply 'kho', the Bhutanese national dress for the male) dressed home minster of the kingdom, who almost chided me for being late for an alleged appointment. I tried to correct him in English and he went on haranguing me in Hindi. With some difficulty I extricated myself from the predicament and ran into the Chief Town Planner. He gave me all the important preliminary information about the 'town' such as there is nothing like a town, total population of Thimphu inclusive of the labourers was that of about 3,500 and that too included the seasonal migrants such as monks, workers, members of the 'assembly' and district and the national administration. In fact, Bhutan did not have a permanent capital till then and that is why Thimphu Township was being built by the town planners from Indian Institute of Technology, Kharagpur (IIT/KH), India. I had recorded my first impression of Thimphu, thus:

I found the Bhutanese capital like a labour camp, in which some casual construction was on. It was (still) not an urban centre, had no market, but possessed a few shops. The 'town' was huddled within a few lived-in buildings in one street. The royal court was secluded away in the dzong (fort) at a distance. It was, windy, desolate and a starving welcome. Unlike Gangtok, there was no crowd in Thimphu at any time of the day. There were few persons to talk to, and

those who were available, were shy, uninformed and reluctant companions ...
Naturally, I decided on the spot that Thimphu was not a suitable universe for a
comparative study with another capital, e.g., Gangtok. Thus, Bhutan and I both
had to wait for a more opportune time for each other. (Sinha, 2001: 10–11)

I went back to the Department in IIT/K and reported that the two capi-
tals of these kingdoms were so dissimilar that no comparison was possible.
In fact, Thimphu was a settlement in making and there was no tradition of
an old urban centre anywhere in the country unlike Gangtok, the capital
of Sikkim, which was almost a hundred years old by then. In this way, my
earlier research proposal to study 'the community power structure of two
feudal cities in the Himalayan kingdoms' stood abrogated. I had to revisit
my research proposal and after a lot of discussions it ultimately emerged
as a combination of intensive field study in anthropological tradition by
concentrating on elite performance in the capital city of Sikkim, Gangtok
and a technique of data collection through questionnaire by extensive
survey of power structure in kingdom of Sikkim. And naturally, Bhutanese
phenomena had to wait for a more appropriate time and research design,
but I had made a mental note that I must do it. To cut the story short, I
had to give attention to my personal affairs for some time: I got married,
got a new job, got my doctorate and my thesis on Sikkim was published
as *Politics of Sikkim: A Sociological Study*, in 1975. As soon as I was on
my legs academically speaking as a lecturer in Sociology in the Department of Humanities and Social Sciences, Indian Institute of Technology,
Delhi (IIT/D), I applied to the Indian Council of Social Science Research
(ICSSR), New Delhi, for a research grant in 1976. Very soon the element
of chance played another trick in my personal life and I had to join the
newly established North-Eastern Hill University (NEHU), Shillong, in the
state of Meghalaya (south of Bhutan and north of Bangladesh) by leaving
the beautiful environment of the IIT/D by the end of 1976. Naturally, I
requested ICSSR to transfer my research grant on theocracy in Bhutan to
NEHU and waited for opportune moment to initiate field study in Bhutan.

Fieldwork in a Closed Feudal Bhutan

I was under the impression that Shillong, where I was located as a faculty
in the University, was closer to Bhutan and thus, it would be advanta-
geous for my study on Bhutan. However, in spite of my best efforts, my

impression that proximity between my place of work and field of study would help me got punctured very soon. I was determined to try my best and complete the chosen theme of the study. Once C.D. Devnesan, the ever obliging first vice-chancellor of the university, came to know about my research interest in Bhutan, he advised me to see 'the universal uncle of the ruling families of Sikkim and Bhutan', Nari Rustomji ICS, who happened to be the chief secretary of the state of Meghalaya. I sought an appointment and Rustomji promptly obliged me. We met over a cup of tea in his office and after a brief discussion on my academic background and topic of research; he promptly agreed to write a letter of introduction to king's cousin brother and the Chief Justice of High Court, Bhutan, Daso Paljor Dorji. Incidentally, my father-in-law knew Jigmie Dorji, Daso Paljor Dorji's father, who had extensive interests in horse racing and who was a known face in Royal Tuft (Race) Club in Calcutta in 1950s. And one of his uncles, Rim Dorji, or Lhendup Dorji, popularly known as Rimpoche, was a friend of a cousin of my wife. Armed with the letter of introduction and copies of an ad-doc questionnaire, I proceeded to Bhutan by bus, rail, rickshaw, and even horse cart in 1977 without much fanfare so that my study did not attract undue attention and publicity. I reached Phuntshilling, the gateway to Bhutan in West Bengal–a shanty town at the Bhutan border, from where one had to secure 'entry permit' to Bhutan. It was also the place from where the road to the national capital, Thimphu, starts. I stayed for the night in a miserable hotel full of mosquitoes and next morning went to the Deputy Commissioner's Office for the required permit. I filled the simple form and wrote in the columns for purpose and places of visit, 'pleasure trip to Paro, Thimphu and Punakha Dzongs', a rather common reason and places for visitors. Sure enough, I got the permit to enter Bhutan without any trouble within no time and I went to book a seat for Thimphu on the 'Vomit Express', the notoriously filthy vomit smelling buses, for the following morning.

Next morning, I boarded the 'famous vomit express', the Royal Bhutan Transport Service bus, which was filthy, foul smelling, and overcrowded for an eight-hour drive to Thimphu. On reaching my destination, I found accommodation in one of the best hotels in the town. I contacted Daso Dorji the next morning, who was getting ready for the Court, and thus, he advised me to meet him in evening at his place. After knowing my purpose for contacting him, Daso responded in this way:

> I know that your research is important and uncle (Rustomji) has written about it. I should help you out, but I have my limits in spite of my position and proximity to His Majesty. Bhutan is a simple, but a status conscious

society, in which formal structures cannot be bypassed. I shall take you to the right person tomorrow morning and he will do the needful.

We had some drinks in the company of another visitor, Col Lam Dorji, the chief of the Royal Bhutan Army, prior to the dinner and I walked back the short distance to my hotel. Next morning, His Lordship took me to the office of the Directorate of Manpower Planning and left me in his care of the director with a promise that we shall be in touch with each other.

Before I proceed further, a few words about my research design should be in order. What I had proposed for my study was a combination of intensive study of three selected villages from north-west (the region under strong Tibetan cultural influence), north-east (Sharchhop region), and southern foothills—Lhotshampa (literally 'southerners', but meaning Bhutanese of Nepali origin) settled region—and a macro-study of the social background of the members of the Tshongdu (National Assembly) and higher level of bureaucracy. My reasons were simple: I wanted my study to be representative and comprehensive enough for the Bhutanese kingdom. And there were serious problems in my proposal. Northern Bhutan neither had thickly populated villages, nor in fact the concept of village as such, as the dominant economy was herdsmanship lashed with subsistence agriculture. Still language was a serious problem and it would be difficult and costly to arrange for an interpreter. Though it was easier to identify the reasonable size of a Sarchhop village, it would be far away from the transport network in the interior and again the problem of interpreter would certainly arise. It was relatively easy to identify and research in a Lhotshampa village, preferably from Samchi or Chukhha districts. However, in the absence of a formal permission to research, it would be almost impossible to travel, find an accommodation, and work in rural Bhutan. Between the two sets of national elite proposed for the research, there were 151 members in the National Assembly, which also included senior monks and almost all the senior bureaucrats of the country. In the absence of a middle class, trading community, mass media, television, newspapers, reading public, educational centres, and professionals such as lawyers, doctors, engineers, professors, managers, executives, and the rest, I had proposed the above two sets of elite as the representatives of Bhutanese nation. But even that too was small in number, say about 175 in all after removing the recurrent names. There was another intriguing problem: that was the nobility, the Wangchuks, but there was no aristocracy in Bhutan like the Kazis (the former Sikkimese aristocrats) in Sikkim. And howsoever hard I tried to solve the mystery, I invariably got the answer: 'Yes, we don't have it.' On this, we shall discuss more in the text.

I explained the purpose of my visit to the Director, Manpower, along with the relevant literature I had come with. He appeared to be a serious person, who promised to study them minutely and handed me some literature on Bhutan and his dissertation on 'Public Administration in Bhutan' submitted to his Alma Mater for the award of Masters degree. We decided to meet in the afternoon; he sent an office peon to show around the offices and Dzong, which was over within an hour and half and I returned to the hotel for lunch. When we met in the afternoon he had my research proposal in his hands and as soon as I was ushered in his presence, he told me that it would not work towards the desired result. He proposed that if I agreed, 'he would re-word my proposal for official purpose'. I found myself in no position to disagree with the suggestion and he immediately read a rough draft on my research proposal, which he had already drafted, and again I found myself agreeing to this affable person. He was kind enough to fix up an appointment for me with somebody known as 'foreign' for the next morning and promised that by then five copies of my research proposal would be ready. I met the said 'foreign' the following morning, who promised to study the enclosure and asked me to see him again after two days. Meanwhile, I spent my days and specially evenings in calling on my potential respondents. The Director, Manpower, was kind enough to arrange an invitation for me to attend the evening celebrations of the Graduate Orientation Course, where I ran into almost 'who is who of Bhutan' quite informally over light refreshments and plenty of beer. I had learnt in my previous field in Gangtok how these informal get-togethers could be used for observing the elite behaviour and factionalism and for establishing rapport for the future. There was also a public library, which I made it a point to visit more to pass the time in the day. The library possessed some faded travel and illustrated books and over-handled inexpensive paper back editions on its almost empty shelves.

Two days' wait was over and I called on the above 'foreign' and he promptly asked me to see him any time that afternoon. When I called on him, I was ushered in the presence of the almighty foreign and he sprang up from his chair, extended his hand for shaking, ordered for ubiquitous tea, leafed through the papers handed over by me, became serious, and turned to me:

Dr Sinha, I must say your study is so significant that I was wondering why such a work was not done by us before. I have studied it and found it very interesting and at the same time very important. This needs serious consideration and we shall get in touch with you at your place. Yes, we have your address over here. Don't worry; we shall be in touch with you. Have some more tea. By the way, have you met our Foreign Secretary? No, please meet him; he is a very fine person. Oh, yes, let me see, when he is free.

He dialled a number, spoke something in Dzongkha (the national language of Bhutan) and turned to me, 'You are lucky, he is free, and he will meet you right now.' He called his office peon, who bent over his waist and uttered: Lah. I faithfully followed him to the office of the Foreign Secretary. That position was occupied by Dr Tobgye, a pleasant person, short statured, heavy built and avuncular in his approach, educated in Darjeeling and Darbhanga in Bihar. It was simply a courtesy call and he promised to do the needful. My impatience solicited his response that I should expect their response within three months. By then, I had developed a sense of estimate on how did the Bhutanese bureaucracy function. I called on my benefactor Daso Dorji in the evening and let him know 'the pilgrim's progresses'. He laughed a lot, invited me for an evening drink and asked me to have some more drink. He enquired whether I had met the Speaker of the Tshongdu. When I replied in the negative, he said, 'You must not leave Bhutan without meeting him. He represents the best traditions of Bhutan.' Then he dialled a number and the next day I was in the company of a mostfriendly, down to earth, tower of a hefty man, who promised to send the list of the members of the Tshongdu to Shillong, which he did.

Meanwhile, as I had done in my earlier study in Sikkim (Sinha, 1975: xiv), I decided not to wait indefinitely for the official clearance and go ahead with my studies, wherever it was feasible. By then, certain points became apparent: it was not possible to move freely in the interior of Bhutan, as there were no roads, no public transport to avail, no towns or markets to buy normal consumer provisions, or public accommodation for hire. I felt the linguistic barrier strongly, as I did not know either Dzongkha or Sarchhop language, though Nepali/Hindi was followed to an extent by the mobile Bhutanese. The written words, even on questionnaires, were soothing like sacred scriptures or the royal commands to most of the Bhutanese. So filling up the questionnaires informally was simply out of question. Moreover, even today after a gap of more than 30 years, there is no literate or otherwise middle class in Bhutan, who could be informally approached for probing questions without raising undue hassles. Thus, in the absence of formal order, conventional fieldwork was not feasible either in the western or in the eastern Bhutanese interior, as I had proposed. So I saw only two ways out for me to proceed. Firstly, to move slowly with the elite, the formal position holders in bureaucracy and the members of the Tshongdu, with my questionnaire and record their response and work on their social background. Secondly, I unpretentiously located myself at the southern shanty and multi-lingual border markets such as Samchi, Phuntsholling, Geylegphu, Sarbhang, and Samdruk Jongkhar and observed socio-economic life-style and various levels of transactions, and work out, if possible, Lhotshampas' marriage, kinship, and family networks. However, like interior of Bhutan, conventional anthropological fieldwork, necessitating long stay, was not possible in the absence of a formal permission from the authorities. So I have no hesitation to confess that my research in Bhutan does not fall in the conventional anthropological style of data collection. Rather, I had to rely heavily on age-old techniques of observation, case study, interview, and a limited operation of questionnaires and for that I had to undertake a number of trips to the Bhutanese field.

Once my study was complete, I informed my readers:

> Bhutan has been termed as 'data-free' country in the sense that social research is entirely a new phenomenon for the Bhutanese. Except the 'religious' text discoverers' accounts, legendary feats of the holy men, Lamaist mysticism, religious texts of Indian and Tibetan origins, biographies of the monk state functionaries, there are not many other sources ... We are frequently informed that fire and earthquakes devastated the dzong repositories. The idea of having an individual or public library is yet to find acceptance. The state archives are in a state of infancy ... Journalism is yet to emerge as a profession even among a few individuals. There is no extensive reading habit among the universally formally uneducated masses. In such a situation, there is no source of authenticity except the statements of functionaries. There is no recognized forum or programmes of public dissent. Even the statements and approach papers and such documents do not represent the existing state of affairs, but they are rather indicative of the state of intentions. It becomes most difficult to locate the copies of the state policies in various decisions, rules, procedures and proclamations ... On the top of it, two more problems for the researchers are added. Firstly, as means of public transport is yet to be established for the most parts of the country, it is difficult to reach the inaccessible interiors, even if somebody is permitted to go to the most of the prohibited regions. Secondly, as Bhutan is a monarchy with a strong input of Lamaist theocracy and is a type of a closed society in itself, it has yet to develop a critical approach to individuals, institutions, decisions, policies and programmes. Consequently, a critical or rather a searching question makes the respondents most uncomfortable. (Sinha, 1991: xvii–zviii)

The Shangri-La Closes Its Door to My Research

I came back to Shillong and got busy in my usual work. Lo and behold, three months went by and there was no response from the 'foreign'. Even when I knew the outcome, I sent letters of reminders, but they were of no avail. After waiting for about six months, I decided to dash in Bhutan once more and I was at Phuntsholing trying to get my entry permit to Bhutan. I learnt that the Foreign Secretary was at the local government guest house. Without caring for a formal appointment, I barged in his presence. He was once more his affable best. He gave his frank advice:

> Dr Sinha, please do not waste your time; we are not going to issue you permission to conduct your research, but we will not formally refuse you. I shall advise you not to proceed to Thimphu, as your knocking at the doors will elicit no positive response. In the given situation, I suggest please drop the idea of conducting research.

Our conversation was conducted in Hindi, my language and in such a brutally frank manner that there was no scope left for any ambiguity. In a way I was thankful to him for his frankness and opening up my eyes to see beyond the horizon. I thanked him for his frank advice and I was about to take leave of him, he blurted out: 'Mr Sinha, I know Biharis are very smart. Don't be depressed. I am sure you will do something much better.' I did not know how to react to this type of unexpected, well meaningful, but unproductive encounter. (I did run into him in mid-1990s when I was on a state visit to Bhutan and he was holding the office of the Minister of Communication, in the Royal Government of Bhutan, prior to his last appoint as the Bhutanese ambassador to Thailand. By then he had already read my book on Bhutan and could slightly recall our encounter at Phuntsholing.) Though I felt terribly dejected with this development, but I decided to take the challenge and not abandon my research. The only thing I decided then and there, was to avoid the Bhutanese dignitaries henceforth.

Before I talk about my field strategy of data collection, I have to complete another aspect of the Bhutanese riddle. I was in Kalimpong with venerable Nepali cultural icon Paras Mani Pradhan and I asked him if he could give me some contacts in Bhutan to begin with. He replied, 'Why, go to Indra Mani, my eldest son at Phuntsholing.' Like his father, I found, Indra Mani a mine of information on Bhutan. He knew almost everybody and everything worth knowing in Bhutan. We became so frank with each other within a few days that one evening I enquired him about the current fortune of the Dorjis. 'We, the Bhutanese, consider Wangchuks and Dorjis as the joint rulers of the kingdom. Don't mistake for the rumours, two are so inter-mixed with every affair (of the state) that they are one and that is all,' said, Indra Mani. Then we discussed the case of the Sikkim's Kazis; how powerful and smooth operators were they with the British in terms of trade and commerce from across the border with Tibet. Asked of how come unlike Sikkim there was no aristocracy like the Kazis of Sikkim in Bhutan? Mr Pradhan gave a thought to it and replied that it was mainly because of the fact that the monarchy in Bhutan was hardly 100 years old and they do marry with the Dorjis and Namgyals of Sikkim. But we did agree that it was not a convincing answer. Incidentally, this was not the first time that I had this type of an answer to my question mentioned previously.

The issue of missing aristocracy kept me puzzled for years and it was solved accidentally. I was working on the archival data in the India Office Library, London in the year 1983. And I found a genealogical table of the royal family of Bhutan prepared by Sir Basil J. Gould, Political Office in Gangtok in his annual report on Bhutan in 1937 (Sinha, 1991: 147). Having drawn lessons from the faction ridden history of Bhutan, Ugyen Wangchuk, the first Druk Gyalpo, who had to struggle hard to succeed, decided not to encourage any family through marital ties to rise as a potential challenge to his supremacy. He solved the problem himself by marrying with the two daughters of his elder sister, and giving his eldest daughter (from his previous wife) in marriage to his sister's son. He got his son and the successor, Jigmi Wangchuk, married to two granddaughters of his previously mentioned sister. That was good enough to set the tradition of marrying within the extended ruling family, a practice, common among the Tibetan social world. His grandson and the third Druk Gyalpo married Kasang Dorji much later, but other than Dorjis, no family had been permitted to rise to eminence in Bhutan. However, Dorjis have as checkered history as the Wangchuks through Ugyen Dorji, the 'Jungta Kazi', an associate and collaborator of Ugyen Wangchuk, who carried the letters from the British to the Dalai Lama prior to the Tibet Expedition, 1903–1904.

I was in the company of the famous Miss Gurung, of the 'Samchi Kazi' family and a highly respected faculty of the Teachers' Training College, Samchi, one afternoon we were conversing leisurely on state of education in Bhutan. Some villagers, apparently known to Miss Gurung, were passing by, they wished her and leisurely squatted on the ground close by. After a while, the august lady asked them the purpose of their visit. They began to talk how the elephants were destroying their crops, orchards, and even settlements. They had been to the Dzongda's office demanding actions against the marauding pachyderms and requested for some reliefs against their damaged crops. I overheard a term repeatedly, *pathy*, in their involved encounter and asked to know about it. I was informed that it was a former official standard grain measuring pot, made of brass, and which could contain around 16–17 kg of paddy, which was still in operation among the southern Bhutanese farmers. It was apparently devised by the Samchi Kazis with a view to measure the output of the crops prior to collecting their own revenues from the tenets. (I was reminded of kerosene tin measurement of paddy in Khasi hills.) I desired to see such a pot for myself and was asked to come back next day. The next day, I had to climb quite a few hillocks to reach an imposing Bhutanese structure owned by a Bhattarai family. Now I was in the company of others, the venerable Nepali Brahmin, the head of the household, who talked non-stop about local history and his family. At last, he asked some ladies to bring the *pathy*, and a shining brass pot with a hanging ring was brought for the inspection. I took it in my hand and upturned it out of curiosity and found two half terms in Nepali: Samch … and V S 20 … Apparently, other halves ('I Kazi' and an unknown year in Vikram Sambat) were rubbed off because of continuous handling of the pot. In this way, I was denied of a potential definite date in the economic history of south-western Bhutan.

I had to evolve my own strategy to collect empirical data in the situation described above. In fact, I learnt later that the Tshongdu (The National Assembly, the royal legislative body) resolved not to permit foreign scholars to study the Bhutanese society till their own scholars were ready to take the challenge. Naturally, in such a situation, I used to visit Bhutan as a tourist to the places, which were open to the tourists; observe people at work, at home, in the offices, in public life; record their economy and try to understand their much acclaimed developmental schemes. It was not possible to visit northern and eastern Bhutan, but the southern foothills were easy to travel to. I travelled extensively and interacted with the respondents from Darjeeling, Kalimpong, Samchi, Phuntsholing, Geylegphu, and Samdruk Jongkhar, all these predominantly Lhotshampa settled districts. I worked on the social background of the higher level bureaucrats in Bhutan (Sinha, 1991: 222–223). But at last, I confess that I was not happy with the quality of data I gathered to write the book. And for that I was invited by the British Council to consult the source material on Bhutan in the India Office Library, London in 1983. I confess that I am not duly trained to handle the archival data, but materials I collected in London filled the important gaps in my study on Bhutan. And that is how I completed my research on Bhutan. I am aware of the fact that my study did not have richer ethnographic data, but in spite of my best efforts it was not possible. However, I could see the clouds collecting over the happy Bhutanese Shangri-La in the form of ethnic conflict, which I had mildly termed as 'ethnic identity and national dilemma'.

I was getting late by the ICSSR bureaucratic time schedule for submission of the report on the research project by the normal procedure. And they were not to be blamed, as I had also given a time schedule for completion of the research project, which was already over, but I was not happy with the progress I had made by then. The intricacy of the Bhutanese field scenario was yet to unfold and the functionaries of the funding agency were hardly aware of the music I was facing in the field. So, there were persistent reminders to file the completed report. I had to file not a very satisfactory report, as far as I was concerned in 1982 (Sinha, 1982). Then I faced the problem of finance for undertaking a costly clandestine visit to Bhutan for the sake of study. An opportunity arrived very soon (1983), when the Department admitted a student from Chukhha district of Bhutan, Sadhna Thapa, and she did a small field visit based on MA dissertation on 'Marriage and Family in a Nepalese Village of Southern Bhutan'. But she informed me also that life was becoming difficult for her family and her father had already shifted to Shillong to do business in horticultural products. I could not gauge the extent of turmoil at the time, as part of her family continued to cultivate their patrimony in Bhutan. She joined MPhil programme in the department and was allotted to me as a research student. But she could not continue her researches, as I and my family were involved in an automobile accident, necessitating my absence from NEHU for some months and I was not in a position to pursue my normal duty in the University. By the time I came back to the department, Shillong was caught in an anti-Nepali ethnic conflict leading to exodus of many Nepali families including that of Sadhna Thapa's in midsummer, 1987. Naturally, that was not the ideal time for pursuing a career in social research, when one's family was uprooted twice within a few years from one's home and hearth. Much later, I learnt that the young lady's family had found shelter somewhere in Kalimpong.

I remember an evening in Thimphu, while watching the cultural evening organized on the completion of the Graduate Orientation Programme in 1977; I had recorded in my diary:

> Most of the Dukpa performances were rather crude, repetitive and without much artistic excellence. However, the audience watched them with rapt attention, ending with a thundering applause. The Nepalese presentations were relatively sophisticated and fine tuned, but in most of these items, there was an uncalled for intrusion by a Dukpa joker with his crude gestures and stupid

mimicry, which deflected attention from the dexterity of the performances. Instead of appreciating the pause, tune, style, and quality of the Nepalese presentations, the audience used to burst into laughter, leaving the artists dejected and sulking in the wings. This will not go for ever like this and one day it may explode.

By the middle of 1980s, it appeared that the Dukpa establishment had made up its mind to call a halt to their policy of ethnic integration of the Lhotshampas in the Dukpa fold. By then, the foreign educated and exposed among the Lhotshampas had also turned demanding instead of waiting for patronage to be bestowed. As if the die was cast and poor Lhotshampas were caught unaware. An aggressive policy of ethnic assimilation was inaugurated without taking the Lhotshampas into confidence. A selective set of 'home department personnel' was taken into confidence to initiate the ethnic cleansing pogrom ruthlessly by deliberate efforts to humiliate the 'target population' and subject them to physical indignities. Overtly, it was maintained that the alleged conflict was caused, as the migrants resisted introduction of the Bhutanese code of conduct, driglam namzha. Moreover, the efforts on the part of the national government was to enforce obedience on the part of the subjects 'to be respectful to the monks, monasteries, royal family, dress properly on occasions, and use national language, Dzonkha, in public'. And those who refused to abide by the 'code' were naturally the illegal immigrants, who deceived the authorities in issuing various sets of documents in their favour. The Lhotshampas could not believe what was happening to begin with and they nursed a feeling that if His Majesty came to know of the details of atrocities caused on his subjects like them, he would intervene in their favour. But that was not the case and an exodus from the Shangri-La to the refugee camps in eastern Nepal was the logical development. However, a sizeable number of the Lhotshampas had no choice, but to stay back and are under threat of cultural annihilation.

A Canadian primary school teacher, who later married a Sarchhop, had a taste of the dictated cultural landscape in 1989 at the grassroots level from the Pema Gatshel district of eastern Bhutan, when mono cultural policy began to be implemented:

> But I am disappointed and puzzled by the sameness of the writings (of the pupils in the class). Every piece begins with a cliché or a mangled proverb. Every piece concludes the same hackneyed piece of advice or fawning praise. Originality seems to count for little; the community is more important, conformity and accordance and compliance. But there must be dissent, I think. I listen more carefully outside class room, and begin to hear different stories.

Some senior girls tell me they were forced to cut their hair at school. They are ethnically Nepali from the southern districts of Bhutan. (According to government policy, students above class VI are sent to schools outside their home districts. Southern students are sent north, eastern students west, and western students south, to promote greater integration.) The Nepali girls tell me that it is their custom to keep their hair long. 'We wept like anything,' they say, 'but what to do? Short hair is driglam namzha' ... But this driglam namzha is appearing more and more. There is new dress law: all Bhutanese citizens have to wear national dress in public or face fines and possible imprisonment ... According to Kuensel, Bhutan's weekly newspaper, the southern people have expressed full support for strengthening Bhutan's unique cultural identity by wearing national dress, speaking the national language, and following the ethics and practice of driglam namzha ... Everyone is always expressing support and gratitude; no one ever seems to have a contradictory point of view. It seems strange, for instance, the people of southern Bhutan would be so keen to wear the (heavy woolen) northern dress in the hot tropical plains, and that not a single person of Nepali origin expressed concern for preserving their own culture and language ... Either dissenting views were felt but not expressed, or expressed but not recorded, but there must have been some people who were not happy with this idea.'

I ask a class VIII student to explain the dress law to me. He says, 'Our national dress is part of our culture.' I ask why it must be legislated then. He is not sure, but says that the Dzongda (the bureaucrat district administrator) recently told his class the question 'why' should not be allowed in Bhutan. 'Why ever not?' I ask, incredulous. 'Asking "why" is not driglam Namzha,' he says. I stare, open mouth, but in the end I say nothing. I am afraid to contradict the district administrator ... Obedience to authority, respect for elders and preservation of the status quo form the bedrock of Bhutanese values. (Zeppa, 2000: 139–141)

And the unhappiness was loudly expressed and the situation did explode very soon within a year of writing of the above lines in Zeppa's diary leading to an ethnic crisis, from which Bhutan is still trying hard to extricate itself even after two decades. And perhaps my writings on Bhutan made some sense even to the otherwise, not used to listening, dissenting voices by the Bhutanese establishment. And that is how I ran into the august company of most of the above mentioned and many more of the dignitaries in 1990s, when the Royal Government of Bhutan used to invite me as a State Guest for discussing the ongoing ethnic conflict involving Lhotshampas. But that is another story (Sinha, 2001).

The story of research howsoever one may try to be objective is bound to be personalized. The individual scholar's family background, educational attributes, empathy to descend to the level of the 'subjects', and above all the elements of chance factor play decisive roles in the ultimate output. I have tried to recollect after more than three decades how I had proposed the study on process of nation-building in a theocratic society by combining anthropological and political sociological techniques of data collection. But it goes without saying that the real socio-political situation failed my strategy to deliver desired result. As a perseverant researcher, every field researcher has to be determined for the cause chosen by him/her, I had to evolve short-term field strategy, far from the ideal one from the textbook point of view, to collect relevant data as much as possible within the given limitations. Though I did not stake a claim to have produced the masterpiece work of excellence on Bhutan, the academics, policy makers, journalists, the Bhutanese underdogs, and above all, the power to be in Bhutan, do read my writings. It is a fact that I do not write to make somebody happy and by the same logic I do not write to hurt somebody deliberately. I try to follow the standards in research set forth by my academic ancestors as per my understanding and the field situation and for that I do not propose to offer any apology to anybody.

References

Gorer, Geofre. 1938. *Living in Lepcha Village*. New York: Mouton.

Sinha, A.C. 1975. *Politics of Sikkim: A Sociological Study*. Faridabad: Thompson Press.

———. 1982. *Theocracy in Bhutan: A Study in Nation-Building*. New Delhi: MSS, ICSSR.

———. 1991. *Bhutan: Ethnic Identity and National Dilemma*. New Delhi: Reliance Publishing House.

———. 2001. *Bhutan: Tradition, Transition and Transformation*. New Delhi: Indus Publishing Company.

Zeppa, Jimie. 2000. *Beyond the Sky and the Earth: A Journey into Bhutan*. New York: Penguin (Paperback).

4

Remembering Fieldwork Histories

Mandy Sadan

Prologue

In the last 18 months, Burma or Myanmar has changed dramatically. Daw Aung San Suu Kyi has been released from house arrest, leading international statesmen and women have visited the country, censorship laws have been repealed, and the international community has been facilitating the re-emergence of the country as a regional presence rather than a pariah. This essay is a reflection upon the fieldwork undertaken in the country at a time, during 1996–1999, when changes of such scale and relative speed could not have been anticipated. Yet, many of the memories of this fieldwork relate to issues that have not been altogether resolved in the country: the Kachin State reverted to a stance of armed opposition after the breakdown of the ceasefire with the Burma Army in June 2011, and the prevalence of communal violence between Buddhists and Muslims has taken on alarming new forms as seen recently in the Rakhine State. In 1997, when this recollection began, there were protracted, frequently violent outbreaks of the communal protest in Burma between various Buddhist and Muslim groups in the country. Some of the most serious of these outbursts were seen in Mandalay, the historic capital of the last Burmese kings and a city proud of its distinctiveness. At this time, I was travelling through Mandalay hoping to get a boat to Bhamo, the important border trading town close to China which had long been a key site on the China to India trade route across the northern parts of Burma and the Kachin hills (Sladen, 1871). The ceasefire that had been signed in 1994 between the Burma Army and the Kachin Independence Army (KIA) had made such a visit viable, although it was still potentially sensitive.[1] That evening, I like everyone else had to remain inside as a night time curfew had been put in place to try to dissipate the tensions that seemed to build on an almost daily basis and to maintain order in face of the recent communal disturbances. In Burma at that time, there was heightened awareness among security officials and local populations that the civic disorder of any kind could trigger more focused political protests, which would be dealt with severely.[2]

As in most urban areas, including the then capital Yangon, electricity was erratically supplied and sometimes an entirely lacking resource. Shut in my guest house room as the curfew descended, the lights went out and it seemed that it would be a long, hot, and dark night. The owner brought a candle up to my room with the kind of embarrassed graciousness that was typical of many Burmese people who found themselves frustrated, angry and impotent in their current circumstances, yet who also had to make explanations to foreign visitors about the things that were beyond their control. Sitting quietly in my room with the candle, I noticed that on the table in the corner of the room was a thick yellow book that looked very familiar. It was the Myanmar Yellow Pages. Today, more than 16 years later, when Internet cafes can be found in many places in the country and when we have become used to seeing images from inside Burma broadcast globally through mobile phones and ICT networks that have been built up within the country and across her borders, it is quite difficult to describe how absurd the concept of a 'Yellow Pages' seemed to be in Myanmar at that time. Telephones were still largely collective social objects where one often queued for a long time to be connected via recalcitrant operators along faulty lines. There seemed to be only a handful of phones in the whole of Mandalay during my visit. Intrigued by this apparent incongruity, I did what seemed the most rational thing to me at that time: I sat with my candle and read the Yellow Pages.

It is remarkable how interesting a text like the Yellow Pages can be when there is nothing else to read. The walking finger trademark had been taken up by IMEX (Myanmar) Co. Ltd after 1993 with the aim of promoting a modern business image of the country and facilitating business contacts with the foreign companies. Yet it could not escape its reality. The idiosyncrasies of the commercial environment at that time were there laid bare for anyone who had the time and rather train-spotterly interest in such things to take note of them. Despite my ongoing doubt that so many working telephones were actually present in the country at that time, after a couple of hours reading through the listings, some strange social shapes started revealing themselves: the place where most astrologers were likely to be present became apparent, the area where traditional medicine sellers lived, and so on. It became a social document on the form and substance of commercial aspirations in Burma in the late 1990s.

Rarely would a lecturer advise his students that a night spent reading the Yellow Pages in the dark was a night spent doing 'fieldwork'. Yet such events were typical of the process through which I started to learn about the intriguing country in which I was now living. First, there was no possibility of controlling a field of research in any long-term way, and second, the aspiration to do so would have been flawed from the outset, so intricate and dense were the complexities of urban life in Burma's towns at that time. I soon learned that asking questions only resulted in receiving answers; in contrast, listening, rather than speaking, following rather than leading, led to questions, answers, discussions, and lines of thought that could not be anticipated, opening up areas of knowledge and learning that were much more vital and penetrating. When stuck in a blackout, in a curfew, one's mind can only turn to trying to understand how that situation had arisen with whatever one has at hand, and to piece together the minute, even infinitesimal fragments of peoples' daily lives to bring out meanings. The mindset that encouraged me simply to sit back and start reading the Yellow Pages if that was all there was at hand, served me well in Burma in seeking out the qualitative embedded in the quantitative, the sublime in the banal, and it is this mindset that ultimately defined the fieldwork journey that I was to undertake.

Fieldwork Memories

A small group of us sat together in an upstairs office in the Kachin-owned company Jadeland in downtown Yangon. In the later part of 1996, it had been just two years since the KIA had signed a ceasefire with the central regime, then referred to by the acronym SLORC (State Law and Order Restoration Council; Zaw and Min, 2007). No one knew at that time what the implications and consequences of the ceasefire would be, or whether it would last or not (Woods, 2011). However, for the time being, it meant an end to armed conflict in most of the far north of the country, large parts of which had been under KIA control following a protracted armed conflict which had started in 1961. The ceasefire was a controversial affair and the manner of its brokerage remains a contentious subject in Kachin politics today. The 'Lahtaw Brothers' as some referred to the ceasefire's principal civilian brokers on the Kachin side, Reverend Saboi Jum and Khun Myat, were seen by some Kachin people as having forced a situation of compliance upon the KIA and its civil wing, the Kachin Independence Organization (KIO), without adequate discussion or foresight of its consequences; self-seeking business interests were sometimes invoked to explain the primary rationale of those promoting the ceasefire. For those negotiating the ceasefire, however, the devastating social consequences of long-term conflict and the need to stop the endless pressures upon Kachin families to give up the lives of their sons and daughters to become permanent, unpaid recruits in a conflict that seemed increasingly unviable as a means of bringing about political resolution seemed justification enough for their actions. Neither was this the first time that attempts had been made to bring about an end to the conflict; other discussions had been held intermittently throughout its three decades or more of destruction, but the collapse of negotiations in the early 1980s seemed to herald a newly brutal and irresolvable phase of conflict that took a decade to turn into another opportunity for a tenuous 'peace' (Smith, 1999). For some, the opportunity presented in 1994 was not a capitulation but an opening that could and should not be shut.

I came to be sitting in the Jadeland office through a surprising and wholly unanticipated set of circumstances. In April 1996, when I arrived to work in Burma as one of the foreign teaching staff in the newly opened Direct Teaching Operation at the British Council in Yangon, there were a host of similar issues impacting upon many so-called 'border' regions of Burma. The country was undergoing some of the most dramatic economic and political changes it had seen for many decades, and, indeed, that was the sole reason we were allowed to be there. Following the suppression of political protests against the military regime in 1988, and the events of the 1990 elections when the National League for Democracy, with Daw Aung San Suu Kyi at its head, won and were then denied power, ceasefires had been brokered with many armed non-state groups across the country. In 1989 the regime had announced a new 'Open Door' economic policy, which was intended to entice foreign business investments and, although rather erratic in its implementation and operation, this resulted in more foreign businesses taking the bold, perhaps rash step at this time of opening trade and other links with the regime. For decades under the Burma Socialist Party Programme (BSPP), which took control of the central functions of the state under General Ne Win in 1962 and which was the only party allowed to exist from 1964 to 1988, foreigners had been allowed to visit the country on seven-day tourist visas, and Burma rightly gained its reputation as being one of the most closed countries in the world to outside eyes. When it was declared that 'Visit Myanmar Year' was to be promoted in 1996, it seemed an odd concept, to say the least. Arguments raged internationally about the need for boycotts and sanctions following the winning of the 1990 election by the National League for Democracy and the subsequent house arrest of Daw Aung San Suu Kyi and others. The Lady's statement that tourists should not come to the country was heeded by many, but tourist-spotting became a strange and even increasingly enjoyable distraction for local tea shop customers in downtown Yangon by the end of 1996, with badly tied, often incorrectly gendered traditional Burmese skirt cloths, with acres of hairy white flesh displayed beneath, apparently being the dress of choice for those who decided to enter the country, as they tried, impossibly, to 'blend in'. This was a time of enormous transitional potential, but it could also be a time of military entrenchment at the centre: the field of play was not clear at this time. However, one thing was increasingly certain, and that was that when any such changes might be introduced, it would never be completely possible to go back to what had previously been.

The British Council had been allowed to bring in three foreign teachers to help improve the standard of English teaching in Burma. As it turned out, the Burmese teachers who had already kept the ship afloat for many years were far better than us in almost every way. The field of action open to the British Council at this point was still not clear and whether the new operation should be primarily oriented towards its business potential or its grant-in-aid functions seemed a point of dispute within the organization and between some of its own staff at that time. In 1996, Burma had only recently begun to loosen slightly its restrictive policies on long-term habitation in the country by foreigners, especially western ones. To live in the country for such an extended period was, during those times, quite unusual, although it is now rather commonplace.

Just after our arrival in April 1996, someone ran into the British Council offices and shouted 'Come and look outside! There's a traffic jam!' It was the country's first. One of the other very noticeable changes in urban Yangon at this time, apart from the mind-boggling speed with which the number of second-hand Japanese motor cars seemed to increase exponentially to clog up every street, was an almost overnight development of the technology 'sector'. When we foreign teachers arrived, our Burmese colleagues were already far more adept at using a PC than we were and they, as in so many other things, led and we had to follow. The opening of some limited trading connections and Burma's entry into ASEAN in 1997 meant that computer shops began to spring up all over Yangon, and gradually other principal urban areas, although the supplies of ink cartridges and other resources varied noticeably from one month to another.

Yet from September 1996, the universities were again closed by the regime following student protests. This time, however, a large body of young people started eagerly to take up the low-cost computer training courses that proliferated, fees being covered by families in the regions or by siblings and cousins working (usually illegally) abroad. Desktop publishing and the availability of better quality printing papers produced an expansion of the printed public sphere that, although still heavily censored, created new opportunities for the subversion of its control than did the time-consuming, labour-intensive process of manual typing, and Gestetner copying. Looking back, these changes were highly significant in bringing the developments that have been seen recently possible on a social level, indeed they contributed towards making them necessary and possibly to a large degree irreversible.

Although I initially worked for the British Council, this role was soon superseded by the increasing involvement I had in an archive digitization project that materialized between myself on behalf of the Green Centre for World Art at Brighton Museum, United Kingdom, and an organization called the Yup Uplift Committee. This relationship was also partly a product of the changes just described which made even thinking about a 'digitization project', a possibility rather than a fantasy. My connection with the museum had developed during a Masters degree in art and archaeology from the School of Oriental and African Studies, London University. This degree was still being completed upon my arrival in Burma. The Masters dissertation analysed a collection of photographs held at Brighton Museum taken by Colonel James Henry Green. Colonel Green had worked as a recruitment and military intelligence officer in the Indian Army in Burma throughout the 1920s and in the early 1930s (Dell, 2000: 9–27). During that time, the officer had collected a large number of artefacts such as textiles and had compiled an impressive photographic collection derived from his experiences. Significant portions of these collections were related to the Kachin region where he had been a recruitment officer for the Burma Rifles and had also been engaged in military survey and intelligence duties along the northern borders with China. Colonel Green's most noteworthy achievement amongst his peers seems to have been the extension he oversaw of the Kachin Rifles recruitment field to the Nung region north of Putao in non-administered territory (Sadan, 2007). His documentation of this expedition through the collection of photographs and items of material culture has subsequently proved to be of significance in the historical representation of this area.

In Burma, I had in my possession a selection of about 300 randomly selected photocopied images from Colonel Green's photo archive and started to make enquiries about them. As news of these images spread to the Kachin communities' resident in Yangon, largely through students who were attending the British Council because their university educations had come to a grinding halt, I was introduced to the members of the Yup Uplift Committee. The Yup Uplift Committee was headed by Pungga Ja Li, a former Baptist pastor and a well-known cultural researcher and a commentator, but it had been initiated and supported by some of the most prominent elders in the Kachin Baptist Convention and Theological College in Myitkyina. Since 1992, the Committee had been attempting to make audio and video recordings of key 'Kachin' indigenous spirit rituals and related performances as part of a cultural documentation project. The assumption today is that 'most' Kachin people inside Burma are Christians of various denominations, the figure of 90 per cent or more usually being cited, although the Baptist and Catholic churches are the largest congregations (Robinne, 2007; Tegenfeldt, 1974). However, certain elites from within the Baptist church (although similar concerns are expressed by members of other church groups) felt increasing concern during the years of conflict that all knowledge of previous non-Christian indigenous cultural practices was disappearing as the rituals were no longer being performed. These elites were typically those who had themselves experienced the process of conversion to Christianity or had direct experiential knowledge of indigenous spirit practices. The founders of the Committee did not desire to restore these former ritual practices but rather desired to 'salvage' the communicative and cultural social memory that was deemed to be embedded in them: knowledge of genealogies, of cultural paradigms, social behaviours, and the indigenized historical experience of place and space affected through the ritual consolidation of social and cultural relationships. This documentation was made possible by the control that the KIA had over the larger part of the Kachin region during the early 1990s but the support that had been given to the programme by these church elders was also critical. Some of the recording activities went under the guise of missionary activity as a means of persuading local Christian nationalist KIA officers that recordings should take place.

The committee had been funded by a local Kachin businessman, called Yup Zau Hkawng. Whilst the ceasefire undoubtedly brought economic opportunities to Yup Zau Hkawng and others of his ilk, they coincided with great pressures upon the economic bedrock of their businesses—the extractive jade trade. A small network of Kachin jade bosses had built up a significant business in mining and selling on jadeite into China, where it would be carved and put into the Chinese, Hong Kong, and Taiwanese market by the Chinese traders (Levy and Scott-Clark, 2001). The wealth from this trade was vast beyond the belief and access to this resource was significant both for the development of the economics of conflict in the Kachin region and for the modern distinctiveness of Kachin society relative to other 'minorities' in conflict with the Burmese military government. Yet ceasefire also heralded greater control of the jade mines by the Burmese military regime. KIA control of the jade mines area was now reformulated through the trading company Buga, and Yup Zau Hkawng and other jade bosses found their worsening economic position started to impact upon their ability to define their own course through the politico-economic minefield (Woods, 2010, 2011). Yup Zau Hkawng, as many other Kachin businessmen, operated a loose ship financially with economic realism watered down by a traditional Hhahku proclivity towards showy, symbolic displays of wealth and generosity, and an ever-expanding circle of needy people and their causes demanded his attentions. The original Yup Uplift Committee, which had undertaken the cultural recordings, had a vision not only of a museum in a computer but also of a giant festival that would establish the Kachin cultural and political space of Myitkyina as a Kachin stronghold. These ideas were still being formulated at this time. This was before the grand manau festivals had become established as a cultural icon, the zenith of which was a reported 300,000 people attending the massive cultural festival and business expo at the end of 2001 which heralded the manau community dance festival as the major symbol of modern Kachin identity. This future was not guaranteed in 1996.

Despite these considerable difficulties, the workers of the Committee had amassed an impressive collection of audio–visual and photographic materials from across the Kachin region, the cultural and historical value of which could not be underestimated. These recordings included ritual performances in ritual context as well as studio renderings of oral performance in ritual language. However, by 1996 the harsh weather conditions as well as an investigative probe conducted by government Military Intelligence officers, who suspected a Kachin nationalist agenda, meant that this archive was in an extremely disordered and vulnerable state. My role became that of facilitating information exchange between the Green Centre for World Art and local Kachin researchers with the objective of enhancing the data on the

UK collections and providing technical support for the preservation of the local archive through its digitization. I frequently found myself from this point sitting in the office in Jadeland, Yup Zau Hkawng's company, talking with a group of later middle-aged Kachin men who had spent all their lives in a conflict zone in one of the world's most internationally isolated countries. It did not at that time seem as surprising as it perhaps should have done, that one of their intentions in wanting to work collaboratively with myself and the Green Centre for World Art at Brighton Museum in the United Kingdom was that they hoped to develop 'a museum in a computer'.

It was this which had brought us together, and this group already had grand, very expensive ambitions as to what they wanted to do with the material they had collated and how it could be used to revitalize knowledge of 'traditional' Kachin cultural practices. The idea of 'a museum in a computer' seemed perfectly logical and reasonable even in Burma at that time, so rapidly had the local communities appreciated the potential of a newly dawning 'digital age' in the country and our whole research project, as it became, in some ways coalesced around this kind of virtuality: we dealt almost entirely with imagined spaces and people of imagined times and their convergence within a technical space that could be used to transcend every day. The Yup Uplift Committee had a notion that the process of 'salvage', affected through digital archiving, might assist, amongst other things, with the production of historical narratives counter to those promoted by the Myanmar military government on the historical integrity of the ethnic category 'Kachin', and thus the historical base of their claims to autonomous control over a distinctive territory within the modern state. In 1998–1999, this developed further into a local publication project, again initiated by the local research committee as a part of their cultural agenda, which transcribed and translated from Jinghpaw ritual dialect into Jinghpaw colloquial idiom a key ritual recitation with explicative commentary, making use of the new desktop publishing facilities that had begun to expand. This was part of the attempt by this committee and its supporters to increase understanding of the non-Christian past and to develop new meaning frameworks for traditional modes and models of non-Christian communicative and social memory in contemporary society. Clearly this was a very particular moment of possibilities, which brought together technological potential, limited international communication, and a respite from conflict to create a space for reciprocal intellectual enquiry and exchange. It was a 'fieldwork' opportunity that was created by our common interests and curiosity and yet could not have been constructed externally or anticipated.

It soon became apparent that for my role to be effective, it would be necessary for me to make a detailed study of the rituals and ritual language that had been recorded by the Yup Uplift Committee so that I could understand the nature of the materials with which we were dealing. From the publication project in particular I learned some of the ways in which non-Burman speech communities, as well as non-Buddhist religious communities, were able to manipulate the state's censorship of cultural output in small but politically significant ways, as well as the modes by which cultural and historical counter-narratives in minority nationality languages can be developed through networks that function beyond the tight grasp of the official censorship board. The value, role, and possible implications of this audio, video, and photographic archive were nonetheless highly contested within many Kachin communities and interest groups at that time. Gradually I learned about some of the problematics of contemporary Kachin nationalist identity discourses, especially when engaged in the representation of Kachin history, the impact of colonialism, the Christian missions, and the meaning frameworks of modernity and 'tradition'. I was privileged to witness firsthand the development of such discourses and to learn about the mechanisms by which these difficulties can be negotiated within local discourses conducted in Jinghpaw, the principal 'Kachin' language.[3]

My encounter with the problematics of ethnic representation was not confined solely to the Kachin context. However, in 1996 I came into contact with the ethnographic video production company, AV Media, run by the Rakhine-born producer U Win Tin Win. The public output of this company, which was designed to be consumed in tourist hotels and airports, gave no indication of the difficulties that were faced by the cameramen and producers to create even this ostensibly 'soft' material; the company subsequently went out of business due to the increasing and unbearable pressures that were being placed upon it. The strict enforcement of censorship and its haphazard and erratic mode of operations rendered all such output open to a bizarre array of random demands for the inclusion and exclusion of material as the censor board adopted a mode not of regulation but of subtle and persistent harassment. However, the public output was but a fragment of a rich collection of videographic material that had been made throughout the country since the 1980s by these local cameramen with local contacts and through local eyes. Through this relationship I had access to one of the most remarkable contemporary visual archives of festivals, places, and customs as the team travelled endlessly trying to record the changing face of Burma and its varied social and cultural life through the lens of Burmese photographers. This uncut footage would be discussed in the office by the predominantly Burman staff as they related their experiences of being Burman in these non-Burman majority areas, their prejudices and assumptions, their sympathies and empathies, and the constraints on understanding within the political and educational framework in which they had been raised. In addition, I learned of the aesthetic–political process of editing and scriptwriting for the submission of ethnographic videos for the official censor; how control was asserted not only over the representation of ethnic minorities but also over the ethnography of everyday life for the Burman communities around the country and the different social, cultural, and historical models that were allowed to pertain in these representations. Over a two and half year period of being involved in this process, I began to appreciate some of the complexities of how the state manipulated its public consumption of ethnographic images in a range of fields and, again, how strategies and networks operated subtly to contest this control.

Without a specific research agenda of my own, the discourses I engaged in with these various groups became in itself a focus of interest for me, as I sought to unravel and understand the confusing complexity of what it meant to be, or be labelled 'Kachin' in the modern Burmese state, why that label itself was objected to and also manipulated by nationalists, as well as how it was interpreted by sympathetically and non-sympathetically minded non-Kachin people. Intuitively I learned that there was a core historical problematic that needed to be explored and the 'fieldwork', if it can even be described as such, was an exercise in defining and unravelling that intuited problematic, as much as an attempt to resolve it. The key element in this 'fieldwork' became the sometimes laborious daily process that we undertook to translate inter-culturally (Jinghpaw to English) and intra-culturally (ritual Jinghpaw to colloquial Jinghpaw) the ritual recitations that had been recorded during the early 1990s from across the Kachin region. It is in this process that I am mindful of my willingness to read the Yellow Pages, for it was this, that made the collaboration possible. These difficult performances, recited in couplet phrases using a now almost disappeared ritual lexis, may last for many hours, are accompanied by complex and intricate sets of ritual practices, and have now almost ceased to take place in the Kachin region of Burma on any significant scale.

Yet it was the triangulation of translation that was critical in this research. From the intra-cultural perspective, the extended amount of time that we spent carefully decoding every word, line by line, became a fascinating process for me of also observing the evolution of explanations, as my understanding increased, as their trust in me deepened, and as my own critical abilities improved. It was about extracting the qualitative from the quantitative and the sublime from the banal. The explanatory commentary was an evolving and transformative process, not a linear one. This experience has perhaps been the most formative intellectually of my life in how I approach understanding this area. A full parallel text of ritual and colloquial Jinghpaw was the outcome of this collaboration by 1999. This was of a translation of a recitation at a performance called Lanyi (Pungga, 1999). The Lanyi, which was recited at weddings after the bride had entered the family home of the groom, was performed by the dumsa, or indigenous spirit priest, Chyahkyi Brang in 1992. This performance is intended both to honour the new bride and to instruct her about the ways of a good wife in a new family. The term Shanhpyi Laika or 'Leather Book' was used to describe the broader series of works that the Committee then hoped to produce. As in many other parts of Asia where similarities of practice are seen, this term evokes missionary ethnography, by which the development of Jinghpaw literature was equated with the recovery of the internalized spirituality that the ancestors had consumed (through the body of a buffalo called Nga Shaga) on their migration from Mahtum Mahta, the point at which humans separated from spirits as they migrated to human habitation. The transcribed text was selected because, as a didactic discourse, it was deemed less provocative towards the still highly sceptical Christian nationalist majority, who still suspected that these research activities would lead to Kachin Christian unity being undermined. Significantly, the recitation was not subdivided into ritual sections around offerings made to a particular spirit but could be abstracted from the ritual proceedings that preceded it during the day of the wedding. This particular recitation was also one of the most complete performances that the research team had been able to record of this ritual, and Chyahkyi Brang was considered to be a very fine dumsa.

The development of this work started to reveal the complexities of how the abstracted text related to the original oral performance and how the colloquial translation should be in turn related to that of the transcribed original form performed in ritual language. In this, there were also significant difficulties arising from the censorship of text over many decades and related socio-educational constraints, due to the fact that a very limited textual corpus in Jinghpaw was available for people to read, other than religious tracts. Kachin people, it was felt, would have multiple difficulties not only in reading the text but also in understanding its structure and how to use items such as footnotes, these being unseen in Jinghpaw texts until that time. Not only would the reader have to be oriented to the recitation and translation as an unusual encoding of Jinghpaw communicative social memory but also they would have to be oriented to the text as a material object. The solutions to these problems were found in making a tape to accompany the book, which presented extracts from the original recitation to help orientate people to the sound and structure of the original language. The transcription and translation were line-numbered and cross-referenced, and a brief introduction described how to use footnotes and other references. Footnotes were used for some of the expository commentary relating to individual items of lexis that might be particularly significant or obscure. Each chapter was also prefaced with a short introductory statement in which the context of the following section was summarized and interpretations given where appropriate. The text was illustrated with drawings made by a local graphic artist, and was produced to the highest standard that was then possible inside Burma, using Kachin technicians and designers wherever possible. As the book was for public sale and use, it had to be submitted to the official censor. This could have been avoided if it had been presented as a religious tract. However, this would have necessitated the formation of an officially sanctioned group or Committee, which would have had to declare itself as 'Animist'. This was deemed to be playing into the hands of those who felt indigenous spirit practices would be divisive of Kachin religious unity in the present. Yet, as a non-Burmese language text, it was possible to submit a summary of the text's contents in Burmese for approval, reflecting the generally poor understanding that the apparatus of the central state had of minority languages and cultures, but which offered a slight window of opportunity that minority language cultures could exploit. It was decided, therefore, to present the text to the censor under the rubric of being a clan or a family history, being the recitation made at the wedding of a particular family, in order to obtain official sanction. If it had been presented as a book on Kachin history, the text would have been prohibited as being a nationalist discourse.

The translation by Pungga Ja Li was criticized by some elites who had personal recollection of these forms by stating that the poetic and aesthetic aspects of the original were lost too much by rendering them in a translated colloquial form. Nonetheless, the text was at the time of considerable significance in providing a new model by which ritual language could be represented in contemporary Kachin society, as well as challenging the boundaries of what it was felt could be achieved intellectually and technologically in repositioning these forms for a new, youthful, Christian-oriented audience. It achieved this partly by the material structure that was given to the text, which elevated it as a high-quality publication evoking academic models of presentation. This directly challenged the Christian nationalist social memory construction of ritual language, which stigmatized it as a form that personified illiteracy and degeneracy (Sadan, 2007). As a result, the social networks in which this text was used demonstrated the transformation of the meaning frameworks of oral ritual in contemporary society that began to take place. In 2002, the text was used in a newly constituted Kachin Culture and Literature Summer School in Myitkyina, which had the support of the Kachin Baptist Church. Most recently, it has been serialized on the principal Kachin language community radio programme Wunpawng Daini over a period of weeks. Significantly, this, like the Summer School, was a youth-run programme, although the radio programme is sponsored by opposition organizations and appeals mainly to Kachin youth in a global diaspora. It was this youth community that was in the late 1990s most antagonistic towards research on historical Kachin culture and dismissive of any attempt to reconfigure understandings of the ritual language. Clearly there had been a shift in contemporary social memory towards this form in the last five years as contemporary nationalist discourse again repositions the meanings of its own past. It is also clear that it was the direct challenge to the representation of the ritual language as a medium of potential disunity and degeneracy that helped to affect this change. However, the transfer from individual memory to social memory of these forms has inevitably necessitated a great loss in detailed knowledge of ritual and cultural forms as the language remains abstracted from its ritual context. Furthermore, the semiotic shift of the forms to the entrenched cognitive encoding of the Christian missions is equally unavoidable, not only in the transfer of semantic ritual domains in the translation of the Jinghpaw Bible, but also through the censorship and social networks within which the text of this recitation has been taken up as a material object with something to say about the social memory of the Kachin people.

The whole process for me, however, was an experience of such daily intensity that I know that I will probably never be able to replicate such an intellectual experience again, and it has remained absolutely fundamental to almost everything I have thought or written on this subject since then. The intensity of the study was critical. It is in this that I think my willingness to sit down and read the Yellow Pages in that dark, hot room in Mandalay is indicative of the kind of mindset that one needs to persevere in these circumstances with difficult but frequently tedious detailed explorations of the minutiae of lives that one does not fully understand. Every day we would spend hours discussing sometimes just a few words from these performances, with long, meandering explanations reaching off into many detailed areas of Kachin cultural history that I could never see either then or possibly in the future. Two lines might occupy us for three or four days, with the heat, with illness, with all the other daily problems that living in Yangon entailed also frequently slowing us down. The process of digitization was equally slow and laborious. As the 1998 World Cup approached, the electricity supply became almost non-existent, with it being widely believed that this was to ensure that electricity could be guaranteed during the event. Sure enough, during that time we had the first steady electricity supply for many months, albeit during the hours of midnight and two in the morning; this then became our working time. During one notable period it took us nearly three months to successfully print out 60 pages of transcriptions as the availability of an electricity supply, a computer without hardware or software problems caused by the surges and slumps in the current, and a working printer with ink proved too much of a challenge to bring together all at one time. It was an interest and a commitment that could not be faked, and that won me many friends. There are still many unresolved questions arising from this time, but we all in our various ways continued with the work that we elaborately constructed together during those three years. Many young people who became involved in the network of those interested in the work have gone on to do significant work in developing cultural projects with young people in the Kachin region, in developing language and literacy courses in advanced Jinghpaw, and in developing education-based projects for young Kachin people struggling to maintain their place in the state education system. It was an unrepeatable experience for all of us concerned, and continues to provide a thread many years down the line, and into the future.

Epilogue

Just before I left Burma in 1999, sitting on the banks of the Irrawaddy River in Myitkyina, the capital of Kachin State in northern Burma, downstream of the bridge that was then being built to improve the infrastructure to the border with China, I was given a Jinghpaw name by means of a short ritual. Ginger had been pounded together with dried fish, and then I and other members of my new family sat together and ate it, swilling back a few cups of rice beer along with it. Following this, I was fully adopted into the Pungga family of the Jinghpaw Maran clan. Ba Li, as I should thereafter refer to the man who was then my elder brother, had given me this name as a means of paying respect to the relationship we had built up over the previous years, but also because he knew it would help me out. 'If you want to do more research about Kachin', Ba Li said, 'you will need this name. Now, wherever you go in Kachinland, when you meet someone who is Kachin they will automatically be a relative and they will assist you.' I had entered into a new social space where the first point of reference with anyone to whom I was introduced should always be a kinship relationship. These kinship terms articulate a complex transnational network of real and imagined historical relationships between Jinghpaw-speaking peoples' spanning territories in North-east India, Burma, Yunnan, and beyond. Ba Li had given me my Jinghpaw name so that I could establish closer relationships with Kachin people across this transnational space that constitutes one of the borderworlds of South, East, and South-east Asia. The Jinghpaw of Burma, the Singpho of North-east India, and the Jingpo of Yunnan were historically and are today socially intricate parts of a commonly understood non-national cultural zone. This zone, whose fluid boundaries may be defined in part by social use of the Jinghpaw language, usually in combination with a range of other national and non-national languages and not necessarily with Jinghpaw as the dominant gloss, has evolved both in relation to the multiple state systems with which it is in contact and in line with its own internal logic of social explanation. In the decade following the gifting of my name, I have had more experience of this space and have entered into it along a number of disciplinary and geographical routes. The more I have done so, the more I am amazed at its ability to integrate and enable articulation of a commonsense of autonomous being in relation to the intersecting vectors of the Indian, the Chinese, and the Burmese states. This was a characteristic that was clearly historically produced, but more than this it seemed to me a process that existed in an ontological relationship with time and the possibilities for consistency within transformation; it was produced within and by state systems, but also above and beyond them. Ba Li was right. As I criss-crossed this zone, within five minutes of meeting any person who might categorize themselves broadly speaking as 'Kachin', my status as either sister, cousin, mother, grandmother, or aunt was established from China to India.

Increasingly I have been able to test the premise of these imagined relationships as my research has extended to the west, east, and south-east of Burma. These experiences remain largely unstructured as I still like to allow for the possibility of just allowing things to happen and unfold and to try to understand the ways in which things happen and unfold, rather than forcing them to unfold in particular ways. As I have done so, I have had to reconfigure and reposition my previous learning in relation to new social situations, new political environments, and new cultural and religious dilemmas. This has also opened up the possibility of looking at lines of discourse and how they develop over time, to introduce a further temporal dynamic into the framework of learning. From this, one can begin to see an alternative model of fieldwork emerging that is pertinent more to the historical than the anthropological, a form of praxis that might take on the name Fieldwork History should its method and reasoning ever become formalized. Such a praxis is vital if we have to understand the histories rather than just the ethnographies of environments that are excluded from our traditional historical gaze. Adding the temporal into our understanding does not always involve a deep chronological framework; rather it can emerge through a process of repeated interaction, of shifting interaction, and which seeks to draw out historical process rather than anthropological constants as its main focus. In this way, slowly it may be possible to begin writing the histories of marginal spaces according to their own internal dynamics and frames of reference.

Notes

1. South (2008) gives an account of the developments around this time at a general level. Smith (1999) remains the classic work on ethnic conflict in the country, although it was written principally before the ceasefires were signed.
2. Lintner (1990) is a well-known account of the 1988 protests and the brutality of the response to them by the military regime, which still defined the possible reactions towards any protests at this time.
3. For a more complete and extensive representation of the full outcomes of this collaboration see Sadan (2013).

References

Dell, E. 2000. *Burma Frontier Photographs 1918–1935.* London: Merrell Publishers.

Ja Li, Pungga. 1999. *Shanhpyi Laika: Lanyi.* Yangon: A Z Offset.

Robinne, Francois. 2007. *Pretres Et Chamanes: Metamorphoses Des Kachin De Birmanie.* Paris: Harmattan.

Levy, A. and C. Scott-Clark. 2001. *The Stone of Heaven: The Secret History of Imperial Green Jade.* London: Weidenfeld and Nicolson.

Lintner, Bertil. 1990. *Outrage: Burma's Struggle for Democracy.* London: White Lotus UK.

Sadan, M. 2007. Historical Photography in Kachin State: An Update on the James Green Collection of Photographs. *South Asia: The Journal of the South Asia Studies Association of Australia*, Special Issue: Northeast and Beyond: Culture and Change, 30(3): 457–477.

———. 2013. *Being and Becoming Kachin: Histories Beyond the State in the Borderworlds of Burma*. Oxford: The British Academy and Oxford University Press.

Sladen, E.B. 1871. Expedition from Burma, via the Irrawaddy and Bhamo, to South-Western China. *Journal of the Royal Geographical Society of London*, 41: 257–281.

Smith, Martin T. 1999. *Burma: Insurgency and the Politics of Ethnicity*. London: Zed Books.

South, Ashley. 2008. *Ethnic Politics in Burma: States of Conflict*. Abingdon: Routledge.

Tegenfeldt, H.G. 1974. *A Century of Growth: The Kachin Baptist Church of Burma*. South Pasadena, California: William Carey Library.

Woods, K. 2010. Community Forest in Cease-Fire Zones in Kachin State, Northern Burma: Formalizing Collective Property in Contested Ethnic Areas. Paper presented at the CAPRI Workshop on collective Action, Property Rights and Conflict in Natural Resources Management, Siem Reap, Cambodia.

———. 2011. Ceasefire Capitalism: Military-Private Partnerships, Resource Concessions and Military State Building in the Burma-China Borderland. *Journal of Peasant Studies*, 38(4): 747–770.

Zaw, Oo and Win Min. 2007. *Assessing Burma's Ceasefire Accords*. Washington, D.C.: East-West Centre Washington and Singapore: ISEAS Publishing

5

Fields of Working Knowledge

Ben Campbell

In the Field

My first period of research took a very literal approach to the idea of fieldwork: I arrived explicitly to take part in the agricultural activities. In 1980, I had first walked up the Trisuli Valley in Nepal and became curious about the Tamang villages, their homes and the ecological setting. The Tamang ethnicity had been relatively under-researched as compared to Gurungs, Sherpas, Magars, Rais, and Limbus. In this period I also trekked to Jomsom, and journeyed to Darjeeling, Kashmir, and Ladakh, coming to appreciate the variable distributions of wet–dry, up–down, rice–barley, *masjid*, *mandir*, and *gomba*. By 1987 the plan for a research project evolved, taking a cue from seeing a rise in the academic and popular interest in indigenous systems of food production and environmental knowledge (and having over several years myself practised organic vegetable growing techniques in a volunteer working organization called Willing Workers on Organic Farms). In 1979 I was staying with a Bahun family in Pokhara, and one morning saw the teenage boy of the house start to hoe the land at the back of the house to plant potatoes. I offered to join in, and as I had worked two summers with small French farmers, was able to keep pace, and enjoyed a meal of maize dhero and saag for lunch break. This had been one of the most interactive ways of spending time socially during my travels. I had probably doubled my Nepali vocabulary in a very short time, and I could foresee that research into the social dimensions of food growing would be a topic for original theoretical reflection on the anthropology of the Himalayas.

Drawn to explore further mountain cultures, I had fled the madness of England at the time of Margaret Thatcher's Falklands war to spend four months in Peru. Above the upper Marañon valley, I had joined villagers and school teachers in their wheat harvest by carrying and trampling the crop under the hooves of horses and mules in a rotating, roped radius I helped to encircle. Later, back in the United Kingdom, I was inspired by reading the account by Wendell Berry (1982) of his sojourn with the anthropologist Stephen Brush in Peru, and saw the value that non-anthropologists can derive from ethnographic knowledge, who are working to rethink human relationships with the land and the food it can produce. Reading subsequently about Andean collective agricultural practices of ayni and minka, I have placed the elements of ethnographic reports of agricultural social practices from the Himalayas and the Tamang in particular (Clarke, 1980; Euler, 1984; Hoffpauir, 1978; Holmberg, 2006; March, 1979; Toffin, 1986) into a frame that had a comparative dimension—to investigate the phenomenon of collective or reciprocal labour groups in subsistence farming systems. Contrary to the two dominant approaches to indigenous subsistence systems within anthropology at the time, that of Sahlins' (1972) domestic mode of production, and French Marxist anthropology's ceding of explanatory primacy to reproduction rather than production, and thereby devaluing 'the labour process' (Meillassoux, 1981), my goal was to investigate the coproduction of food and social relations from toiling in the fields.

Leaving aside consideration of the time in which I was beginning my fieldwork (the hiatus of India's blocking of trade and transport to Nepal, the run-up to the jana andolan of 1990), I chose a village where I had stayed one night during a trek through the Trisuli and its side valleys in November 1988, and had received a good impression as a community which was of a reasonable size, and the people had been approachable. In basic Nepali, I explained, I wanted to learn Tamang words for farming activities, for foods, livestock, plants, and trees important for the subsistence system, for aspects of domestic architecture, and kinship terminology. Naturally enough, a significant village faction did not accept this version of my purpose, but a man who was married to a classificatory 'daughter' of the father in the family I was lodging with, and who had a position of haldar in the Nepal army, conducted diplomacy on my behalf, not that anyone could dispel all mistrust of motives from living in such a community. The veteran Tamang ethnologist MacDonald told me in 1988 that the Tamang 'probably wouldn't kill me'.

Cultivating Knowledge

With most of the development literature on rural Nepal being focused on poverty, and the chronic insufficiency of mountain farming systems, it came as something of a surprise that in my first day's work in March 1989 joining in with field labours of weeding terraces with a hoe, and clearing gravel from the soil that had spread from a stream, diverted after rains, the tone of conversation among the small groups dotted across the fold of terraced hillsides was decidedly ribald. Sex was the main interest for conversation. My marital status was inquired into, and when I said that my wife had stayed in Britain, I added that I was perhaps like a lama. The reply came, 'The lamas in this village sleep with their wives every night!'

Having cleared the gravel covering on the terraces by the edge of scrub forest, our family group continued with hoeing along the terraces ploughed and sown with maize. During the clearing of weeds (*mraa*), the woman beside me noticed some uncovered maize seeds in the ground and saw that they had germinated. Makai piiji! She called out to the other small groups up above. This appeared to be a celebratory moment, an instance for declaring to those in earshot the evidence of this turning point in the year, when new life comes from people's scratching and sweating labours, from their daily rounds of trotting up and down the mountain paths to coax sustenance from the varied patchwork of fields and forests on whom the lives of villagers depend.

Within a few weeks, I had learned to recognize enough faces and names to realize that the small groups that had been within earshot that day of the maize germinating were the families of the Shyangba lineage, with one of which I was staying. The great grandfather of the man whose house I had been welcomed into had first cleared the area of fields we had been working in, known as Braa-di. The other families working in Braa-di that day were the elder brother's and their father's brother's son's family. More lineage land was held higher up, and similarly aligned against the edge of the cultivable slope by Tengu shyong, the stream marking the southern edge of the village territory. These fields had first been cleared for swiddening (*mrangshing phyeeba*). Several years later, I was able to see a shift of focus in where people were cultivating, due to the wholesale relocation of the clustered village houses by the dirt road built 15 minutes walk above the original village, and due to the market prices that were attracted by growing potatoes for sale. The better potato land was on or above the altitude of the road, and old 'clan' fields were brought back into cultivation after a generation of fallow since the practice of swidden had been banned by the

Langtang National Park in 1976. The Shyangba lineage claimed their fallow clan land had been illegitimately cultivated and then registered by members of the more numerous and powerful Bongtso Ghale lineages. This way of speaking about ancestral clan land suggested that the institution referred to as kipat, and which is historically associated with ethnic groups in the east of Nepal, could have been more widespread.

The Shyangba married with Ghale clans, and the woman of the house I had become closest to was Ghale. She did not eat beef (*me shya*). The Shyangba do. She would not cook it if it came into the house. She did eat water buffalo (*mai shya*), and chicken (*naga shya*). What was I to eat? Nepal was then a Hindu kingdom, and the Tamang clans who ate beef were consequently held in low regard by high caste Nepalis. In the United Kingdom I have been a vegetarian since 1981, but moving beyond Europe my penchant for cultural relativism kicks in, especially when people offer you food which is a non-everyday item, and it is often difficult even offensive to refuse. In this case though, the first time beef arrived in the house the question arose of dietary coming out. Would the Desi eat beef? I made a strategic decision not to join the beef-disparagers, and play into the game of minor status differentiations whereby the Ghale present them to the Nepali mainstream as a rank above the Tamang proper. If I was to break my normal vegetarianism, was it not right to follow the diet of my host lineage?

This was one form of deliberate self-marking required from fieldwork, of becoming a persona given shape and characteristics from response with field conditions and relationship dynamics. Another major step came with a question some men had begun to ask me, often after rather a lot of drinks, and very insistent that I should comply. Would I become their ritual friend (*leng laba*)? There could well have been some collective pressure towards the men who asked me this question, as after a couple of months of being around, villagers were perhaps getting tired of this indeterminate foreigner who was acting as if he had integrated, joined the work groups, even tried to carry head-loads of finger millet stalks as livestock fodder, but without a connection that would ascribe to me a normal location within the placing of clan-kinsmen solidarity and affinal alliances. The option of rolling out dyadic fictions of 'brother' or 'sister' in reciprocal appellations made no cumulative sense if I was calling two men brothers, who were actually brothers-in-law to themselves. Tamang kinship practice needs to add up, and comes to be a constantly worked at, readjusted, making-place-for and logically explicable collective enterprise that enfolds and contracts with new arrivals.

A further factor played into my move to accept the ritual kinship with my Shyangba host. It was not simply my non-classifiable kinship status that had caused discomfort. My motives of wanting to learn the Tamang language, the names of plants, the practices of farming, the kinship terms, the histories of clans, the memories of trading with Tibetan nomads, and the places and rituals of significance to the bombo and lama had not convinced the villagers of Tengu of my purpose. The idea of an anthropologist living among them in this way was not a locally credible subject position. Well yes, they did recall someone who had lived in Manigaon years back, an American 'David [Holmberg]?' I asked, 'David' that's right. He could speak perfect Tamang, well, 'western' Tamang! (*nuppa shimmm*, they parodied the accent). Did you know someone in Shyabru Andrew [Hall]? Ah Andrew he spoke perfect Tibetan, and could lead the singing in a funeral dance. But for all these cases (some remembered that David had been compelled to leave the district and accused of cow killing), the innocence of observer neutrality was not a persona of any credence. I had to be intent on taking off with my host's wife, or worse. The gossip mill was running in overdrive. 'Small village, big words'. 'People say bad things', 'those witches cause me grief with their talking, saying one thing from the mouth, another from deep down'. My enquiries about what the *leng* relationship entailed and my observations of other relationships of *leng* and *romo* (as contracted between women, or the term used for your *leng*'s wife) led me into receiving local explanations of the institution: substituting the precise equivalence of terms of address as people would use for your *leng*, mourning when kin are lost, and polite verbal honorifics to be used at all events; and in an observation of sociological comparison I was told that in contrast to the practice of Khampa Tibetans, making *leng* or as the Tibetans call it—*robo*—does not entitle a man to sleep with his *leng*'s wife—*romo*. I was told other villagers had become *leng* precisely to make this ethical categorization. So the big day came, I went through the wedding-template ceremony of Nepali *mit laune* (Tamang *leng laba*), applying *tika* marks on each other's foreheads with eyes averted, and passing plates of rice and coins in exchange beneath a separating sheet held between us.

The integration by ritual kinship gave moral clarity to the relationally dense world in which I had arrived. I was initially taken aback by quite how many people called me 'grandfather', often people just 10 years younger than me, but they were the children of Shyangba lineage 'older' brothers from previous generations' older brothers. Then there was the flip side to respect honorifics. Elder brothers' wives enjoy taunting and 'joke'—flirting with their husbands' younger brothers. If the elder brother's wife—husband's younger brother (*tsang teba*—*tewar*) relation has a formal structure and code for its proper conduct of impropriety, the more generic interface between cross-cousins was far more spontaneously explosive. Ribald verbal exchanges and playful assaults could erupt at a moment's notice, and contests of advance and repulsion, or counter attack could result in a rolling tumble of bodies on the floor. Suddenly my social world was split between the siblingship and own clan world of lineage generation and age hierarchies, as opposed to those others who provide space for alterity at a number of levels: erotic, aggressive and contestatory, but affinally constitutive from the outside of the core conditions of possibility for the lineage's own social and biological reproduction.

How far did all this extend in practice into the literal fields of knowledge, it was my task to investigate—with 'the social context of agriculture' as my research project title. At one level, the flip back between parallel and cross kinship ties laid the basic warp and weft for the forms available to social discourse. Did the subsistence economy entirely concord with these forms? At the apical point of the socio-agricultural construction is the legitimate inheritance of property, confirmed at the mourning feast (*gewa*) of a household head. It is the arch affine, the mother's brother, who performs the central validating role of dispelling grief among patrimonial land—and livestock-inheriting sons, giving an external moderator's blessing to the passage of herds and fields of productive earth to the next generation of agnates. But the truth is that mourning feasts are often punctuated by violent outbursts among tired and emotional siblings. The fit between formal kinship patterns of expectation and actual events of who gets what can be variously scripted. The idea that structures of solidarity and actual co-operation emanate in onion rings of agnatic proximity as depicted in Sahlins' writings on the domestic mode of production and the sociology of exchange, and which had been applied as if this was the way things are in Fricke's (1986) study of Tamang demography and subsistence in Ankhu Khola, did not account for what I was seeing in the deep tensions that reverberated between siblings in particular.

The core evidence I gathered to look into these issues was from the observation of field labour, from a village-wide survey of all households' socio-economic data, and from a specifically focused survey of domestic labour activities during the most intense working seasons. By holding back the bulk of my survey work to the last third of my time in the field, I had built up the linguistic and social competence to ask the right questions, knowing the terms and idioms for asking questions of measures such as *dhaka* (carrying basket-loads of grain harvest), *borak* (bamboo mats tied into cylindrical silos to hold potatoes or maize cobs), also the place and field names, and the calculation of field areas in *hal*. Furthermore,

I was able to draw on observations of process and change from a previous year's activity. So when it came to compiling the survey of facts from questions such as 'who belongs in this household?', I was able to see the actual domestic arrangement in front of my eyes as processually on the move. There were already several households where children had moved between their main place of eating and sleeping, from one to another. There were young couples who had tried to make themselves economically independent, but had collapsed back into the larger extended family frame. There were domestic workers on contract for households that had insufficient labour of their own, but where the worker in question was also a clan relative of the mother or father of the house, and it was entirely through the idiom of kinship and the coproduction of daily life that the relationship was conducted. Though it was clear there was to be the gift of a water buffalo or cow after the period of service, this was not to taint the qualitative subsumption of working hands as an activity between people of close kin relations. This worked the other way too. A 12-year-old son from a previous wife was told by his father he could stay in his house if he worked. 'Work and you will be fed.' Even direct agnatic consanguinity was not enough to merit belonging to a household.

The resolution I came to while writing up the research was to posit an irresolvable tension between delimited domestic circuits, against extensive kinship networks. The actually existing units were further complexified by the Tamang agropastoral transhumant economy. At the time of my first fieldwork there was only one domestic unit among 44, that did not have a livestock *godi* (Nep. *goth*). To focus research on the domestic economic sociality primarily on structures of four stone walls would miss the importance of the fact that people moved their de facto residence on an average of about 12 times a year (sometimes no more than a few metres at a time to camp on a different area of fields, to cultivate the ground or manure the terraces by tethering the animals over night; sometimes to decamp further to high pastures or down to where some villagers held fields by the Trisuli River itself). But the movement, the reforming of micro-neighbourhoods, the decisions to open up some old fallow, plant potatoes next to a family with a loud, bellowing voice for scaring crop-raiding wildlife, or to make a new cooperation with a family with whom some marriage might be contemplated led to a special dimension of constantly remaking effective social groups of everyday conviviality and work. Therefore, in terms of social composition and in terms of how the 'domestic' was processually 'done' in recombinant memberships and place locatedness, the community of mobile human and livestock dwellings came to be seen as moving through the shifting patterns of transhumance, and by fieldwork days consisting of walking the pathways and stopping at encampments to understand why and with whom the next recampment was to be made.

In April it was like there was a return to the forest. With maize and potatoes already sown, and the wheat not yet harvested, the *godi*s retreated off the fields to scrubland where the finger millet seed beds were prepared. Set among overhanging rocks, or in openings of woods at the field margins, the beds would be manured, ridged up and sown. The *godi*s of the lineage clusters would come closer together than when spread out across their field-holdings. Then a first period of intensive *nangba* would begin, weeding the maize and potatoes in April/May.

The sociality of *nangba* came to dominate the last phase of my fieldwork. On any day when I was present in the village, I would try to keep up with how many *nangba* were working and where. *Nangba* dominate the agricultural season for the villagers. If people ask what time it is in the morning, the *nangba* takes over time reckoned for the synchronics of daily life: 'it is time to go to *nangba*', 'it is nearly time for *nangba* to return'. When I had figured out which were the participating households in any given group, I usually only needed to know one or two names before having a good idea of who would be involved. Of course not every household could send the same member every day, to the one or more *nangba* it participated in. Here was the interest. If normally a 30-year-old woman goes to the group, but is indisposed one day with other tasks or illness, she might send anyone, a male or a female between ages 11 and 72, in her place. Some nangba groups worked after eating a solid meal, starting about 10:00 am. Others began from early in the morning (*sho ense*), taking snacks of toasted maize or wheat with them, returning in the late afternoon to gorge on boiled potatoes dipped in chilli and salt.

In the spirit of *nangba* the household is the primary unit of account, but in the spirit of *nangba* the household is insufficient to itself and its members. The normal hierarchies of the household's kinship forms are placed in the background, to be replaced by a more vigorously egalitarian and rowdy ensemble, focused on completing a day's work in a round of reciprocal exchange. It was moreover in the *nangba* that one found characters with somewhat ambiguous domestic belonging: the people in 'service' to the house, for contracted financial reasons, or absence of a primary alternative residence. Some widowed women came to join their daughters who had married in the village, making their contribution to the daughter's marital household by saving another household member the unrelenting toil of day upon day of hoeing and weeding. In fact there was one *nangba* where the

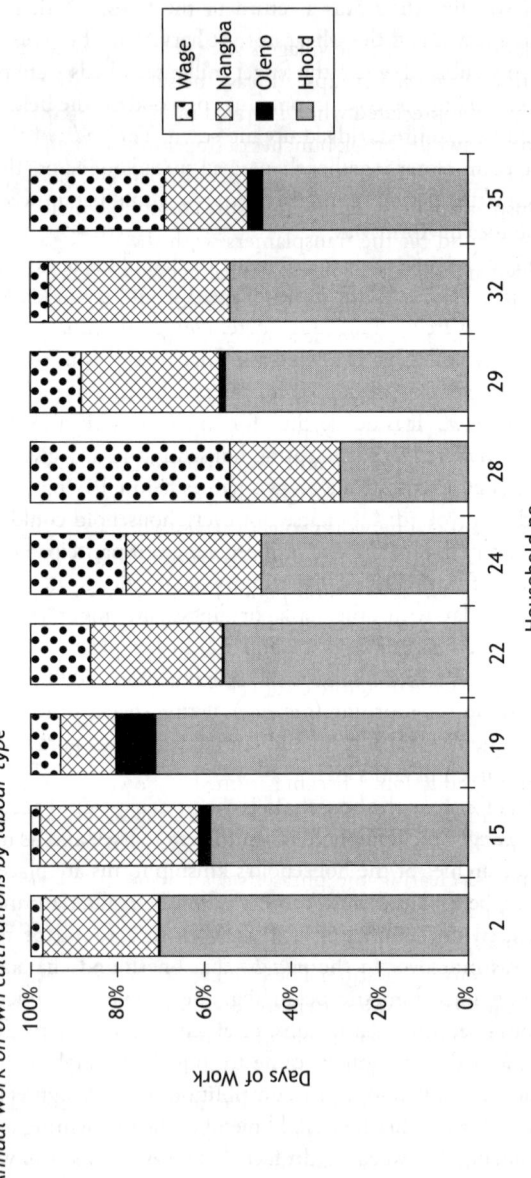

Annual work on own cultivations by labour type

Household no.

Days of Work

Wage
Nangba
Oleno
Hhold

Source: Campbell (1993).

women of 60 years plus all gathered to keep each other company, just as the teenage girls had their own informal club, but never quite as formalized as one reads in reports of *rodi ghar* among the Gurungs (Messerschmidt, 1981; Pignède, 1966).

My own relationships with the villagers were possibly eased by a willingness to spend time in *nangba* groups. At least the supply of cigarettes I had with me was always appreciated when I arrived in the company of a group. If I had time to stay awhile, I took bunches of finger millet seedlings to plant in rhythm with the women who mostly do this work, or I would help set the pace of the transplanting by adopting the more commonly male-performed role of clearing ground for the transplanters, with the rapid hoeing of the previously ploughed terrace. The *nangba* social networks were evidently the way into the village life for strangers. One woman who had not turned up for several months and had not made a success of running a shop of a friend who had given her the responsibility of it, was told by a village woman pointedly, 'if we don't have money or food, we go to work with *nangba*'. For the months of April through September, there is a living to be had, in terms of food and shelter, for any able-bodied person. For the duration of the growing season, the immediate 'short-term' (Bloch, 1973) pragmatic interests of effective social networks to get the work of primary subsistence completed are foregrounded, and the boundaries of domestic inclusivity are flexed. For less intensive agricultural periods of the year, the longer-term alignments of domestic enterprises, and the principles of kinship hierarchies reassert themselves to protect household property (*sampatti*).

Forms of sociality were therefore creatively in play over different times of the year, and in fieldwork over two years I was able to monitor the contraction and expansion of residential units, and their periodically co-operative arrangements for production. I became attuned to how the imagery of the house was far from that of a fixed edifice, constructed on firm foundations, but one of the most malleable and tactically performed institutions for social purposes. Hearing the phrase 'we are of one house' invariably signalled using a past reality, that at some level of calculating appropriate exchanges in rituals, gifting, and kin terms will play a role, but as an everyday reality was a rhetorical gesture. The Himalayan 'house' of the Tamang-speaking communities of Rasuwa emerged from research as a lively and dynamic enterprise. It was given shape and moulded to meet the diverse and demanding needs of producing livelihoods and social relationships from an ecological setting where food production has to be spread across different altitudinal zones and crafted to attend to familial, livestock, and crop needs. To understand the role of the *nangba* in Tengu village was also to recognize that this institution maintained distinctly egalitarian modalities within the village community. When compared to Tamang villages with more powerful and wealthy local families, it was evident that one distinguishing feature of this different class was the fact that these households did not join *nangba* groups (the other locally salient feature was not sending their members to go portering for wages).

Research into domestic subsistence production gave a grounding to my understanding of social life among the Tamang. However, as the production-oriented ways of understanding social life gave way to more environmentally contextualized approaches, my second phase of fieldwork became an exploration of strands of enquiry I had begun pilot work on: that of social reflections on encounters with non-human others.

Natural Affinities

With fieldwork on environmental relationships, the research picked up on elements of mythological storylines, and narratives of historical oral accounts which spoke of how the Tamang interaction with other communities was frequently ecologically coded. My interest at this stage was less in describing the details of how people live in close daily proximity with biodiversity, and more in finding a characterization of the qualities of the relationship with non-human others. The immediate context for this research was the political and cultural impact of the Langtang National Park criminalizing much of the villagers' traditional subsistence practice, including hunting, swidden farming, and bamboo barter. The global messianic spread of biodiversity protection made people like the Tamang into iconic 'degraders' of the natural environment. Their supposed ignorance of forest depletion and loss of species, their reckless use of the forest species and habitual encroachment into the forest spaces with utilitarian motives all signalled environmentally indisciplined populations that nature needed to be protected from.

There were two obvious strategies I knew could be taken to counter this view. One was to discuss the reports I had heard of the ways in which Tamang villagers had been historically forced into productivizing the forest environment. Royal dairy herds pressing village labour into providing stabling and equipment for their annual passage was one example of this. Another was the mobilization of village labour for hunting *tahr* and *ghoral* with rope trap nets. In general, though the Tamang areas in the immediate hinterland of

Kathmandu's trading economy had been left deliberately underdeveloped to reproduce the labour force of porters, from their own resources in the areas of temperate forests of no value to commercial interests. The other strategy was to question the way in which 'Nature' has been introduced as an organizing concept for framing human/non-human interactions. What alternative ways of talking and behaving signified was that perhaps the Tamang notions of their humanity did not involve the kind of dualism so directly prevalent in the contrast between biodiversity and human culture, which arrived in Nepal in the 1970s pre-scripted with narratives of imminent eco-perdition, and the default boundaries of fragile nature to be defended by armed soldiers.

Fieldwork now took the form of amassing numerous accounts of interaction with non-human species, and also the quasi-humans, such as ghosts, territorial spirits with inclinations to anger or retributive acts of malice, manifest in disease, or untoward events such as hailstorms or landslides. I went on the winter pilgrimage to balance my knowledge of the summer pilgrimage to Gosainkund, and see how mountain verticality provides an image of fertile abundance in space and time, that attracts diverse ethnic communities to participate in. As it happened, this was almost the last chance I had to learn from the *bombo* (*shaman*), to whom I owe most of my understandings of the non-human species. I spent so much time in his company and many people asked me if I was planning to become a *shaman*. In fact he was reckoned to be so efficacious with spells and mantras that I was strongly warned not to continue with some of the medical aspects my curiosity had led me to enquire into. I was warned I would go blind if I chanted those words I was recording. This was another point I reached in the field when the notion of an objective, distanced observer merely gathering information about another culture in a disinterested manner did not convince many in the community, and I was told to stop this line of research for my own good. The *bombo* was, however, a source of remarkable mythological tales, which opened a door on an indigenous imaginary of interspecies exchange and metamorphosis.

The majority of these tales, chants, and local myths of place were explicitly categorized as coming 'From the time when people spoke with gods and spirits' (*Lha deng lu batiba bela ri*). Many were to do with the original processes of cosmogenesis, of adding difference in the forms and relationships of life. Such was the case in the myth of two sister yaks who used to return in summer to ever higher pastures for grazing. However, one time the younger sister decided against her sibling's repeated calls, and even cautions, to stay below. She stayed, but transformed into a water buffalo and became the demonized sacrificial animal of humans. The options for analysing this story are intriguing, and as with tales of how rhododendron trees attempted to make marriage alliance with alder trees, there is an analogical possibility for interpreting the non-humans as metaphorical substitutes for human counterparts. There is obviously a parallel to the Tamangs' migration from Tibet, and their acclimatization to lower altitudes where they have been ritualized victims of lowlanders' organized violence (Holmberg, 2006). But the parallel narratives of human and non-human do not admit the ways in which many of these tales point to something altogether more ambiguous than analogy. There is a becoming aware of other beings' outlook of the world, which carries the recognition of non-humans into a different ontological realm than one of parallel substitution. Perhaps the most powerful of these accounts was the *bombo*'s very own story of how he became a *bombo*.

He tells the story in the film I made with my cameraman brother, 'Shamanic Pilgrimage to Gosainkund'. The *bombo* was captured by *lo-ngai*. These are anthropoid beings, sometimes known as *nyalmo*, the Tamang equivalent of 'yeti'. They captured him in the forest and kept him for days. He spoke of seeing the *lo-ngai* children talking with their parents and threatening to eat him. They were all staking claims to which part of his body they would eat, 'the arm', 'the leg', 'this nose', he says feeling his body as chunks of meat for the predatory intent of the savage creatures. With this 'capture on the far side', the bombo was able to take up the position of other beings, and had an empathic curiosity for stories of species interaction, conflict, and deceit. But this perspectivism does not make a stable cosmology as has been argued for Amazonian relations with non-human others (Viveiros de Castro, 1998). Indeed with Himalayan ethnography the vertical factor of ecological, linguistic, economic, and power differentials provides a sectional provisionality to any attempt by local or state actors, or even external analysers, to encompass or reduce local realities to wider complexes, or generative causes (Campbell, 2013a). There is rather a listening to neighbours that passes elements of myth and narrative history through transforming exchanges of borrowing, imitation, parody, and retelling.

The Way of the Road

Will this fragmented array of relational positions adopted according to who or what one is confronted with all be flattened by how a road will be driven through to the China border? This was the scenario facing the second film I made, again with my brother, in 2007. 'Making links' in circumstances not of one's choosing is the Tamang disposition to accommodate travellers through their lands. The speed of the road traffic and its possible routing along the main river course rather than through Tamang village locations and the subsequent risk this would pose to livelihoods of small traders became the film's subject matter. Fortuitous timing, and an invitation from a VDC chairman in Bharku village to film the biennial re-enactment of ancient wars between Nepal and China, generated an arresting set of images that call for reflection on the Tamangs' upside/downside, flip-around vision of the radically different universes they mediate on a daily basis.

Fieldwork using film provides a wholly different relation of access to the possible sense that can be made of recorded material. This was already realized by the village *lama* in Tengu, who saw how the deceased *bombo* lived on through the previous film we had made. Therefore, on our arrival with cameras, he chose the most important story to tell us—that of the passage up the valley of Guru Rimpoche, defeating the demons on his route to bring Buddhism to Tibet. With this story on film, he knew his unborn descendants would be able to hear him telling it.

Unlike the faulty memory that struggles in field notes to leave a trace of observation and the gist of conversations, with smatterings of verbatim phrases, the filmed interviews especially bare repeat viewing when each time the chances of layering meanings and points of reference accumulate. As the composition is, however, watched through repeatedly to communicate organized messages of linked conversation, text and image, there is a danger of missed perspectives dropped from the preferred edit, and a risk that untidy but significant surrounding material is left out. The more powerful interviews, and their performative impression, work an interpretive line. In the film, there is a sceptical opinion of the possibilities that road building, even in the name of the poor, as avowed by the Asian Development Bank, will seriously bring improvement to the economic well-being of the district. This perspective is actually delivered mostly by the traders whose enterprises stand to lose more, and they will have to adjust to the new landscape of small profits in different ways than the villagers, whose products might find markets they could not previously reach, or shift their production to activities like fish farming. However, the confidence of the Asian Development Bank's literature that the road would alleviate poverty for this northern district of Nepal was shared by none of the people we interviewed except those most connected to the state (Campbell, 2013b). It was an accident of the timing of our filming trip that in capturing the festivities of the war dances between Nepal and China, we missed the occasion to interview the chief district officer, who was on holiday. Among villagers there was considerable doubt that the local population would stand much chance of competing with richer and more experienced transport businesses, while the effective labour power of the local population had, in the economic crisis facing the rural population during the Maoist People's War, mostly departed for Malaysia and the Gulf years before.

Conclusion

From reciprocal labour groups to roadside development, from a cosmogenic storybook of ancestral figures in the forest to Gulf-bound migrant workers, the fieldwork experience over two decades never ceases to change shape according to shifting priorities, and unforeseen events. New techniques and forms of enquiry and new geopolitical contexts of explanation refocus the ethnographic accounts and explanatory potential. While looking back over 20 years there has clearly been a process of rapid globalization for a district once considered relatively 'remote', yet the fieldwork experience has constantly reiterated the discovery of perspectives on locality that were not always previously apparent, or did not hold salience in the same way. As the *janajati* movement took hold in Nepal, and all ethnic groups found new reasons to review their own histories, the work of anthropologists in presenting fieldwork-based accounts of the realities of economic, environmental, and ethnic complexity in the Himalayan societies has served to vitalize certain forms of the cultural production. This has been quite dramatic in the case of filmed fieldwork episodes, in villages that had no electric supply a dozen years ago, and the complaint is now heard that people are no longer active in their cultural institutions because they are inside their houses watching DVDs. That is one side of the story. Another is the phenomenon I saw of a DVD of the wedding conducted between a clan nephew of my ritual friend and his wife from a Sherpa village far to the east. I watched the flickering images of the big day, the *khata* scarves aplenty, and marvelled at the sharing of subjectivities between the anthropologist-cum-part-time-local and the observational practice of watching and commenting on a cultural production of the Himalayan communities in ritually inventive communicative interaction as to how Tamang and Sherpa can marry on mutually satisfactory terms. A new era had come in which the evidence of novel social practice in its grounded Himalayan variety has acquired extensively shared popular value.

References

Berry, W. 1982. *The Gift of Good Land: Further Essays Cultural and Agricultural.* New York: North Point Press.

Bloch, M. 1973. The Long Term and the Short Term: The Economic and Political Significance of the Morality of Kinship. In J. Goody (ed.), *The Character of Kinship*, pp. 75–88. Cambridge: Cambridge University Press.

Campbell, B. 1993. *The Dynamics of Cooperation: Households and Economy in a Tamang Community of Nepal.* PhD thesis, University of East Anglia, p. 188.

———. 2013a. *Living Between Juniper and Palm: Nature, Culture and Power in the Himalayas.* Delhi: Oxford University Press.

———. 2013b. From Remote Area to Thoroughfare of Globalisation: Shifting Territorialisations of Development and Border Peasantry in Nepal. In J. Smadja (ed.), *Territorial Changes and Territorial Restructurings in the Himalayas*, pp. 255–271. Paris: CNRS Editions.

Clarke, G. 1980. *The Temple and Kinship among a Buddhist People of the Himalaya.* Thesis. Oxford: Oxford University.

Euler, C. 1984. Changing Patterns of a Subsistence Economy. *Contributions to Nepalese Studies*, 11: 63–98.

Fricke, T. 1986. *Himalayan Households: Tamang Demography and Domestic Processes.* Ann Arbor, Michigan: UMI Research Press.

Holmberg, D. March 2006. Violence, Non-violence, Sacrifice, Rebellion, and the State. *Studies in Nepali Society and History*, 11(1): 31–65.

Hoffpauir, R. 1978. Subsistence Strategy and its Ecological Consequences in the Nepal Himalaya. *Anthropos*, 73: 215–252.

March, K. 1979. The Intermediacy of Women: Female Gender Symbolism and the Social Position of Women among Tamangs and Sherpas of Highland Nepal. Thesis, Cornell University.

Meillassoux, C. 1981. *Maidens, Meal and Money: Capitalism and the Domestic Community.* Cambridge: Cambridge University Press.

Messerschmidt, D. 1981. Nogar and other Traditional Forms of Cooperation in Nepal: Significance for Development. *Human Organization*, 40: 40–47.

Pignède, B. 1966. *Les Gurungs, Une Population Himalayenne Du Nepal.* Paris: Mouton.

Sahlins, M. 1972. *Stone Age Economics.* London: Tavistock.

Toffin, G. 1986. Mutual Assistance in Agricultural Work among the Western Tamang of Nepal: Traditional and New Patterns. In K. Seeland (ed.), *Recent Research on Nepal*, pp. 84–96. Munich: Weltforum Verlag.

Viveiros de Castro, E. 1998. Cosmological Deixis and Amerindian Perspectivism. *JRAI*, 4: 469–488.

6

Reflections on Fieldwork in Three Cultures*

Arjun Guneratne

I am sometimes asked by well meaning American anthropologists why a Sri Lankan would study Nepal. This has always seemed to me an odd (and tiresome) question for what they clearly find curious is why someone of my nationality would wish to work somewhere other than his country of origin. They seem not to find it odd, however, that someone raised on the prairie of Nebraska or in a suburb in Massachusetts should also want to study Nepal or some other place remote from the United States. The assumption that underlies this question is that Americans (and in particular, white Americans) can study whosoever and whatsoever they please and need justify it only in terms of their interests as individuals, while those anthropologists who hail from places that historically have been the object of anthropological study are supposed to (or assumed to) study their own society.

This assumption has to do in part with the history of anthropology itself, as European discourse about 'native' others, but it also reflects the way political and economic power is organized on a global scale. It is because the United States is a global power that American anthropologists are able to take for granted that they may do research where they please (especially if they are recipients of a Fulbright grant, which smoothes the logistics

---

* This essay previously appeared in Seneviratne, H.L. (ed.). 2009. *The Anthropologist and the Native: Essays for Gananath Obeyesekere*. Firenze : Società Editrice Fiorentina. It has been reprinted with permission from the University of Florence Press.

and bureaucratic hassles wonderfully). The flip side to this is that many 'natives' who are the object of the gaze of American anthropologists assume the ethnographer is motivated not by individual curiosity but by ulterior motives; given the power and the ambitions of the United States in the world, American anthropologists, for instance, often run the risk of being taken for agents of the CIA. Why else would someone leave home and family to spend a year or more among strangers to no apparent productive purpose? The question asked of me by certain American anthropologists, with which I began this essay, is second cousin to the suspicions of a 'native' confronted by an inquisitive American ethnographer. Both are curious about the behavior that seems out of place and which must be accounted for in terms of some ulterior purpose that transcends mere intellectual curiosity or individual motivation.

I have carried out anthropological fieldwork in three different cultures, two in Sri Lanka and one in Nepal, and each has presented me with different challenges and opportunities. My first fieldwork was as an undergraduate, when, with funding from my American college, I spent five weeks in a peasant colonization scheme in the Anuradhapura district. My next and major fieldwork was in Nepal, where I spent almost two years living in a village in the Chitwan district, doing the research that led to my dissertation and subsequently to a book (Guneratne, 2002). Both these stints of fieldwork fall within the rubric of what anthropologists conventionally have understood by the term: I lived in a village, I worked among people who did not share my social background and like all good anthropologists I strove to understand two cultures that were to varying degrees alien to me—one more so than the other. It can be said that in both these cases I was engaged in a study of 'the other'.

My third phase of fieldwork however, in which I am currently engaged, is a study of my own milieu: I am working on a history of the environmental movement in Sri Lanka, focusing on the central role of the English-speaking middle classes in it. I happen to have been actively engaged in environmental issues in Sri Lanka, am a member of the same social class that I am now studying, and am working with a culture with which I am intimately familiar—in fact, it is my own, and the social network I draw on to pursue this research is more or less the one into which I was socialized. This presents challenges and opportunities that are quite different from those posed by working with farming people in the Anuradhapura district, even though both take place within the political confines of Sri Lanka.

My aim in this essay is to examine the problems and opportunities that arise for the fieldworker when working both in his own culture and society as well as ones that are alien. Important to successful fieldwork is (a) having one or more key informants and (b) the ability of the researcher to insert himself into existing social networks; these two things are usually related, for the key informant's social network will typically become that of the anthropologist. In Nepal and rural Sri Lanka, I had to start from scratch to create the networks I needed to do my research successfully; in my current research, the network I draw on is my own, created as part of my own socialization as a Sri Lankan. How the anthropologist is perceived, what his identity is taken to be, and whom he associates with in the context of doing fieldwork inevitably shapes what he is likely to learn, and this has different implications depending on whether one is working in one's own society or one that is foreign. In Nepal, what was salient was my identity as a Sri Lankan; in rural Sri Lanka, my status as an educated person from Colombo and my membership in a particular social class; and in Colombo, my own positioning in the politics of environmentalism in Sri Lanka.

Doing Anthropology at Home and Abroad

We take for granted that culture is multifaceted and fragmented, being inflected along lines of class, gender, status, age and in whatever other ways are locally relevant. I take culture to be a system of symbols that enables human beings to apprehend and give meaning to the world and by so doing, to act on it. The culture of urban, English-speaking middle class people in Sri Lanka is very different from that of monolingual Sinhala-speaking farmers living in settlements in the Dry Zone, and for the first to study the second is in fact to engage a culture that, despite its superficial familiarity, is alien in many of its assumptions and ways of being. Urban middle class Sri Lankans can be as uninformed about rural life as the foreign anthropologist arriving in Sri Lanka for the first time; more so perhaps, as the foreigner would at least be familiar with the relevant ethnographic literature.

Anthropologists in both Nepal and Sri Lanka are drawn to the discipline because they see it as a useful way to understand how their own societies work. In this they are no different from American anthropologists, many of whom now work within the confines of the United States. Even so, there are anthropologists based in South Asia who have carried out research abroad. The Nepali anthropologist Rajendra Pradhan, for instance, studied the care of the elderly in a village in the south of Holland, while Dilli Ram Dahal, who is also Nepali, worked with the Center for the Ethnography of Everyday Life in Michigan to study American families in the Midwest. And it is by no means uncommon for South Asian anthropologists to do research in communities outside their countries of origin. The Indian anthropologist Triloki Nath Pandey, having studied the Tharu in India, turned his attention to the Zuni and the Navajo for his major fieldwork, studying anthropology's historical other in anthropology's own backyard (Pandey, 2002). Sri Lankans tend to stray abroad in search of their subject matter to a greater extent perhaps than other South Asian anthropologists: one thinks of Chandra Jayawardena in Guyana, Stanley Tambiah in Thailand, ViranjaniMunasinghe in Trinidad and Val Daniel in South India, among others. What they have in common of course is that they are (or were) resident abroad and thus have (or had) access to resources that would allow for such fieldwork.

That most anthropologists outside Europe and the United States and a few other related places tend to study their own national society reflects economic circumstance as much as it may do the inclinations of the researcher. Doing fieldwork is expensive and going abroad to do it is more expensive still. Analogous institutions to the western ones that support and facilitate research abroad—for anthropologists based in the United States, these would include the Fulbright commission and the offices of the United States Educational Foundation abroad, the member institutions of the Council of American Overseas Research Centers, the Social Science Research Council and others—simply do not exist in Nepal and Sri Lanka. It is not surprising that Sri Lankan anthropologists who work in other parts of the world are all located—as far as I know—in academic institutions outside Sri Lanka.

It is reductionist to assume, however, that because one does fieldwork within the boundaries of one's own country that one is studying one's own culture. For instance, Indian anthropologists who study India (which is to say the majority), can only loosely be described as studying their own society; India is so vast and varied a place that an anthropologist born and raised in India will find no shortage of social and cultural 'others' on which to focus his anthropological gaze. While anthropologists who find their research subjects in places for which they do not need a passport are studying some subgroup of their national society, very seldom do they actually study their own society—that is, the community into which they themselves were socialized and in which they have networks that predate the ones all anthropologists create in the process of doing fieldwork. This is true of American anthropologists researching the United States as much as it is of South Asian ones. For instance, approximately 27 per cent of doctorates (70 of 260) in cultural anthropology awarded by American universities in 2000–01 were for research carried out in the United States (American Anthropological Association 2001)[1]; most of this work, if one can fairly judge based on information contained in the dissertation title and the author's name, was not on societies with which the author had any organic connection.

This is true also of Gananath Obeyesekere's Sri Lankan work, from that on land tenure to the Pattini cult: they are studies of subgroups in Sri Lankan society that are different from the social milieu into which Obeyesekere himself has been socialized (Obeyesekere, 1967, 1981, 1984). But Obeyesekere's work has also gone beyond his Sri Lankan ethnography into the realm of the historical anthropology of the Pacific, to which he has made theoretically significant and characteristically erudite contributions (Obeyesekere, 1997, 2005). Susantha Goonatilake's (2001) recent tirade (a word which captures quite precisely the tone of his book) against Obeyesekere and other anthropologists of Sri Lanka was based on his assumption that his own imagined urban, middle class society and its culture was the model for Sri Lankan culture in general, and insofar as he was prepared to accept that Sri Lankan culture is multifaceted, it was on the basis of a hierarchical ordering of this difference in which other ways of being Sri Lankan (or more narrowly, Sinhala Buddhist) were consigned to the margins, the domain of 'oddballs' and the 'lower classes'. I mention Goonatilake because the implication of his critique is that the 'native' anthropologist's subject should not be the 'other' in his society but his own subgroup—in this case, Westernized, urban, middle class Sri Lankans and their own version of Buddhism. But this goes against the historical grain of anthropology, which has always seen itself as an enterprise in cultural translation or mediation, through which the anthropologist renders an alien logic in terms that members of his own society can understand. The advantage a (typically urban, English-speaking, upper middle class) Sri Lankan anthropologist who studies Goonatilake's oddballs has over a foreigner who wishes to do so is (usually) a native command of the language, citizenship in the political space in which research is to be carried out (which relieves one of the necessity to obtain a visa and engage in other bureaucratic minuets), and some degree of familiarity with many of the symbols in the culture, although perhaps not a complete understanding of their local semantic structure. He also has a more intangible knowledge of the overall context in which the culture is situated. It is true however that much anthropology in Sri Lanka done by Sri Lankans remains largely an urban, elite, middle-class enterprise that find its research subjects among those segments of the population that do not share those attributes.

Informants and Networks

Doing fieldwork is fundamental to anthropology but it is by no means a simple or straightforward task. The anthropologist, unless he or she is a native speaker, is usually hampered by an imperfect command of the language, particularly if it is not a language taught in universities. Many anthropologists pick up their language skills in the field; the corollary to this is that the longer they stay there, the better their language skills are likely to be and the more insights they are likely to develop into the society and culture they are studying. If language is an obvious barrier to understanding, another, more subtle one, is that of class and social position. In most fieldwork situations, the anthropologist arrives as a relatively powerful and influential outsider, with resources at his or her command that most local people cannot hope to match (most anthropological research, usually through force of circumstance, involves studying down rather than up). In addition, the anthropologist is likely to associate with the wealthier and more powerful people in the local society. This association is likely to erect further barriers between the anthropologist and many of the people he or she must interact with in order to understand the local culture and social system. If this relationship is not overcome, the ethnographer is likely to come away with a skewed picture of social life.

When I arrived in Nepal in 1989 to begin fieldwork for my dissertation, I had little knowledge of the language. The country was unfamiliar; I had been there only once before, for about a week, and what I knew of the place, I had learned from books. My language skills were based on ten weeks of intensive Nepali taken at the University of Wisconsin, followed by a year of reading Nepali texts on an informal basis with two other like-minded people who wished to work in Nepal. I could barely make polite conversation, let alone carry out ethnographic interviewing. I had no knowledge of Chitwan Tharu, the language of the ethnic group whose culture I wished to study, a minor language spoken by some 50,000 people. And finally, I had no idea where to find a field site. So I headed to Tribhuvan University in Kirtipur, to seek advice. I owed the relative ease with which I found a field site to the help of Mr. Thapa, a lecturer at the agricultural college in Chitwan to whom I had been referred by a professor at Tribhuvan. He had a Tharu student, Surendra (a pseudonym) who he said, had a good command of English and would be able to introduce me to people in the Tharu villages of Chitwan and help me find a fieldsite. I borrowed a bicycle and accompanied Mr. Thapa to Surendra's village several miles away, close to the boundaries of the Chitwan National Park.

The village turned out to be an eminently suitable field site. The core of it was entirely occupied by Tharus, the original inhabitants of the Chitwan valley, which lies sandwiched between the imposing blue massif of the Mahabharata range to the north and the lower and gentler slopes of the Siwaliks to the south. The periphery of the village however had been settled by immigrants from the hills, mostly Brahmans, who had been moving into the area since the 1970s. It was a few miles away from the nearest market town and paved road (the East-West Highway), but was connected to it by a well-graded dirt and gravel road, which has since been paved. It had no electricity at the time I did my fieldwork; it has since been electrified. Surendra was enthusiastic about my settling in the village and his working as my research assistant, and promised me he would make all the arrangements necessary for me to stay there for a period of almost two years. He gave me the choice of a room behind the granary next to his house or a small hut in the middle of a neighboring field on the village's outskirts, which had once served as the watcher's quarters for a failed chicken farm. Being very aware that I was the object of curiosity to everyone in the village (a phalanx of little boys and girls had formed in front of Surendra's verandah, where we were sitting on wooden cots, and were contemplating me with unblinking interest), I opted in the name of privacy, a concept that, of all the people in the village only I seemed to appreciate, for the hut.

My first fieldwork in Sri Lanka also benefited from an intermediary, in this case the Sarvodaya organization. I wanted to study the problems of state-sponsored resettlement of landless peasants in Dry Zone irrigation schemes for an undergraduate thesis, and the Sarvodaya District Centre in Anuradhapura helped settle me in one of their fieldsites: their health clinic in the Mahakanadarawa colonization scheme in the Anuradhapura District. Unlike the nucleated village of Pipariya, the settlement in Mahakanadarawa was dispersed in a ribbon pattern, each house standing in its own two acres (0.8 hectares) of high land close by the right bank main channel of the Mahakanadarawa tank, with three additional acres (1.2 hectares) of paddy land as part of a separate tract. I was somewhat familiar with such schemes, for as a boy growing up in Sri Lanka, I used to accompany my father, who was Director of Land Development, when he went on tours ('circuits') to inspect the work being carried out by his department in the Dry Zone. I welcomed the opportunity to get to know one from the inside.

Unlike in Pipariya, I did not have a key informant in Mahakanadarawa. I was in the settlement for a total of five weeks in two separate visits, in 1984 and again in 1985. I stayed first in the Sarvodaya clinic with the health-worker, a young woman named Seela who was a year or so older than I was, and during my second visit, with a local villager known as Piyum Mama (he was a retired postman), with whose family I had established a good relationship during my earlier stint in the field. His son Lalith, studying for his 'O' levels, became my principle conduit to village life, and it was largely his family's network and the Sarvodaya network, to which Seela introduced me, from which I benefited. Lalith was not an informant, however, in the sense that I learned very much from him about village life, and what I learned from Seela had mostly to do with the Sarvodaya organization.

To return to my experiences in Nepal, although I guessed that Surendra's family must be well-to-do to afford to send him to college, I did not realize at first that his was the largest landowning family in the village. It would, of course, have not made any difference to my decision to work with him if I had, but there was certainly nothing to show, to my untutored, naive eye that the social standing of his household was in any way different from that of his immediate neighbors. Surendra's house was not significantly bigger than theirs, and was built in the same fashion, with the same materials: walls of elephant grass plastered with a mixture of cow-dung and mud, with tiled roofs. I had seen brick houses in other villages; there were none here. After a few months in the village, I learned to read it differently: Surendra's house and those of his patriline were located in the very center of the village, in a much larger compound; they had a tractor parked in the shed behind the house, more cattle than their neighbors, and a number of the men had white-collar jobs as schoolteachers.

Having made arrangements to stay in this village, I returned to Kathmandu to collect my belongings, and also to make a foray into the far western Tarai that delayed my return to Chitwan. I returned to Pipariya to find that my little hut wasn't quite ready yet; it lacked a door, and the latrine, a pit surrounded by a wall of elephant grass for modesty's sake (most people simply used the fields) had not been completed. Surendra told me he hadn't wanted to complete the job until he was sure I would return. In the meantime, I was to stay with him. The house where I had been entertained during my earlier visit was occupied by his large joint family headed by his older brother, who, as I was soon to discover, was an important political activist in the village. I was to occupy a little room opening off another building next door, which was used to store grain. Although I soon moved to my hut, I spent much of my time in this old Tharu area of the village, in the company of Surendra and his friends, eating my meals in his house, and (as I discovered later) becoming associated with the households of the movers and shakers of village life. Their network became mine.

Surendra was well respected in the village. He was a year or two younger than I was, a forceful man and a natural leader. His father, who had died recently at the age of 75, had been, in his younger days, the chief revenue collector (a jimidar or local official who, in addition to collecting the tax, also exercised some juridical powers) and an important local political figure. Surendra's family and that of his father's brother, who lived next door, were by far the largest landowners in the area (with about 24 hectares, their combined holdings would be considered minute by American standards, but substantial in terms of the more modest landholdings in Mahakanadarawa, where land distribution was, thanks to government regulations governing allotments, more equitably distributed). Average landholdings in Pipariya, excluding the two jimidari households, were just under a hectare per household during the time of my fieldwork.

My life soon settled into a routine. I would spend the morning working at my language skills and in the afternoon would visit people or hang out with the young men of the village, usually accompanied by Surendra. Although I often met poorer villagers, I never got to know them well. Because I was interested in tracing the social and cultural changes that had taken place since the valley had been opened up to development and settlement in the 1950s, Surendra drew up a list of the old men in the surrounding area, who could talk to me about what life had been like before the malaria eradication project of the 1950s and comment on the changes since, and we arranged to interview them. Many of these men were former revenue collectors like his father or important in some other way. In that first phase of fieldwork, the social networks I explored were those of Surendra and his friends. The weddings I attended, for example, were those of fairly well-to-do people, never those of the poor. During those first few months in Pipariya, struggling to master the language and adjust to my surroundings, I relied heavily on Surendra. Because I ate in his household, I had also come to be regarded as a member of it, or at least as Surendra's guest. While people were always friendly and willing to talk, poorer people in the village tended to keep their distance at first. Thus, while I accumulated much good data about the lives and opinions of the village elite, I learnt relatively little about the village poor during that first year.

The villagers, I discovered, were divided, in their own estimation, into three social strata. At the top were the families of the former revenue collectors; at the bottom was a landless class that had formerly worked as household servants for landholding peasants and now tried to eke out a living any way they could: some worked as servants, others as wage labor, and others found menial work in the tourist industry that had grown up around the national park. In between were 'middle' peasants who owned some land, ranging from those who had enough of it to guarantee their requirements of food, clothing and shelter, as well as education for their children and sundry other necessities of modern life, and those whose land was inadequate for year-round subsistence and were always in danger of slipping down into the category below them. My social circle in the village during my first year of fieldwork was drawn mainly from people of Surendra's social background and the households of the better off 'middle peasants' (see Guneratne 1996).

Surendra was an exemplary key informant. In the first place he was knowledgeable in his own right about various aspects of Tharu social life and could speak with authority on a variety of different topics. He once told me he would listen as a boy to his father's conversations with his peers, and learned a great deal that way. He was also eager to learn more, and during my first six months in the field, when he was interpreting for me, he would ask his own questions of the person we were interviewing. In addition to interpreting, he would transcribe the taped interviews (which were conducted in Tharu) and then translate them into Nepali, thus providing me material to teach myself the language. As the son of one of the most important jimidars in Chitwan and a forceful personality in his own right, he was well known throughout the Tharu villages in the district, and was able to introduce me to people all over the valley. After working with me for about six months however, Surendra returned to his studies in Rampur, and I was on my own. By that time my knowledge of Nepali had progressed to near fluency, and I had a modest working knowledge of Tharu, and I was able to do my interviews without the need of an interpreter. His older brother Ram Bahadur was also taking a keen interest in what I was doing, and would sometimes arrange for me to interview people he thought would be useful to my work. It was he, in fact, who told me about the Tharu Kalyankarini Sabha (Tharu Welfare Association) that eventually became the focus of my research.

My work among the Tharu was made even easier in that they are an extraordinarily hospitable people, and many were interested in inviting me to a meal and in talking with me. On one occasion the headmaster of the village school, who was also Surendra's cousin, introduced me to two Brahman visitors as "our anthropologist." My presence in the village, I soon realized, gave it a certain cachet. In a context where high caste Nepalis tended to dismiss the worth of Tharu culture, it meant something locally that a well-educated foreigner would choose, at some expense, to live among Tharus and record those very aspects of social practice and cultural beliefs about which Brahmans tended to be dismissive.

A salient fact about Tharu experience that I learned early on was the tension that exists between them and Nepali hill people, principally of the two high castes, Brahman and Chhetri. The Tharu were once the principal inhabitants of the Chitwan valley, whose reputation for malaria discouraged other groups from settling in it. Once malaria was eradicated, thanks to a USAID funded project in the mid-fifties, the valley was opened up for settlement and the Tharu quickly became a minority. One of the consequences of that influx was that many Tharu lost land to settlers from the hills, often through fraud and chicanery, compounded by their own lack of education and literacy. When discussing these matters with me, two people cited one particular individual as an example of how Tharus were exploited: a large landowner in a neighboring village, who had lost all his land and been reduced to the status of a woodcutter. I decided I would like to get his own version of events, and Surendra agreed to take me to see him.

Budhan Mahato (a pseudonym), then in his fifties, lived in a hut in a village in another part of Chitwan. Although neatly built, it was smaller than my small hut in Pipariya. He, and the family of his only surviving son, occupied that space. A fondness for alcohol and for consumer goods, to purchase which he had got into debt, were reputedly the cause of his undoing. It was not a very successful interview for me since I felt ambivalent about the whole enterprise as soon as I met him and for the first time since I had begun my fieldwork began to wonder about this business of prying into other people's lives that is inevitably an aspect of trying to understand another culture.

Budhan had owned almost 10 hectares (a substantial estate by local standards), and then, through his own folly, had lost it all and been reduced to near destitution. Surendra felt that Budhan was not giving us the whole story of his misfortune, which was not to be wondered at; he must have been trying to present himself in the best light possible. Budhan himself attributed his misfortunes to his karma; Surendra to his fondness for liquor. We talked in the tiny front room of his hut, seated on a gunny sack (another indication of his poverty; even in the poorest Tharu homes that I'd been in before, a blanket is spread for guests to sit on). He worked away at making a fishing net while we talked, watched by his son, daughter-in-law and various grandchildren. When we got back to Pipariya, the headmaster, Surendra's cousin, asked to listen to the tape (Budhan, after all, was a byword) and I explained to him that I couldn't let him do that, given the subject matter of the interview. The headmaster didn't press the point.

This was the first time in my fieldwork that the power relations inherent in my situation were made visible to me, to my discomfort.

Like most anthropologists, that I was able to do fieldwork was dependent on the hospitality shown to me, and that I was introduced to Chitwan Tharu society through the medium of one of its more important families worked in my favor in gaining me acceptance in Tharu society at large. But while most people were willing to talk to me, there were a few, like Budhan, who undoubtedly felt constrained to do so, not because of who I was necessarily, but because of the people who were prepared to exert themselves on my behalf.

During my first year in Pipariya, I came to be identified, as I've said, with Surendra and his social circle. I was not aware at first of these evaluations and I did not begin to develop a more complex picture of village life until the second year of fieldwork, after my wife joined me. We moved into a small house that Surendra's elder brother had had built for us on his property at a little distance from the main house, and quite separate from it, and we began to cook for ourselves and establish ourselves as an independent household. One day Surendra's mother's brother's wife, who, being quite poor, worked for his family as a servant (bahariya), came to visit us in our hut. She'd been afraid to come before, she explained, out of deference to her nephew, but now that we were living on our own, she felt more comfortable about doing so. I was now working on my own, without need of Surendra's interpreting skills, and that helped as well. Towards the end of my stay in Pipariya, I carried out a socio-economic survey of the entire village (about 84 Tharu households); with help from another young Tharu, a man named Chulahi (a pseudonym). Chulahi was well-educated and fluent in English and was a student at Tribhuvan University; while he was a member of one of the more important local lineages, he was not of a jimidari family. Unlike Surendra, who was a supporter of the Congress party, he supported the Communists. My association with Chulahi encouraged many of the poorer members of village society to speak with me.

In both Pipariya and Mahakanadarawa, I was associated with the better-off stratum of village society, but in terms of power, prestige, and relative wealth (by village standards) there was little comparison between the two situations. To begin with, the right bank settlement of the Mahakanadarawa scheme lacked the long history and organic development of Pipariya. Surendra came from a long line of *jimidar*s, people with wealth, power and influence in village society, and although the family was no longer as rich or as powerful as it had once been, it was still a major force in village life. In Mahakanadarawa, on the other hand, I stayed first with the young woman who ran the Sarvodaya clinic and then with a retired postman, both of whom had come to the settlement (along with all its other residents) from outside, like everyone else, and who had no particular clout in the community. There was no way that the situation I had encountered with Budhan in Pipariya could have been replicated in Mahakanadarawa. The settlement, following the restoration of the ancient Mahakanadarawa tank, had been created in the 1960s and class formation had proceeded along different lines.

The class structure, as I determined it over nearly two months of field-work, was, like Pipariya, tripartite. At the top (the closest thing to a village elite) was a labor-hiring class, consisting of both colonists and non-cultivators who had access to capital, such as mudalalis (businessmen) from outside the colony and some colonists who had salaried jobs, for example as minor employees of government offices. They used this income to employ others to work their fields for them. Then there was a large middle order of people I call poor colonists; they had legal rights in their land but no capital to cultivate. They leased or rented their land to the first group and sought employment as wage labor, more often than not outside the settlement. Finally, at the very bottom were encroachers, who had not title to the state-owned land they occupied and seasonal agricultural workers from neighboring and desperately poor *purana* villages.

The Ethnographer's Identity

Being a Sri Lankan in Nepal had its advantages. Most Nepali villagers I met, wherever I traveled in the Tarai, knew a few things about Sri Lanka that they would bring up with me. The first was the assumption that it was the Lanka of the Ramayana and I would be asked what traces of that famous conflict were still to be found. Had I seen the ruins of Ravana's palace and did Sri Lankans worship him? Someone once observed during one of these conversations that Lanka had been completely destroyed along with Ravana, and rebuilt anew, and, therefore, vestiges of Ravana's time could not possibly exist. Once that matter had been dealt with, the conversation would turn to Sri Lanka's reputation (in Nepal at least) as a well-educated and developed place and from there it would inevitably turn to the ethnic conflict, and the next question would invariably be some variation on why such well-educated people should be fighting. Nepalese had few preconceptions (other than those mentioned above) about Sri Lankans, a generally favourable view of them, and they were always especially interested to meet one. It was better to be a Sri Lankan in Nepal than an Indian, and I did not fit anyone's preconception about what an American should look like.

There were, however, less positive images about Sri Lanka that were circulating in some quarters and they had to do with the stories that Nepali Gurkhas serving in the IPKF during that time were bringing home. A Tharu in a village near Pipariya told me there was a Gurung home on leave from the Indian army in the next village who had been recounting his experiences in Sri Lanka, and he wanted my opinion on his veracity. The Gurung had reportedly said that while they were fighting and killing Tamils, their officers were giving the Tamils, including young boys, military training. Could such things be true, he asked me, and I replied that I thought they could. The Gurung was reported to have said that Sri Lanka is the sort of place where you come across a child crying, and you pat it on the head to comfort it, but as soon as you turn your back, the child whips out a pistol and shoots you. Such images of Sri Lanka were not in wide circulation, however, and as I've said, the general impression village people had of Sri Lanka wherever I went was overwhelmingly positive.

In general, people who did not know me took me for an Indian or perhaps a madeshi (a Tarai person descended from Indian immigrants who had arrived in the 19th and early 20th centuries). This was certainly how the police saw me, in my only encounter with Nepal's blue-uniformed fraternity during my fieldwork. It happened during the *jana andolan* (the people's movement that forced King Birendra to restore parliamentary democracy to the country) shortly after I had begun my fieldwork. The police were constantly coming through the village searching for party activists, one of whom was Surendra's older brother, Ram Bahadur (who was lying low and constantly moving around to avoid them). An officer saw me walking across the schoolyard with Surendra one day and presumably recognizing me as matter out of place, stopped to interrogate me. He insisted on questioning me in Hindi, which I understood well enough at the time but barely spoke, and I replied in Nepali, which did not, however, lead him to switch to that language. This pas-de-deux continued for a few minutes until Surendra intervened to say that I was an American researcher studying Tharu culture and that I had the government's permission to do it. Surendra possibly realized that in the current context, dealing with the awful majesty of the law required an identity with a little more 'source-force' as they say in Nepal, than Sri Lanka could provide me. As a Fulbrighter, I had a U.S. embassy-issued ID emblazoned with the stars and stripes in one corner to demonstrate my American affiliation to the policeman and we eventually satisfied him as to my bona fides.

Occasionally, early in my fieldwork, village children, especially those who were not from the Tharu neighborhood, would take me for a tourist; this usually happened when I ventured forth with my camera bag, day pack and sleeping bag, to visit another village (these, of course, are the material attributes of the tourist). On one occasion I set off with a group of young Tharu men to attend a wedding in another village (they travelled light), and one enterprising child returning home from school said hopefully, as he passed me, 'Hello, one rupee?' which raised roars of laughter from my companions. On the other hand, I was invisible to the (mostly white) tourists; one 'native' looks very much like another.

I was also invisible in Mahakanadarawa to outsiders, but that was because I was in fact a native. From time to time Sarvodaya would send foreign visitors to the clinic on tours of one sort or another and on one occasion, we were visited by the local head of the U.N. Volunteers Program, a Filipino, who turned up in a chauffeur driven, air-conditioned Volvo, accompanied by two women from Sarvodaya and an interpreter. I was not introduced, and dressed as I was in a tee shirt and sarong, blended nicely into the background, where I held my peace, not wanting to upstage Seela. The interpreter did less than an adequate job; he modified the responses that Seela gave him to the Filipino's questions and simply failed to translate others. I was tempted on several occasions to intervene, as I was the only one among the 'Mahakanadarawa' people present who could perfectly understand both languages, but I refrained, deciding that it was not my business. The U.N. representative learnt little from that interaction. I told Seela afterwards that she should have been franker in her answers, but she commented that the interpreter would only have modified her responses. Both she and another villager present felt, given my knowledge of both languages that I should have interrupted to correct the interpreter. I felt that if I had, as an English-speaking person from Colombo, the focus of the meeting would have shifted away from Seela to me, which would have been undesirable.

On a very few occasions in Nepal, however, people recognized me as a Sri Lankan. On the first occasion, I had just got down from the bus in Bharatpur, Chitwan's administrative center, when I heard footsteps come up behind me and a man hailed me in fluent Sinhala. I turned around, to find, to my astonishment, a Nepali man who seemed to be in his mid fifties. He introduced himself (in Sinhala, the language in which we carried on our conversation) as the chief lay disciple of the Theravada Buddhist temple in Lumbini, and invited me to his house by the road, where we talked for almost an hour, the business that had brought me to Bharatpur momentarily set aside. He had spent four years as a young man studying Buddhism at the Vajiraramaya in Colombo, which was where he had learnt Sinhala and he could still speak it with near fluency. How he knew I was Sri Lankan, I have no idea, and I did not think to ask. I had not spoken in that bus either except to tell the conductor (in Nepali) where I planned to get off. On another occasion, I was accosted on the streets of Kathmandu by a young man who wanted to know whether I was from Sri Lanka; he was a Nepali student in India and had roomed with a Sri Lankan and thought he saw something of his roommate in me. On both these occasions there were no overt indications of my Sri Lankanness: it could not have been my clothing or my accent that gave me away. It had to be what bird watchers and First World War aviators, who both have (or had) to identify distant flying objects by their size, shape, and movement, call 'jizz'. The fashionable anthropological term for this is habitus. What exactly about my habitus-or, to be nautical, the cut of my jib-marked me as Sri Lankan I do not know. But another encounter on the streets of Kathmandu suggested that my habitus may have been more complex, after eight years in the United States, than even I had imagined. On that occasion, a young tout on the streets of Kathmandu, frustrated by my refusal first of his offer to change my money, then of various prohibited substances and finally of the services of his sister, said something quite derogatory about Americans, presumably in the hope that it would get under my skin.

The question of habitus is discussed a great deal in anthropology and regularly invoked, but to the best of my knowledge (which admittedly is limited) no one has yet described habitus at the level of subtlety indicated above—that would, for instance, allow a Nepali intimately acquainted with Sri Lankans to pick one out where his compatriots saw only an Indian. And yet, anthropologists do recognize the habitus of the people they have studied; they can recognize someone from the culture they have studied even when that individual is devoid of the overt cultural cues (such as dress or adornment) that would betray her origin. It is extraordinarily difficult to reduce to writing the subtle clues in how one carries oneself, or moves (for an excellent effort in that direction, see Geurts 2002). This is perhaps the next frontier in ethnographic writing.

If I was recognized as a Sri Lankan by some in Nepal, rumor in Mahakanadarawa had me pegged as something else. When I had arrived in the settlement, I had explained to the Sarvodaya Committee why I was there. I was, I told them, a student in an American university and I needed to write a thesis to complete my degree and I wished to write it about Mahakanadarawa. This went over quite well, and in fact, towards the end of my stay in the settlement, I was invited to declare open the new primary school that the villagers had collectively built (an indication also of my status in their eyes). I also distributed a questionnaire which I asked people to fill out and return to me; many did. One evening, well into my fieldwork, a man rode up on a bicycle to the clinic where I was staying. He introduced himself as someone who had grown up in Mahakanadarawa and was now a Sarvodaya worker in Matale. He was home on a visit and had heard of me. After a pleasant hour chatting, he got up to leave and confided that he had heard there was a white man from America in the village handing out a questionnaire, and rumor thought it possible that he was from the CIA. Having met me, he was now able to put that rumor to rest. This incident suggests that this particular cross is borne not only by American anthropologists but also by those with American affiliations, although it is worth noting that at no time in Nepal was I ever taken for a CIA agent, even though, as a Fulbright grantee with a US embassy-issued ID, I had closer ties to American power. I attribute that in part to being identified in Pipariya as a Sri Lankan and not an American.

The Ethnographer as Culture Broker in the Field

An ethnography is the art of interpreting to members of one culture, the lived experience of life in another, and the anthropologist's role is that of a culture broker who mediates between his own milieu and that of the culture he is describing (and in the history of anthropology, this has typically entailed two quite different cultural contexts, necessitating some degree of translation). This fact has been widely commented on in the discipline. What has been less widely commented on, even though I expect most anthropologists have experienced this to varying degrees, is that the anthropologist is often seen as a culture broker in the field by some members of a host society that wishes to know more of their neighbors (their immediate 'other'), and who see the ethnographer as having special access to those domestic others. This was brought home quite forcefully to me in two different ways.

As I've discussed elsewhere (Guneratne, 2001), Pipariya village was on the tourist circuit as the site of a 'village walk' for tourists visiting the national park. Many Tharus were ambivalent about being objectified in this way, and women in particular were resentful of the intrusiveness of the practice. Based both on what Tharus told me as well as what I had occasion to overhear, I knew that a great deal of misrepresentation of Tharu society and culture went on in these excursions, based on the stereotypes and prejudices that the typically high-caste tourist guides had of Tharu society. When these guides discovered my presence in the village and what I was about, they approached me on a number of occasions-often in the presence of Tharus-for information that they could incorporate into their discourse to tourists. On every occasion I refused, and suggested instead that they should ask their neighbors directly rather than come to me, a foreigner.

The other occasion on which my services as a culture broker were solicited happened in this way. One morning, the child of one of my neighbors came to tell me that some people had come to see me. My visitors turned out to be an American and two Nepalis, one a Tamang, the other a Limbu. They had heard about me from some of the village boys and had sought me out. The American told me he was a carpenter and construction worker from Seattle, currently self-employed. He was evasive however in telling me why they had wanted to see me; he claimed that his Tamang companion, Mohan, was interested in learning about Tharus. Why? I asked, but got no satisfactory reply; the reason emerged over the course of the conversation. They wanted, he claimed, to find out what it was like to live among Tharus; was it easy, for instance, to establish oneself among them? While the American was evasive, the Tamang was not; when I asked him, he said quite forthrightly that he wanted to teach the Tharus about Christianity. He was a convert and gung-ho about his new religion, and wanted to spread the faith.

The American told me he had come out on his own, not as a member of some missionary society, and had found his way to Nepal, after participating in a cultural orientation in Mussoorie on 'the people of this region' (and he volunteered no further information than that). Mohan had only a vague idea of what denomination he belonged to; when I asked him what his church was, he said he was a Protestant, and became confused when I pressed him to be more specific. The American explained to him what denominations were and Mohan said he didn't know anything about them, he just believed in Jesus Christ-certainly an adequate answer.

Surendra invited our visitors to lunch-his usual response to strangers in the village-but told me afterwards that he had not been favorably impressed by them, mostly because he felt that Mohan had not been honest with him. On this occasion too, my services as a culture broker was sought out by other members of the host society, in this case to determine how hospitable the

Tharus would be to outsiders wishing to reside for a while among them. The quick answer is, of course, that the Tharus are very hospitable, and I have found this to be true wherever I have travelled in the Tarai, but having no sympathy for evangelization, I ceased to be forthcoming once I learnt what they were about.

In a culturally complex and plural society like that of Nepal, the foreign anthropologist can emerge as a cultural broker (should he choose to) within the host society because he is perceived as having inside knowledge that could be useful or instructive to other segments of the population. The fieldworker must then decide whether he will share that knowledge or not, and under what circumstances. In both cases described above, I was skeptical of the uses to which the knowledge to which I had access was to be put, and chose not to cooperate. I also pointed out to the tourist guides that with reference to the specific kinds of information they were looking for-about festivals, social organization and the like-they would be better off asking their Tharu neighbors directly; I was only a bird of passage, and the relationships they needed to develop were with their neighbors and not with me.

The long-term answer the Tharus themselves came up with for the whole issue of the village walk and their own exclusion from participating in it except as the passive objects of foreign curiosity about the primitive was to set up a Tharu Culture Museum in Pipariya, which was opened in 2005, both to tap into the tourist market as well as to engage in self-representations of their own. Unsurprisingly, the venture was funded in large part by the King Mahendra Trust for Nature Conservation, which has a vested interest in promoting tourism in the valley. The Tharu Culture Museum has become the venue not only for the promotion of research on the Tharu (the museum includes living quarters for foreign research-ers) but also a wholesale objectification of Tharu culture by the elite Tharu who promote it. At work, here is a process similar to the objectification of culture described by Barney Cohn in his seminal paper on the Indian census (1987), except that here, it is not the administrative curiosity of colonial officials that has encouraged local elites to think about their culture in a new way, but the curiosity of an anthropologist, of tourists, and of tourist guides, as well as the opportunity to make 'culture' profitable. It is not a coincidence, I think, that the idea for a Tharu culture museum emerged in the village in which I did fieldwork; this village, far more than any other in the vicinity, was the focus of attention for various outsiders who, for various reasons, were interested in 'Tharu culture.' That, coupled with the presence of an energetic and activist group of local Tharu men, provided the conditions for the project to emerge and take root.

Researching One's Own Milieu

The fieldwork experiences I have described so far have concerned my work among people who, in many fundamental ways, were different than I was in their way of being in the world: in their assumptions, their values, their cosmology and indeed, in their habitus. I want to turn my attention here briefly to some of the issues that arise in researching one's own milieu-the context in which one is socialized and enculturated, the social networks in which one is embedded by virtue of that process-and to indicate some of the ways that it compares with what I've described above.

Firstly, of course, gaining an entrée into the society or putting together a network presents few difficulties. Who I am is well-known or easily ascertainable. My current research focuses on the development of environmentalism in Sri Lanka from colonial times to the present (and in that sense it is a work of historical anthropology, requiring work in the archives as well as interviewing) and the role of Sri Lanka's westernized bourgeoisie in that process. Many of the people I need to talk to are already known to me, and through them I am able to gain introductions to others (the snowball sampling effect). My own involvement in environmental issues in Sri Lanka and my active participation in a number of important environmental organizations, such as the March for Conservation, the Field Ornithology Group of Sri Lanka and most importantly, the public interest law firm Environmental Foundation Limited, which I helped to start as a law student at the University of Colombo in 1981, as well as the involvement of various members of my kin, now and in the past, in these activities, provide me with the credentials and the connections to pursue this work. Here too I have key informants. I depend on these individuals to provide me with documents which I would otherwise find it hard to obtain, to give me leads to other people I should talk to, and give me their interpretation of the events I am trying to chronicle.

One significant difference between my current research and my work in Nepal and Mahakanadarawa is that it concerns a subject—environmental conservation—with which I have been involved for much of my adult life. My involvement in these issues in Sri Lanka has provided me to some extent with an insider's knowledge of what the issues are, and the factions that are skirmishing over them. There has been, of course, a great deal of water under the bridge since then and my own thinking about the issues has evolved since I left Sri Lanka 25 years ago. My thinking in particular has been shaped by the experience of living with village people in Sri Lanka and Nepal who suffer from the depredations of wild animals; my views have evolved in an anthropocentric direction, while much of Sri Lankan middle class environmentalism continues to be grounded in eco-centric thinking. While some things about this micro-culture remain familiar, others are new to me. Nevertheless, the phrase 'participant observation' applies to this research in a very fundamental way.

There are, however, pitfalls in this kind of participant observation that did not exist in my other fieldwork. To become a participant in an activist micro-culture is to take sides, and to be identified with a faction (or a particular point of view) inevitably shapes the research that can be done. In this sense, the ethnographer who works in his own society (defined in the narrowest sense) is at a disadvantage compared to the foreign anthropologist, who, while she may have her sympathies, does not necessarily have any dogs in the fight and can afford to be dispassionate about it. The nature of this project is thus different from my earlier work in Nepal. The eventual written product of this research is meant to be read by those same people about whom I am writing; it is an intervention in an ongoing debate that is taking place within the culture I am studying. This is an important difference with my work in Nepal; that was primarily intended for a scholarly audience and not written at all for the Tharu themselves; although some Tharus have read it (I sent three copies of my dissertation to various people in Pipariya and copies of all my publications to the Tharu Culture Museum).

Anthropology, it is often said, is the art of making the strange familiar and the familiar strange. The two ideas are linked, but for the second to be realized, the strange must be made familiar first. One must travel outside of one's own society to truly appreciate that it is only one among innumerable other ways of being, all of them perfectly rational by their own lights. The deeper the immersion in these other ways, the more profound one's understanding of this basic anthropological insight. The familiar will always remain familiar in the absence of a yardstick by which to gauge its strangeness. That is why immersion in unfamiliar places among people who operate according to different logics should remain an essential part of anthropological training; it is probably the most effective way to call into question the categories into which one was socialized, for one's assumptions do not make sense in places remote from where one grew up, whether those places are found in a Dry Zone settlement or a Tharu village in Nepal, and it is in the field that one comes to terms with that fact.

Note

1. The figures exclude doctorates granted in applied anthropology (seven, of which two were for work done in the U.S.) and medical anthropology (19, of which 11 were for U.S. based research. These figures are approximations, as it is not always possible to tell from the title where the research was carried out).

References

American Anthropological Association. 2001. *Guide: A guide to Programs, a Directory of Members*. Washington: D.C.

Cohn, Bernard S. 1987. The Census, Social Structure and Objectification in South Asia. *An Anthropologist among the Historians and other Essays*. pp. 224–254. Delhi: Oxford University Press.

Geurts, Kathryn. 2002. *Culture and the Senses: Bodily Ways of Knowing in an African Community*. Berkeley: University of California Press.

Goonatilake, Susantha. 2001. *Anthropologizing Sri Lanka: A Eurocentric Misadventure*. Bloomington: Indian University Press.

Guneratne, Arjun. 1985. *Water, Rice and People: Problems and Constraints of Peasant Colonization in the Dry Zone of Sri Lanka*. A Thesis Submitted to the Committee on Senior Fellowships. Hanover, New Hampshire: Dartmouth College.

———. 1996. The Tax-Man Cometh: The Impact of Revenue Collection on Subsistence Strategies in Chitwan Tharu Society. *Studies in Nepali History & Society* 1(1): 5–35.

———. 2001. Shaping the Tourist's Gaze: Representing Ethnic Difference in a Nepali Village. *Journal of the Royal Anthropological Institute*, 7(3): 527–543.

———. 2002. *Many Tongues, One People: The Making of Tharu Identity in Nepal*. Ithaca: Cornell University Press.

Obeyesekere, Gananath. 1967. *Land Tenure in Village Ceylon: A Sociological and Historical Study*. Cambridge: Cambridge University Press.

———. 1981. *Medusa's Hair: An Essay on Personal Symbols and Religious Experience*. Chicago: The University of Chicago Press.

Obeyesekere, Gananath. 1984. *The Cult of the Goddess Pattini*. Chicago: The University of Chicago Press.

———. 1997. *The Apotheosis of Captain Cook: European Mythmaking in the Pacific*. Princeton, N.J.: Princeton University Press.

———. 2005. *Cannibal Talk: The Man-eating Myth and Human Sacrifice in the South Seas*. Berkeley: University of California Press.

Pandey, Triloki Nath. 2002. The Anthropologist-Informant Relationship: The Navajo and Zuni in America and the Tharu in India. In M.N. Srinivas, A.M. Shah and E.A. Ramaswamy (eds), *The Fieldworker and the Field: Problems and Challenges in Sociological Investigation*. Second edition. Delhi: Oxford University Press.

7

Return to Rengsanggri*

Robbins Burling

Technology, Work, and the Physical Village

I first traveled to the Garo Hills in the western part of what is now the
state of Meghalaya in 1954. I lived there for two years, for much of
that time among the people of a village called Rengsanggri. This village
lies about 20 kilometers northeast of the town of Tura, and it was there
that I gathered the material become the basis for my Ph.D. dissertation in
anthropology and, later, a book (Burling, 1963). Living in the Garo Hills
and coming to know the Garo people and their language was one of the
most exciting adventures of my life, but in 1956 I returned to my home
in the United States, and for almost two decades I hardly thought about
the possibility of returning. When, in the 1970s, I finally did try to go
back, unsettled conditions in Northeastern India had made visits difficult
for foreigners, and I had to wait for two more decades until my opportunity finally came. Then, from the end of December 1996 through most of
February 1997, more than forty years after I had finished my original field
work, I was able to visit Rengsanggri once again. I could see that extensive
changes had come to the village in the forty years that I had been away, but
I was at least as impressed by the continuities that had persisted through

* This essay (revised) is republished taking permission from Prof. T.B. Subba, editor
of the *NEHU Journal of Social Science and Humanities*, Vol. 2, July–December,
1998, pp. 21–46.

all those years. I want to describe both the changes and the continuities that I found.

My return to Rengsanggri was made possible by a generous fellow-ship from that wonderful institution, the Fulbright Foundation, and by the warm hospitality of North-Eastern Hill University and especially the members of the Anthropology, Linguistics, and History Departments. I am particularly indebted to Dr. Milton Sangma, Professor of History and Pro-vice Chancellor of the Tura Campus of NEHU. Professor Sangma eased my visit to the Garo Hills in more ways than I can count, and he and his family repeatedly welcomed me to their home. Many other friends, both old and new, made me welcome in Tura. I am also deeply grateful to Anne Hvcnekilde who accompanied me to Meghalaya and to Rengsanggri. She and I worked together to gather the data that is reported in this article, and it was she who collected the statistics on both church membership and educational achievement. That left me free to work on untangling the gene-alogies. Most of all, however, I give my thanks to the wonderful people of Rengsanggri. For forty years I have known how important they have been in my life and nothing has ever been more gratifying to me than to discover that I seem to have been almost as important in theirs. In a way that defies my understanding, their lives and mine were intertwined for forty years with never a single word of direct communication passing between us.

In many respects, the Rengsanggri that I found in 1997 was a radi-cally changed community. Wet rice, Christianity, education, literacy, and even other languages had all reached the village. At the same time, much remained familiar. In the forty years that I had been away, many people had died, of course, but some of my contemporaries still lived to welcome me back, and the older people who had died had been replaced by their chil-dren and grandchildren. These people dealt with me, and they seemed to deal with each other, in much the same way as they had forty years earlier. They organized their families much as they had when I first knew them, and in the essentials of life, they remained resiliently the same. I will begin this paper by describing the changes that have come to Rengsanggri, and that are certainly startling to a visitor who returns after forty years, but I will then turn to the continuities that I found just as impressive.

The most obvious change that had come to the village during my long absence was the dispersal of the households across its entire land area (a 'king). Every one of the sixty households that constituted Regsanggri in the 1950s was located in a single well defined central location. The village had taken its name form a tumbling stream that flows beside it and that is called the 'Rengsanggri', and a mile of unsettled territory separated the settlement from the nearest village, Songmagri, to the south. In other directions, settlements lay even farther away. By 1997, the sixty households of the earlier village had increased to 105, but only twenty-six of them, about one quarter, were still found at the site of the old village. The other seventy-nine households were scattered over much of the village land. The villagers described these households as belonging to eight or nine named hamlets (git-im), and if a map of the village existed, it would show the house to be partially grouped into clusters that corresponded to these hamlets.

Villagers told me that a few families had begun to move their homesteads away from the site of the old village about 20 years before my return visit, probably during the 1970s. Villagers had always built temporary field house on their slash and bum plots where, during the periods of most intense farming, they could live for a few days, and so avoid long daily walks back and forth from the main village. Their field houses were small and temporary, however, and they were never occupied for more than a week at a time. When villagers began to construct permanent fields, some of them moved to live permanently beside them. In the nineties, a few people looked back nostalgically to the days when everyone lived together. They remembered those times as more friendly, and they recalled with joy the village festivals that were once held in the old central village. Still no one proposes that people should move back. The residential pattern of Rengsanggri has irrevocably changed.

Architectural style has also changed. By 1997, only one house in Rengsanggri was still built in the style that I remembered from my earlier trip. That one house, like the older ones, still had a central fire place in the main room, and a separate room at the front that would once have served as a barn for the cattle. Even in that house, people no longer cooked at the central fire place. Instead, they prepared their meals in the front room and kept their cattle in a separate building.

Other village house had different plans. It had become fashionable to have the main door in the middle of a long wall of the house instead of at the narrow end where it had always been placed before. This required a more level plot than the older houses where only the narrow front end had to be at ground level. Most houses were still constructed from bamboo, and many were built with the same construction techniques as older houses, but some had new type of bamboo mat walls, some had tin roofs, and a few were built, in part or entirely, from wooden planks.

In the 1950s everyone cooked at the central fireplace in the main house. By 1997, most people had separate cook houses. Houses are more comfortable without the smoke of a fire, especially if people sit high on chairs and benches instead of on the floor or on low stools as they invariably did in the 1950s, but without the cooking fires, houses also lose the protection that smoke gives against destructive insects.

I was startled by the dispersal of the houses around the old village land, but this was only the most obvious reflection of the more fundamental changes that have been taking place in agriculture. When I took my census in 1956, 293 people lived in Rengsanggri. By January 1997, the population had climbed to 673. The land area of the village remained the same, of course, and the older slash and burn agriculture was incapable of yielding sufficient food to feed the growing population. New fields were needed each year, and this forced people to clear and burn scrub land before the forest cover had a chance to regenerate the soil's fertility. By 1997, hardly any real forest remained within the boundaries of Rengsanggri. Every family still cleared and burned a plot each year but, as everyone was all too grimly aware, their harvests had declined disastrously. The slash and burn fields no longer yielded enough rice to feed a family. The most important cash crop had once been cotton, but it did poorly by the nineties and was little grown. People told me that chili, peppers and some tubers could still be grown successfully. Ginger does especially well, and much is sold to traders in the market, but the traditional agriculture can no longer support the village.

Rengsanggri has been saved from disaster by the new agriculture of permanent fields: wet rice, pineapples, tea, and some area nuts, but permanent fields were less evenly distributed among the population than the fields of shifting cultivation once were. The people of a few enterprising households had been clever enough to seize a new opportunity and to invest the labour needed to construct rice fields and to plant gardens. Others have lagged behind. Villagers told me that only eight or ten households of the 105 in Rengsanggri had enough irrigated land to supply all the rice that their families needed. Another dozen or so had smaller amounts of irrigated land. Most had none. Only five households had tea gardens. More had pineapple gardens but even pineapples were grown by only a minority of the villagers. Government agencies have distributed seedlings for orange and cashew trees but these had not yet sufficiently matured to yield significant income to anyone in Rengsanggri. Many households had no permanent fields at all.

Several of the households that have adapted most successfully to the new agriculture had already been among the villages more prosperous households forty years earlier. Perhaps their relatively ample resources allowed them to invest, or to hire, the labour that was needed to level the fields, plant the crops, and wait out the years until their investment paid off.

In 1997 many villagers told me that they were planting permanent gardens of one sort on another, or planning to do so. They could all see that permanent gardens offered the best agricultural opportunity for the future, but it is difficult to know how many of their plans will be carried out. Some of the plans seemed quite vague-little more than a wishful nod in the direction that they felt would be sensible.

Villagers were free to plant permanent crops on any land that was not already in use. Village men with title of 'nokma' hold a kind of title to plots of village land, but they hold it in trust for the villagers, all of whom are free to use it even if that makes it unavailable for later shifting cultivation. By 1997 the amount of land that had been converted to permanent fields was not great, probably less than five per cent of the total village property. The best spots for wet rice had already been claimed, however, and it is not clear whether terraces can be constructed that climb up the hill sides. Some families have already missed the best opportunities. Permanent land ownership has already given a decisive economic advantage to the households who have seized the chance. Their houses are larger, their food supply more certain, their possessions more numerous, and they have sufficient surplus to invest in their children's education.

When first constructed, ownership of permanent fields is not formally recognized by the government, but the villagers recognize planting as conferring effective rights to the land. Eventually, the district government was expected to send in a surveyor to map the plots and register them in the owner's name. This is a bit of a mixed blessing, since once the land is registered the owner must start to pay tax. Nevertheless, registration secures the right to use the land and people were generally quite willing to pay the tax in return for this official recognition of ownership. Most permanent land in Rengsanggri was not yet formally registered in the name of the cultivator, but people took it for granted that it 'eventually would be'.

My visit to Rengsanggri in 1997 was too short to give me a clear idea of the extent of wage work within the village, but many people told me that day labour was their main source of income. Even forty years earlier, people sometimes worked for a few days on the fields of their richer neighbours, but at that time labourers were more often paid in rice than in money. Working for others has certainly become more common.

Wage work outside the village constitutes a more radical change from earlier practice than working for fellow villagers. In 1997, one villager had a responsible job with the government's soil department. At least two had menial jobs in the neighbouring settlement of Asonanggri where there are shops, schools, and government offices. I was told about a number of other people who had taken work in Asonanggri, Tura, or other places and who had moved permanently away from Rengsanggri. Among those who still count Rengsanggri as their home, a number of men have also had periods of work in the coal mines that have opened in the southern part of the Garo Hills. The men stay at the mines for as much as several months at a time, but then return home. Some have cut coal and some have worked as carriers. They are paid by the amount they cut or carry, and I was told that a carrier who works hard can earn as much as ₹100 per day. A skillful cutter can earn even more. This is high pay when compared with the ₹35 per day that is the government mandated wage for menial labour in the village.

Even in the 1950s Rengsanggri families differed in their wealth, but nobody had permanent rights to their fields so nobody had the security that is conferred by permanent land ownership. Everyone could hope that, with enough hard work, they could build up their resources and join the more prosperous families. By 1997, a minority of families had secure income from permanent fields. The poorest families seemed no poorer in 1997 than those I remembered from 1956, but the gap between rich and poor had certainly grown. That must give a greater poverty to the poorest families.

The new forms of agriculture and the new pattern of settlement were the most dramatic of the visible change that had come to Rengsanggri during my forty years absence, but modern technology had arrived in a number of other forms. First came the road. In the fifties, the closest motorable road passed through the market town of Rongram, a five kilometer walk to the northwest. During the years that I was there, however, a new road began to be cut that went right past the village. That road later became a part of the paved highway that connects Tura to the town of Willialnnagar in the eastern part of the Garo Hills. In 1997, cars, trucks and buses passed just below the site of the old village.

Other changes were more recent. In about 1991, a water supply system was built by a government Department. From a collecting place on Arbela hill above the village, pipes, often leaking at the joints brought water to a number of points around the old village, and even to many of the outlying hamlets. This greatly eased the burden on the women, who once had to carry all of their household water from one of the streams that flowed past the village. Water still had to be fetched from one of the taps, but these were generally much closer than a stream.

Three or four years before my 1997 visit, electric wires had followed the water pipes to Rengsanggri. The idea that an electric motor might do the work of human muscle had not yet come to Rengsanggri, but seven households had TV sets, the only purpose, except for light bulbs, for which I saw electricity used. Early one morning, high on Arbela hill to the east of the old village, I was treated to American sports news, courtesy of CNN.

Many people cannot yet read a calendar, but they are hung for their pictures, so an outdated calendar is as good as a new one. Some families had several identical calendars with pictures of a smiling Purno Sangma, the most successful of all Garo politicians, who was at the time the speaker of the lower house of the national parliament. A few displayed photographs of family members.

Recognizing the many technological changes, I was impressed by the absence of plastic and the absence of litter. The villagers were also able to keep the village surprisingly free of the debris of modern materials. The wrappers and broken artifacts that refuse to rot, and that litter the towns and cities of India, were rarely seen in Rengsanggri. Most houses were still built of Bamboo, and their unpainted natural colour made them fit comfortably into the landscape. For all its Changes, Rengsanggri still looked like a village.

Education

Less visible than the changes in settlement pattern and agriculture, but at least as important in the lives of the people, have been the changes that have come in religion and in education. Christianity and formal education have come together in Rengsanggri, just as they have come together everywhere in the Garo Hills.

When I first arrived in Rengsanggri in the 1950s, no villager had any formal education, and no one had adopted Christianity. Everyone in the village and everyone in the surrounding villages still practiced the traditional Songsarek religion. Change was soon to come, however, for the first school teacher was sent to Rengsanggri by the District government during the time I was working there. For an hour or so each morning, a few village children would assemble at the little rest house that villagers maintained for visitors. These children received the first introduction to the alphabet and had the first taste of literacy that had come to Rengsanggri. Like all educated Garos, the teacher was a Christian, and even though he had been sent by the government, he took it for granted that, along with the rest of the curriculum, one part of his job was to teach Christianity. No child of Rengsanggri could have been called literate by the time I left in 1956, but the first steps in that direction had been taken.

When I returned forty years later, a three room masonry school build-ing had been constructed near the road at the bottom of the old village, and almost every village child received at least a few years of schooling. 149 adults had attended school, in some cases only briefly. 122 adults (not in every case those who had attended school) claimed to be able to read, and another twenty-five said that they could read 'some'. An additional 153 village children and young people were still enrolled. Sixty-nine of these attended the Rengsanggri school, and about forty attended schools in Asonanggri, just to the north., The rest found their way to a dozen other schools, some in neighbouring villages, some in Tura, and a few even further away. Education in the Rengsanggri village school ended with Class four, so any child who wanted to continue had to go elsewhere. Many of those who attended school in Asonanggri and most of those who were studying further away were in higher classes.

Education represents a considerable commitment of time and energy, and it was clear that education was regarded as important. It was something to be encouraged in children. The practical goals of education were not so clear, however. Most of those who claimed the ability to read were limited to the Gam language. Children received instruction in English from an early age and a few even attended schools that were described as 'English medium'. Classes at all the available high schools were conducted in English so everyone who advanced as far as high school (Class 7–10) had to control some English. Very few had learned to read English easily, however, and no more than one or two people in Rengsanggri could read it easily enough to do so for pleasure. On the other hand, not enough has been published in the Garo language to encourage people to gain a reading habit. Periodicals in Garo were limited to thin weekly newspapers, and neither newspapers nor magazines in any language had become a part of village life by 1997.

By the standards of the West, this amounted only to marginal literacy, but people found the symbols of literacy to be very important. I doubt if many people could really read their bibles. The few bibles that I saw did not look well thumbed.

Christianity

For all the formal education that people in Rengsanggri had achieved, the village was not yet, in 1997, much dependent on written language, but educa-tion could claim one notable achievement: the introduction of Christianity.

The connection between education and Christianity was clear to everyone. Men and women who become educated also become Christians.

The first baptisms took place in Rengsanggri during the 1960s, then Christianity progressed only slowly at first. Church records and people's memories suggest that only about fifteen villagers had become Christian by the end of the sixties. A decade later, another twenty-five had joined them. Baptisms picked up somewhat in the eighties but the real turning point came only in the early nineties when more than a hundred people were baptized within a brief two year period. All but small children and the most stubbornly resistant adults had by then been baptized and with fewer remaining non-Christians, baptisms inevitably slowed once more. Rengsanggri had become a predominantly Christian village. Many of the remaining non-Christians were older people who had never had a chance for education.

In early 1997, 541 of the 673 people of Rengsanggri could be counted as Baptists. This number includes not only those who had been baptized but also their younger children, who will almost certainly be baptized once they are old enough. Thirty-four villagers were Catholic and ninety-six people of Rengsanggri still counted themselves as Songsareks, adherents of the traditional Garo religion leaving a few linked with Hinduism or Islam through marital linkages.

I had been surprised in the fifties and I was surprised again in the nineties by the lack of resistance to Christianity even in the part of old people who had resisted conversion for themselves, but whose children had been baptized. Everyone seemed to regard it as only natural that, as their children became educated, they would also become Christians.

Many people told me that they had become Christian simply because everyone else was doing so. One older woman told me firmly, and with a touch of irritation, 'I don't know what this Christianity is all about, but my children wanted me to be baptized, so I went along'. A few suggested that they believed it was important to be baptized before they died and they seemed to fear that some dire fate awaited those who missed the chance for baptism. A number of people pointed out that I was getting old and that I had better hurry and be baptized before it was too late. From only a few did I hear any more thought full consideration of the values and ideals that some christians elsewhere take to be the hallmark of their religion. It was clear, nevertheless, that becoming a Christian was a sign of becoming modem.

The changes in formal practice that had come with Christianity were clear, but I was not in the village long enough to feel confidant that the changes had penetrated very deeply. I attended the funerals of two old people during my visit in 1997. The ceremonies were largely Christian in form, but they seemed little in spirit from Songsarek funerals. Parties of kinsmen from other villages came bearing food. Feasts were prepared and consumed, and then the bodies were carried to the graveyard beside the river where graves had already been dug. A number of people had told me carefully that while Songsareks had cremated their dead, Christians buried theirs. What I had not been told was that Christians placed little paper flags attached to small sticks on the grave. When I asked what these were, I was told that Songsareks had used feather fans to keep flies off the dead body until it was burned. Christians use paper fans instead of feathers, and it is these fans that are placed on the grave.

The Songsareks lacked any sort of institutionalized priesthood. Some men were regarded as particularly skilful at sacrifices, but no restrictions kept others from performing them as well. No group of specialized priests had a vested interest in defending their position or in persuading people to adhere to the old religion. There were no spokesmen for the Songsarek religion who urged people to hold to the older ways or who could reinterpret old beliefs so as to adapt them to a changing world. Quite apart from its teaching, the older religion could not compete with the superior organization of the Christian Churches.

Continuity of Custom

The changes that came to Rengsanggri in the four decades between my visits have been profound, but even more than the changes, I was impressed by the continuities, and these are nowhere more striking than in the practice of kinship. The matrilineal kinship system of the Garos has always been one of their most distinctive characteristics. It was, indeed, the trait that first persuaded me to work among them. Most people of India, even most hill people of the northeast, are patrilineal, tracing their decent from their fathers. The Garos trace descent through women, from a mother to her children, and they are well aware that this distinguishes them sharply from most of their neighbours. The matrilineal kinship system that I learned about in the fifties remained very much alive in Rengsanggri forty years later, and if, in the following pages, I emphasize the points where changes have taken place, it must be understood that the changes have occurred within a context that remains, in most ways, much as it was.

It did seems that a number of rules that were once quite strict have been somewhat relaxed. Most startling to me was a relaxation in the rules of exogamy. Garos divide themselves into several large named groups of which the Sangmas and the Maraks are by far the largest. In the 1950s everybody in Rengsanggri was either a Sangma or a Marak, and every single marriage united a Marak to a Sangma. Sangmas were not supposed to marry other Sangmas, nor Maraks to marry Maraks. I was told of one Marak-Marak marriage in the neighbouring village of Songmagri, so even then, people who were sufficiently stubborn occasionally got away with a marriage within one's own group, but such marriages were rare and they were not really respectable. I was also told about cases of two Maraks or two Sangmas who were known to have had a sexual relationship outside of marriage, people did not approve of these affairs because the partners were not married. But their common kinship group made the matter even worse. Still these relationships did not evoke the kind of horror that so· many people show toward incest.

The Maraks and the Sangmas are both divided into dozens of smaller named groups or 'lineages'. In the 1950s everyone in Rengsanggri belonged to one of just four of these lineages. About half of the adults belonged to the Chambigong lineage of Maraks and the other half were divided among three lineages of Sangmas: A'gitok, Manda, and Ti'gite. Garos have been much more strongly opposed to either sexual relations or marriage between two members of the same named lineage than between two Sangmas or two Maraks who belonged to differed lineages. Their attitude toward a relationship between lineage memberships came closer to the feelings that incest often evokes. In the 1950s I never knew a couple who shared a lineage name, although people were able to report a few cases from other villages.

In 1997, I was astonished to find no fewer than eight Rengsanggri couples, both of whom were Chambigong Maraks but who nevertheless lived together and jointly cared for their common children. These couples had never been officially married because the Garo Baptist Church will not give its blessing to marriages between people who share a same lineage name, even when no literal kinship tie can be traced. Even without church blessing, these Chambigong-Chambigong relationships were regarded as marriages by their neighbours. The partners were easily referred to as 'husband' and 'wife', and their children were accepted as Chambigongs. People did seem mildly embarrassed by these relationships. I remember a few giggles when I showed my surprise the first time I realized that a husband and wife were both Chambigongs. Each person's lineage membership is so well known, however, that the impropriety cannot possibly be hidden.

I find it difficult to understand how villagers in this part of the Garo Hills could have enforced almost perfect exogamy of Sangmas and Maraks in the 1950s while, forty years later, they failed to prevent unions within the much smaller named lineage. A more modest break with tradition would have accepted marriages between Maraks or between Sangmas, while still forbidding marriage within the lineages. There are, to be sure, a great many Chambigongs in Rengsanggri, and the choice of spouses from other lineages may seem to be a bit limited. Most people marry outside the villages, however, and an ample supply of appropriate spouses should have been available nearby. All these marriages were, I believe, initiated by the young people rather than by their parents, and most of the couples probably started living together without community or parental blessing. This is the kind of marriage that the Garos describe as 'stolen'.

In 1997, the great majority of married adults in Rengsanggri belonged to the same four lineages that were found people there forty years earlier, but travel has become easier and more young people now have periods of residence away from home either for work or for education. This has allowed some of them to find spouses from more distant places than they had in earlier years. Nine men and three women in Rengsanggri belonged to eleven named lineages other than the four established ones. The composition of the village has become just a bit more cosmopolitan.

In 1997 it was still felt to be desirable for a man to find a sister's son, or at least a classificatory sister's son to marry his heiress daughter, but I found more exceptions to this rule than I had in 1956. A few men of entirely different named lineages than their fathers-in-laws were described as nokroms (heirs), something that I did not find in 1956. In 1997 I was also surprised to find one very old women who was being cared for by her son and daughter-in-law, a startling departure from earlier practice when it was always daughters rather than sons who cared for their aged parents. I asked why the son was performing a job usually given to a daughter but I learned no more than that the family found it convenient. All other dependent old people were still living with daughters.

In the 1950s the heir and heiress always lived with the wife's parents or with her widowed mother. A few large families built a separate building for the younger couple, but these buildings were always placed next to the main house of the family, and the two were counted as belonging to a single homestead. In 1997, when the homesteads had become much more scattered, five two generation families had buildings in widely separate locations, most of them in different hamlets. The couple that had been designated as heir and heiress lived in one place and the young wife's parents or widowed mother lived somewhere else. People assured me that this was done simply as a matter of convenience and they said that whenever the widow or the older couple grew feeble enough to need help, the two parts of the family would move back together.

The balance of decision making seems to have shifted somewhat since the fifties, and the young people probably have more ability to make their own selection of spouses, or at least more power to influence the selection, than they did before. That may have allowed the marriages between chambigongs and it may also have forced some men to accept heirs who not their own nephews. Young people may have gained more freedom to maintain a house at some distance from the residence of the girl's parents.

It is not impossible that Christianity has changed some people' attitudes about the selection of spouse, but I see no obvious signs of this. Indeed, as far as I can see, Christianity has been directly responsible for only two changes to the kinship system: it brought an abrupt end to polygyny, and the older practice of bridegroom capture was immediately abandoned. Neither change brought any radical upheaval. Polygyny, of course, is forbidden for Christians, but since polygyny was never common among the Garos, its prohibition did not affect most people.

Upon becoming Christians, a few men with two wives had to stop considering one of them as a wife. I asked one man who had been married to the daughter of his first wife, and who had children by both women, whether he had been obliged to divorce one of his wives when they all became Christians. Both the women were sitting with us when I asked the question, and everyone burst out laughing. They told me that, yes indeed; he and the older women were no longer married. This woman, however, continued to live in the household with her daughter and her former husband, and except that she was no longer considered a 'wife', she had much the same status as she had before. She continued to work as much as her advancing age permitted, and she could look forward to being cared for by her daughter and her son-in-law, formerly her husband, just as if she were still married. I presume that the man and the older woman no longer had a sexual relationship. But perhaps her age would have limited that even without Christianity.

Christianity may do more to change the way people talk about their families than to change their practice. Older women still live with their daughters and sons-in-law and they still play much the same role within their families. It is possible that the, prohibition on polygyny will make it more difficult to find younger men, who are willing to marry widows. That could make it more difficult to provide good care for some elderly women. In 1997, twenty-nine women lived in Rengsanggri who had been widowed or divorced but who had not remarried. Eighteen of these lived with a daughter and son-in-law, and one lived with a son and his wife. six lived alone or with their unmarried children. Given the expansion of population this is not very different from the eleven widows who lived with a daughter and son-in-law, and the three, who lived alone with their unmarried children in 1956. Four widowed or divorcee young women with small children lived with their parents in 1997, and three women who were no longer married lived with parents or other relatives in 1956. Again, this does not represent any great change.

The other change in kinship practices that Christianity brought was the end of bridegroom capture, but that has been even less disruptive than the end of polygyny. In 1956, marriage arrangements began when a girl and her parents reached an agreement about whom to select, but the wedding itself began when a half dozen unmarried youths, ideally the brothers and cousin-brothers of the young woman, were sent out to find the chosen bridegroom. They would surprise him at an unexpected moment and force him to come with them to the bride.

Bridegroom capture disappeared with Christianity, but the more important preliminary process of selection was little changed. The only change was the abandonment of the rather stylized bridegroom capture itself. Among Christian, the marriage was supposed to be publicly agreed upon ahead of time, and the boy did not have to be captured.

Continuity of People

I was impressed by the continuity of the kinship system, but I was equally impressed by the continuity of particular families. There had been sixty households in Rengsanggri in 1956. Forty years later, people who had been married adults in twenty-three of those households still lived in the village. Many of them had moved to a different hamlet, but their households were clearly recognized as the same as those I had known before. In each generation, a new heir and heiress should be appointed. They should maintain the household until they pass it on to still another generation. All of the adults of fifteen of the sixty households I had known in 1956 had died, but their households had survived, maintained by surviving heirs.

Another six of the 1956 households had moved to Asonanggri, just north of Rengsanggri. Asonanggri had been a tiny settlement in 1956, with no more than half a dozen houses. The area of those villages, however, had been selected by the government as the site of a development block, and by 1997 it had shops, schools, and government offices and it must have had many more residents than Rengsanggri. Sometime between my visits, probably during the 1970s when wet rice was just beginning to reach the area. A sizable patch of land in Asonanggri was brought under irrigation. Asonanggri and Rengsanggri were regarded as sister villages, and for a family to move from Rengsanggri to Asonanggri was only marginally more disruptive than to move from the site of the old village to one of the new hamlets in Rengsanggri itself. In 1997, of the six households that had moved to Asonanggri, four had at least one adult who had survived from 1956 and the other two households were maintained by heirs.

When one looks backward form 1997, the continuities are as impressive as when one looks forward from 1956. The village had grown, and of its 105 households, only 38 were identifiable as the 'same' as households that were found in Rengsanggri in 1956: the twenty-three original households with surviving members, together with the fifteen that have surviving heirs. The great majority of the remaining sixty-seven households had at least spouse who had grown up in Rengsanggri, but who had not been chosen as an heir. As non-heirs, their families did not continue earlier households but formed new ones instead.

In the years between my visits, very few people had moved to Rengsanggri for any reason except to marry a Rengsanggri man or woman. In the 1950s, more husbands than wives changed villages at marriage, and the same has been true more recently. There were 108 married couples in 1997. (Eight of the 105 households had no married couple at all, nine had two married couples, and one had three. All the rest had one each. All marriages were monogamous). Seventy-two of the rest of the husbands, but only eleven of the wives, had moved from other villages to join Rengsanggri spouses.

Men sometimes leave home for a few months for work. A few people move to a neighbouring village, and a few move further. More often, people move when they marry. Most Rengsanggri villagers, however, have remained, year after year, in the same village. This is a degree of stability that mobile Westerners find difficult to imagine. Rengsanggri had 248 adults who were married or who had been married in the past. More than half of them had lived there all their lives, and with a handful of exceptions, the rest had lived there since their marriage.

Of course, they also know the people who live in the surrounding villages. They visit the weekly market in Rongram where they meet people from dozens of villages, and they meet Bengali and Nepali traders as well.

Songsareks once visited other villages at the times of festivals and Christians now attend intervillage services and meetings. When people need help, and when they get married and die, kinsmen from other villages assemble. Almost everyone occasionally visits Tura, twenty-five kilometres away, although one woman did tell me that she had ridden a bus three times, become sick every time and resolved never to try again. She said she had never gone even as far as Tura. A number of villagers have been further, to distant parts of the Garo Hills, and a few to other cities in the north east. Handfuls have even been to Delhi or Bombay, most of them on government Sponsored trips where they took part in multi ethnic festival. Government official, vaccinators, and school teachers all pay visits to the village.

Prospects for the Future

What of the future? Are more extensive or more disruptive change in store for the people of Rengsanggri? My suspicion is that the most important pressures for change will be economic. As long as the population continues to expand, less and less of people's subsistence can come from shifting cultivation. More people will probably have to find paid work away from the village. Families without permanent gardens or rice fields may become impoverished and forced to find menial work somewhere else, as a few already have. Others will gain enough education to claim more prestigious and better paying job in government service. Some day, perhaps, people will even find work with private concerns. It is difficult to predict the impact of employment on the traditional family system, but if, in the search for work, people become more residentially mobile, it may become more difficult to maintain the kind of mutual support that the members of an extended kinship network can provide when they live near to one another.

The greatest threat to the traditional family system, however, is likely to be the ownership of permanently cultivated fields. If fertilizer were to allow land to be used every year for other crops than wet rice, pineapples, tea, and fruit trees, shifting cultivation might be quickly abandoned. All cultivation might then be done on privately owned fields. The impact of permanent land ownership will depend on how it is inherited. If property continues to be inherited by a single daughter, some women will be much wealthier than their sisters, and wealth differences might rigidify. That, in turn, could increase the social inequality among households.

In a society where people have been accustomed to reasonable economic equality, however, serious inequality among siblings might cause considerable strain. The unequal inheritance of earlier days was seen as no more than fair compensation for the care of the old people. With enough hard work, even non-heirs could hope to improve their position. It is one thing to accept wealth differences that can be credited to hard work and cleverness, but quite another to endure differences that are due to nothing but the luck of inheritance. If property so given only to daughters, the disruption to the matrilineal system should not be great, but if couples feel that they would also like to give something to their sons, the present kinship system could be undermined. Young men might become less dependent upon the kinship groups of their wives. Sons who are lucky enough to inherit land from their parents might want to bring their wives to live near their fields, and wives might move to their husbands' villages more often than they do now. When it is usually men who move, women can often live near close female kinsmen even when they are not a part of the same household. If women move more often, the security that comes from living in a neighborhood among friendly parents, aunts, sisters, and cousins could be undermined.

By 1997, private land ownership was too recent in Rengsanggri to have had a dramatic effect on income inequality, inheritance, or residence patterns. People told me that the rule of inheritance remained unchanged: the heiress and her husband were supposed to inherit all the property of the older couple, including all their permanent fields. The few instances of inheritance of rice land that I heard about seem to have followed this rule. In, most respects, the family system that I had learned about in the fifties remained intact in the nineties. The possible changes about which I have speculated are for the future.

Old Friends

It was an extraordinary experience, to return to Rengsanggri after four decades and to find that its people remembered me as vividly as I remembered them. For forty years, I had been writing stories about them, and through all that period they had been telling stories about me. Many people had died, of Course, but some of those I had known were still living, and others who had been children still remembered me. Some who had not yet been born in 1956 said that they had heard about me from their parents. I had almost become a legend. I was repeatedly reminded that I had carried my own basket hanging from a thump line across my head, and that I had once climbed onto a roof during a thatching party and helped the other young men to tie on the thatch. Far from having grown away from the villagers, I felt that I belonged with them more securely than I ever had. I remembered their parents and grandparents. We shared a history.

In December 1996, on the morning of my second day in Rengsanggri, when most people had not yet heard about my return, I climbed off the bus that had brought me from Tura and met a woman who looked at me for a moment and then said in astonishment 'Raven Marak'. Raben, a Garoized version of my first name, was the way they had always addressed me, and I acquired the 'Marak' one day when I was sitting with some men, one of whom suggested in a joking way that since I was living a village with so many Chambigong Maraks that I, too, should be a Chambigong Marak. People would refer occasionally to my membership in the Chambigongs and the Maraks, but always as a joke. People would laugh heartily at the idea; they and I knew that there was no way in which a foreigner could really join a Garo kinship group. When I returned the woman I met on the road was only the first of many who called me 'Raben Marak' and, I noticed with surprise, they no longer laughed. During the forty years that I had been gone, they must have talked about me now then, and after referring to me often enough as 'Raben Marak' it stopped being just a joke. They began to think of it as my real name.

I found it easy to deal with these old friends and with their children. Their melting smiles reflected the joy that I felt. I had learned how to behave. I knew how to be courteous and how to joke; I needed no new learning to take on old habits. Everyone, whom I remembered, of course, had grown forty years older, and so had I. We had all undergone the change that forty years bring, and we seventy years-olds did not act like the thirty-year olds we once were. But the community in 1997, like the community in 1956, included both thirty year-olds and seventy year-olds, and young and old alike continued to play the familiar roles of their ages. Young and old men and women still divided the work in the same way. As far as I could see, they still behaved toward one another in the same way, and they accepted me with the same curiosity and tolerant good will that I remembered so well.

Garos are a wonderfully pragmatic people. Things that Westerners gloss over are faced with no nonsense. I remember with delight the man, some-what older than I, who asked if I would ever make another trip to the Garo Hills. He thought about his question briefly and then, with a matter of fact good cheer, he answered it himself, 'No, probably not. You are old and you will probably die soon'.

Garos are less concerned with status and less worried about their own dignity than many of the people of the subcontinent. No caste difference divide them, and they treat each other, and even outsiders with a kind of symmetry that Westerners miss in their dealings with many Indians. Garos can laugh at each other because they can easily laugh at themselves. I can tease them because they can tease me, and some of my happiest memories of the people of Rengsanggri are times when they laughed with great good nature at my expense, or when I was able to laugh at them. On my last day in Rengsanggri in 1997, I passed a woman on a path who asked me the same question as the older man had asked. 'Will you ever come back again?' She too answered her own question but she answered it a bit differently: 'If you do come back you will probably come like this', and she held up her hand with her index finger tightly crooked, in a gesture they use to suggest the bent backs of old people. She burst into gales of laughter, and so did I.

After my return in 1997, but when I had made only two short visit to Rengsanggri, a man in the district headquarters at Tura asked me whether the villagers were happier or less happy than they had been forty years earlier. I replied that I did not know 'Yet', but even then I realized that I would never be able to answer that question. Happiness is much too subtle and subjective for a visitor to measure. Does it make any sense to ask whether life had improved in those forty or become worse, or to ask in what ways it had improved and in what ways grown worse?

The most important single measure of improvement that I can point to is in the ability of people to keep their children alive. In both 1956 and 1997, I asked as many adult women as I could find, how many children they had borne and how many had died. Their answers have too many ambiguities to inspire much confidence. I cannot confidently separate late abortions, still births, and early infant deaths, for example. Nevertheless, it seems clear that people had become considerably more successful at keeping their children alive by 1997 than they had been in 1956. More than half of the women in 1956 reported that at least as many of their children had died as were still living. In 1997, I asked 110 women who had ever borne children how many of them were living and how many had died. 'Only' 19 of these 110 women reported that as many or more had died as were alive. They reported a total of 567 births, 407 still living and 160 dead. Most of those who had died had done so as babies or very small children. This is still an appalling infant mortality, but it is a marked improvement on the earlier level.

So life has, in some ways improved, but in other ways, people looked back upon the earlier years as better. Some felt that the scattering of the houses away from the old village had brought a loss of a sense of community. They missed the old village festivals, and some Christians admitted to missing the joy that rice beer once brought. Permanent land ownership has widened the difference between rich and poor. As the tempo of change accelerates it may become more difficult for parents and children to understand each other's worlds. But Rengsanggri survives, still beloved by its permanent residents, and still beloved by me.

Reference

Burling, Robbins. 1963. *Rensanggri: Family and Kinship in a Garo Village*. Philadelphia, Pennsylvania: University of Pennsylvania Press.

SECTION II

The Indian Experience

8

Researching Garo Death Rites

Erik de Maaker

In this essay I am focusing on the fieldwork that I did between 1999 and 2001 in the Garo Hills of western Meghalaya (India). I am exploring how I, in the course of this PhD research, have related to the people I met. I describe how relationships emerged and developed, and how people reacted to my involvement in their lives. I conclude by arguing that, although my research did not have the intention to expose the village concerned, it has certainly contributed to it being put on the map as a 'traditional' village. As far as I can judge, this seems to have worked out positively for the villagers. It has made people more aware of the importance that is being attributed by an outside world to their cultural practices, and ensures that they receive a positive kind of attention from state organizations and the like.

Over the last two decades of the previous century, anthropology has moved away from the kind of fields that it used to cherish before. Where previously anthropological research was typically linked to a single field site, now a multi-sited approach became the standard (Marcus, 1995). This provided better possibilities for the comparison of data collected, enabling a better and broader understanding of the topic being studied. Nevertheless, there are certain research topics that continue to benefit from (predominantly) single-sited research. The fieldwork that I have conducted on death-related practices required close engagement with a limited number of people. Not only because of the level of 'trust' and 'rapport' required for the fieldwork but also since the research demanded that I took multiple dimensions of the relationships maintained by the people concerned into account. To achieve this, I had to meet them in various roles: in relation to their land, as traders, as kinsmen, or when acting in accordance with their religious responsibilities. This could be achieved best by interacting with a (more or less) single set of people over a prolonged period of time.

First Encounters

It is not easy to say where my journey to north-eastern India started. I guess that an initial interest was raised by the long talks that I as a teenager had with a secondary school teacher who told me about his extensive travels in India. In his stories, North-east India invariably surfaced as a region that was for its political instability forbidden to foreigners.

My interest in death rites developed several years later, when I was working on an ethnographic film project in Indonesia. We made a film (or as it later turned out—a series of films) based on the research by Danielle Geirnaert, an anthropologist who had done extensive research among people for whom ancestor centred belief systems played a major role (Geirnaert-Martin et al., 2007). These beliefs inspired people to participate in a complex cycle of annual rituals, which were, however, increasingly difficult to maintain, because the younger generations converted to Christianity. While conversion to Christianity ended people's participation in the annual ancestor-oriented rituals, it had much less impact on the death rituals that were conducted. We attended the mortuary ritual of a man who belonged to the local gentry, and what unfolded was a performance stretching over several days, which combined care for the deceased's soul with complex interactions between relatives, neighbours, and friends. Following that occasion, it dawned upon me that in societies where social relationships are primarily framed in kinship terms, funerals are often attributed much greater importance than is the case in the West.

In 1995, the restrictions which the Indian state had imposed on foreigners for entry into the north-eastern region since decades were partly abandoned, allowing travel on a tourist visa to the states of Assam, Meghalaya, and Tripura. Access to the four other north-eastern states (Arunachal Pradesh, Nagaland, Manipur, and Mizoram) continued to be subject to a special permit. In 1997, I had the chance to go to Shillong, the capital of the Indian state of Meghalaya. During this trip, I met many of the people who would come to play an important role in my PhD project. One of them was Tanka Subba, a prolific scholar attached to the Anthropology Department of the North-Eastern Hill University (NEHU). He would later become my local academic supervisor. I also met Milton Sangma, a historian, who belonged to the community (Garo), which I would decide to work among. Furthermore, I met anthropologist and linguist Robbins Burling (1963/1997), who was at that time a visiting professor at NEHU. He had just retired as a professor from the University of Michigan. His engagement with the Garo had been lifelong, resulting as early as 1963 in the monograph *Rengsanggri*, which was followed by a large number of articles and several other books.

It soon dawned upon me that most of what had been published on the Garo community religion (the practitioners of which are referred to as 'Songsarek') is to an important extent based on interviews with 'knowledgeable people'. Interviews tend to force people to generalize about beliefs and practices. Rather than taking such generalizations as a starting point, it seemed worthwhile to attempt the research of death rites with a focus on what people actually do (rather than what they say they do). A mortuary ritual demands the involvement of relatives, friends, and neighbours of the deceased, allowing them and at the same time forcing them to express their relationship with the deceased and his or her closest relatives. Moreover, a death calls for gifts to be offered, some of which are attributed great symbolic value. Therefore, I supposed that an analysis of the conduct of Garo death rituals would reveal people's perspective not only on notions such as life, death, and the ancestors, but also on practices and ideas relating to kinship and exchange.

During my first visit to North-east India, I did not have the time to actually visit the Garo Hills. A couple of months later, I had another chance to go to India, and I spent about a month in the Garo Hills. Accompanied by Rafael Marak, a local folklorist, I visited many places, notably in the east and west of the Garo Hills. We did not have a car, so we used public transport or—where that was absent—went around on foot. Moving around like this, carrying backpacks with a sleeping mat and some food, allowed us to stay over whereever we were invited, and meet a large number of people. This also facilitated meeting the local underground. Or rather, they met us, but at that time I was blissfully unaware of that. Rafael did not tell me about this until a couple of months after the trip, and at the time I had only registered a couple of young men who were curious to know my whereabouts. One afternoon we reached a village named Sadolpara. When we came in the vicinity of the village, we heard gunshots. Rafael identified these as an announcement of a death that had occurred, and told me that according to his knowledge it would not be impertinent to attend the event. As compared to other villages that we had been travelling through, this one had several courtyards, divided by stretches of forest, areca nut gardens, and even a paddy field. The courtyards were large sandy patches. Houses were located at the fringes of the courtyards. Near the house from where the gun had been fired was a small group of people, centred around a frail old woman. She was walking slowly towards the house, keeping her body bent to point stick with feathers towards the house, while raising her voice in lament.

The particular village and the larger region in which it was located had a good number of Songsareks (practitioners of the Garo community religion). Along the way to the village we had come across many remnants of sacrifices, but this was the first time that I saw a Songsarek ritual. Rafael asked the bystanders whether we could record the chant of the old lady. Much to my surprise, they had no objections. Perhaps they were used to people being attracted by the exoticism of Songsarek practices. And perhaps they recognized Rafael Marak—who is a famous Garo folk singer—and they wanted to be forthcoming to a local celebrity. Moreover, as I understood much later, they simply did not see any harm in a foreigner making video recordings of the chanting old lady.

The woman whose chanting I recorded did not blink at the sight of the video camera. Once she had finished, we asked her a couple of questions, which she answered briskly and self-confidently. Her chanting had concluded a certain phase of the death ritual, and she asked us to come over to her house for a cup of tea. The house was located on top of a low hill, at a slight distance from the part of the village where we had just been. Inside the house we were joined by children, grandchildren, and in-laws. They joked with Rafael about me. At one stage, half as a joke, half serious, the woman told me, 'You will be like a son to me.'

The old woman's name was Jiji. Jiji's position in life was a delicate one, as her husband had died about a decade ago, leaving her with the responsibility of five children. Attempts to find a new groom for her, as a replacement for her deceased husband, had not worked out. Jiji and her children survived, but in the bargain she lost much of the wealth that had previously belonged to her household. Moreover, she and most of her children lacked the funds to invest in newly emerging forms of cultivation. By and large, they remained dependent on the swidden agriculture that had made previous generations of Garo villagers wealthy, but was for various reasons quickly becoming less rewarding.

Jiji invited us to eat and sleep in her house, but we could not do so. Early that afternoon, before we went to the funeral, we had met a young man who lived in one of the only brick houses of the village. We had left our bags with him, and had agreed to eat and sleep in his house. Notwithstanding my boldness when it came to videography, I was careful not to offend people when it came to commitments regarding food and stay. I was afraid that our going back on an earlier made appointment might harm my future relationship with the young man.

Now, before I continue these fieldwork-related accounts, I want to fill in the reader on the social topography of the area in which I conducted my PhD research.

Between Town and Village

North-east India consists of broad river valleys surrounded by hills and mountains.. Differences in mode of agriculture and so on create a divide between people in the plains, and those in the hills or mountains, although there are also abundant inter-linkages. Notably among the people who live away from the plains, great cultural and linguistic diversity exists. Opinions differ on what sets apart a language from a dialect, and on how to define an ethnic group, but according to the official classifications the region consists of several dozen communities, many of which have their own language (Singh, 2002). Most of the people who live in the hills and mountains have, by the various state governments, been classified as 'tribal'. They belong to numerically relatively small groups that do not only have their own language, but are also in a social, economic, and religious sense believed to differ from the more mainstream Hindu and Muslim communities. For instance, 'tribal' groups would have a more egalitarian social structure. Also, it is generally assumed that 'tribal' groups attribute greater importance to kinship as a model for social organization than 'non-tribal' groups. Most states of North-east India have a 'tribal' majority, and quite a few 'tribal' communities have a certain level of administrative autonomy within the state.

The concept of 'tribe' as used in India is rather problematic, since there is no single set of criteria that applies to all that have been categorized by the state in such a manner (Bates, 1995; Karlsson and Subba, 2006). Hence I have used quotation marks around the term 'tribe', to indicate that it refers to an administrative category that does not necessarily link up to the ways in which anthropologists have been applying the term elsewhere in the world. Rather than representing groups that share certain traits, 'tribe', as a category, seems to act as an umbrella for all those groups who do not satisfactory qualify as a Hindu or Muslim community. Since the Indian state considers 'tribes' to be 'less advanced', or even 'backward', in comparison to the majority communities, they qualify for positive discrimination. People who belong to a 'tribal' community tend to have access to a certain quota of dedicated 'seats' in schools and universities, but usually there are many other benefits associated with having a 'tribal' status as well. These kinds of benefits are accessible to every member of a given community, without considering individual needs. The Garos have qualified as 'tribal' from the time since the category came into use, even though there is great cultural and linguistic variation within the community, and it is not always clear who qualifies as a Garo and who does not.

Early on, in the 19th century, when the colonial state expanded towards the northern edge of Bengal and into the plains of the Brahmaputra valley, at times Garos maintained tense relationships with the inhabitants of the plains. The ensuing violence provided an excuse to the colonial state for the conquest of the hill area. Garos, who had their own community religion, proved susceptible for conversion to Christianity. Australian and American missionaries (predominantly) came to play an important role in the emergence of an educated Garo middle class, as well as the formation of a Christian Garo cultural identity. From the second half of the 20th century onwards Christianity became the majority religion, leaving the remaining adherents of the community religion as a relatively marginal group in the rural hinterland. The village in which I had met Jiji was located in one such a region.

Most of the Garo live in the four easternmost districts (collectively known as the Garo Hills) of the state of Meghalaya. These four districts have a Garo majority, but they are home to people belonging to various other communities as well. Some of these are categorized as 'tribals', such as Koch and Hajong. Others are the descendants of migrants from Assam or Bengal, among others.

One of the things that I noted during my first weeks in the Garo Hills was the great disparity that existed between people's lifestyle in the towns, as compared to that in villages such as the one in which I had met Jiji.

With about 60,000 inhabitants, Tura is the largest town in the Garo Hills. It harbours about one-tenth of the region's population. Tura is the political, administrative, and educational centre of the Garo Hills. It is here that all major government offices are located, as are the principal hospitals, colleges, and even a university. In Tura town, people lived with the comforts of small town-India. Electricity (although with frequent power cuts), telephone (often out of order), running water (during the dry season only for a couple of hours a day), cable TV (about 40 stations from India, Bangladesh, and the United States), shops selling a variety of food and consumer items, and so on. Most importantly, in contrast to the villages where everyone knows everyone else, a town like Tura has such a large number of people that there is a scope for anonymity and to have contractual, non-personalized relationships.

In villages such as the one where Jiji lived, modern day comforts were absent. There was no electricity, no telephone, and water had to be collected with a vessel or a bucket from a well. In Jiji's village of about 1,600 inhabitants there were less than 10 TVs (operating on solar-charged batteries). There were two shops, but these only sold basic items such as rice, lentils, salt, dry cells, cigarettes, and soap. Once a week there was a market at which villagers sold their produce to wholesalers, and could buy rice, clothing, and sometimes vegetables.

Most of the villagers had very little access to money, and would not be able to buy much from the shops or in the market. People did, however, have free access to the forest that belonged to their village and the produce it yielded. Most people cultivated their own land, but if they worked for money salaries would vary from ₹30 to ₹50 a day (US$0.75–1.25). Some families did not have food security throughout the year, which was notably an issue in the months immediately preceding the start of the rains. Tura had the Garo elite, but there are also many poor Garos, as well as a substantial number of poor non-Garos. Many townspeople commanded by way of their salaries a steady flow of money. Notably the incomes of government employees and traders could be substantial, and allow them to build large houses, maintain servants, own cars, and travel.

In villages such as the one where Jiji lived, educational facilities would be basic or non-existent. During the first year when I went there, there was one primary school in Sadolpara. The teacher would only give classes for one or two hours a day, if at all. Educated in proper schools, townspeople had access to book-based knowledge, which was out of bounds for the mostly illiterate villagers.

There was a government health dispensary in a village close to Sadolpara, but its doctor would not be present for more than a couple of hours a week, if at all. A larger community health centre was slightly further away. It did have doctors and medicines, but the villagers did not like to go there. This had a variety of reasons, one of these being that the medical staff of the community health centre tended to be quite harsh towards the villagers, who in their opinion lacked basic knowledge of hygiene and so on. Regarding medical care, villagers by and large managed on their own. Several people were knowledgeable about the use of medicinal plants, and in addition practitioners of the community religion solved their health problems through sacrifices to the animist deities.

One way to look at the town–village disparity is that the medical posts and schools were exponents of an urban culture that extended into the rural area. From the perspective of the government-salaried medical personnel and the teachers, the villagers were illiterate, backward, and ignorant. Songsareks were referred to as immoderate when it came to drinking rice beer, and lacking the disposition to create savings. From the villagers' perspective, however, educated townspeople had little idea or interest in village life, and the difficulties faced by the villagers. Unless townspeople had spent their childhood in a village, they would invariably lack what was for the villagers basic knowledge of animals and plants. Townspeople normally lacked the skills required for life in a village environment (bamboo working, house building, hunting, fishing, etc.). And what they lacked most of all, was the sheer physical strength and endurance required for doing these kind of tasks.

Although the contrast between townspeople and villagers was in many respects pretty sharp, this did not mean that there were no connections. Some townspeople enjoyed to visit the villages. And some villagers would travel every now and then to the town for trade, talk with their political representatives, and see all that money can buy. Village youth would move to town to work as a domestic helper and get the opportunity to attend a reasonably good school. Likewise, towns had many people who during earlier phases of their life lived in villages, or who owned agricultural land and went there regularly. Most importantly, people living in towns and villages were connected through kinship ties. This allowed them to call upon each other for help and assistance. It also implied that they would meet every now and then at events such as funerals or—in urban Christian settings—weddings.

The disparity between town and village was particularly big where villagers were Songsareks. More and more, for urban youth, the Garo community religion is something of the past. It is an important part of what makes Garos 'different' from others, and therefore attention is given to it in textbooks used in schools, through documentaries shown on the regional subsidiary of the state broadcaster Doordarshan, on local radio stations, or at exhibitions or festivals that display 'traditional' Garo culture. In these representations, Garo culture tends to be shown in a rather essentialized manner that has only a distant relationship with the way in which Songsarkes live their lives today.

For the fieldwork that I did among Garo villagers, I depended upon university-educated Garo students for linguistic assistance. In the first couple of months, I worked with Sengjrang N. Sangma. Later, I worked with Henysingh A. Sangma and with Nixon Dango. They were aware of the particularities of village culture, and had a positive disposition towards animism (even though they themselves were Christians). Not surprisingly, both of them were former students of the Department of Garo language of the NEHU (Tura campus). Not only were they willing and able to live in a Garo village for a prolonged period of time, they also accepted that animist Garo villagers engaged in practices and used language that is at times not readily understandable to people who belonged to the same community, but have been brought up and live their life in quite a different setting.

Getting Organized

After the second trip to Meghalaya, I had an outline of what I wanted to do my PhD research on, but it took me a year to secure funding. I applied for a PhD grant with Leiden University, but my application was turned down in the first round of the selection process. 'Theoretically not sufficiently innovative,' was the reason given. Fortunately, an improved version of the proposal passed the first of the two rounds for funding from the Dutch National Science Foundation. I reworked the proposal, collected feedback from many scholars, and reworked it some more. Once I had submitted the final version, it took many months before I received the reviews, and then again more weeks before the committee decided which proposals to fund. Throughout this period, I worked as a freelancer on an ethnographic film project, the earnings of which were just enough to pay for my monthly bills. After more weeks of waiting and worrying, word came that I had received the much desired scholarship, and could embark on my PhD research.

In the meantime, my personal situation had changed. Earlier that year, I had met my wife-to-be. She was an Indian, at that time residing in Mumbai. A couple of months later we got married, and whenever her activities allowed, she would stay with me in the Garo village. Instead of being alone, which had been my earlier prospect, I preferred to be with her. This had important consequences for my position in the field, in a positive sense, as it worked out that she could have a kind of contact with women that was out of reach for me.

Now, in order to do research in India, I needed a research permit. Anticipating that I would eventually manage to secure a grant, I had put in an application for such a permit immediately after having returned from my visit to North-east India. One and a half years followed. The problem was, not surprisingly, a certain apprehensiveness on the side of the Home Ministry about the safety of a foreigner residing for a prolonged period of time in a north-east Indian border zone. These were justified concerns, as I found out once I started reading the local newspapers. Nevertheless, the Home Office eventually relented and granted the visa required.

By the end of August 1999, I returned to Tura, this time with my wife. We took classes in Garo, and after a couple of months we could shop in the market, ask for directions and so on. However, more complex conversations continued to be cumbersome. Moreover, in Tura it proved very difficult to practise simple Garo, since almost everyone who had been educated beyond primary school would for convenience sake talk to us in English. English is the language of tuition in many secondary schools and colleges in the state of Meghalaya. To improve our Garo, we had to move out of town. It was, anyway, time to leave Tura, since my fieldwork would take place in rural West Garo Hills.

To prepare for the move, we made a two-day visit to the village in which Jiji lived. The rainy season was at its height, and the humidity was suffocating. The mud paths were extremely slippery, while the abundant rains chased snakes out of their holes. I nearly stepped on one that crossed the path we walked on. A little while later, there was another encounter with a snake when I was walking on grass (I had not yet learned that one should not do so in the rainy season). As a European, used to nature as pristine and beautiful (since it has been 'cleared' from dangerous animals), I was not at all prepared for this. In addition, on the day we left I developed a high fever: I had contracted malaria.

It took about a month for me to recover from the malaria. By then, the rains had stopped, the mud was dry and hard, and the snakes had retreated to their holes. Now, how to move to Sadolpara? Who had the space to put me up, and where was I supposed to keep my laptop, video camera, and other equipment? At that time, I was alone. My wife had gone to work in Mumbai, and I had not managed to find a research assistant. To start with, I took a room in the partly abandoned government health dispensary. From there it took about 10 minutes on a scooter, to reach the village in which Jiji lived. An attendant maintained the dispensary. In the absence of medical staff, relatives of the attendant occupied most of the rooms. Others were used as storage space for firewood and so on. The attendant granted me a room that was still vacant.

From the dispensary, I began to make trips to the surrounding villages. In this way, I thought, I could meet people and begin my research. However, right from the start people discouraged me to drive either after dark or before sunrise. They warned me for tigers, and herds of wild elephants (neither of which I ever saw). This meant that I could not be out after six at night. Likewise, I would never be in any of the villages before six or seven in the morning. Around eight in the morning, and sometimes earlier, people left for their fields, to return by four or five in the afternoon. During the day, villages tended to be depopulated, except for children less than four years of age, people who were so old that they could hardly move, and those who were ill. In order to collect the kind of data required, there was really no other option than to move to a Garo village.

I did consider other villages than Sadolpara, but, nevertheless, almost instinctively chose the village in which Jiji lived. More than two years later, her 'You are like a son to me' still resonated in my ears. She herself repeated that statement on virtually every occasion that I met her. My wife had joined me again, and we discussed our wish to stay in Sadolpara with some of the villagers. Jiji (or perhaps one of her sons) told me that we could construct a house next to that of hers. She appeared to be a title holder to land (as we then found out), which gave her the right to decide so. We discussed this proposition with the village head (nokma), who cautioned us that we should not 'depend on the village for our rice'. When we reassured him that we would buy our rice from the market, he did not object to us staying in the village.

We requested various people if they were willing to construct a house for us, but that proved rather difficult. No one had the time for it, they explained. Thatching grass and wood were scarce, so it would take a lot of effort to obtain these. A long discussion followed, and in the end a group of men offered to build a house that would last for at least a year, for the price of ₹5,000 (about US$125). They did a good job. The house outlasted our entire stay, and after three years it still stood, but was dismantled since people wanted to use the spot on which it was built for something else.

I expected people to get down to building the house straight away, but this was not at all the way it went. The men could only work on our house for one or two days a week, whenever they had some spare time. Dependent on who was available, the size of the party varied from day-to-day, and from week-to-week. To begin with, the men went to a part of the forest that had many different kinds of bamboo. There, they harvested particular kinds of bamboo for distinct parts of the house. I tried my best to help, but it was hard work and I was of little use to them. I could not even carry half their load of bamboo. Then the men collected wood for the pillars and beams of our house. A good part of the bamboo that had been collected would be used as a weave for the walls, and had to be flattened before the actual building could commence. All these preparations took many days, in the course of which we got to know more and more people. It was a good starting point for an extended stay. After several weeks of construction work, the house was finally ready, and we could move into it.

Gaining Relationships

Moving into the house transformed the relationship with Jiji and her relatives. From the first day, the youngest daughter of Jiji, who lived with her, provided me with drinking water and firewood. Notably, the drinking water involved no small effort, since it had to be collected from a well at the bottom of the hill at which the house stood. I asked a granddaughter of Jiji, who lived next door, if she would be willing to help mornings and evenings in the house. She was ten or perhaps twelve years old, which is an age that children are anyway expected to contribute to the running of their household. Every day, she would cook lentils and a vegetable, and later on wash the dishes. We would pay her some money, and provide her with her meals. She readily agreed, and so did her parents.

I used my time in Sadolpara to talk to people, take pictures and so on. Also, I spent many hours a day typing away on my laptop. Obviously, people were curious as to why I was living there. Rather than trying to explain the theoretical framework of my PhD project, I would stick to the much more general (but not inaccurate) statement that I intended to learn about their 'customs and culture' (*niam aro dakbewal*). I tried to explain that I was affiliated to a university, but very few villagers could imagine what such an institution might be about.

At the time, Sadolpara did not have much of a place on the tourist map (there were other villages within which the majority of the people were Songsareks closer to Tura), but its inhabitants were well aware of the importance attached by the townspeople and foreigners to the Garo community religion. Every year, the villagers participated in the annual Wangala dance competition, a festival organized by the government of Meghalaya state. These dances originated as part of the most important annual celebrations of the Garo community religion, and the dance competition as a whole in many ways presents that religion as a main source of 'Garoness'. Villagers were not unaware of the importance that was being attributed to their practices and beliefs of the outside world, and I guess that the interest I expressed in their customs and culture was in line with this.

The villagers were very proud, and would never ask to be given any-thing, even though it was obvious that money provided us with access to a seemingly unending supply of tea, milk, rice, lentils, vegetables and so on. I knew from earlier fieldwork experiences that this could prove to be enormously uncomfortable, so consciously set up an unequal exchange. We agreed with Jiji and her daughter that they would cook our rice. That is, we bought rice (at least 10 kg at a time), or gave them money to buy rice. In return, we received a number of shares of cooked rice twice a day. The amount of rice that came into Jiji's household this way covered our needs as well as those of Jiji and her daughter (compensating them for their cooking effort). In addition, it allowed them to share or lend rice to relatives and neighbours. For Jiji and her relatives it was obvious from the outset that we would leave again, and they made sure never to depend on us in any structural manner.

The granddaughter of Jiji who helped us in the house collected food from us, to have it with her own family. So her family had access to our food as well. In addition, there were the less regulated food exchanges with other people living in the same area of the village. People would offer us eggs, or a bowl of curry. Invariably, we would reciprocate such gestures. Since there was always a more substantial flow of food (and money) from us to the others than the other way round, we did not burden them in this respect. For us, it contributed to being tied in a web of exchange relationships that extended far beyond food.

Our household helpers would never stay for more than a couple of months. When Jiji's granddaughter decided not to work for us anymore, her elder sister volunteered to replace her. After the elder sister followed the daughter of another neighbour, and then again others. That these commit-ments were short lived was not unusual. Every now and then, village youth in search of adventure and an education would go to one of the towns in the Garo Hills (such as Tura). There, they would combine work as a domestic helper with attending school. Very few of these youths stayed on for more than just a couple of months, while they actually had intended to be there for several years. The most common reason for leaving was referred to as *krachaʾa*, which can probably best be translated as 'being ashamed' or 'made to feel ashamed'. My reading is that after some time, they felt humiliated when they had to accept orders from someone who was not a kin-senior to them. It would normally not be a problem to take orders from relatives who are senior in the kinship hierarchy, such as parents, grandparents, uncles, and aunts. However, taking orders from people who are not truly consid-ered kin would for many of the village youth after a while become difficult to accept. Although Jiji projected a kin relationship between me and her, we were not truly kin, and our household helpers would after some time feel uncomfortable with us telling them what to do.

My relationship with Jiji, which had had such a quick start two years ago, continued to be important. She remained very committed to me, and whoever came with me to the village. She was self-confident, witty, helpful, caring, and at the same time able to advance her own interests.

Jiji was a well-respected person in her village, who knew an immense number of people. My affiliation with her and her children and in-laws provided us with a starting point from where to negotiate relationships. During the first couple of months, I often went out with her to meet people. Later on, this happened less, as I had grown confident enough to go out on my own. It was also with Jiji that I attended my first Garo funeral. Funerals were by and large public events, but Jiji was obviously well aware of any sensitivity, and knew where and how she could take me without causing offense.

For close relatives of the deceased, the loss of someone dear had a great impact on their lives. But mortuary rituals were not only attended by close relatives and friends, also by many people for whom it was also, or perhaps primarily, a social occasion. It allowed them to express their position within their social network. For me, it was possible to legitimately attend funerals by being included within this latter group. A death was in itself 'bad' (*namja*), but that did not mean that funerals did not have enjoyable elements as well. Funerals involved a lot of waiting and hanging around, and provided people with an occasion to catch up with friends and relatives. Funerals also implied a relative abundance of food, since close relatives of the deceased had to provide at least one meal to everyone, and if the funeral was hosted by Songsareks, there would be rice beer as well.

Sadolpara had about 1,600 inhabitants. Nearby, that is, within a couple of hours walking distance, were at least 6 other villages with around 200 to 600 inhabitants. Throughout the nearly two years that the fieldwork lasted, I was notified of about 15 deaths. I attended at least eight mortuary rituals. Most people died inside the house where they had lived, usually after a period of prolonged illness. Quite often, given the course an illness had taken, people expected a death to occur. They would gather in the house of the ill person, and provide him or her with water or medicines. Immediately after someone had died, the nearest relatives would wash the dead body, and lay it out in state inside the house. Once this had been done, gunshots were fired, and people would send out messengers to convey the news. Soon after, relatives, friends, and acquaintances would begin to drop in. Funerals lasted normally two days, the dead body being buried or cremated at the end of the first day.

Rather than just attending funerals, I intended to record them on video. For Jiji, my making of video recordings was not at all a problem, which had become clear from our very first encounter. This was also what she communicated to other people, and at funerals I was generally more or less directly allowed to make video recordings. The video recordings became an essential source for the research. They allow for a detailed observation (both visual and auditive) of the events witnessed, and to ask people to clarify what they or others had said, and why certain things were done or avoided.

Sustaining Relationships

Throughout the period that I stayed in the village, I did a lot of work in the house that had been built next to Jiji's. There, the research assistants would work on transcription of the Garo dialogues. It was also there, that local people volunteered to discuss the video material shot, or just dropped in to chat over a cup of tea. Every now and then, I tried to make appointments with people to come over and work with us, but that proved quite difficult. They usually had other, more important things to do. However, our house was located at a crossroads, and many people passed by when they were on their way to somewhere else. Luckily, our house turned into a welcome place to stop, chat, smoke, and drink tea. Dropping in was then a spontaneous decision on the side of the person who did so, and they would generally be very committed to the discussions we had.

Certain people proved to be so resourceful, that they gradually became key informants. One man made himself available day after day, freeing lots of time for us. After many weeks, I decided that I wanted to compensate him for the time he spent with us. After all, if he did not stay with us, he would spend his days working his fields, or earn money as a day labourer. He had an amazing memory, and provided me with the names and kinship designations of an enormous number of people. He could place relationships between people in a historical perspective, providing insights into their economic, social, and ritual dimensions.

After a couple of months in the field, I had collected many hours of video material. Analysis of the tapes took time, and soon a considerable backlog developed. Consequently, we would mostly be working on events that had been videographed months ago. By then, these events had become 'history', and the sorrow that people had felt at the time that a specific mortuary ritual took place had waned. One category for which this did not hold, were widows and widowers, and the parents of deceased children. People actively discouraged them from watching the video recordings, since it was believed to be unfavourable if they would relive the grief and sorrow that they had felt at the time of the funeral. These sort of emotions, when relived, were said to make people vulnerable for diseases and affliction by ancestral ghosts.

Although our relationship with Jiji and her close relatives was the most profound, gradually many other people befriended us as well. Friendship involved sharing time and food, as well as helping each other out whenever that was necessary and possible. If people came to us with requests, which could vary from headaches and infected wounds to the repair of a radio or a ride to town, we tried to accommodate these. I was also regularly asked to loan small sums of money, and much to my surprise, everyone but a single person paid back their debts, without me reminding them even once.

Of course, there was also envy. Garo villages are face-to-face communities, in which people have little choice than to get along with one another. This particularly, since land ownership rests with the resident kin group as a whole, and techniques of agriculture and animal husbandry are such that people have to take joint decisions. No one can do without the co-operation of others, but that does not mean that people do not have their likes and dislikes. Some people talked dismissively about the benefits that Jiji and her relatives had secured by having us residing with them. They mentioned the food that Jiji and all had obtained through us, and the monetary inputs that we provided (which were even by village standards very modest). But then, everyone acknowledged that it had been Jiji and her relatives who had come forward and provided us with a very explicit invitation to stay with them, while other people had at that time been much more reserved.

Conclusion

I don't think that any of the villagers had ever thought that a book might be written on mortuary rituals, or that it might be interesting and worthwhile to videograph these. The analysis of the video recordings, and their use in the research process, resulted in extensive discussions on people's involvement with the mortuary rituals, the activities they engaged in, and the conversations they had. Often, we found that these activities and conversations revealed core principles (*niam raka*), which were not normally formulated. Among the villagers, there was a general consensus that these principles were poorly understood by townspeople (who had lost their connection to the Garo community religion), and even by the village youth (who tended to move towards Christianity, if they were not already Christians).

Most of the people in Sadolpara were illiterate, and those who did read, only read Garo. My PhD thesis is in English (de Maaker, 2006), and they could unfortunately only appreciate the pictures. I have shown the DVD which came with my thesis to the people filmed, as well as to others. The DVD has video recordings of a mortuary ritual, and I feared that people would not like to watch it. However, between the occurrence of the death filmed, and the finalizing of the DVD at least five years had gone by, and the events filmed had become part of their past.

Some of the people among whom I did my fieldwork developed an increased interest in ritual practices, and the kind of explanations that people provide for these. After all, I spent a lot of time talking to old and knowledgeable people (these were also the ones who were more or less granted the authority to do so by the community). And perhaps, my listening to these people, and meticulously writing down what all they had to say, resulted in other people paying more attention to their explanations as well.

My research also had other consequences. It resulted in an increased interest of townspeople in the village. Some of these came to visit us, others were perhaps drawn by the stories that were doing the rounds about us. NEHU's Department of Garo shifted its annual outing to the village in which we resided, which meant that about 50 students and staff would attend the most important of the annual year cycle rituals. Sadolpara gained a name with various state organizations, which led to journalists and foreign tourists dropping in to be guided around. In addition, even more than before, the village came to be used as a set for documentaries and docudramas shot by local TV stations.

The attention that was drawn from the outside world contributed to the early inclusion of the village in projects run by International Fund for Agricultural Development (IFAD), an ambitious scheme funded by the United Nations Development Programme (UNDP). This brought professionals engaged in development work to the village, who have guided people in creation of savings schemes, management of natural resources, creation of a joint agenda for village development and so on. The results of some of these programmes appear positive, but it remains to be seen what their effect will be over an extended period of time.

Over the years, Jiji has shown great hospitality to many of the strange visitors who came to Sadolpara. Her good natured, sincere curiosity made her a natural talent when it came to engaging people. She would never give anyone the feeling that they had to support her in one way or the other, but I know from her stories that many of the visitors did. After all, these visitors saw the relative poverty in which she lived, and felt that they should not take her hospitality for granted.

On the whole, villagers reacted positively to these developments. They appreciated the interest shown in their way of living, laughed about the silliness and clumsiness of the outsiders, and tried to benefit from the visits. Many years later, Jiji told me how she had once received an older couple, he an American and she Japanese. Jiji enacted how the old man and woman had with great difficulty climbed into her house (which has its entrance about 1 m from the ground level). Clearly, it was not the first time that she narrated this story, as the other people listening knew what was coming and laughed their heads off long before she had made her point. Likewise, Jiji told me about a Mumbai-based filmmaker who had stayed for days in a tree hut in order to shoot a herd of marauding wild elephants—that did not show up. In relation to myself, one of her most popular stories was how I had tried to make rice beer, but burned the grains that I had to roast. The rice beer tasted so bad that it had to be thrown away. I take it that the continuing recounting of these sorts of stories, are an expression of what have become lasting relationships.

I, on my part, do not only cherish the memories of the time that we could spend in Sadolpara, but also hope that relationships with its people will continue in the years to come. The writing and films that have come out of the fieldwork, and will most probably continue to emerge over the next couple of years, will hopefully contribute to an appreciation of a rich culture among a broad audience.

References

Bates, Crispin. 1995. Lost Innocents and the Loss of Innocence? Interpreting Adivasi Movements in South Asia. In R.H. Barnes (ed.), *Indigenous Peoples of Asia*, pp. 103–120. Ann Arbor, Michigan: Association of Asian Studies.

Burling, Robbins. 1963/1997. *Rengsanggri: Family and Kinship in a Garo Village*. Tura: Tura Book Room (Original Publication with the University of Philadelphia Press).

Geirnaert-Martin, Danielle C., Erik de Maaker and Dirk J. Nijland. 2007. *Ashes of life: The annual rituals of Laboya, Sumba 1996.* An Ethnographic Multimedia DVD. Göttingen: IWF Knowledge and Media (DVD-video, colour, 277 minutes).

Karlsson, B.G. and T.B. Subba. 2006. *Indigeneity in India.* London: Kegan Paul.

de Maaker, Erik. 2006. *Negotiating Life: Garo Death Rituals and the Transformation of Society.* Ph.D. Dissertation, Leiden University, Leiden.

Marcus, George E. 1995. Ethnography in/of the World System: The Emergence of Multi-sited Ethnography. *Annual Reviews of Anthropology,* 24: 95–117.

Singh, K.S. 2002. *People of India: Introduction.* New Delhi: Oxford University Press.

9

Memories and Reflections on Ethnographic Fieldwork in 'Conflict' Setting

Debojyoti Das

Doing fieldwork in frontiers and borderlands has always been challenging. However, most of the ethnographic projects of the colonial period were sponsored by the imperial states to understand and control native life in their colonies. In the post-decolonization phase, anthropologists got involved in the practice of 'studying backward tribal communities' within newly independent nation-states and were implicated for aiding 'espionage' and 'spying' in the masquerade of anthropological research. Nonetheless, things have changed with the turn of the century, with strong ethical guidelines set by the research ethics communities in United States and Great Britain (AAA, 1973). On the other hand, armed conflicts all over the globe have proliferated and as Jeffrey A. Sluka (1995: 276) rightly observes,

> [A]bout one third of the world countries are currently involved in warfare and two third of the countries routinely resort to human rights abuses as normal aspects of their political process to control their population. it is clear that few anthropologist will be able to avoid conflicting situations and instances of socio-political violence in the course of their professional lives.

Therefore, doing fieldwork in politically disturbed fields means negotiating and surviving from dangers that often come without warning. Anthropological ethics committee in the United Kingdom as elsewhere is unenthusiastic on setting practical guidelines that could defend the interest of anthropologists doing fieldwork. The conventional ethical requirements in anthropology do not speak of the researcher's safety, security, and well-being in violent environments. Anthropologist's well-being is often taken for granted as 'common sense knowledge' in violent field site.

It is this dilemma that I would like to explore by narrating the ethnographer's 'hostage crisis' while doing fieldwork in Nagaland, North-east India by being reflexive on the fieldwork practice. I will also draw on personal experiences of other professional native anthropologists and social scientists working in these perilous field sites. Ethnographers often find themselves caught in the crossfire between the state's armed forces and the rebel guerrilla warlords of borderland of north-east India. Negotiating access in such environment thus becomes critical for conducting successful fieldwork. I will try to show why ethics committees should emphasize on this very aspect of researcher's security in their fieldwork methodology and practice. Similarly as anthropologists we should make serious efforts to negotiate the challenges posed by violent field sites, where the success of ethnography depends on gaining trust of the respondents and study the community at large.

The essay engages with the practice of pursuing ethnography in communities torn by traumatic violence, suspicion, and aura of militarized control juxtaposed with insurrections—'ethno-political' and 'ethno-nationalistic' mobilization in India's North-east frontier state of Nagaland. Here, I am referring to the colonial 'blank space' places of Indo-Burma, which remained as frontier till quite recently. The reference communities are the Nagas and the landscape they inhabit 'Naga Hills' is politically fragmented with interstate boundaries (that act in some ways as an international border that divides the Nagas between India and Burma). The colonial and post-colonial state interventions in Naga life since 1860s were marked by people's resistance to colonial administration and thus began an era of armed conflict between the Nagas and the Indian state post 1947. Their political demand for self-rule has produced decades of violent rebellion and guerrilla warfare with the state police and paramilitary forces.

My 14 months fieldwork during 2008–2009 among the *Yimchunger* Naga tribe who inhabit the Tuensang district close to the Saramati mountain range, carry salient memories of doing fieldwork in a trouble torn borderland. On paper the Naga nationalist and underground groups had declared cease-fire with the government, however on the ground everyday crime, arson, taxation, vandalism, street harassment, factional clashes, drug trafficking, and suspect killing are common, threatening life and security of people in villages and remote areas. The multiple check gates of the police and the paramilitary force in all district headquarters and even at the entry point of many sensitive villages makes mobility difficult for people and terrorizes everyday life. On my part, I had to constantly show my Inner Line Permit (ILP) to prove that I had permission to travel and stay in the district.

My interest to conduct ethnography in the Naga Hills developed in 2006 when I submitted my MPhil in Science Policy at the Jawaharlal Nehru University, New Delhi, and was applying for a PhD programme abroad. I was spellbound by a lecture delivered by Professor Emeritus P.S. Ramakrishnan in Environment Science Department on the project Nagaland Environment Protection and Economic Development Project (NEPED) that he was initially part of, but had remained unevaluated in Nagaland. His eloquent understanding of the development practice in Nagaland fostered my interest in the project. Before embarking on my doctoral research, I had conducted a short reconnaissance of my field site in 2007. I had been to Kohima, the state capital of Nagaland and had spent a good time in a small hotel and met few people who were on deputation in the project.

Streets would desert early in the evening and the roads would become dark, with markets shutting down before dusk. Inmates in the hotel were particularly advised not to come out of the hotel premises after dark. Occasionally drunk men would squabble in the streets just facing my hotel room, break glasses, while speeding police vehicles would run in the veins of residences. The aura of fear and tension was reflected in people's everyday talk. In the hotel room, messages were circulated that unofficial checking would be carried out by student unions and police to verify people because of which they had to carry their Inner Line Pass. People who failed to produce their pass were picked up in trucks and handed over to the police, sometimes detained and tortured. Almost all of these 'terror talks' seemed to me as hearsay but some people gave oral testimony, that in the past they witnessed such violence. I came back from the field with memories of despair and confusion on how to conduct fieldwork in such perilous and high-risk environment.

If we look back at the post-independence context of state administration in the Naga Hills, the Nagas were put behind a security cordon by the Indian state and any outsider doing research on the Nagas was closely monitored. During the summer of 1970s Christopher Von Furer-Haimendorf (who conducted his fieldwork in 1938), was granted permission to visit his field site as a state guest for a month. Furer-Haimendorf writes in his private papers about the confusion and fear that existed when he revisited Nagaland. Reading his unpublished papers and notes I got the impression that he had by then taken a neutral stand on the Naga issue and disassociated with the political question. I had the extraordinary privilege to live and work among the *Yimchunger* Nagas being an Indian national and a person who was born and brought up in North-east India, with little social capital in the form of networks I had developed with my Naga friends since childhood in school and later at the undergraduate level at college.

At the School of Oriental and African Studies (SOAS) during my PhD coursework in Anthropology, I was made aware of research ethics as I read through volumes of books on ethical requirements in Anthropology. The ethical guidelines as I realized reading the literature had become stringent ever since the discipline came under condemnation for being a conduit of American neo-imperialism. Anthropologist's engagement as spies during the Vietnam War and their involvement in espionage in Latin America had brought to limelight the ethics in ethnological fieldwork and questioned the very inner working of Anthropology as a discipline (Berreman, 1968). The crisis in Anthropology is very well summed by Levi Strauss as, 'Anthropology is a daughter to [an] era of violence' (1966: 126). The increasing ethical misconduct demanded stringent regulation that would restore academic faith in the discipline. Out of this crisis has emerged a strong ethical guideline set by the American Anthropological Association (AAA) soon after the disclosure of Project Camelot—the massive US government sponsored counterinsurgency research project (see especially Glazer, 1970; Horowitz, 1967, for a good discussion on Project Camelot). In South-east Asia, these controversies have continued with time. Central Intelligence Agency (CIA) involvement in covert military and counterinsurgency activities in Thailand for example in the early 1970s has led to some restriction on research activities and a five year embargo on publications and results coming from Chiang Mai's Tribal Research Institute (Hinton, 2002; Wakin, 1998; Wolf and Jorgensen, 1970). Similarly, the Himalayan Border Countries Project engaged many anthropologists to gather strategic information on border life and practices of mountain communities (Berreman, 1973).

In response to these revelations and as attempts for retrospection over the years, both the American and the British anthropological fraternity have evolved with strong ethical guidelines and codes of conduct based on informed consent, respect for traditional institution, responsibilities towards future research, legal approval by host nations and so on. In the United Kingdom the academia has perhaps gone a step further. The Economic and Social Research Council (ESRC) required a full documentation of fieldwork notes for any post-doctoral application. Similarly, graduate researchers are accountable for keeping all records of their fieldwork in their home archives, to produce as value for defence if ever prosecuted. Any objections or complaints registered by the respondent (participants in research) could easily jeopardize the researcher's career in academics. The checks and balances, however, talk scantily of guidelines or prescriptions that would look at the researcher's well-being, and assess under which conditions researchers perform their field study. People organizing fieldwork in violent environment are the most affected lot, as often the ethical guidelines bring ethical dilemmas by prescribing 'ideal peace time fieldwork environment' and the scientific idea of maintaining neutrality in research. Within the university system in Britain the usual practice is to gain consent from the researcher, on a fieldwork application form. The researcher has to confirm whether he is safe in the environment where he is going to conduct fieldwork. The application reads like this;

> The candidates should declare whether there are any issues that threaten physically or mentally while in the field.[1]

While most researchers involving risk to life commit to such regulation on a voluntary basis, they undermine the cost of the dangers and uncertainties prevailing in the field. If certain trade-off and risk are not undermined during research in politically charged and conflict zones, it would become an ethnographer's nightmare. Moreover, given the contemporary political scenario, with more than 120 'armed conflicts [globally], it is clear that few anthropologists will be able to avoid conflict situations and instances of socio-political violence in the course of their professional lives' (Nordstrom and Martin, 1992: 15). In the British anthropological tradition, the consent is arrived between the PhD adviser and the researcher planning to embark on fieldwork. However, there are no guidelines on how researchers cope with unexpected circumstances in the field. When flexibility in research guidelines means a breach of research ethics there is very little room left to conduct 'ethically pure' and 'scientifically detached' ethnographic research. Anthropology is perhaps the most intricate fieldwork based discipline that throws up unique challenges to questions of morality, ethics, and subject position (agency and reflexivity). In the 21st century with growing concerns on bio-piracy, informed consent, photographing indigenous community has attained such critical sensitivity that often the concerns of the researcher's well-being is predisposed and never given a serious thought. These issues are seen as too complex, generic to the anthropologists' field site to be addressed under a broad framework of 'ethics in research'. This brings forth the need to explore the contextual dimension of what it is like engaging in ethnography in violent environment, in communities that live in perpetual fear and where violence, lawlessness, and state's panoptic vigilance has become a recipe of everyday life.

Working with Complexity: The Dangers of Doing Research and Meddling with Ethics

While doing coursework in Anthropology I was made fully conscious of research ethics. The research methodology course was tailored to inform students with illustrative reading list on ethical issues, research methods, and methodological guidelines to conduct fieldwork. However, these guidelines and framework of fieldwork were quite silent and naïve to address questions of violence, insecurity, and the practical day-to-day encounter of researchers with their subjects in insecure field situation. It was often presumed to be 'common sense'. Nonetheless, in the past two decades this question has gained some attention when discussion started surrounding an unpublished paper on 'Occupational Safety and Health in Anthropology', 1986, where Nancy Howell for the first time flagged ethnographers' attention to the need to discuss the issue of personal dangers involved in doing research. Howell appealed for a practical piece of research that would produce a comprehensive survey of occupational safety and health hazard which was quickly accepted by the AAA. Her expended work was published as AAA special report titled 'Surviving Fieldwork' in 1990.

The study evaluates over 80 separate variables, from sunburn experience, robbery, venereal disease, and stinging ants to frostbites, arrest, malarial, and military attack. It proved to be a compelling data on human hazard very difficult to quantify—suspicion of espionage, acute conflict, political turmoil, and other risks—since there have been scanty attempts to explore the debate on ethics and fieldwork dilemmas in hazardous and perilous environment. As Kovarts-Bernat has argued,

> [W]e continue to do research in increasingly hostile and dangerous regions, the very real possibility of victimization in the field presents a challenge not just to the practicalities of personal safety but also to the ethnographic method and ethics that we are retrofitting for use in cultures in which ordinary inter-relations and social institutions are overshadowed by unrest, instability, and fear. Even exposure to low intensity repression or harassment over a course of research threatens to adversely affect the ways in which we approach the field and interpreted social phenomena within it. (Kovarts-Bernat, 2002: 208)

In South Asia like elsewhere, there has been very little attention paid, if any, to the trials and tribulation of doing fieldwork. With the exception of Srinivas et al. (1972), pioneering volume on *The Fieldworker and the Field* (1979/1991, 2002) and some other works by Nita Kumar (1992), Panini (1991), Thapan (1998), Lobo (1990), Shrivastav (1991), there are no other significant texts, which discuss this very crucial issue within the discipline— 'self reflexivity'. The problem that arises in performing fieldwork in violent and politically charged environment is more an epistemological one. The questions that unsettle my mind while reflecting back on my fieldwork practice were: How do anthropologists cope with the ethical requirements of scientific neutrality in 'abnormal'-dangerous field sites? What are the moral dilemmas surrounding individual's 'subject position' that confront anthropological research in such uncertain fields? And, what kind of methodological and ethical issues emerge from the practice of a research collecting fieldwork data in a chaotic and dangerous situation? I will explore these questions and the risks that encounter anthropological research in hazardous and violent fieldwork situation.

Once in the field (Nagaland), I was overwhelmed with similar dilemmas that I had experienced during the short visit to Nagaland before my research began. The field was riddled not only with dangerous stories of how outsiders are treated but also there was a general suspicion towards research. As one individual expressed, 'outsiders come and misrepresent our culture, tradition, and write whatever they like and wish to write'. His claim seemed reasonable to me as most of the writings on the Nagas by Indian writers have been based on secondary research and without much fieldwork. The writings take a nationalistic tone. Even colonial ethnographic work carried out by administrator anthropologists such as J.P. Mills and J.H. Hutton— the most prolific among colonial civil servants—often misrepresented Naga culture, customs, and traditions, by presuming certain cultural truths as presenting 'the savage other'. Abraham Lotha (2007: 7) highlights how Mills misrepresented a *Lotha Naga* tradition that has been amended from his monograph *The Lotha Nagas* quite recently after a public declaration by the Lotha elders (*hoho*). The latest reprint of *The Lotha Nagas* comes with an amendment, published by the Directorate of Art and Culture, Government of Nagaland. Similarly, other scholars in recent years working on Naga culture have faced impeachment and were punished with fines for misrepresenting local culture and custom. Some researchers got away with paying for a feast arranged for the whole village while others had to offer animals for sacrifice. These worries also lurk in my research. Colonial official representations of the Nagas were products of authoritarian knowledge of the white master and the Nagas had little knowledge to resist. In the contemporary context people read their ethnographies and make sense of the 'misrepresentation of Naga culture' and register their protest. In fact, for many elderly Naga Nation Workers (ex-Naga National Council activist) whom I interviewed during the course of my fieldwork these manuscripts produced by colonial administrator anthropologist carry the only written history of the Nagas. But, they have come under critical scrutiny because of the various misrepresentation and misconceptions that emerge while understanding the history through oral narrative, folklore, and trick star. As Sluka (1990: 114) observes that 'there is always the possibility of dangerous cultural misunderstanding arising between researchers and subjects. Yet in the existing literature on methodology, almost no mention is made on the various dangers inherent in many if not all fieldwork situations.'

In the field I was challenged with proving my identity. My racial features that resembled Aryan traits often disappointed villagers who memorialized the dead and remembered the crimes committed by the Indian armed forces in the Naga villages in 1950s. The post Indian independence decades saw violent resistance and deployment of the military to quell Naga national sentiments. The soldiers who were engaged in subverting violence and counterinsurgency operations were mostly from north India regiments. Daily patrol and raids were common to nap Naga nationalist (Naga National Council [NNC]) workers who had gone underground. Similarly, since 1956, villages were regrouped to isolate the rebels from the public. This led to mass massacres and villagers retreated to the forest. Often the general practice was to burn granaries that would starve the whole village. The post-independence government adopted the colonial official tactics adopted by the frontier administration to punish trans-frontier Naga who were head hunting and slave takers.

A senior retired schoolmaster, NNC well wisher whom I visited during the early days of my fieldwork, was sceptical on my entry to his house in Mezoma village. He jokingly said 'are you from north India. The north Indian army people who raided our village in the 1950s were very bad. They killed, raped, and destroyed our people. We were terrorized by your people.' Our successive encounter made him feel more relaxed and happy as he realized that I had roots in the region and that he had mistaken my identity as a north Indian Hindi speaker. The other experiences in the field were equally interesting. Once a tour operator in Khonoma village explained that people from mainland India visit their village as spies. He narrates the story of a south Indian tourist who came with his Tata Safari jeep and stayed over in the village for couple of days. His suspicion grew, as he was constantly interested in exploring the workings of the underground groups rather than his initial interest in Naga culture. Similar stories were narrated by villagers who encountered freelance journalists, media people, and seasoned travelogue writers and backpackers, who behaved unusually in the eyes of the villagers. In one encounter, a village bird watcher, again a tour operator from an Angami village in Kohima explained that outsiders come and steal their 'bio-diversity'. He explained that they seldom take the permission of the Village Council before entering the village and do whatever they want. He was hinting at the new economic opportunity provided by 'bird watching' in the village nature conservation site that had become a contested terrain of interest for tour operators and guides from the village and outside who were the obvious beneficiaries of 'green village' project in Khonoma. The entry of outsiders with differing purposes and intentions made my defence precarious.

My claim as an anthropologist doing research on Naga farming practice gave rise to enthusiasm as well as doubts. There were angles of bio-piracy that were raised by certain people. Few years back an Australian anthropologist had conducted his fieldwork in one of my initial field sites, Khonoma village. After he left from the field there were rumours mongering surrounding his fieldwork practice. He was hosted by a respected villager in Khonoma and had carried out Global Positioning System (GPS) survey in the village, to map its vegetation and resources, particularly land use. When he left the village people started complaining about his presence. Some of the respondents whom I interviewed claimed that he never shared his information. Everybody acknowledged that he was a great researcher as he had put his best efforts to understand the practice of farming in Khonoma, getting down to the paddy fields and overcoming leech bites to succeed in his scientific experiments. He bothered least about the hardships he undertook to accomplish his scientific experiments. However, he never disclosed his research findings with the villagers who hosted him and gave him all logistical support for his anthropological and ecological research. This secrecy annoyed many villagers who complained about his clandestine behaviour. Majority of the villagers tarnished his image as a pirate of local knowledge excepting the people who hosted him. He was supported under a transnational conservation and livelihood programme. Hence, villagers did not dare to speak much about him during the project phase.

In Tuensang district, where I conducted most of my fieldwork, there were stories of repeated short visits by German and Swiss museum ethnologists, curators, travelogue writers, freelance anthropologists, graduate researchers, and backpackers—all interested in anthropology but were entering the field in the guise of tourists. In the last decade the interest in Naga ethnography has seen a new high with a renewed interest in Haimendorf's visual ethnography of the 1940 and a series of curator exhibitions carried out in the west particularly in mainland Europe and London. Tourists are reinventing Naga customs and traditions in the era of ceasefire. The Ministry of Tourism and the Department of Art and Culture host annual programmes in December called the 'Hornbill festival' to celebrate the Naga Culture that attracts international tourist to promote its own brand of cultural tourism highlighting 'unity in diversity'. A new arena where tourism has gained popularity in Nagaland is 'bird watching' because of sustainable eco-tourism initiatives mostly undertaken by international tourists, Indian ecologists, and bird watchers.

Frequent short trips made by international scholars with the aim to record Naga oral history and those undertaking visual ethnography documenting social change in the Naga society have come to be looked with suspicion by the local communities. Many of my respondents suspected that these good hearted and benevolent tourist researchers would take their portrait and do business back home. In Upper Konyak village of Sanyou, that has become the symbol of Naga tourism with the iconic Chief's hut that lies at the boundary of India and Burma, local people are not eager even to be photographed. As one tour operator narrated people demand good money for taking their photograph. This has primarily happened because of the lack of reciprocity. While tourists come and extract local produce they do not give anything in return except breaching trust and goodwill.

Violence over the years has emerged as a norm in Nagaland. However, the context of violence and the ways it is produced by the state, military, development organizations, pressure groups, and underground factions needs empirical intervention to understand its implication on the overall psychology of the public. The critical stands taken by the people against the state, their narratives of violence, and the violent talk were rooted in the personal experiences and memories of the past and the ceasefire environment of the contemporary present. One enterprising Angami villager in Vesema village in Kohima district stated that their life has become more miserable, stressed in hardship, and uncertainty during the decade of everlasting ceasefire. His only wish was to end the ceasefire. These narratives give accounts of the amount of uncertainties people were experiencing in the area. A few months later, I was also to encounter a violent episode under the low intensity velvet of ceasefire.

Ethical Guidelines

Stories narrated till now reflect that in Nagaland past ethnographers have flaunted and abused ethical requirements. In light of limited access to the field and the strict security check imposed on the fieldwork, researchers have resorted to fast-track often piecemeal visual ethnography, that has produced shallow ethnographic details and eroticized representation of Nagas through mediums such as under-researched coffee table books sold at travel bookstores in Europe and America. The repercussions of these insensitivities have also been disastrous leading to breach of trust and crisis in individual research work. Given the background of the past intervention it brings me to a dual dilemma of protecting the interest of respondents as well as working in perilous field environment that also enshrines protecting oneself from the dangers of fieldwork. Both the military and the factional rebel groups pose tantalizing danger towards the collection of information and the performance of ethnography.

In the next section, I will adopt a narrative style to communicate the memories of my fieldwork experience from the time I entered the field. Second, I will describe the hostage crises and the bricolage of information that I had put together months after, that helped me in reconstructing my ethnography of violent encounter and the lessons I learnt. The final act will be to understand how we make sense of participant observation when the evidence is gathered months after the events had taken place? Interconnecting these propositions, I reflect upon the practical and common sense measures I undertook to minimize the risk and the lessons learnt in the field.

On 18 March, while travelling from Kohima to Dimapur, as a regular check on the National Highway Number 39, I was stopped by the Indian Reserve Police (IRP) *jawans* (soldiers) because of the material I was carrying in my bag. I had just attended a history conference in Kohima Science College and was carrying the programme list along with the abstract of papers. As the paramilitary persons glanced through these documents they were suspicious of me carrying vital documents perhaps information linked to the rebel groups. For most of my field notes I used pseudonyms and often camouflaged the locations and villages where I conducted fieldwork. After a long look at my papers and hand written notes the cab was allowed to go. Other passengers in the cab were staring at me as a suspect. Similar embarrassing incident happened at police check gates while passing from one district headquarter to another in Nagaland State Transport (NST) buses. Harassments and demands for petty bribes were common, despite holding proper documents and permits that allowed me to travel all over the state. Such troubles were quite common and it always made me feel like a trespasser, on an espionage mission.

In the streets and bazaars such panoptic vigilance often interrupted my mobility. I remember while withdrawing money from an ATM (Automatic Teller Machine) in Kohima, a stranger who had queued up for cash withdrawal requested me to show him the PhD thesis I was carrying. He soon became glued to the thesis and started cross-questioning me. Finally I had to explain to him that the thesis does not belong to me and he should contact the author of the thesis in Nagaland University. The reader was an Angami and he expressed that he did not like the explanation of their history given by an Ao scholar who had no right to speak on Angami culture. I politely ended the confusion by giving him the address of the teacher from whom I borrowed the book. The matter was temporarily relieved.

These experiences greatly influenced my ethnography as I became conscious of the ground reality and it made me think twice before saying, writing, or recording the events I witnessed in the field. People with whom I interacted were welcoming. My ethnic identity often doubted my host and he thought that I had not come with good intentions. The 'identity' formation of an 'outsider' a plain non-tribal population has been memorialized in people's mind through the brutalities carried out by the armed forces and the common sense of exploitation and misrepresentation of the Nagas in Indian academic writings. Often my rescue point was my association with SOAS and at times my native place Shillong. On one hand people were pleased to share information with a person from a UK university but there was also rumour mongering that why should a person travel such long distance just to know about us.

But the major challenge came in the later part of my fieldwork when I established my base in a village in Tuensang district that was considered by the Nagas of Kohima and Mokokchung as backward places where underdeveloped Naga tribes lived.[2] My interest in these colonial unadministered Nagas grew after I met a member of the *Yimchunger* community while I was returning from Tuensang town to Kohima in the middle of January 2009. The young lad was an energetic arts graduate and worked as Facilitator of Community Conservation (FCC) at the Nagaland Environment Protection and Economic Development (NEPED) through People's Action Department. As my initial ethnographic interest linked me to the inner working of the NEPED programme in Nagaland, the FCC was an important link in my fieldwork. On his invitation I travelled to the land of the *Yimchunger* Nagas that lay nearly 300 km away from the state capital (Kohima) close to the Indo-Myanmar Border few days after I reached Kohima town.

Research in a Dangerous Setting

To many of my colleagues, friends, and relatives, me going to Nagaland itself appeared to be an act of bravery, adventure, or foolishness. While this attitude was largely the result of the media-based and common perceptions of people about Nagaland in mainland India but I was more intrigued by what my Naga friends and well-wishers told me about eastern Nagaland. They saw it as a misadventure given my status as an outsider, someone who had come from London to do research on the unadministered Nagas of colonial times. To many of my Naga friends these were the 'wild spaces' where people still practised *jhum* (slash and burn) cultivation, wore less cloth, and were less civilized. My cultural network would bring in hardship. They instead suggested me to conduct ethnography in a nearby village close to the town where commutation would have been easy and life would be safe. But I had already promised my *Yimchunger* friend that I shall visit his native village and he seemed to be eagerly waiting for my arrival. The dangers that I would encounter were already in my mind and they were encrypted when my supervisor and I discussed on the ethic form that was submitted prior to my departure from London.

After returning back from the field when I looked back at the colonial archives in British Library, I felt euphoric that I was one of the few fortunate people who got the opportunity to study the *Yimchunger* Nagas. Before me J.H. Hutton conducted his trans Dikou tour into the territory of Kolyo-Kongan Nagas in 1923. The details of his tours and visit to *Yimchunger* villages appear in *Dairies of Two Tours in the Unadministered Area East of the Naga Hills* (1929). Following him J.P. Mills, the Deputy Commissioner of Naga Hills and a prolific writer on the Nagas conducted extensive tour in 1936–1937. During this period of insurgency and Naga independence movement (1950–1960) for self-determination a number of tours were conducted by the Political Officers of the North Eastern Frontier Agency (NEFA) administration who were working for tribal welfare. Chiefly among them were Major Kathing, Verrier Elwin, and Bal Bahadur Rai who produced confidential Tour Reports of their pacification and reconnaissance tours. They were kept secret and are classified documents in the National Archives, too sensitive to attract the attention of Human Rights Organization. These Tour Reports besides describing the life and culture of the people are classic records of how violence was produced by government forces engaged in counterinsurgency operations and intelligence gathering.

The annual tours were used as 'governmental' tactics to warn the Naga villagers from facilitating the reactionary forces. Villages were segregated and regrouped for night vigilance. Young men from regrouped villages were recruited as Village Scouts to defend villages where government sympathizers and peddlers outnumbered the rebels. Forced labour was imposed by law as punishment for helping hostiles. Development grants and assistance were selectively rewarded to government followers and political agents— *Dobashis* as well as government servants (particularly agricultural demonstrators and village level workers). The other objectives of the frontier administration were to sedentarize and territorialize Naga settlements by grouping villages and through demonstration of wet terrace rice technologies. Nagas practised slash and burn farming and were highly mobile and often invisible in state 'hostile management'.

The objective was to quell violence by creating an aura of terror by touring villages that had information of hosting rebels. The annual patrols were primarily geared to educate people of the rebel activities and to warn them of bitter consequences if found guilty of hosting rebels. Many villages were burnt to the ground on the suspicion that they were hosting rebel leaders. The paranoia continued till a settlement was reached in 1961 with the NNC leaders and the birth of Nagaland as a new state within the Indian federation. Even since then there has been a low-intensity warfare between the Naga underground factions and the government paramilitary troops (Assam Rifles) and the Nagaland Armed Police (NAP) including the Indian Reserve Police (IRP).

I entered the field at a time of peace. However, peace was only on paper. During the long time span of 14 months while I was pursuing my fieldwork of which a significant part was spent in archives, travelling and in dedicated participant observation, the aura of fear and insecurity was felt at every moment. Visit to village was at first facilitated by the local FCC. After travelling to a randomly picked up village I stayed with a family which was politically influential. The village was close to the sub-divisional headquarter and was overlooked by the Assam Rifles camp. The village was well-connected with memorable *kacha* (non-black topped) roads build just before the 2003 elections. There was also a footpath that connected the government school in the town to the village. There was a network of small roads that connected the town with the village and the village with the surrounding settlements. During my first day in the village I saw villagers engaged in a road building project that would connect the village settlements with the stone hill from where they collected stones for the burial memorial for the village symmetry. Most of the settlements were beneficiaries of the

Indira Awaas Yojna (IAY), under which two bundles of corrugated galvanized iron (CGI) tin roof sheets were provided to the villagers to build their house. The village looked pretty clean. Pigs were restricted within the household failing which the village council and the students union imposed fine on the trespassers. Every shop in the village was registered with a valid license and prohibited to sell tobacco-flavoured betel nut (*ghutka*). Yet, the sale of *ghutka* through informal means was rampant. It was mandatory on the part of the student union to impose a symbolic fine on the sellers of *ghutka* whom they knew very well. Occasionally, the village was visited by armed guards who would have tea and lunch in my host's kitchen and talk for hours. Often they were curious to know about my research.

One faithful evening as I was returning from my usual household survey from the lower *khel* of the village, my interpreter, the village headman's son, and me, nearly confronted an alcoholic who had chased him to his house last night. These unidentified men annually collected ransom from the villagers, circulated demand notes and were violent at night. We scarcely missed their uncanny eye and ran off fast in the dark. The village had banned the drinking of local beer at its golden jubilee year celebration in 2008. Nonetheless some villagers still continued with the practice of making beer. It is in these huts where the villagers interested in evening leisure and occasional squabble mixed with town gangsters and occasional rebel soldiers who visited on their official duties of reconnaissance and information gathering. Their secret visit to villages on reconnaissance was a normal annual event. These visits were followed up by the Assam Rifles men who gathered information about the mobility of underground factions. The danger of clashes and tribal feuds under the cease-fire environment was ever present. It just needed an ignition.

I recorded stories of violent clashes in the past between the government forces and the rebel groups. In 1993, the village was turned into a battle-ground between the government forces and the rebels who had taken shelter. On the tip off from a local villager the Assam Rifles platoon launched a sudden attack and killed one underground member in the village, while the rest managed to escape. The village headman's son took me around the village to show bullet punctures in electric post symbolizing the violent encounter. Following that encounter the rebel leaders circled village elders and insulted them by exposing their bottoms for passing information to the military. The stories narrated by one of the village Gaun Burrah (GB) were full of sorrow.

The *Yimchungers* have been in news in recent years because of the ethnic cleansing that took place within the tribe. Head *Dobashi* of Shamature town explained to me that the *Tikhirs* are our brothers and sisters, our neighbours poison them out of jealousy, so they become venomous. Since the 1980s, the *Yimchunger* Nagas have been involved in an ethnic struggle to establish their pan-*Yimchunger* identity. The *Yimchunger* identity was challenged by the *Tikhirs* who claimed for a separate underdeveloped backward tribal status. The *Yimchunger–Tikhir* conflict reached its peak in late 1990s when there were violent clashes between the two groups supported by their local guerrilla extremist. The *Yimchunger–Tikhir* conflict, as many Nagas argue, emerged out of the cultural inferiority complex that *Tikhirs* had and is interceded by the politics of the state. The *Yimchungers* emerged as the major beneficiary in government programmes and employment schemes. Although the *Yimchungers* have been shown as a separate linguistic identity, they were never recognized as a separate sub-tribe of the Nagas under the Indian constitution. The political turmoil in Shamatur subdivision, headquarters of the *Yimchunger* pitched hard in recent years with violent clashes between the two groups.

In my study, in village Leangkangru every villager was armed with 0.2 rifles. Prosperous household owned multiple guns. These guns were locally manufactured in the village, by the village blacksmith who manufactured the Naga machete and nobody carried a license for their use. Guns were also household assets. According to my household survey they were assets for mortgage. They were most commonly used for hunting wild animals during peacetime. Guns had replaced bows, arrows, and spears that were previously used by the Nagas in their resistance with the British. Local politicians (MLAs) were one of the main suppliers of *Cartoos* (ammunition) to households as a part of their patronage politics. Village party workers constantly received packets of bullets as gifts from the party leader. During elections, the villages are transformed into a battleground between rival political affiliations. I was informed that foreign liquor, guns, and money were the main things in circulation during election fever. I deliberately avoided the 2009 parliamentary election month not staying in the village, as it was reported to have been too dangerous.

Life in the village was networked towards new development schemes and projects. Influential village people from the Village Development Board and the Village Council would explain me the schemes and the new crops introduced in the village in their fields. They also highlighted the need for more agri-link road and better marketing facilities of their agricultural commodities. A massive central aid under the Department of Underdeveloped Areas (DUDA) programme and an ingenious community driven development in the guise of new legislation like the 'Nagaland Communitization of Institution and Public Services Act 2002' had brought in new power dynamics in Naga Villages (Angami, 2008: 31–38). Jealousy, greed, clan ego, corruption, and *Khel* groupings based on lineage and political affiliations were emerging and were part of people's back talk in their drawing room and in private gatherings.

Some were extremely happy with the new arrangements while others were completely unsettled with the unfolding situation that empowered some while marginalized others. The Mahatma Gandhi National Rural Employment Guarantee Scheme (MGNREGS) that provided 100 days employment to the village was in full swing with the construction of the village road. The village was divided into *Khels* (wards) for this job and job cards were distributed unequally. Some 25 job cards were yet to be distributed as the construction came to an end in June 2009. Villagers complained, argued, and quarrelled on the gross mismanagement and corruption in the distribution of funds and every village institution from the village Church to the Village Council were deeply implicated with the mismanagement. The links were also connected higher up in the bureaucracy. In the surrounding remote villages, jobs were taken by contractors and village intermediaries, the powerful Village Council members and the Village Development Board Chairman. Work was completed by bulldozers bypassing the beneficiaries. When some knowledgeable outsiders visiting the villagers made them aware of the Right to Information Act (RTI) villagers were terrorized with severe consequences by the council and the head GB (village headman) who controlled the village. Many people like my host who had previously a say in the local administration of the village appealed to the Additional Deputy Commissioner (ADC) for internal audit of various schemes in the village, but their petitions fell to deaf ears.

During my stay in the village the local factions made two reconnaissance visits and each time they demanded food grain to sustain the marching party. This march was followed up by the Assam Rifles *jawans* (soldiers) with their commanding officers who visited to gather information of militant mobility and insurgent activity in the area. During peace times as the villagers stated there were annual visits by the army, so were the visits of underground groups, restricted towards the realization of annual tax. Nonetheless, rogue people would often visit the village carrying pistols inside their shawl and would demand the village headman to pay cash. Often their threats were averted in villages where the council stood strong. In other villages people often submitted to these splinter rouge underground militias.

My engagement under such circumstances was difficult and strange. I chose to live with powerful, the most respected families in the village.

The choice though obviously carried certain disadvantage which was practical to the ground realities. In the neighbouring villages that I visited I would usually stay with the village pastor, in his house. Pastors were not questioned by the villagers too often. I also attended the village Sunday service and enthusiastically participated in the Church programmes and was slowly exposed to the inner working of the Church. It generated trust among the community. After a couple of months, the Village Women Leader one day smilingly replied, 'You have now become a member of our *Yimchunger* family'. These supports were built upon months of intense negotiations and struggle to fit into the local complexities. Often I travelled with my hosts' children, his brothers, or distance cousins, who were attuned to the morphology of the village, the clan dynamics within the village, and different shades of people.

I also developed good rapport with the village headman's son who was also a respected citizen of the village and the members of the village student union, who in numerous encounters made me understand the local complexities of land relations and farming. My friendship with the Village Citizen President, a body established by the Baptist Church, was crucial as he had extended patronage with the village people from all ranks. These associates were helpful in reducing the risk inside the village from getting hurt, while the danger of travelling between villages was still a big question. As I got mesmerized with individual life testimonies of people narrating their origin stories, I felt the need to travel to their origin village to reconstruct the migration flow and changing social relations. However, here in lay the danger. My attempts to visit *Tikhir* dominated village were shattered by reports of violence and rumour-mongering. Several plans to visit a nearby village that had been hostile to surrounding *Yimchunger* village had to be altered and finally cancelled. However, I managed to visit other *Yimchunger* dominated village to record the migration history to my study village and how migrants and hosts redistributed land to produce complex land rights in the village. The contemporary land use has a direct impact on people's livelihood and land relations.

In a neighbouring *Yimchunger* village, *Tikhir* villagers were engaged in ambushing visiting *Yimchunger* villagers by poisonous arrows that were kept hidden on the village pathway to harm unknown guest. These terror conditions were quite common which changed my mind for good. Safety and security of me and my co-workers (guides) were the top priority. As part of the reconciliation effort between the two villages (study village and the origin village) during my fieldwork, the *Tikhir* village Church Pastor was invited to the study village Church association to participate in one of their Sunday service. These efforts were few and far between to deescalate the tension that had been implanted in people's heart and were claiming human lives.

Besides ethnic difference and growing hostility between the *Yimchunger* and *Tikhir* dominated areas, the village itself was on the brink of a split between the Baptist majority and a Catholic microscopic minority. For many to convert to what they qualified as 'Roman' Catholicism was a 'sin', undesirable in the true Baptist spirit. In fact the first Catholic Church that was set up in the village a few years back had to be withdrawn under public and Baptist Association's pressure. Today the village is divided between a Catholic *khel* (ward) and a Baptist *khel*. The Baptists and the Catholics have a sublime relationship as their interests often clash. Conducting ethnography in such a sensitive environment demanded empathizing with each subject position. In their private talks the Baptist pastor would complain against the town parish, while the Church father would highlight the lack of accountability between the Baptist. These competing narratives often complimented to the fears I already inhabited. To de-escalate the politically and emotionally charged conversation I often diverted my discussions to practical concerns of daily life that pastors and fathers faced in their monastic life. The art of gaining access to the inner working of the Church with its followers was crucial towards understanding land relations and the tributes paid to the Church, that now sanctified farming and fertility, which regulated the crop calendar and labour distribution through free man days. Understanding the politics of the Church became crucial towards reflection on land relations and their ties of patronage within the village.

Negotiating 'Exceptional Circumstances'

Often the fieldwork complexity may blow out of proportion, and at that time it is common to manoeuvre strategies that meets the practical needs of the researcher. Thus it is important to survive the fieldwork by adopting a plan that would protect one from being shot (Leopold, 2005: 16). This often could mean manoeuvring the methodological premises and ethics of research. The ethical guidelines have been archived to suit a social context scientifically weighed and rationally ordered towards an emic understanding about the field's site and its cultural agents (Kovats-Bernat, 2002). Thus these ideal conditions do not exist in dangerous fields and one is forced to engage with manoeuvring the risk of violating ethical guidelines at the same time protecting one's life and limb.

The contradictions have not yet been addressed in the discipline's core discourse but it does not stop field researchers from innovating to an acceptable limit. Phillippe Bourgois (1991/2007) has argued more provocatively on the question of 'ethical exceptionalism' within anthropology that has kept its professionals 'cozy' away from the arena of politics. This has affected the ethnographer and his respondent to make meaningful shifts and practice innovative methods that would mean a radical transformation of both the ethnographic method and the anthropological ethics. The subject has been considered before with relative unaccomplished debates within the discipline. The problem that dangerous fields pose to ethnographic ethics have been addressed by Nash (1976) and Jenkins (1984) and more recently and radically by Bourgois (1990). There has apparently been very little discussion on the ethical dilemmas that researchers confront in violent field site that could stimulate methodological innovations in studying violence, terror, and the resultant impact on communities.

The need of contemporary research ethics within Anthropology is to debate and make its domain of classification flexible, malleable, and elastic that responds to unknown contingencies of fieldwork. This would also mean questioning the epistemological base of postmodernist deconstructivist approach of hermeneutics and reflexivity devoid of the political, economic, social, and historical context. Nilan (2002) has shown in the context of her fieldwork that it is not the bricolage of events that takes place in violent, high risk encounter that shapes our ethnography, but the post encounter secondary information gathering that feeds into the ethnography reconstruction of 'events' and in framing the ethnographer's narrative. Ethnographic encounter under strict, controlled scientific detached practice can inhabit the researcher's practice and often create ethical dilemmas and emotional vulnerability. Nilan (2002: 364) highlights several ethical dilemmas in her 'participant observation' and reflexive action pointing at the 'subject position' and questioning the 'prompt' practice of 'reflexivity'.

Here I use Nilan's fieldwork dilemmas to reflect on my own engagement in the field and what I learnt for the 'exceptional circumstances' that I faced in the field had a great bearing on the remaining conduct of my fieldwork.

To continue with my preceding interlocks of surviving fieldwork in a *Yimchunger* village, by March 2009, I had established firmly in fieldwork practice, 5 km away from Shamatur town. I was constantly in touch with district officials, project co-workers, and village big man. It is here that I met a local politician, whose father served as minister for two decades and was now taking rest after being defeated in the last election. He invited me to visit his plantation farm spread over 270 ha. The plantations were carried out in Teak, Gamori, Cherry, Acacia, and Manjam. The minister's son reminded me of the dangerous field I was working in and made me aware of the hostile parties who often barged into his plantation and destroyed his newly planted saplings. He also revealed that human-induced forest fires had destroyed his plantation nearly three times in the last 17 years. On one occasion he lost 30,000 saplings. As his father had been in the horticulture ministry, this loss rarely bothered the family. He also explained the relentless caring that he undertook for the success of his plantation which the local people disregarded. They would poach in his forest and extract valuable trees. The plantation was not well guarded given the paucity of funds. Valuable trees now ran the high risk of going in the hands of poachers and other lumber smugglers.

The minister's son was also indicating the dangers I faced and advised me to accompany local villagers during my travels. But my short day's visit raised more curiosity on land rights and how hundred of hectares were brought under plantation over a period of 17 years. These questions, coupled with his request to visit the plantation again were very tempting. I instantly promised that I would visit his farm again. In a couple of weeks I was ready to revisit his plantation farm. This time I had planned to take a short biography of his plantation activity and was curious to know how he had acquired land and the modus operandi that were used as practices for compensating the land loser. I had already gone to another town outside the state by the time I had to return back to his farm. Initially, I adopted this approach as my village host would get uneasy after few weeks of hosting me and later I adopted it as a method to negotiate with the tension and to supplement my archival research in the local archives. This time round I had been to state archives in Shillong to gather historical records on the *Yimchunger*. On 9th of May I reached Dimapur, where I was greeted by my host. The same day we travelled through the doggy mountain highways of Nagaland towards my host's plantation field in Shamatur. His plantation farm lay some 10 km away from Shamatur headquarter. Before leaving, the minister and his family had prayed for our well-being and wished us good luck by holding the Bible in their hands. They seemed to be worried yet tried to be cheerful. Every journey into the wilderness of Tuensang district entailed not only a physical danger of land slips and landslides but also a practical threat of being ambushed and threatened on the way. I felt for a moment we all are God-fearing people. The blessing was a bonus adding to our safety and security, much needed for such a treacherous and stressful journey on mountain roads.

As we reached Tuensang town after much struggle it was already evening. In the morning when I reached Dimapur, I was informed by one of my respondent's driver that his boss has left. This was originally a miscommunication but perhaps internally done to mock the mobility of people. I later learnt in the field that our journey was kept secret to the host family and between us. The vehicle in which we intended to travel was also different from the one used commonly in such long journeys. I felt quite uneasy, unprotected, and visible to crowds passing by travelling in an open jeep for such a distant journey. The off track road conditions had already made me lousy. After the ordeal of travelling over 270 km in 10 hours I was falling asleep. As fuel had gone infinitesimally low after reaching Tuensang town, a refuelling was urgent. Being Sunday the sole petrol pump in Tuensang town was closed. However, soon it was opened by the owner on request. In Tuensang town, my host in the village who had accompanied us in the vehicle with his young daughter was to see off his daughter. We then reset ourselves for the onward journey. On our way, we witnessed some drunk men waving at us to stop on the road. The situation was averted by our driver who passed by at accelerating speed. As our vehicle left the petrol station and was taking swirling curves across the corners, I was feeling drowsy. Suddenly I saw our car being stopped by two armed musketeers. The person on the left was carrying a revolver while the man on the right was carrying an AK 57 pointing at the vehicle. The rushing vehicle immediately stopped with an immediate violent jerk that tossed us up from our seats. Next followed a loud bang, within minutes the unidentified armed men took control of the vehicle. They had destroyed the vehicle headlight and there was complete blackout. Before I could murmur a word our driver was bleeding from his forehead after a pistol button was being smashed into his forehead. My host who was trying to stop the assailants was dragged out of the front seat. In the meantime a group of armed guard came to my side of the seat and ransacked my belongings. In the midst of confusion I nearly popped out of the vehicle but resisted the scuffle. The driver was completely drenched in blood. The militants were constantly shouting, 'Don't you respect us as soldiers, we are in civilian dress, you don't respect us. You will have to pay for it with your blood.' The driver pleaded for mercy but he could hardly escape. In the mean time the assailants held my village host and ransacked him giving blow after blow. The man in his mid-fifties had already developed a bloated forehead. I was the only person who remained unharmed. In the midst of this crisis one of the armed guard commanded, 'Run, run, before you are beaten up too, run for your life.' I pulled the driver out of the trouble and started running in the darkness with a dim torch in my hand. The torch was a lucky guide. After running for around 10 minutes, in the dark road, I called a teacher whom I had contacted during refuelling of the vehicle, to come out of her house for help. The lady, a college teacher responded promptly as we rushed towards her hut. As there was a blackout people came out with lanterns (night lamps). Quickly we rang the police but to no avail. It was Sunday night and no constable was around to respond to our call. Even her political connections with the town politicians were not working.

Soon I received a frantic call from my host. Under the press of gun, he was calling us to come back. He pursued me that the situation was now settled and we would be soon returning back to the village. He urged us to return back to the spot. But we were utterly in despair worried about the well-being of our host. I immediately informed the children of my village host and they reached the streets with shock and horror. As we proceeded to the site where the incident happened, most of the people left including the college teacher who appealed that, we shouldn't return back. But, we hardly had any alternative. The driver was reluctant to go back, but my host's children convinced that I should return back, otherwise the suspicion would grow. I felt it was morally incorrect to leave my host alone with the assailants. Life was at risk as I was approaching the site. As we moved the armed guards had blocked the road. My host was coming down with a loincloth across his face all in blood. He identified us as the inmates who had ran away, out of utter panic. The next moment we were escorted to an unidentified place, detached from the host's children who were asked to go back home. The town people who had gathered there were threatened to retreat. The underground town commander reappeared with his man, this time with a Spanish assault pistol to terrorize us. One of the hosts had run away to a local village headman's house and informed him about the incident to the town elders. Soon the town elders were also in communication with the miscreants. My host dialogued with the underground Town Commander who was incredibly drunk and hallucinated. His gun was pointed towards the driver who was a Nepali. The driver prostrated before the commander for mercy who kept on asking where to hit the bullets. He self-loaded the rifle to prove that the show was real. Intense negotiations were on both from our side and by the village elders. Occasionally he contacted the militant headquarters from where instructions were given for further action. The hostage crisis had just begun and we were all trapped in a small room. He even ordered his men to strip our clothes and this humiliation further drenched my heart. At one point I felt this was the end of my fieldwork that was just midway through.

I had no idea where my field notes, my camera, and laptop were thrown out of the vehicle. Even the vehicle was declared missing. All mobile phones were snatched and switched off. We were at once disconnected from the outside world. The dialogue that followed was emotionally charged and explosive, sentimental and quiet. The town commander narrated the story of his hard life as a rebel leader haunted by the military. Pointing at me he claimed that you are an Indian, and your government has repressed our aspirations for self-rule. He also accused my host of misunderstanding them. The Naga army has been cursed to be *musafir* (traveller) in the forest and jungle of Saramati. Amidst this violence I could make nothing of the cause. In the pitch end of the night the commander decided to release both of us but had no plans to release the driver, who was taken to another destination. As we were being drawn out, the village tribal council leaders had found their way to the spot. This made the town commander furious and he immediately called off any discussion and decided not to release us. However, the paramilitary forces had made their move. They reached the area and rescued us from their trap. All the people were immediately taken to the hospital for medical aid in armed vehicles.

In the following days, there was intense deliberation. Many people visited the host's house and demanded that he should not spare these rouge assailants. The *Yimchunger* Tribal Council leaders gathered and passed resolutions securing the safety and security of common civilians. A compromise deed was signed between the two parties for reconciliation. I was requested by my well-wishers to return back from the field. However, my conscience never permitted me to go back. My host assured me that these were exceptional events. The cool we maintained during the hostage crisis not only minimized the dangers of confrontation but also saved our lives.

Reflecting back on the whole event there was very limited inference that we can draw excepting that the pure scientific participant observation was not helpful. There were ethical and moral questions involved. One of the host's children asked me why I ran away initially when the town commander had beat up his father. I had no simple answer but I felt it was more appropriate to have run away as I survived the violence and I could inform his children along with other town people who then rushed to the spot with other townsmen. In the next few days we again became good friends, but a question still struck me whether I was a betrayer initially. The intensity of violence demanded quick action, which under siege, we dialogued as victims under gunpoint. The information I registered in my mind varied widely from colonialism by the Indian state to questions of suffering that common people often do not understand, that the guerrillas undertake to survive as resisting forces against the state. The question is of repression and hegemonic control and I being an outsider was unaware of the Naga problem.

However, many things were unclear. Why did they take their own community people hostage when they constantly uttered that we Nagas are one? What were the self-contradictions? What were the issues of conflict that led to this terror? Was the plot pre-planned? What were their motives? The situation was terrorizing to enquire about this. Whatever was spoken in that tensed environment, I tried to memorize. As there was no scope to transcribe or scribble the discussion of the town commander and our response, I realized a loss of an interesting but terrorizing captivity. Reflecting back afterwards on what had happened that night; I felt I had no control on the production of ethnography. The information derived from this violent 'participant observation', I took moral and ethical judgments without really following the 'exotic' and 'profane' scientific detached ethnographic practice. The decisions were based on the practicalities of the ground situation and I was less bothered about research ethics than the moral responsibility of protecting the interest of my well-being and my respondents who were my host. The 'hostage crisis' was obviously not directly linked to my research activity, but was embedded in the day-to-day violence produced in this borderland.

In the days that followed, I had determined to go back to the village. It was during this visit that my hosts slowly came up with their narratives that linked one by one to complete the whole text of my ethnography. Their personal accounts of guerrilla encounter during election campaigns and other moments of critical despair made me realize that there was logic to this kind of violence. It was ultimately enmeshed in the local political power struggle and resource extraction strategy that every individual was interested in. The crisis busted out of one of these mismatches. My host exclaimed that the guerrillas had pre-planned the ambush. He was reflecting on the terror that these areas produced. Interestingly, nothing appeared in the local newspaper on this event. Every information was concealed from the outside world. It helped my ethnographic exercise and I never made it public. I thus acted as a good 'participant observant' in the entire research exercise. The information was restricted to my research committee who showed their empathy and worries of conducting fieldwork in such perilous field.

In the whole event that unfolded on that night, the government forces did not apprehend the perpetrators; rather they acted as go between in the hostage crisis. So was the role of the *Yimchunger* Tribal Council. As nothing appeared in the media it further raised worries of how people survived such violent encounters. The negotiations were skilfully articulated as 'misunderstanding' between my host and the 'rebel groups'. A treaty of apology was signed to end the crisis. The other ways in which my ethnography was shaped lay in secondary information of the event. The events became clearer and my ethnographic resource sets were framed when I returned back to the fieldwork village. My decision to return back to the fieldwork in the village remains crucial towards the narration of my story.

Working within a Violent Social Context

My intentions were clear to continue with my research activity on farming. I developed a hunch that the hostage crisis had wider ramification and interconnected stories that linked with the broader political economy of borderland aid and the local politics within the tribe. The MGNREGS project had already created quarters of fracture within the village. My host, who aspired to stand for the next Legislative Assembly election from his father's constituency, was long opposing the functioning of the programme and had lauded his voice for transparency in public spending in the district. These cries were overheard by the people who led the ruling party. The district administration and the bureaucracy were obviously not happy with his activities. In the village, my village host was agitating on this issue. He had already created a faction within the village who were opposing government plans and were accusing selection of beneficiaries based on favouritism. The political context was very charged. Two months before the incident took place, in the village the local Sub Divisional Officer from the Public Works Department (PWD) inaugurated the MGNREGS road in the village. On that day my host had kept himself absent from the function. He had moved to the nearby town for his personal work. The growing tension was innate. My host's social position within the village made him an important prestigious person who would participate in all important government functions and was the main link in the reception of officials. His invisibility in the occasion raised doubts in people's mind. During the MGNREGS programme, he never participated in giving man-days. However, he was the first person who enthusiastically showed me the places around the site.

Over the years, the village has evolved as an important site of political activity. Roads, personal benefactors, jobs, and contracts came to villagers just before the elections. Political intermediaries in the village selected beneficiaries for government programmes. Often they acted as Village Council Chairman and Village Development Board Secretary. The underground factions were also agent in the sharing of funds. The Church subtracted 10 per cent of the grant value as was otherwise being offered by the household. The political economy of the village and the local bureaucracy was dependent on aid. My post 'crisis' fieldwork revealed the kind of patronage and nexus people maintained with the project officials and project officials maintained with the underground groups. Most of the information was not 'outcome of participant observation per se' much were derived from interviews, testimonies of my respondents, and at times hearsay or as complaints registered against the beneficiaries in the village by others who competed for it. I was at times dependent on my respondents to gather the data. Nonetheless, I was eyewitness to the politics at times as to the culture of violence. My finest opportunity came just a month after the MGNREGS project was completed. It was time to collect wages for the man-days. The scene turned grim as reports poured in from the Village Council that the government had decided just to give ₹650 instead of ₹1,500 as part of the project commitment of daily wage fixed at ₹100 under the programme. When the money actually got distributed to the houses of *Khel* leader, people received just ₹600. The *Khel* committee further made cuts for the meals and tea they provided during the work. The Church made a 10 per cent deduction as offering, which was mandatory under all projects as the pastor commented; villagers are too lazy to offer to the Church if they are not deducted at source. The council made a deduction of ₹300 and justified its action by claiming the money kept aside for annual tax payment to underground factions. The beneficiaries were busy in back talking, and grumbled with their family members on the issue. They had learnt by now the political economy of patronage. One of the village's land-less labourer who I interviewed while accepting the case said, 'My family is landless in the village. If I raise voice my job card will be cancelled and I tend to lose whatever I get.' He further said 'with this cash I even cannot send my child to school, but I have no option but to accept it … Something is always better than nothing.' These stories reverted back to the incident that happened that night. As a pure scientific observer I was thought to be 'emotionless', 'unbiased', and committed to an objective scientific enquiry. But the practice of scientifically detached observer obscured and made my ethnography least introspective. I was always tempted to become an activist or a revolutionary. However, I was always compelled to draw the line. The romanticism was deeply distorted and challenged the 'non essential personal'. As a good anthropologist I never reported it to the press. Although I seem to successfully fulfil the ethical requirements of the ethnography, morally I was questioned by my conscience. My fears became real one day when I met a Kheingmun lawyer in Tuensang town. He had invited me to his subdivision Thunuk, one of the most backward areas in Tuensang. His main intention was to persuade me to independently report about their suffering and marginality incomparison with advanced districts. He was extremely friendly. The requests had put me in the strangest of situations and I was utterly at a loss. All I could do was continually reiterate that I wanted to remain neutral in order to do objective research. As written by Frances Henry (1966: 553) from her fieldwork in Trinidad, 'this answer was not satisfactory to some people. In fact when I refused to write an *exposé* of the situation, one person accused me of being a CIA agent in disguise.' On my part I was questioned by my Kheimungen Naga friend what relevance my research will hold when I cannot independently report on the facts that he considered were facts of borderland communities, neglected by state elites. I made a sorry excuse that my focus of attention was the *Yimchunger* Nagas and it was too late to conduct fresh fieldwork on the Kheimungen. If I would have reported on these issues that were close to my heart, I would have faced similar sanctions returning back home as many past anthropologists faced in their research (see particularly Bourgois, 1991/2007).

During the rest of my fieldwork, rumours with occasional true stories poured in as the connections of violence became ever clearer. Democracy and electoral politics produced more messy outcomes in lineage-based society of the Nagas. In the last few months of my field stay in *Yimchunger* village yet another sad news reflected on my hostage crisis. A team of agricultural engineers and surveyors visited my study village from the government to survey land for a minor irrigation project. The villagers were ever jubilant to this new economic opportunity. One of the members who were accompanying the team was from the village. He had studied in a Catholic school and joined the government service a few years back. He had been responsible for persuading his agricultural department colleagues to bring projects to his village farm and the village at large. The study village had well-developed paddy fields but had suffered from acute shortage of water in the past years. The irrigation survey was just in time. Elaborate arrangements and multiple cuisines were prepared to satisfy the officials. The survey went well and in the evening we all were tired to return back home. The villagers even learned to use the GPS I had borrowed from my FCC friend. A few days later the villagers reported that the agricultural officer was badly beaten up in a local wine store by the underground town commander. The reasons were unknown but people hinted at possible cash connections. They also started narrating stories of the town commander's life that he was a murderer, his beloved had committed suicide and that his father a former village guard command had deserted his mother. The whole family was cursed with misfortune and violence. These gossips were informative and at times seemed exaggerated and based on the 'agency' of individuals who narrated them.

As Nilan has emphasized in fieldwork, the question on the control over the production of data often worries qualitative ethnographic fieldwork in 'exception setting', where emotional detachment, objectivity, and control over the production of data are difficult to achieve in unique emergency situations. She further emphasized on the fact that it is often data collected after the event or in quieter moments which turns out to be the most evocative in the final production of ethnographic details of 'unfamiliar' and dangerous fields (Nilan, 2002: 383). In my case, the political economy of violence surrounding my fieldwork was not very clear after the 'hostage' event had taken place. The ethnographic lessons learnt were latent and called for self-reflexivity. However, it also opens up the dilemma of ethics and the risk of being naïve and emotionally detached from the political. The dangers of remaining scientifically detached from the practice of politics is well spelt out in Fances Henry's paper where she highlights the problems of conducting real world fieldwork in fractured settings. She states that:

> the situation of being caught between two rival factions is certainly not a new one for the anthropologist; but when this occurs in the political arena and involves the policies and legislative programme of the government of the country, these problems take on a new and sometimes threatening significance. (Henry, 1966: 554)

The moral dilemmas remain to be resolved in the discipline and need discussion that perhaps spills over the discussion of this essay.

Reflections and Recommendations

Given the emotive position of my fieldwork, survival was the last wish in such violent settings. The possibility of surviving such fieldwork is determined by the factors that are beyond human control and comprehension. But we can always take steps that do not stop at the 'common sensual' 'rhetoric', nonetheless, transcend the idiosyncratic standpoints of anthropological research determined solely by professional ethics. I will argue that 'professionalism' should match 'humanism' and our study among the 'poor, marginalized and powerless' contribute to their empowerment. It would be dangerous and utter falsehood to think that there are definite answers to any of these ethical questions. We need to think about them in both practical and theoretical terms.

Over the last decades, there has been some rigorous introspection towards the methodological and philosophical concerns of fieldwork in unstable places from Nancy Scheper-Hughes' (1995) call for anthropology 'with one's feet on the ground' to Antonius Robben and Caroline Nordstrom's examination of *Fieldwork under Fire* (1995). We must think critically how we deal with 'violence' in the field alongside ethics issues without undermining our obligation towards the society. These may seem certainly value loaded but if anthropology as a disciple has to progress in the 21st century it should very well address these critical issues towards fieldwork practice in violent environment. In South Asia research ethical guidelines have never been structurally formulated within the academic setting, but the series of literature on fieldwork practice also demands a fresh insight into violent and abnormal field sites.

When the debate of researchers well-being and ethical dilemmas were first discussed by the American Anthropologists in the 1960s, the British Anthropologist were avoiding the timely questions arising out of research work emanating from violent fields. Today the complexities of the debate have gained new grounds, so has the political climate of the world. With multiple counterinsurgency programmers operating globally, anthropologist task of conducting 'scientifically detached objective fieldwork' sounds profane. Violence is part of our everyday life and to decontextualize violence as an objective agent brings in the anxiety within the anthropologist. Violence thus in the first place should be understood as subjective to the human condition. Similarly violence is produced as much as it is experienced. In my fieldwork I was more fearful psychologically then actually hurt. This has implication for one's research. Much of my understanding of violence was negotiated by its articulation by different actors in the field. While under siege by the underground commander violence was understood quite different from what I later learnt in the field. The practice of fieldwork therefore becomes critical towards producing valuable data set substantive for research. Ethnographers thus working in dangerous fields are pressed with the challenge of innovating new strategies for the preservation of their well-being while at the same continuing to identify and explain the unique social inter-relation that arise amidst crisis and strife. In my own 14 months fieldwork in Nagaland I engaged with the problems and steered my way through at times adopting alternative root that were quite unconventional and dared to experiment with new methods of data collection quite unconventional in ethnographic research. The end result has been a reflective memory that perhaps is a humble exercise towards the understanding dangers in conducting fieldwork.

The journalist taking photograph during the Hornbill Festival under tight security cordon

Source: Photos by Debojyoti Das.

A villager showing the AK 47 bullet piercing a thick iron lamp post in the village

Source: Photos by Debojyoti Das.

Notes

1. SOAS Fieldwork and ethical guidelines form, 2008.
2. In the Naga Hills there are today six 'backward' Naga tribes; Yimchunger, Sangthans, Kheingmungen, Chekasang, Phom, and Konyaks. Out of these six sub-Naga tribes, the Yimchunger inhabit the Saramati range with their administrative headquarter in Shamatur sub-division, where I conducted most of my fieldwork. Five underground factions today influence the Yimchunger territory. Three of these factions have international presence NSCN (IM), NSCN (K), Federal. The remaining two underground groups are supported by these major factions and are armed to fight for a local cause of ethnic identity and for backward tribal status. Limusung underground guerrilla fighter represents the Tikhir tribal group who claim for a separate tribal status separate from the pan-Yimchunger identity; while the YLA pleads the pan-Yimchunger unity. During my fieldwork there was relative peace in the Yimchunger area. There were occasional rumours of gun battle and violent clashes between the two guerrilla groups in the surrounding Tikhir dominated villages. The NNC old man were the only silent non-violent group unarmed, who only lived on annual taxes that they collected once in a year from the villagers. Their living leader Father Lakham is the only surviving warlord of Chasoor village, but their role has been limited by the control exercised by the international groups who have their presence across the international border.

References

American Anthropological Association (AAA). 1973. Principles of Professional Responsibility. In T. Weaver (ed.), *To See Ourselves: Anthropology and Modern Social Issues*, pp. 46–48. Glenview, Illinois: Scott, Foresman.

Angami, Z. 2008. *Nagaland Village Empowerment Laws*. Kohima: Novelty Printing Press.

Berreman, G. 1968. Is Social Anthropology Alive? Social Responsibility in Social Anthropology. *Current Anthropology*, 9(5): 391–396.

———. 1973. Academic Colonialism: Not So Innocent Abroad. *The Nation*, 10 November. Reprinted in Thomas Weaver (ed.), *To See Ourselves. Anthropology and Modern Social Issues*, Glenview, Illinois: Scott Foresman.

Bourgois, P. 1991/2007. Confronting the Ethics of Ethnography: Lessons from Fieldwork in Central America. In Fayeh V. Harrison (ed.), *Decolonising Anthropology: Moving Further Towards an Anthropology for Liberation*, pp. 110–126. Washington, D.C.: American Anthropological Association.

218 Debojyoti Das

Glazer, Myron. 1970. Fieldwork in a Hostile Environment: A Chapter in the Sociology of Social Research in Chile. In F. Bonilla and M. Glazer (eds), *Student Politics in Chile*, pp. 313–333. New York: Basic Books.

Henry, F. 1966. The Role of the Fieldworker in an Explosive Political Situation. *Current Anthropology*, 7(5): 552–559.

Hinton, P. 2002. The 'Thailand Controversy' Revisited—Anthropologist as Spies. *The Australian Journal of Anthropology*, 13(2): 155–177.

Horowitz, Irving Louis. 1967. The Rise and Fall of Project Camelot. In J. Deviance Douglas (ed.), *The Rise and Fall of Project Camelot*, pp. 35–70. New York: Random House.

Jenkins, R. 1984. Bringing It All Back Home: An Anthropologist in Belfast. In Colin Bell and Helen Roberts (eds), *Social Researching: Politics, Problems, Practice*, pp. 147–163. London: Routledge and Kegan Paul.

Kovats-Bernat, J.C. 2002. Negotiating Dangerous Fields: Pragmatic Strategies for Fieldwork Amid Violence and Terror. *American Anthropologist*, 104(1): 208–222.

Kumar, Nita. 1992. *Friends, Brothers, Informants: Fieldwork Memories of Beneras*. Berkeley, California: University of Californian Press.

Leopold, Mark. 2005. *Inside West Nile: violence, history & representation on an African frontier*. Oxford: James curry.

Levi-Strauss, C. 1966. Anthropology: Its Achievements and Future. *Current Anthropology*, 7(2): 124–127.

Lobo, Lancy. 1990. Becoming a Marginal Native. *Anthropos*, 85: 125–138.

Lotha, Abraham. 2007. *History of Naga Anthropology 1832–1947*. Nagaland: Chumpu Museum.

Nash, June. 1976. Ethnology in Revolutionary Setting. In Micheal Rynkiewickh and James Spradley (eds), *Ethics and Anthropology: Dilemmas in Field Works*, pp. 148–166. New York: Willey and Sons.

Nilan, P. 2002. Dangerous Fieldwork Re-examined: The Question of Research Subject Position. *Qualitative Research*, 2(3): 363–383.

Nordstrom, Carolyne and Joann Martin. 1992. The Culture of Conflict: Field Reality and Theory. In Carolyn Nordstrom and Joann Martin (eds), *The Paths to Dominatio, Resistance and Terror*, pp. 18–36. Berkeley, California: University of California Press.

Panini. M.N. (ed.). 1991. *From the Female Eye: Accounts of Women Fieldworkers Studying Their Own Community*. Delhi: Hindustan.

Scheper-Hughes, N. 1995. *Death without Weeping: The Violence of Everyday Life in Brazil*. Berkeley, California: University of California Press.

Sluka, J.A. 1990. Participant Observation in Violent Social Contexts. *Human Organization*, 49(2): 114–126.

———. 1995. Reflections on Managing Danger in Field Work: Dangerous Anthropology in Belfast. In Caroline Nordstrum and Antonius C.G.M. Robben (eds), *Fieldwork under Fire: Contemporary Studies of Violence and Survival*, pp. 276–294. Berkeley, California, and Los Angeles, California: University of California Press.

Srinivas, M.N., A.M. Shah and E.A. Ramaswami. 1972. *The Fieldworker and the Field*. New Delhi: Oxford University Press.

———. 1979/1991. *The Fieldworker and the Field: Problems and Challenges of Fieldwork Investigation*. New Delhi: Oxford University Press.

Thapan, Meenakshi (ed.). 1998. *Anthropological Journeys: Reflections on Fieldwork*. Delhi: Orient Longman.

Wakin, E. 1998. *Anthropology Goes to War: Professional Ethics and Counterinsurgency in Thailand*. Madison, Wisconsin: University of Washington, Centre for South-East Asian Studies Publication.

Wolf, E. and J. Jorgensen. 1970. Anthropology in the Warpath in Thailand. *New York Review of Books*, 19 November, pp. 26–35. www.nybooks.com/.../a-special-supplement-anthropology-on-the-warpat. Accessed on 21 May 2014.

10

In Search of Storytellers among the Khiamniungan Nagas

Anungla Aier

Background

The Naga tribes inhabiting the northeast most corner of India were a subject of great interest to the European anthropologists during the later phase of British rule in India. The field diaries and monographs on the various Naga tribes written by the British administrators turned ethnographers as well as by such greats as Christoph Von Fürer Haimendorf (1939) and Milada Ganguli (1984) take the reader, even native Nagas of the present generation who have no knowledge of the ethnographic reality of the their ancestors, on a journey in which they can feel the emotions and experience the struggles they and the subjects they study went through. Those early writings combined with the vibrancy of their culture have been responsible for the continued interest on the Nagas.

The anthropological and sociological literature on the Nagas, written both by non-Nagas as well as native Naga writers have provided a wide array of information on the Naga society and culture. No amount of theoretical conceptualization, however, can replace our understanding of culture that can be arrived at only through the field experience. The importance of field-work in anthropology or for that matter in any discipline that engages itself with the study of human society at work cannot be emphasized more than what has been described in such lucid terms as seen in the personal accounts of fieldwork presented in the edited volume, *Encounter and Experience: Personal Accounts of Fieldwork* by Béteillé and Madan (1974). Accounts of fieldwork experiences among the Nagas during the early- and mid-20th century such as by von Fürer-Haimendorf in *The Naked Nagas and Return to the Naked Nagas*; Tour Diaries of the British administrators, continue to provide useful information about the people among whom he worked. Nevertheless, there is a lacuna concerning accounts of field experiences of researchers (natives or outsiders) among the Nagas in the more recent times. Although native Naga researchers have been writing about their own culture and society which are published in the form of books, journal articles, and book sections, there is a conspicuous gap of accounts and experiences of the native researchers. The aim of this essay, therefore, is to initiate and make a small effort in filling that gap which future researchers, I hope will fill in basing their own experiences.

As a student of anthropology, every field experience has always something new to teach. This aspect of the discipline and the way it engages with the study of human society and culture never fail to amaze me because as a Naga, and working as an anthropologist for the last 20 years, I believe every fieldwork still unfolds something unexpected. At such junctures, we are reminded of what Béteillé and Madan (1974) have stated, 'fieldwork remained central to anthropological research and has often been described as the anthropologist's rite de passage. This suggests a degree of personal involvement unmatched among other scholarly pursuits.' As Geertz (1973) observed, 'All Ethnography is part philosophy and a good deal of the rest is confession'; I have to admit that though a native, like most people of my generation living in the towns, a product of the formal system of education with set college and university guidelines, my understanding of Naga culture, was picked more from the published works of non-Nagas and the rest was grasped from my everyday life as Naga, which many a time escaped my notice. Since my introduction to anthropology in the 1980s, my whole perspective towards my own culture changed as I began to realize how little I know, much less understand many of the things I had taken for granted as being 'Naga'. Since then I had been undergoing a continuous process of 'returning' or trying to 're-enter' into my own culture and society.

So when I embarked on a project for documentation of the Naga folklores in collaboration with the Department of Art and Culture, Government of Nagaland, it gave me the opportunity to travel to the less known tribes living in the areas bordering Myanmar. This particular essay talks about some of the personal field experiences of working among the Khiamniungan Nagas, a transborder tribe of Tuensang district in Nagaland. According to the locals, the number of Khiamniungan villages on the other side of the border is much more than their numbers living on the Indian side of the border. As a child, I grew up during the 1960s and 1970s listening to my parents telling stories about the Khiamniungan people among whom my father worked as a government school teacher in Noklak village during the first half of the 1950s. It was a time when the Naga movement was just starting to pick up momentum. And from my parents I learnt how the Khiamniungan village of Pangsha was burned by the Indian army. During that time one family of my tribe, the Ao was working as a pastor in Nokhu village who were completely wiped out during a head hunting raid and my father along with some friends went searching for the dead bodies so that they could give them a proper burial. My mother told stories of how they witnessed the return of a victorious war party and how the heads were dressed and put up on the head tree. So I grew up with a lot of fascination coupled with fear about this particular Naga tribe. As an adult, the fear disappeared but the fascination remained.

Preparation for the Fieldwork

As I began gathering as much information about the Khiamniungan, I realized that among the Naga tribes, they are one of the least written about tribe and I could not get much other than what I already knew. The next thing was selecting the villages to visit and making the necessary contacts with the villagers. As a Naga and also from all my earlier fieldworks among other Naga tribes, I knew that first I must obtain the permission of the village authority to visit their village. In this, my Khiamniungan neighbour in Kohima was a great help. He gave me the general layout of the location of the villages and also a little historical background on the establishment of villages. This was important because oral tradition pertaining to the village establishment is critically important for the Nagas as it also involves issues of land control and many a land disputes between neighbouring villages always go back to it. Considering the time and financial constraints, I decided to conduct the fieldwork in four villages—Noklak and Nukho in the upper range and Sanglao and Peshu in the lower range.

The next on the list was to make an arrangement for a translator. Although many Ao pastors and school teachers had worked among them, there was no guarantee that I would meet some in the villages I planned to visit. There was always the possibility that we may be able to converse in Nagamese; however, Nagamese lacks depth of expression and has been found to be completely useless to communicate matters of cultural value and more significant issues that can best be described only in local terms. Fortunately, my Khiamniungan neighbour once again came up with the solution and allowed to let a Tokpoa, the girl who lives with his family, to come with me. She also happened to be from one of the villages I was going to and spoke perfect English as well as the 'indispensable Nagamese'. Along with us also came Binthunglo, a Lotha girl who had worked as a research assistant and proved to be more resourceful in more ways than one.

Arriving at the Village

From Kohima it took two days of travel to reach our first field target, Sanglao village; having stopped in Tuensang for the night. Tokpoa said that it usually takes five to six hours to reach the village from Tuensang but it took us 10 hours and we arrived at night only and found the village in total darkness with no electricity. The next day, our first call in the morning was to make the mandatory visit to the village head Gaonbura and explain the purpose of our visit. Word had been sent to him about our coming and we found him waiting for us, he had delayed going to the field for our sake and I was grateful for it. In all the subsequent villages we went to, the same procedure was followed. By doing so the village authority was made officially aware of our presence in the village and should any untoward incident were to happen to us or otherwise should the need arise to seek the help of the authority in any situation; we would come under its protection and care as guests.

This is Customary in All Naga Villages

My research objective being the documentation of folklore, I needed somebody to identify the key informants who I presumed would be the elderly persons who would have better knowledge of the origin mythology, migration narratives, and various other oral stories that I sought to document. Earlier, Tokpoa had already told me that among the Khiamniungan the stories are 'given' only to the selected/chosen persons. This was confirmed by the head Gaonbura of the village who took upon himself to call all such persons in his village so that we could talk to them. Unfortunately, some of them had already left the village for their field and it was only 7:00 am. I tried to meet and talk with one such person who was still in the village but he refused to tell any stories. The reason behind this, which I came to know only in the evening, was that it was my first visit to a Khiamniungan village and I only had a few hours to explore it. Though I had known from stories told by my parents and grandmother as well as reading of the various monographs, it still evoked a wistful feeling to find that all the *khels* still had their Morung with the log drums in its compound though it was in a state of disrepair.

The slate roofed houses for which the Khiamniungan were famous in the olden days were not to be seen in Sanglao, in Nukho, or in Noklak village. Except in Peshu where still some houses were built with slate roofs, in all the villages I went to, it was completely replaced by thatch or the roofing tins which the government had provided through the housing schemes of the rural development department. Other than this, signs of development were very scanty. The village paths and steps, which in most of the Ao, Angami, Lotha, or the Sangtam, Chang, and Yimchunger villages were either paved with tar or plaster, fine stone works by the local masons were not seen. I could not shake off the feeling that the dusty and narrow village paths had been just the same they had been for centuries without much improvement. Electricity was a rare luxury, it was fortunate that I had brought battery backups for the camera and recorders. Health care facilities were miles away.

Meeting with the Storytellers

In my earlier experiences I had already encountered that all elderly persons are not necessarily walking libraries of traditional knowledge and oral stories, because it takes years to accumulate such knowledge and one needs to have a disposition to take an interest in such matters from a young age. It is, therefore, not possible for all elderly persons to have the confidence to narrate such stories even if they may have some knowledge of oral stories. However, when I found out that among the Khiamniungan the 'one who knows the stories' is a special person, I was curious and interested at the same time to know more.

Storytelling always happened in the evening because day time is reserved for their agricultural toil. In every village, the head gaonbura or the chairman of the village and in their absence the village development board secretary would take the responsibility of informing all the knowledge keepers (those who had been chosen to be the keepers of the stories). Curiously, though I met some of them during the day, I could not get much information from them. In the evening also, I had to wait for everyone to arrive before any discussion on the subject could be initiated. Later from Tokpoa I learnt that all those who are recognized as knowledge keepers must be present before any discussions on the stories began. Considering the fact that oral transmission involves the possibility of alteration in the stories, it is probably a precautionary measure to ascertain that all the clans are in agreement with each other concerning the stories before it is divulged to someone from outside their community. While working among some other tribes, I had encountered similar attitudes earlier where the storytellers insisted that other storytellers should also be present there to corroborate and also to fill in lest they fail to remember the entire story. There were also situations where no agreements could be reached and I had to settle with a more generally acceptable version that veered away from the more controversial issues. Sometimes the differences among them were so deep and politicized that it became doubtful and even impossible to verify the validity of a story. And so having gone through all those in my earlier experiences, I presumed it was worthwhile to wait for all the storytellers to arrive for the good of all concerned. It was quite dark by the time we could sit down to the serious business of storytelling. As in all other Naga tribes, all the knowledge keepers were men only. Also it was not possible to get a straight answer to any of my queries as they wanted to confer with each other first and only when all of them were in agreement, a story would be narrated. I had anticipated this based on earlier experiences. This was a very time consuming process but if I wanted to document their oral stories, this was the only way I could get an authentic story. Besides, by doing so whatever stories I recorded had the official sanction of the village authority and all those who are recognized as the keepers of such stories.

Considering the great disputes that sometimes erupt in some Naga villages due to non-acceptance of some versions of the same story, I know how important it is to have all the parties in consensus to the recorded stories. In this connection I may refer to an incident that happened in Sangpur village of the Yimchunger tribe. We had stayed in the village for several days and the head gaonbura of the village narrated the migration story of their village. We left Sangpur and went to Shamator and were staying the night in Shamator town. That night around 7:00 pm one man from Sangpur came to meet us having walked the distance between Sangpur and Shamator. The reason of his coming was that, after we left the village he and the head gaonbura had a discussion regarding our coming to the village and they realized that there was a slight mistake in the story narrated to me. Therefore, he had to walk all the way from Sangpur to make the necessary correction before we left for Kohima. This probably describes the seriousness with which such stories are narrated and all precautions are taken to ensure that no misrecording of the stories takes place. Encounters such as this further underpin the importance of the responsibility of researchers to report correctly.

Coming back to our Khiamniungan storytellers, one of the fascinating aspect of the way they authenticate the stories is that first each person will tell the story that has been passed down to him by his clan's ancestors through his father to test whether it matches with the other's or not. If the first story is the same as the other ones and there is no clash in the details of the stories, it is good news for me. But if there is a difference of opinion, they get into a long discussion, taking references from other narratives till all of them come to an agreement. Sometimes it took hours and I had to resign myself to listening patiently to a discussion that I could not understand a single word of. For instance, in Sanglao village on one such storytelling evenings, Kongkhao a 70-year-old elder, narrated the origin myth of the Khiamniungan tribe and how they dispersed and establish the different villages. All those gathered allowed him to narrate the story, listening attentively. After he finished, there was some moment of silence, all were busy with their own thoughts perhaps. After the short moment of silence all started talking, pointing out how it differs or is the same as the story told to them. What is interesting about the whole process is that everyone seemed to be careful not to impose themselves and their version of the narrative upon the others. They all agreed that as the knowledge keeper of their clan, the story held by each one of them has been passed down to them by their ancestral knowledge keeper and therefore it is not wise to ignore or consider wrong the story held by the other person. More importantly I think it was also a matter of diplomacy to maintain communal harmony.

The custom of recognizing certain individuals as the authorized storytellers of the clan was something new to me and I have worked on folklore among 12 of the 14 Naga tribes of Nagaland. The anthropologist in me was curious to know more about the manner in which such individuals were chosen and whether they have to go through certain customary procedure to be given the title or to be recognized as the official storyteller. What I found out was far from what I had speculated. The story of Tangsoi, a *gaon bura* as well as one of the storytellers explain why. Tangsoi was the youngest among 10 of his father's sons. His father tried to give the stories to his elder brothers: Stories and other traditions concerning the village, their tribe and most importantly their clan stories about land rights, boundaries with other clans and all other stories known to him. But none of his elder brothers gave their 'heart' and did not retain the stories. His father suffered from an illness brought about by the 'evil eye' and so he was sick for a long time. Being the youngest child, he got to stay at home to look after their father while his brothers went to work in the field with their mother. As he spent a lot of time with his sick father, the knowledge was passed to him slowly. I found out that he has only one living son who also lives in Tuensang, a few hundred kilometers away from the village. The chances of the son coming back to the village and living there were less. He also said that his own son was not interested in the stories. So I asked him, to whom will he pass on his knowledge and I was quite relieved to hear that he has already chosen the son of his clansmen. I was told that the father would observe his children and his brothers' children and will make a mental note of who should be the next person to keep the stories. Once he makes up his mind and has chosen one of the children, he makes it a point to spend more time with that particular child. Going for hunting together, spending days in the field together and in the process little by little the knowledge is given to the child. The process continues till the father dies or becomes too frail or advanced in age. No formal or ceremonial declaration is made as to who will be the next custodian of the oral stories and traditions. However, as the child grows up and matures enough to participate in the various matters requiring the knowledge, such person displays his knowledge and gradually the community comes to know and gives him due recognition as keeper of the knowledge and teller of the stories.

Among the Khiamniungan, the most important origin myth is the story of the great deluge. The importance of this narrative lies in the fact that all Khiamniungan settlements are believed to have occurred only after the flood waters had receded. According to this narrative, the first humans emerged from under the earth in a place located between Lengnyiu village and the present township of Noklak. The people after having emerged from the under the earth established a village and named it as Khiamniungan because it was near a water source (Khiam = water; niungan = mighty source). While residing there, a maiden fell in love with a handsome young man who visited her during the evenings. But her parents saw that whenever they sit together, a bright light encircles them in a halo. Also he was never to be seen in the village during the day. So they forbid her to see him again. So they asked her to find out where he lives. Subsequently, the following night, when he left after visiting her, the girl followed him and to her horror she saw him jump into the river and turned into a fish. So she told him that she can never marry him but the young man (now turned into a fish) replied that he will never leave and will come and get her. Sometime after this, the people experienced a great flood that inundated the whole village. In order to escape from the flood people fled to the high hills but the water keep rising and making a sound that sounded just like the girl's name. So the villagers demanded that she must be thrown into the water to satisfy the water spirit and save the lives of the villagers. The girl's parents with great sadness pushed her into the water and then only the flood waters receded. After this the people returned to their villages and later dispersed and established the different villages.

This narrative is one of the foundations on the basis of which the Khiamniungan identity as a person is established as all those villages founded out of the ancestral village of Khiamniungan identify themselves today as the Khiamniungan Naga. Although slight differences are prevalent in terms of narrative styles depending upon the personality of the narrator, but the story told is the same. There were two elements in the story that baffled me at first—one was the name of the maiden who fell in love with the water spirit. In the lower range villages such as Sanglao and Peshu she is identified as Monyiu, daughter of Lütiak. In the upper range villages of Nukho and Thangnokking her name changes to Themoi. The other element in the story that differed was the name of the high mountain to which they went up to escape the flood waters. Again in the lower range villages, the mountain so identified is called Longshioking but in the upper range it is called Yakaoking. I had asked in Peshu and as well as in Sanglao whether the mountain is nearby and can be seen or not. From both villages the mountain is seen clearly though quite far away and was pointed out to me. So in Nukho and in Tangnokking I asked the same question and the mountain which was nearer was pointed out. The mountain they pointed out to me looked familiar so I called Tokpoa and pointing at the mountain asked whether it look familiar to her too or not. And she said with a surprise that that mountain is what her villagers call Longshioking—the saviour mountain. Given the fact that the villages in the lower and upper ranges speak slightly different but mutually under-standable dialects, differences in the nomenclature of places like the one described above or persons in stories that are more widely told among the tribe such as the name of the maiden because of whom the flood occurred and whose sacrifice brought it to an end are understandable so long as there are no major divergence from the accepted version of the story. However, within a single village, they are careful about the narra-tives regarding the history of village establishment, status and functions of clans and their relationship with other clans, land rights and control, and matters concerning inter village linkages.

Encounter with the Legendary Tiger Men/Women

The first time I heard stories about persons with tiger spirit was from my father. He used to tell us children stories about an aunt he had who had a tiger spirit. One of his favourites was about the time he was sent to a Mopungchuket village about 15 km away from our village for some work. He hesitated to go because he did not find anyone to accompany him but his aunt told him that she will go along with him and urged him to go ahead. All the way he kept looking back for her but she did not come. After he came back to the village, he confronted the aunt for not keeping her word but she told him how she travelled with him all the way and back. He did not believe her but when she recounted where he rested on the way and what he did, he knew that she truly went along with him but could not understand how. It was only much later that he came to know that she was a tiger woman. Accounts of such men and women among the Ao and Sumi (Sema) tribe are also given in great detail by Mills (1926) and Hutton (1921). Although the phenomenon of lycanthropy is still not understood and many are sceptical about the association, to the Naga mind it is a very real part of their past. We also keep hearing that there are still some people with such spirits and special abilities. So when we were in Peshu village, I asked Mr Pukho, the Secretary of the Village Development Board whether tiger spirit men are still found in his village and what he thinks of it. He spontaneously replied that it is very real and that there are several such people in his village, both men and women. Hearing this I wanted to meet at least one of them. Seeing my curiosity and interest, he took me to a tiger man but he had gone to the next village. So we went to see another tiger man. We found him cutting yam and tapioca to be prepared for the pigs that almost every family rear in the village to supplement their simple meal of beans, rice, millet, corn, and job's tears plant. As he was too old to work in the field, his son and his wife with their children take care of him. His wife expired several years back and lives with his son's family. Nagas in general are very tolerant towards children and the aged and even in very remote villages like the ones I have visited I found that elderly parents are usually taken proper care of despite the hard life. Our second tiger man was quite advanced in age, probably in his eighties and had gone deaf, so we could not talk with him. Luckily for us, the son and his wife returned from the field and we could get some information from them. According to the son, his father had never revealed the tiger to him saying that it might scare him because of its size. But he knows that his father has the tiger spirit because they sometimes find tracks of the tiger outside their house. If the tiger is wounded, for no reason wound marks would appear on his father's body also. Sometimes their pigs were also taken away by the tiger and father would forewarn them about what was to come. While at his house Pukho pointed out a rectangular wooden plate placed on the earthen floor near the door, similar to the plate they use for cutting meat but smaller in size. I have seen those meat plates which were always kept hanging on the side wall of the house and never on the ground. He said that in the house of tiger men only those wooden plates were kept and in the evenings before retiring they fill it with water so that should the tiger spirit visit its human body, it can go after drinking. This was a philosophy I find very hard to grasp and understand but to the people it was just how things worked and nothing to waste their time thinking about. We did not spend much time there because it was getting dark and we could see that both the husband and wife were tired and they still had to cook their evening meal, feed the pigs, and do other chores. So we left the house and went to another house, this time to a woman who also has a tiger spirit. She lives near Pukho's where we were also staying, so we could stay late or even go back without much trouble if she was not in. Our luck was in and she was home but not alone. It was already dark and they were in the process of cooking the evening meal. There were two young men besides her husband and our tiger woman was sitting beside one of the young man. Soon as I saw her massaging his back and stomach I realized that she was also a traditional healer. Through Pukho, I learnt that the young man met with an accident some months back and still suffers from severe abdominal and back pain. So he comes to her regularly for treatment. I asked if it works and he said that since she started treating him the pain had subsided and occured less frequently. Reference to the phenomenon of lycanthropy and persons with the tiger familiars functioning as traditional healers and soothsayers among the Naga tribes is to be found in several colonial writings as well as by local authors (von Fürer-Haimendorf, 1939; Imchen, 1993: 69–71; Mills, 1922a, 1922b, 1926; Smith, 1925). Although the phenomenon is almost disappeared in most Naga tribes, it is still practised among the Khiamniungan tribe as well as in other eastern Naga tribes such as the Yimchunger, Sangtam, Konyak, Tikhir, and other smaller ethnic groups. Although persons with tiger familiars or spirits often function as traditional healers, it needs to be clarified that all the people with tiger familiars are not necessarily healers. Although healing abilities and lycanthrophy are not necessarily linked, such people are believed to be endowed with special abilities such as foretelling the success or failures of hunting expeditions. Later I learnt that all tiger men and women were not healers except some of them, though healing abilities and tiger spirit are not necessarily linked.

It has been told to me that people with such spirits were normally not willing to talk about their condition and since Pukho was known to her who also happened to be an important person in the community, I convinced her that we wished her no ill wishes and she could explain it to us. She had lots of scars especially on her legs, thighs, and some on the stomach which she claims were the result of the tiger's wounds. The enigma about the phenomenon is further deepened by the fact that the human person of the tiger knows exactly where it is at any point of time. I asked the woman where her tiger spirit was as we were speaking and she immediately said that it was located nearby Tuensang. How she knows it, is hard to tell but more baffling was what appears to be a situation where the human and the animal seem to be one but occupying different bodies. She said that at any time she is aware of the tiger—where it is, what it is doing and in what health condition and likewise the tiger is fully aware of her.

Majority of the population in Peshu were Christian, even the woman with the tiger spirit. Interestingly, she converted to Christianity because she thought that by becoming a Christian her connection with the tiger will be broken. But she said that she was unfortunate because by the time she converted the hold of the tiger had become too powerful that she could not be separated from it. This reminds us of what Hutton observed with regard to lycanthropy among the Sema Naga that, 'the habit is far from desired. No one wants to be possessed by the habit, and it is, on the contrary, feared as a source of danger and a great weariness to the flesh.' From another woman from Sanglao I learnt that she had been tricked into acquiring the tiger's spirit but it was discovered few days later by her father who happened to know all the tell tale symptoms of such persons. And the person who tricked her was also a kin of her father and so he convinced the giver to remove it. Although the presence of the phenomenon is far from rare, it was evident that it was not a desired power. These encounters with real people who are reputed tiger men and women was overwhelming in the sense that there is still so much we do not understand about this particular aspect of the culture. For instance how do they actually connect with the tiger? Apparently the tiger and the human control each other in some ways even though physically they are hundreds of miles apart. How does it happen? How do such persons behave and live their everyday life, is it any different from normal persons? Can this be explained within the medical and psychological science? Or is it a pure case of spiritualism and magic? These and many more questions may be answered by an in-depth study of the last remaining tiger men of the Naga Hills but I have to wait for another opportunity for such a study, if the opportunity ever comes.

References

Bèteillè, André and T.N. Madan (ed.). 1974. *Encounters and Experiences: Personal Accounts of Fieldwork*. New Delhi: Vikas Publishing.

Ganguli, Milada. 1984. *Pilgrimage to the Nagas*. New Delhi: Oxford & IBH Publishing Co.

Geertz, Clifford. 1973. *The Interpretations of Cultures: Selected Essays*. NewYork: Basic Books.

Hutton, J.H. 1921. *The Sema Naga*. London: Oxford University Press.

Imchen, P. 1993. *Ancient Ao Naga Religion and Culture* (pp. 69–71). New Delhi: Har-Anand Publications.

Mills, J.P. 1922a. The Were-Tigers of the Assam Hills. *Journal of the Society for Psychical Research*, 22: 381–388.

———. 1922b. *The Lhota Nagas* (pp. 164–165). London: Macmillan & Co.

———. 1926. *The Ao Nagas* (pp. 247–249). London: Macmillian & Co.

Smith, W.C. 1925. *The Ao Naga Tribe of Assam: A Study in Ethnology and Sociology* (pp. 93–94). London: Macmillan & Co.

von Fürer-Haimendorf, Christoph. 1939. *Return to the Naked Nagas*. New Delhi: Vikas Publishing.

11

Experiencing Mortuary Practices in an Anthropological Journey

Gautam Kumar Bera

Death is the ultimate reality in all societies. Amidst this unified feature there lie diverse cultural practices that are unique to each society. As an anthropologist of structuralist persuasion, I find pleasure in discovering the symbolism connected with human culture and in deciphering the ideational systems present in the social organization. With a different bent of mind, the present experience looks into the functional character of myths and beliefs associated with the mortuary practices in a particular frame of time and space. I have attempted here to delineate the mortuary practices of the Riang, one of the Primitive Tribal Groups enlisted by the Government of India living in the State of Tripura through a personal experience. Along with the actual practice of performances of the rituals, a narrative has also been brought into light to understand the ideal that lies in their cognition. For the Riang the ideal present in their mind does far more than to explain their institutions and the actual is their motive power and their authorization. The narration leads anthropologists to experience the human ideational systems that manifest a literary expression of the total social facts. I have not contemplated here to bring a dichotomy between the ideal and the actual; rather it is an attempt to understand the shift of paradigm that actually happens through performances of the rituals. To understand the process in a better way, I have taken the help of a narrative based on empirical experience in anticipation of doing justice to the subject. For me, Tripura, the homeland of the Riang, is an enchanting place that exists in my everlasting memory. I have been to this land over the last one and a half decade during the years 1994, 1996, 2005, and 2007—still continuing in 2009 to gather my anthropological experiences on various aspects. The place lingers in my memory and I live on with it, enveloping its existence. In one such sojourn, I experienced death of one of my informants before hand, the memory of which still haunts me even after so many years.

During the twilight hours of a gloomy winter more than a decade back I heard the sound of *khamkhaja* (drum) in the rhythm of *nouhkcham baihkhlu kamcham baihkhlu*, on my way back to the base camp from the field. As I approached the *hukka* (smoking apparatus) group of elderly people in the village meeting place, I heard the whispers of death message in total silence. It was Saturday, 9 November 1996, when Purnaram Riang, father of one of my informants, Daindrung, passed away at 4:00 pm at the age of 107 years. He lived over a century to see the transformation of his village Gardhang, from *huk* (*jhum* or slash and burn cultivation) to *kheto* (settled cultivation), from a preliterate society to the establishment of a primary school and from his Riang brethren only to outsiders like me, an anthropologist with a temporary base camp. The entire village mourned the death of Purnaram in silence for the whole night preparing for the funeral the next morning.

Tripura, a small hilly state, having an area of 10,486 sq. km, is situated in the north-eastern sector of India, between 22° 56′ and 24° 32′ north latitude and 91° 10′ and 92° 21′ east longitude. The state bears an extreme length of 183.5 km and extreme breadth of 112.7 km. During the erstwhile colonial rule the area was known as Hill Tipperah. Bounded by the Cachar district of Assam and the Mizo Hills of Mizoram in the eastern side, by Comilla and a part of Noakhali district of Bangladesh on the western side, by the districts of Chittagong and a part of Noakhali in the southern side, and by the Sylhet district of Bangladesh in the Northern side the state forms its jurisdiction. Under this backdrop of the state entity the area of present experience is delimited to the uniethnic village of Gardhang, comprising the Riang only, lying under Bagafa Block of South Tripura District. Before going into the details, I take the opportunity of introducing the ethnographic background of the Riang, which may help in understanding the situation in a better way.

The Riang are the second largest tribal group of Tripura with a population of 1,65,103 according to the census records of 2001, which forms 16.6 per cent of the total Scheduled Tribe population of the state. At the present day, they are enlisted as the only Primitive Tribal Group, inhabiting the state of Tripura. The Riang call themselves *Bru*, which, in their language, Kau *Bru*, means 'man'. The term Riang is, however, the widely used appellation to denote this second largest tribal group of Tripura. As evident from their legend, they migrated from Burma to Tripura through the forest-clad regions of Chittagong hill tract. After settling down in Tripura, the Riang got patronage from the ruling Tripuri kings of Tripura as defence personnel in the army of the State. But primarily the Riang are shifting hill cultivators. They have a dialect of their own, and have still retained their individual identity by clinging to their traditional core cultural markers. Today the Riang are not only numerically the second largest tribal group of Tripura but they are also an important group from the cultural point of view who have carved out a special position in the whole of the human surface of the state in general and in the map of the scheduled tribes of Tripura in particular.

The social structure of the Riang can better be understood through the study on Riang clan structure and kinship system. They accommodate a number of consanguineal kin group units called *panji* (clan), which are based on the rule of patrilineal descent. The *panji-haro* (clan structure) seemingly assumes the form of a bisection of the community having two segments of Molsoi and Meska clans.

The Riang kinship system embodies two basic concepts, *sandai* and *houchu*, which broadly refer to agnates and affines. It is also contemplated here that all consanguineal kins do not necessarily belong to *sandai* and all *houchu* members are not affines too. These two fundamental principles are explained in their language, *Kau Bru*, as *buithithahani erungtungha bududuhaphaim* meaning they are of the same blood and the same tree, and *houchuthaha kailaimi* signifying those who could be married. The sandai encompasses persons of the father's agnatic lineage group comprising primarily of two ascending and two descending generations from the ego. It also includes collaterals like a man's father's father and his brothers and their children, his father and father's brothers and their children, his brothers, his own and brother's children and their grandchildren (Bera, 2003, 2009; Bera and Bera, 2009).

In classifying the relatives as *houchu*, the principle of bilateral reckoning has been employed. The concept of *houchu* includes some of the relatives on the father's side and most of the relatives on the mother's side, who are affinal kin in the general sense. Affiliation to a clan although signifies consanguinity in a general sense because of the belief in common descent, in reality all the clansmen are regarded as *sandai*. Invariably the *sandai* must be of the same clan, whereas the *houchu* may be of the same or a different clan (Bera, 2003, 2009; Bera and Bera, 2009).

The creation myth of the Riang says that the life created by Achu Sibrai and Toitaochungchaoma from *hlongha-motai* (two stones) has its ultimate reality in death. It is also believed that Achu Sibrai, the Supreme Being causes death. Buraha, the incarnate of Achu Sibrai and Toibuma, the goddess of water and incarnate of Toitaochungchaoma, are responsible for life and death. Two sons of Buraha, Sisi and Mangji, are the guardian spirits of the *kothoi* (dead).

The Riang distinguish between *laotak* (spirit of the dead) and *rangma-nawba* (human soul), which comes out from the body with death. The spirit wanders about at the crematorium and its neighbourhood under the command of Sisi and Mangji, till the charred bones are immersed in the river after the completion of the post-funeral ritual. The spirit finally enters the *toi* (water). Contrary to this, the soul becomes *nawba* (wind) and ultimately vanishes in the void.

Reincarnation of soul is the common belief among the Riang. They believe that those who follow the path of righteousness in their lifetime are reborn as human being, and those who attain divine primacy by virtue of the spiritual attainments go straight to the temple of god in heaven. On the contrary, a sinful man is reborn as an animal. The dead may also be reborn as a new member in their old homes. The mother often marks the body of her dead child with black ink with the expectation of having him/her back as a new member in the family. It is believed that a pregnant woman, when cremated after death, never bears a child if she is reborn as a woman unless her husband plants a plantain tree with its flowers at the place of cremation, on the following day. In the backdrop of the theory of reincarnation, the nature of rebirth is determined by the past life.

Interestingly, the dead who turn into *puskrah hammi* or *motaihaia* (evil spirit) may trouble the descendants, in case they retain the material belongings such as *dah* (dagger/billhook), tobacco pipe, utensils, clothing, etc., which are supposed to be put into the pyre during cremation. It is expected that the dead may not find any difficulty without these material objects in the next life. This theory reflects intimate association with material cultural objects in the lifetime.

Unnatural death caused due to diseases or a fall from tree is believed to be caused by the deities and spirits and death due to an attack by tiger, wild animals, snake bite, or suicide is attributed to the sin committed in the life time.

Purnaram, a widower, aged 107 years, with whom lived his daughter Daindrung and son-in-law Brajalal, expired on 9 November 1996, at 4:00 pm. The beating of drum in the rhythm of *nouhkcham baihkhlu kamcham baihkhlu* signified the death of this centurion. In no other occasion this rhythm is played. With the beating of the drum two persons carried *riwasa* (bamboo stick) and *rusamphi* (small plant) in their hands and danced to ward off evil spirits. They put on *jama baju ha* (loose garment) as a special dress to encounter evil spirits. A messenger spread the message of death. Since Purnaram died on Saturday, the villagers did not consider it a good omen, as they believe the day to be of prosperity and progress. They anticipated evil spirits to invade the village, which they called *puskrah hammi*. Had it been Sunday too, they would have anticipated the same thing since the Riang consider these two days inauspicious for death. People carried *neem* leaves and *horkhu/dah* (dagger) and circumambulated around his house for seven times, which is done in case of death on Saturday or Sunday only. It was done to ward off *puskrah hammi* and the process was called *puskrah karbeing mi*, that is, purification of *puskrah hammi*. Fear roamed through the peoples' minds for two more counts, like death of a centurion and death on Kartick Chaturdasi otherwise called Bhut Chaturdasi as per the Hindu almanac when normally evil spirits move around. He was cremated on the northern side of the primary school on the *tilla* (hillock) on the following day,that is, 10 November 1996, the date coinciding with Kali Puja (*Deepavali*) on the Kartick Amavasya Tithi.

The next morning, the funeral procession moved towards the hillock at the base of which lies the stream of the river. While taking out the dead body from the house the carriers took out the feet first followed by the rest of the body. Since Purnaram had no son at all, his daughter Daindrung bathed the corpse and thrashed a fowl to death on a stone slab. It was done in anticipation of a belief that the death of the evil spirit should also be like that of the fowl. Purnaram's corpse was dressed up in dhoti and a turban and placed over a new mat covered with a new cloth. His head was kept towards the east on the *mangchouh* (pyre) and a *horkhu* was kept beside his chest. Since Purnaram lived a long life that too over a century, six *pala* (layer) of wood was arranged for *mangchouh*, instead of the general practice of five *pala* ascribed to men. It indicated that he has used more wood in his lifetime by way of cutting, carrying and using it as fuel wood. A *panga* (thread) was tied to the ears. Cooked rice and roasted fowl were kept near his feet along with two birds made of bamboo splits, named *Betaosa* (male) and *Betaoma* (female). Women sang *kahsmang* (funeral song) in chorus when the food was served to the deceased.

A *swmang nouh* (temporary memorial hut) was erected in front of the funeral place and a *thapa* (hearth) was kept inside it. A *nouh khai* (basket) and a *kala* (pitcher) covered with white cloth were placed on the roof of the *swmang nouh* for keeping fruits, comb, oil, and other daily needs. The *mangchouh* was arranged in front of the *swmang nouh*. Just in front of the hut a *yakhli* (ladder) was kept. Besides that a basket full of paddy and cotton was kept. At the lateral side of it a hearth was made for cooking *maiyohmi* (food for the deceased) to be served in the morning and evening by the *laotao* (a woman believed to be a spiritual person who mediates between the deceased and the afterworld). A *pohla* (white cloth of the height of the deceased) was tied to the pole of the *swmang nouh* like a flag.

After the completion of initial formalities fire was lit and put to pyre. All watched for more than three hours to see Purnaram being turned into ashes. With tearful eyes Daindrung made up her mind for *thafla huh mo*, that is, collection of bones from the ashes. The ashes and bones were carried through the village and were kept in the courtyard where villagers paid last homage to Purnaram. For the whole night women sang *kahsmang* in chorus.

The next morning members of both the *sandai* and the *houchu* came to the house to pay their last homage to Purnaram by way of sacrificing a fowl. Daindrung, as the chief mourner, visited the *swmang nouh* and deciphered human footprints on the ashes of the *thapa*. Jubilantly she declared that her father would be reborn as a human being as per the mythical belief of the Riang society.

The *maiyohmi* was repeated both in the morning and in the evening on the second day. It continued till the tenth day but from the third day onwards they observed *horsni* (pollution for closed group only), where members of Purnaram's *sandai* and *houchu* only observed pollution. They abstained from consuming *barmaing* (dried fish) and other non-vegetarian items and oil was not used as the cooking medium. They did not even perform worship of the deities at their respective houses.

On the tenth day all the observers were served food during daytime. Later on, the bones and ashes were brought from the *swmang nouh*, after its demolition, to the *charni nouh* (temporary hut designed to keep bones and ashes) erected at the middle point between the funeral place and the house. In the *charni nouh* a cot was kept where the bones were kept on its way back to home. It is a temporary resting place for bones. After the formal rest the cot was kept aside on the eastern side of the *charni nouh*. Women sang *kahsmang* in chorus and danced circumambulating the *charni nouh* for seven times. Men grouped themselves together and sat together at one place and were called *taukha* (crow), while the females formed another group to sit in a different place and were called *taoleing* (eagle).

On the floor of the *charni nouh* another pig was sacrificed, which they called *lungkhlai youh nai*. With the lungs of the sacrificed pig, they offered food near the bones and ashes as if food was served to the soul of the deceased. A woman from the group called Taoleing and then placed the bones and ashes in the *waphaing* (raft) as the last rite before taking it to the stream of the river. The cot was then turned upside down and kept on the western side of the *charni nouh*. Both the cot and the *charni nouh* were later demolished before proceeding towards the stream for final immersion of the bones and ashes.

The members of both the *sandai* and the *houchu* placed coins, rice cakes, and inscriptions of birds and animals on bamboo shaft in the *waphaing*, which was carried by Daindrung as the chief mourner. The male members who formed *taukha* group and the female members who formed *taoleing* group danced through the way towards the river. This dance was performed to ward off evil spirits who are believed to put obstructions in the path of the *waphaing*. At the riverside, Daindrung pushed the *waphaing* to the flow of water and subverted it. Daindrung, like other Riangs, believed that Purnaram's affection for his past home and village may redirect the *waphaing* towards the village. But the *waphaing* overturned deep down the stream carrying the last reminiscences of Purnaram.

The male members who formed *taukha* group and the female members who formed *taoleing* group again danced on their way back to the village as a gesture to ward off evil spirits. At the entrance of the village, a boundary was made to purify the people who were polluted by the death of Purnaram and the group of men and women called *taukha* and the *taoleing* respectively by sprinkling holy water. The *kothoi aukchai* (priest for the dead) sprinkled the holy water on them with a type of leaf called *khumphla msouh*. The members of the *sandai* and *houchu* formally received them after the ritual of purification of *taukha* and *taoleing*, with the belief that the evil spirits were not permitted to enter the village.

At the village all members of *sandai* and *houchu* sat together for a communal feast, which comprised rice, pork, *arouh chow mtouh* (rice beer), and other things. With this feast the whole part of *chormow bai lukhlai mo* (death ritual) came to an end, and Daindrung was ritually accepted as free from death pollution.

While understanding death ritual through narration one comes across the ideal in Riang cognition. This ideal may not resemble the actual practice as seen earlier at all times since the notion of system is always not a prerequisite qualification. My experience over a varying period of time is that the Riang have not always been accepting the ideal system, as a normative behaviour. I, therefore, take the advantage of mentioning a few lines about the ideal lying in their cognition, without going into the details since it does not enrich the personal experience as an observed behaviour. Moreover, I have discussed it elsewhere (2009) and to avoid repetition I have purposefully dropped the idea of depicting it in detail.

Two elaborate phases namely, *broksokmi* concerning cremation of the *kothoi* and *kothoi neimi* meaning post funeral rite comprise the mortuary practices. The Riang cremate the dead. Children below 1 year of age and death from small pox and cholera receive the treatment of burial. But the bones are dug out after a few months, when the flesh decomposes, and are kept in the *swmang nouh* for final immersion in river. The place for disposal of dead is always selected near a river/stream. The corpse is laid in supine position with the head directed towards the east.

The discussion on narrative understanding of the mortuary practices carries samples and specimens of an oral literature that the Riang ideally believe. I have permitted myself the luxury of drawing parallels with the actual practice that has been experienced in the field where I have taken latitude because of the rarity of the data and also because of the fact that such comparisons may be of some practical value in the discipline of social–cultural anthropology. One may presume that the myths and beliefs produced by the Riang were under the influence of such processes that are regular and normative for their particular mental condition. This condition may have gripped the Riang by imagery, and may indeed have portrayed some natural phenomenon or process at a time when mankind had not learnt to probe nature's secrets or to decipher the endless properties of matter. However, these properties like religion, among other social institutions, existed for some reasons, for the contribution to the cohesion and stability of the social group. Since these are developed from collective consciousness, a comparative analysis may yield formative structure underlying this sort of phenomenon. It was not, therefore, possible to analyse the situation in isolation. I supported the data with a narration to give an intelligible abstract idea. However, the practice provided a concrete reality that they observe otherwise also in the face of struggle and disaster.

References

Bera, Gautam Kumar. 2003. The Riangs of Tripura in the Changing Scenario. In Jayanta Sarkar and Jyotirmoy Chakraborty (eds), *Transition, Change and Transformation: Impacting the Tribes in India*, pp. 139–168. Kolkata: Anthropological Survey of India.

———. 2009. *The Land of Fourteen Gods: Ethno-cultural Profile of Tripura.* New Delhi: Mittal Publication.

Bera, Gautam Kumar and Nishi Bera. 2009. *Echoes from the Hillocks: A Compendium on the Tribes of Tripura.* Agartala: Tripura Bani Prakashani.

12

Making Senses of the Organizations and the Experiences of Anthropological Practices in a University of India

Arnab Das

Whenever contemporary scholars of our university engage in serious discussion about the past genres of anthropological practices in a guarded rhetoric, they set to leave a gloomy recent past (since mid-1960s) bequeathed from a blurry and legacious remote past (before mid-1960s). Their recapitulation would lead to a desirable future of anthropological practice which, nonetheless, would remain fraught with uncertainties. The 'present' lies in-between. Some common digressions of such discussions are the recollection of the experiences with the past faculty members, contemporary students and scholars of the department, interactions during fieldworks with them and all the remarkable bits of their lived experience of anthropological circles. The present author being an insider had regular experiences of joining such casual discussions, which are constituents of the organizational memory. Most of the times, we do it to be happy with the memories in either being critical or being proud of or being lost somewhere in the past without any end. Do we regress much? Is there any identity of such regression? All of us feel, at least if reminded, an inner voice of the reflective memories. Those, who have shared anthropological careers in such a prestigious university of India, have always been in some form of struggle about their identities, either with oneself, or among themselves, or with the 'others' in the academy. Being a faculty of science, anthropology has suffered from the hierarchic subjugation by almost all other scientific disciplines in the university either in a covert or in an overt manner. A threat of multidimensional marginalization had always been borne with. We assume that there was a past, when the scholars made good positions within the institution and abroad. The campus, where it is placed, started in the first half of the 20th century with a few disciplines of science. Anthropology was one of them. There was much such loosely found and co-constructed information with revivalist inputs in those discussions. But they failed to revive or replicate any definitely 'effective' local past for the present. Rather the uncertain effects of the remote and recent past commence to take recourse to certain practicable and slow shift of practices at present with growing ruptures from the past. The attempts to link the present works with those of the past have always been random and have hardly received any centre stage in the research.

The Memories of the 'Present': Why, What, and How

The essay is in search of the 'present' as it may be depicted with the practices and voices about them in order to understand the development of (inter) subjectivity of anthropological students and scholars in an institutional context. The memories[1] of fieldworks in that context, especially the socialization of students in seeing and knowing fieldwork for a period of 'present', intend to reflect and review mainly the methodological practices in 'social and cultural anthropology' of a significant university of India. It concentrates on the 'present' in order to add rigour to the facts. I prefer the temporal confinement of the 'present' since mid-1980s from when I engaged in fieldworks as a student till now when I am a faculty member of the same university. The institutional contexts and the culture that socializes the students of anthropology in fieldworks are no·less significant than what happens in fieldworks and how the fieldworkers deal with them. Thus appears a wider frame of making the memories of fieldworks more meaningful with respect to the institutional anthropological practices, which reproduce them and are yet to be reflected on significantly.[2] In that sense, it is almost the first endeavour to interpret and analyse the organizational process of knowing anthropology, doing fieldworks, and (re)thinking anthropological practices in that university.[3] It covers the similarities and differences of memories in diverse contexts of anthropological fieldwork[4] that we, the insiders of the institution, count. It is also about 'going native' about the organization of practices of social and cultural anthropology from inside. The search of the 'present' (Abu-Lughod, 1991; Whittaker, 1992) is both analytical and critical with a view to interpreting the backdrop of the earlier hegemony of positivism and the significance of emancipation of anthropological practice from that.

Methodologically, the present work is reflexive,[5] qualitative,[6] and an insider's account of different subject positions[7] at the organization of anthropology at an Indian university, which has been premier in establishing anthropology as a department in India. The objective of interpretation could not avoid some reductionist stances in being substantive about the lived experiences. In between the completion of my undergraduate study and the initial stage of doctoral work I started to recall the particular fieldworks. I started interpreting those situations of certain specific field experiences, which I didn't analyse during those particular fieldworks. The formative random thoughts developed over the years as basis for actions as they are discussed below. Recalling that way, the interpretation of experiences transforms the context of fieldwork. This writing with obvious auto-ethnographical slant in an organizational context of experiencing anthropology does focus on the shared interpretations and (dis)agreeable references of facts, but does not intend to close space of the same.

I experienced anthropological fieldworks as a student, as a researcher, as a teacher, or as a supervisor of field training and doctoral fieldwork, as a colleague in the department in an undergraduate college under that Indian university, as a colleague in the department of that university now. More explicitly they include (1) getting training in fieldwork in rural India at both the undergraduate and postgraduate (Masters) levels, (2) helping the supervision of training of fieldworks of the students at undergraduate and Masters levels, (3) directly supervising the fieldworks of the undergraduate students and students of an Indian university at Masters level, (4) supervising the doctoral works of the research students, (5) exchanging the experience of the same with the colleagues and the seniors, and (6) my own studies principally in urban areas, (7) 'going native' among the fieldworkers, associated with the research in the department, and above all (8) experiencing fieldwork not isolated from the wider organizational milieu in which the anthropological practices take place.

My responses to the recast memories emerge both as additions to, advocacy for fundamental modifications of anthropological practices and consequent actions in institutional context. I selected to follow a general framework of certain positions adopted by the participants in the local anthropological practices. My experiences intend to address critically the position(s) and their reflections, as shared among the fieldworkers at different levels of the institution. This participatory interpretation with insiders' criticism of the process is neither to challenge nor to defend any side of the contending practices. It might only help in opening a discursive space for a virtually interminable journey of interpretation along with their terminable presence on paper.

The shared understanding of the process emerged from the positions of the students and scholars, where anthropological practice is born and socialized. Nonetheless, the representation is more from the position of teacher-supervisor. The initiation into fieldwork means a lot to the forthcoming individual studies of anthropologists of an institution. At first, I shall focus on the anthropological field training and fieldworks in that Indian university till a few years back that would be able to explain the critical urge for the emergence of certain more recent practices in curricula and other academic actions.

Broadly I assign the genre that I have passed through and I shall reflect critically in this essay on the moment of qualitative research, named 'The Traditional Period (Early 1900s–Second World War)' (Denzin and Lincoln, 2000).

The Premises in the Beginning

There are two types of undergraduate courses in Anthropology; in one, the students do not take Anthropology as major or with honours and do not usually continue higher study in Anthropology. In this undergraduate course, the actual training in the field takes around seven days and students have to incur relatively less expenditure of their own. Due to pan-Indian uniform formatting of undergraduate courses for nearly the last decade the students with Anthropology as a 'General' paper (without 'honours'), like those with honours in Anthropology, may choose to join some other universities for Masters degree, but this university selects only the undergraduate students with honours in Anthropology on the basis of merit of the scores in examination. Although the future prospect of such general course is somewhat broadened, for most of the students taking up the 'General' paper, the fieldwork is, though compulsory, not a very serious concern for a career. In the other undergraduate course of Anthropology (with Honours), the students according to the merit of the results are enrolled to Anthropology in any university, after which they can continue their research career. In this undergraduate course with honours in Anthropology one field training would take a longer period, ranging from more than two weeks to more than three weeks. The students incur almost the whole bulk of the expenditure, except the expenditure of the journey to the field. Till four years back, there was only one fieldwork for the students with honours in Anthropology.

The students studying Anthropology in the said university at undergraduate level come from science background, especially in combination with biological sciences. Most of them are weak and sensitive to their inadequate practice in English language, which emerges as a barrier to descriptive practices. The previous experience of learning natural sciences principally ingrains the conceptual structure of anthropology and the fieldwork as well. 'Facts' or data are supposed to be out there in the field similar to that of matters outside. The human facts are also presumed to appear systematically like that, either descriptively, analytically, explanatorily, or objectively in a pre-given format but unlikely to undergo conscious introspection, reflexivity, and (inter)subjective processes. The undergraduate course till four years back had nothing conspicuously beyond an unclear combination of positivist and realist limits of understanding anthropology. The teachers and the students since mid-1980s, so far I know them as a member, came from the understanding of science, which demonstrates empirical objectivity in a deductive format of reasoning about the truth. Such a format of choosing, observing, recording, knowing, and memorizing things socialized them, especially with the grossly digested 'structural–functionalist' understanding of social and cultural anthropology as a 'science'. It provided them with minimum capacity to respond to or to internalize later growth of the social sciences in general and anthropology in particular,[8] especially of qualitative research.

The Continuing Premises

In this university the students before taking up social–cultural anthropology in the second year as a special paper during the postgraduate (Masters) level go through 'fieldworks'[9]—either a study of a population of caste(s) and/or tribe(s) settled in particular village(s) and the impact of environment on the 'material' life of such a rural population. The observable aspects of the 'settlement', 'population', 'kinship', 'economy', 'religion', 'political organization', 'Lifecycle' practices, and other structural and developmental aspects of the collective life in certain conveniently selected village(s) remain central to the empirical enquiry. The enquiry is based principally on quantitative measures of the population and descriptive 'normativity of tradition' with the use of household survey schedules, interviews of different types, case studies, genealogical techniques, and observation. Before and after going to the field and staying there in a camp for a duration varying from not less than one week to approximately three weeks the teacher-supervisor takes some classes for teaching the methods, phases, and issues of collecting information and presenting them in the form of a report. Precisely, with little or no actual reading of any ethnography, and hardly ever reading any available book of updated methodology, the trainees try to learn 'field' as equivalent to 'laboratory' or natural setting for 'scientific observation'. In the field, the objective truths are supposed to exist in a systematic order, which had seemingly been already there either as universal or as particular pattern. This would happen less as a product of systematically generalizable observation of the students, more as hegemony of a narrowly alterable template of structuring such Indian village(s) or rural population. This 'thin' template providing both a process and a structure of practices is less consciously reproduced and transmitted by the teacher-supervisor(s). Such reproduction is aided by the students with their 'Indian' submission to the authority of 'teacher', lack of enriched anthropological subjectivity to analyse and interpret experience otherwise. The teacher-supervisor, on the other hand, with or without some exposure to any particular field, though staying with the students in the field camp, dictates the structure of the report in which the data are fit into. Till five years back in postgraduate theoretical syllabus regarding research methodology, there was only a meagre part of basic statistics for all the students before they would take up any specialization in the final year. The students with social and cultural anthropology as their specialization in the last year of the Masters degree could hardly be aware of different research approaches, methodologies, styles of fieldwork, writing, and even any referred conceptions of ethnography, qualitative and quantitative researches, as these were absent in the syllabus and training of fieldwork. The students are informed about certain terms by the supervisors, such as 'participant observation' and 'rapport establishment', 'emic–etic' and 'insider's view', etc. The classroom training altogether would mean explanation of the purpose and the span of visit, to pose cordiality and respect to the unknown villagers for achieving their trust to some extent, which might help them give valid description of 'things' in their life and if possible help us to participate in their daily activities. The criteria of selection of field become a post-hoc construct of purposes derived from and linked with the objectives of the syllabus.

The Close Encounters

From a field camp, arranged and administered by the supervisor(s), the students would travel to the neighbouring village(s), selected by the supervisor(s). The criteria of selection of any village follow the priority in convenience of collecting data within a stipulated period. A team of male and female students of the ages around 20 years—generally 18–23 years— would be introduced to the headmen and/or to the individual villagers by certain local mediators, by the supervisor(s) or by means of certain prior arrangements done by the supervisor(s). The villagers sometimes quickly overcome the suspicion about the group of young strangers and accept that they will face minimum risk and problems in giving information about the questions asked by unknown young students for their educational purpose assigned by any certain urban institution, if the time for their livelihood jobs is not 'wasted'. In addition, the villagers coming to understand the cooperation of the local administration might remain hesitant at the initial periods of responses to the inquiry of the students. Afterwards, members of individual families who become close to individual students develop certain levels of interpersonal emotional proximity. Usually, the villagers are found to be co-operative during the enquiries.

In search of 'traditional' knowledge and experience, the investigators lead the rural informants to certain kinds of normative perception of their own lived experiences. It becomes a communicative tussle between informants and fieldworkers. The tussle is for more 'information' of the (hypothesized) normative fields of facts on behalf of the investigating students. The strain is more because of the short span of fieldwork. The descriptions in the report conceal the fact that the so-called 'valid information' depended on the informants' understanding of how, what, and why they are asked about themselves. The informants, who were previously exposed to such enquiry, responded more readily than the newly exposed ones to fulfil the target of the students. For getting organized information in a preconceived format within the short span of field training, the priority lies in fulfilling the target. The students, who intuit better the virtual construct of representing 'data', are more effective in executing the required observational and interviewing roles while collecting the data. Such 'aptitude' of gathering and representing the data is reinforced in the subsequent fieldworks. Finally, data collection becomes the flexible and easier interaction of the young students of an urban institution with the rural people for certain types and magnitude of valid information during a fixed period.

Certain known discourses of power in the dyadic relations—urban–rural, aged–young, acquaintance–stranger, affluent–poor, guest–host, administrator–administered, more literate–less literate, etc.—with or without certain minor alterations are reinforced each time on both the fieldworkers and the rural subjects in the name of 'rapport establishment'. Unknowingly both the interviewers and the interviewees face advantages and disadvantages of the combinations of the dyads in varied situations. The 'rituals' of such enquiry, like rapid foraging activities, that too involving competition among the students, have their ends in their successful presentation based on the 'standard' methods and techniques of data collection and their 'systematic' patterns of reporting.

With(out) some minimum exposure of particular ethnographic work and awareness of the people to be studied, the students move to the fields according to the arrangements and directions of the supervisors. Till a few years back, the students had been learning and writing about methodology only as the methods and techniques of collecting data without being aware of their constitutional relations with theories, ethics, analysis, or anything else. A manageable template of objective structure of 'traditional' society based on unwritten consensus guides them to supervise the fieldworks. The field notes[10] are excerpts or detailed descriptions either given by the informants during interviews or taken as accounts of observation, especially on objective materiality. As it has been mentioned earlier, in the name of field diary we usually have a timetable of tasks performed each day, in most cases written in phrases. The students would not know and mention any understanding in the form of jottings, methodological notes, theoretical notes, personal notes, memos, codes and so on till some years back. The ideas and implications of different notes,[11] except field notes and field diaries,[12] were completely absent. Consequently, exclusive notes on methods, theories, personal experiences, and their significant relations with the dissertation and afterwards with the doctoral research are unlikely to be available. Those, who would get very much engrossed sensitively with their encounters of the fieldwork, had optionally maintained personal diaries for own subjective scribbling of significant moments. Such a diary as a chronicle of contacts, activities, and other memories is not meant for any core part of the fieldwork and the data 'proper'. However, such practice is also a sequel to the training of keeping a field diary, quite similar to a timetable of contacts and activities during fieldwork.

Like the students of Anthropology and the anthropological supervisor(s), the informants would also care to function safely as demanded by the situations. The exchange, however, is not balanced. The villagers finally accommodate to respond positively to the cordial insistence of the unknown urban team of young boys and girls, who are 'strangers', yet appear harmless, interesting, and interested in them. Their price-free job of giving scarce information serves the career and profession of individual students, scholars, and supervisor. Only the tears in the eyes of the young students and some key informants at the departure from the fields and gradually fading memories of emotions would mark the sudden ruptures of newly grown relations between the team of fieldworkers and villagers. We have seen no reports encouraging any narrative on those (inter)subjective contexts of emotion[13] and relations between these two parties.

A Look Back at Appraisals

The reports, which conceptually may be termed as qualitative one, of a group of fieldworkers on any particular group/community would comprise the similar objective data of the 'same' real society according to their similar socialization in 'ideal'/'standard' anthropological practices. As examples of the variation some might consider certain discussion under titles such as 'limitations of the work' to mention where they failed to meet the 'standards' and why. The situational contexts in the fieldwork for relating the 'observer' and the 'observed' as two (non)-equivalent categories of subject have never been 'relevant' issue of methodology in the report. The experiences of concrete situations of collecting data are completely marginalized by merely mentioning the application of the methods and the techniques (only for collecting data) in a few paragraphs. Some of the central elements of anthropology, such as 'fieldwork traditions', 'village', 'tribe', 'caste', 'material culture', 'technology', 'area and people under study', 'kinship', 'political organization', etc., according to the coverage of study are briefly mentioned, almost copied from certain books or previous reports. Such minimal use of books or papers goes on without any essential training of writing 'references' that is finally learnt while writing doctoral thesis.

The authenticity of 'data' presupposes the standard authentic mechanism. The 'key informants', who can provide the students with the 'scarce' authentic information about their traditional past and present, would again be the key subjects or intermediate objective means to the facts in the desirably 'objective' articulation. Other members of the community, who are instantly judged by the students as unable to do so, seemed to represent the same culture or community with less capacity to represent culture.

I have seen none questioning how the members of a village or a community having different responses to and knowledge about the past and present are accepted as representatives of the one/same culture or whether the concept of culture is questionable coherence/homogeneity. The commonest experience regarding any inquired aspect differs in details, even if they are put in group interview. The students do not learn how to conduct any group discussion and how to derive the points of consensus and of disagreement. In most cases, the students or the supervisors could make the way to readily assumed gross consensus among the interviewees. In the name of 'scientific objectivity' the report officially becomes subject-independent, bias-free, but conscious representation of the reporter's readily made interpretation of information. Anybody, even a non-participant fieldworker might write such a report. The problems are somewhat handled in doctoral research of much greater duration, but any accurately updated training of methodology does not build them up.

The students according to individual merits urge for being provided with, rather than actively shaping gradually, the skeletal structure of fieldwork for better collection of information for systematic presentation. The presentation is theoretically guided by the 'ideals' of the local academic tradition of giving a synchronic, but with the normative picture of contemporaneity. The many-sided (holistic) empirical portrayal of village people, with more emphasis on their normative traditions of behaviour, has been the obsession of local anthropological training. The absence of any guidance on relating those aspects is also a feature of that 'holism'. Those aspects of 'settlement', 'population', 'kinship', 'economy', 'religion', 'political organization', 'lifecycle' practices, other structural and developmental issues, etc., remain as unrelated isolates in that 'whole'. Thus, (un)knowingly it would portray 'present' as mere assemblage of isolates. It becomes more a continuity and/or reference of the past traditions than a relational description of the aspects of 'present' intensively by itself and by analysing whether and how it is a continuity of tradition. On the other hand, the 'scarce' and 'relevant' facts constitute the descriptive report in a preconceived, least analytical, and unfocused format. The experience of differences including (inter) subjective ones is said to be irrelevant and not qualified for representative attention. The data of a very few reports had secured the attention of the public(ation) and most of them are dumped in the department and/or the copy is preserved by the respective student. However, all the experiences in the field would remain as unwritten experience and memory. Some of the principal reasons of inadequate output belong not only to colonially precipitated blindness and under-productive methodological input, but also to the colonial aftermath of adopting weakly internalized English language as a medium of reading and writing. All of them reappear in any subsequent fieldworks, but again (con)textualized in the same old 'pattern'. One may hardly know, during the last 20 years or more, anybody in this local anthropological circle to give serious academic attention to the significance of such practices and their memories, other than using them to arrange and repeat such processes. The rural informants are also subjected to a framework of questions and observations according to which they learn to inform about 'facts' about themselves. Yet, both the interviewers and the interviewees keep it unnoticed that there emerge altogether always some new constructions about themselves in context of such interactions.

In the reports and the theses, the initial one or two chapters introduce those relevant 'facts' of learning from books, which are thought to precede and guide the collection of the 'facts' from the field, their presentation in the subsequent essays. The dissertation fieldwork always of more than a few months during the final year specialization in social and cultural anthropology follows a similar approach to the field with some open options for appropriate methods of collecting data, though much obsessed with the 'normative' image of empirical area under study, thus tending more towards structured enquiry with the presupposition of a general and lasting construct of any group or community or culture. The introduction is more focused on the topic of research, though usually devoid of any clearly reasonable analysis of the previous works for reaching the methodology or the approach adopted for the research. In case of doctoral thesis, only the degree of refinement and checks on the coherence of the texts increase. Every report of the 'ethnographic facts' becomes the variation of the similar logical framework. Methodologically they exemplify that there are certain definite tools for searching, collecting various—known to be anthropologically—definite objects to be reported following certain standard 'pattern'. The reporters take care of the quality of presenting the 'objects' and worry about their ability to reach close to or beyond the 'standard', which is solely mediated and governed by the perception of the teacher-supervisor, not usually obtained by their own understanding of suggested readings.[14]

All the specific subjective experiences of collecting 'facts' are dissolved in the depiction of the traditional generality of a community or of individual cases representing the generality/community. The 'ritualistic' presentation of case studies intends to suggest only a direct collection of a variation of the general whole. For the individual dissertation in the final year of the Masters course, the students only know that fundamentally a subject-alienated reception and depiction of the said people or culture is the average task, which indicates to avoid the inherent 'possibility' of true copy of another report. Every student seems to remain unaware of the analytical and introspective attitude to such a practice. They are unknowingly accustomed to inheriting the laboratory procedures of demonstration of facts. It remains the sole 'tested' experience of scientific search. Despite a strong ethical resistance and solidarity against any attempt of reducing the importance of fieldwork in the courses, faculty members of both the undergraduate colleges and the university feel that there are many limitations in the training of fieldwork and methodology that they have allowed to be conferred on themselves and subsequently on their students. Never facing any serious challenge from inside, everyone suspends any effective interrogation about the consensual conviction that the present guidelines of fieldwork comprise near to the best feasible and applicable format for the training. There is hardly any reflexive assessment of the whole. If the supervisors and subsequently the students would identify and consider the intersubjective and other situational contexts relevant to their purpose, they would have to record details of the situations and interactions. These would clarify their positions with respect to the data. However, such opening for particular experiences to appear intensively in representation would problematize the over-simplistic practice of generalization and result in moving towards theoretical alternatives to positivism.

Constraints, Emancipation, and Actions

The social position of anthropology as a discipline is different from that of the classically and contemporarily 'principal' disciplines of natural sciences and humanities in the said university. It is considered as a natural science discipline in the university, thus providing less ground to develop it otherwise. As a natural science discipline it has not been able to be a forerunner. Both the lack of infrastructural provisions and consequently mediocrity were some contributing factors to the present state of anthropological practices. One might wish to be analytical about the grand local and global backdrops that problematized the present state of anthropology and its disciplinary identity. One might like to analyse the chronicle of phases through which anthropology at the said university has gone through. With all due regards to the prevailing sensitivity about the ethical, analytical, accountable, and creative dimensions to these practices of anthropology in a span of the last 20 years and presumably more, except last few years, the above framework has been stable/stagnating and underproductive. One of the excuses acting in support of the underproductivity is that a nation like India could only respond more supportively to the more 'modern' disciplines of 'higher education'. In consequent dearth of external attention, the previous generations could only try to make the students learn their 'standard patterns' of anthropological practices. The urban institutional students and scholars begin their anthropological careers with the empirical search for the 'others', usually any rural group or community less known to them. They learn that anthropology, like other natural sciences, needs at least an embodied otherness for its exercise and demonstration/description. The Indian students practise this mostly among the Indians, within their Indian culture and society as such without considering the historical and theoretical implications of the relation between themselves and the 'observed insiders'.[15]

One might argue that there is little or no problem in such relegation of reflexivity to the realistic discourse on the objective externality of culture or of society in a 'discipline of science'. There is no problem if this 'culture of science' may only speak and discipline the practices. I would not imply to reject this 'culture', rather I would argue that one needs to get equipped to reflect on this 'culture'. If our purpose is to maintain epistemological gesture of knowing and reporting objectivity, it is not necessary to stop rethinking the contexts and the situations of collecting more valid and meaningful data in relation to one another, even if we set aside other theoretical, epistemological understanding of research. I find to argue that alternative ethnographic subjective positions of fieldworker could be operative within similar infrastructural constraints. In the sole effort of an outward shielding of the positivist norms, any inwardly existing reflexive force could not be unleashed.

We know that every participant and every teacher-supervisor in the so-called 'stable' framework of interaction has her/his own different memories of the field situations that remained unreported and irrelevant due to the 'stable' (stagnating) practices of 'anthropology'. The emancipation of anthropological practices from such a cycle of 'stagnation' needs to engage more subjective, shared, and critical interpretations of individual anthropologists so that these memories can be used in future anthropology. I recollected moments of my studentship during Masters level while rethinking about the 'present'. I found myself further engaged in exploring and inquiring the experience interminably one in relation to the other, than to assume the rigid and taken-for-granted boundaries of the facts. I experienced that the rational boundaries of valid facts would collapse as a result of the shift of context of relatedness. The contextual details of experiences might at least explain the real opening for a lot of different understanding. As a trainee fieldworker I was a member of teams of students, ranging from six to twenty-four, in all my fieldworks till the end of my Masters level. The fields were respectively (1) at a tribal forest village in Bastar, Madhya Pradesh, (2) at multi-tribal villages near Ghatsila, Jharkhand and (3) among the Juangs (Das and Bagchi, 1992), Saharas (Sengupta et al., 1994), and (4) among the agriculturalist caste people in three different villages at Keonjhar district, Orissa. I could not come out of the so-called 'unknowing positivist' methodological positions interpreted earlier in collecting and reporting the data. In the subsequent two years, I went to the fieldworks of later batches of students as an assistant (5) among the tribal and caste population in Jamtara, Jharkhand, (6) among the tribal people of Keonjhar, Orissa. I was virtually in charge of supervising some individual dissertations of Masters students in both rural and peri-urban fields for two consecutive years. I came to understand that the intersubjective sharing of contextual interactions taking place always produced different agreements about 'the concerned objectivity'. The people we study participate in the contexts of the investigation first to assume the positions from where they are being inquired. While they respond attentively and submit to the expected position of informants, a discourse is persuaded for reaching an agreement about it. I tried to extend a sort of reflexive account of my Jharkhand experience (1993) with the same people. After the examination was over, I went to them with the report in order to understand whether they would like to agree with the report. They stumbled and did not feel like identifying with our construction of the experience with their previous agreements of discourse. They added much information to the previously 'valid' agreements on objectivity. The disagreements and differences were collected in the same 'pattern' of the previous agreements. I saw that the data got modified. I have already said that such interviewer–interviewee discourse of anthropological search for knowledge does not imply any balanced exchange. Both the parties may try to manage a balance in order to come to an agreement. In search of such specific discourse-centred disagreements between the researcher and researched I selected some different 'others', who are not rural and to whom 'my' public identity belongs. In such urban studies, every informant, including myself, is supposed to possess the principal criteria of becoming the key informant(s). The experience is somewhat different if one has to accept both agreements and the related disagreements (i.e., more subject positions) on the same discourse. One has to accept the different and even contradictory meanings sometimes of the same signification. Therefore, the account of exploring the differences of meaning in the space of one's own culture gives priority to interpretation and rethinking the agreed meanings. Such a kind of journey took me closer to some observational and analytical tool, psychoanalysis, whereby it was finally possible to find out my desired mode of perceiving a work in terms of my own experience of enabling myself and others to relate different, even contradictory experiences rather than talking about a work as fixed, necessary, and instrumental disposition.

However, the principal themes, which emerged from my critical rethinking about the fieldwork practices around the mid-1990s, might be memorized as such:

1. Not only the syllabi were not updated for nearly 20 years. They needed compulsory exposure to contemporary theoretical, methodological, and ethnographic issues and works, even about the tribes, caste, kinship, and village.
2. Due to this crucial undernourishment for addressing varied contexts of fieldwork and the data, we were unable to articulate our lived experiences of 'differences' and 'relationship' between our regularly inhabited Indian setting and another Indian setting studied.
3. We had to ignore the nuances of emotions and feelings in varied situations of interactions of engagement with the rural or urban 'strangers' and ourselves being strangers to them.
4. There was no scope of assessing the roles we exert aggressively to establish 'familiarity', in the name of rapport, with the people for 'foraging of data' and the consequences of parting relations at the end of such fieldwork.[16]
5. There was no practice of recording the dialogical narratives of data and particularly relating it to the gender or age of the fieldworkers.
6. Those which are presented as objective, especially the qualitative, facts about the people in the report are almost never identified by the students as 'qualitative' and checked by the people studied.
7. Consequently the issues of methodology, theory, ethics, and personal experiences appeared either gross or ignored.
8. Above all, the inherent weakness of the students in English language as a medium of reading and writing worked as a central criterion for most of the problems discussed above.

The lack of realization of the anthropological implications of the above issues and above all the absence of any formal capacity for implementing any consensual academic actions wasted nearly one decade from the mid-1990s to come up with the updated dimensions of research and theories in undergraduate syllabus and later in postgraduate (Masters) syllabus. While joining the university nine years back the consensus on modifying the practices of anthropological enquiries led to the following modifications in the syllabus:

1. Updating the syllabi with emphasis on theories, concepts, research methodology, fieldwork, use of computer, contemporary issues of local, and global significance for anthropological attention and intervention.

2. Extensive coverage of 'traditional' Indian elements of anthropology, such as tribes, castes, weaker/backward sections, rural society, religions and contemporary problems.

3. Since the beginning year of undergraduate course with honours, introduction of compulsory training of fieldwork and/or student's seminar and/or building of research proposal based on ethnographic materials in every year up to Masters level to enhance individual capacity to address, present, and interact.

4. In postgraduate (Masters) theoretical course emphasis on the works of individual anthropologists, ethnographies, philosophical underpinnings of anthropological works in both Western and Indian contexts, subjective and shared reflections of lived experiences of anthropological practices during coursework of the students, writing research proposals based on contemporarily significant topics and applied anthropology.

5. Recording the subjective and intersubjective aspects of field experience.[17] Some supervisors have started to teach how to relate and articulate the notes in the field reports, especially at the postgraduate level and thesis.

6. Expanding the choices of dissertation and doctoral topics based on diversity and contemporarily significant issues and encouraging interdisciplinary works with added emphasis on strong theoretical articulation.

Conclusion

The points listed above have been in practice only since the last four years as possible avenues of emancipation from dominantly existing confinements and constraints. It would be too early to talk about the consequences. Rather, before writing the essay while sharing the above memories and interpretations with the students, scholars, and my present colleagues, trying to reach consensus for action, there were some worth-mentioning points of evaluation of the memories:

1. The rigorously maintained empirical practices of fieldwork had great roles in enhancing the capacities of communication of the students, realized later either in academic or in non-academic professions.
2. In enhanced theoretical and methodological training of the course-work, the emphasis on collecting 'objective' and 'verifiable' standard of the data is given equal priority to the emphasis on subjective and intersubjective constructs of the data.
3. The silent and local post-colonial past in memories of anthropological practices[18] needs to be voiced in the light of the 'present'. It is needed both in order to unearth the local Indian anthropological selves in relation to the respective cultural milieu and to look for other different interpretations and frameworks[19] of accounting for the past practices apart from critically rating them as 'stagnating', 'under-productive', 'non-reflexive', underdeveloped tradition of colonially mediated 'unclear' positivist subversion of science.

It is, however, held valid that memories are productive resources, means and guides of (dis)agreements and actions in anthropology.[20]

Notes

1. Not as Mayer (1989) and Kumar (1992) used it in the sense of revisit and reminiscence of the lived relationship respectively, but closer to that in Rosemary and Jack Lévy (2001) and Bacchiddu (2004).
2. Jeremy Beckett (2001) puts it differently in a wider context of national anthropological practices. Similarly important are the attempts of Daphne et al. (ed.) (2000) and Soto and Dudwick (ed.) (2000) in showing the changing practices and moral concerns of fieldwork respectively with changing nature of state.
3. I found a very relevant discussion in Moeran (2009).
4. Vered (2000) provides a wider construct on the same.
5. Davies (1999) is worth mentioning here. I could call it self-reflexive auto-ethnography (Reed-Danahay, 1997) as well.
6. The books of Sanjek (1996), Denzin and Lincoln (eds) (2000), and Stewart (1998) inspired me a lot.
7. A nice example is the collaborative experience of Buford et al. (2000).

8. A few of the notable ones, which are not assimilated in teaching and learning of anthropology, in spite of their availability, include Clifford (1988), Clifford and Marcus (eds) (1986), Geertz (1973), Gupta and Ferguson (eds) (1997), Marcus and Fisher (1986), and Marcus (1998).
9. Srinivas et al. (eds) (1979) have an enriching account.
10. We thought of suggesting reading of the following just a few years back: Emerson et al. (1995), Malinowski ([1989] 1967), Powdermaker (1966, 1967), Evans-Pritchard (1976), Maybury-Lewis (1965), Mead (1977), and Rabinow (1977).
11. We could not make them read so far Marcus (1999), Moeran (2006, 2007), Sanjek (ed.) (1990), and those others available in the library.
12. Not in the sense of the process as found in Newbury (2001), Okely (2007), and such others.
13. The writing of Hedican (2006) is a nice example to mention in this context.
14. The commoner list of references of reading fieldwork would include Notes and queries (BAAS, 1874), A.L. Epstein's *Craft of Social Anthropology* (ed.) (1967), Pelto and Pelto (1978), and a few others mostly on 'scientific' social research methods. The addition of references of started nearly 10–5 years back, especially in postgraduate course: Ellen (1984), Hammersley and Atkinson (1994), Spradley (1979, 1980), Asad (1973), Keesing and Strathern (1998), and Bernard (1994, 2001).
15. Three writings by Chatterji (2005), Sundar et al.(2000), and Berger (2012) may be referred in this regard.
16. Gary (1993) makes a good note on assessing the moral dilemma in fieldwork.
17. We need to add to the reading materials, like Quinn (ed.) (2005).
18 Sider and Smith (eds) (1997) may be remembered. Institute of Ethnology, Academia Sinica and Anthropology Department (2007) may be enlightening.
19. Chatterji's (2005) review of Indian Anthropology has been a very recent incorporation in their list of readings.
20. I deeply acknowledge all my colleagues, students, anthropological researchers, and above all those numerous people in my previous fieldworks, whose memories enlightened and strengthened me with the conviction of (re)thinking differently.

References

Abu-Lughod, L. 1991. Writing Against Culture. In R. Fox (ed.), *Recapturing Anthropology: Working in the Present*, pp. 137–162. Santa Fe, New Mexico: School of American Research Press.
Asad, T. 1973. *Anthropology and the Colonial Encounter*. London: Ithaca Press.
Bacchiddu, Giovanna. 2004. Stepping between Different Worlds: Reflections Before, During and after Fieldwork. *Anthropology Matters Journal*, 6(2): 1–9.

Beckett, Jeremy. 2001. Some Aspects of Continuity and Change among Anthropologists in Australia or 'He-who-eats-from-one-dish-with-us-with-one-spoon'. *Plenary Address to the 2001 Meeting of the Australian Anthropological Society,* University of Sydney, AAS, Sydney.

Berger, Peter. 2012. Theory and Ethnography in the Modern Anthropology of India. *HAU: Journal of Ethnographic Theory,* 2(2): 325–357.

Bernard, H.R. 1994. *Research Methods in Anthropology: Qualitative and Quantitative Approaches* (2nd edition). Thousand Oaks, California: SAGE.

———. 2001. *Research Methods in Anthropology* (2nd edition). London: Alta Mira.

British Association for the Advancement of Science (BAAS). 1892 *Notes and Queries on Anthropology.* London: Royal Anthropological Institute.

Buford May, A. Reuben and Mary Pattillo-McCoy. 2000. Do You See What I See: Examining a Collaborative Ethnography. *Qualitative Inquiry,* 6(1): 65–87.

Chatterji, Roma. 2005. An Indian Anthropology: What Kind of Object is it? In Jan Van Bremen, Eyal Ben-Ari and Syed Farid Alatas (eds), *Asian Anthropology,* pp. 162–178. London and New York: Routledge.

Clifford, J. 1988. *The Predicament of Culture: Twentieth-Century Ethnography, Literature, and Art.* Cambridge, Massachusetts: Harvard University Press.

Clifford, J. and G.E. Marcus. (eds) 1986. *Writing Culture: The Poetics and Politics of Ethnography.* Berkeley, California: University of California Press.

Daphne, Berdahl, Bunzl Matti and Martha Lampland (eds). 2000. *Altered States: Ethnographies of Transition in Eastern Europe and the Former Soviet Union.* Ann Arbor, Michigan: University of Michigan Press.

Das, Arnab and S.S. Bagchi. 1992. From the Forest to the Market: The Means of Subsistence of the Juang. *Journal of Indian Anthropological Society,* 30: 59–66.

Davies, C.A. 1999. *Reflexive Ethnography: A Guide to Researching Selves and Others.* New York: Routledge.

Denzin, N.K. and Y.S. Lincoln (eds). 2000. *Handbook of Qualitative Research.* Thousand Oaks, California: SAGE.

Ellen, R.F. (ed.) 1984. *Ethnographic Research: A Guide to General Conduct.* London and Orlando, Florida: Academic Press.

Emerson, Robert M., Rachel I. Fretz and Linda L. Shaw. 1995. *Writing Ethnographic Fieldnotes.* Chicago, Illinois: University of Chicago Press.

Epstein, A.L. 1967. *The Craft of Social Anthropology.* London: Tavistock Publications.

Evans-Pritchard, E.E. 1976. *'Some Reminiscences and Reflections on Fieldwork,' Appendix to the Abridged Paperback (ed.) of Witchcraft, Oracles, and Magic Among the Azande.* Oxford: University of Oxford.

Gary, Alan Fine. 1993. Ten Lies of Ethnography: Moral Dilemmas of Field Research. *Journal of Contemporary Ethnography,* 22: 267–294.

Geertz, Clifford. 1973. *The Interpretation of Cultures.* New York: Basic Books.

Gupta, A. and J. Ferguson (eds). 1997. *Anthropological Locations: Boundaries and Grounds of a Field Science.* Berkeley, California: University of California Press.

Hammersley, Martyn and Paul Atkinson. 1994. *Ethnography: Principles in Practice* (2nd edition). London: Routledge.

Hedican, Edward J. 2006. Understanding Emotional Experiencein Fieldwork: Responding to Grief in a Northern Aboriginal Village. *International Journal of Qualitative Methods*, 5(1): 17–24.

Institute of Ethnology, Academia Sinica and Anthropology Department. 2007. *The Future of Ethnographic Practices (June 2–3)*. Puli, Taiwan: National Chi Nan University.

Keesing, Roger and Andrew Strathern. 1998. Fieldwork. *Cultural Anthropology: A Contemporary Perspective* (3rd edition). Fort Worth: Harcourt Brace.

Kumar, Nita. 1992. *Friends, Brothers and Informants: Fieldwork Memoirs of Banaras*. Berkeley, California: University of California Press.

Malinowski, Bronislaw. 1967/1989. *A Diary in the Strict Sense of the Term*. Stanford, California: Stanford University Press.

Marcus, George. 1998. *Ethnography Through Thick & Thin*. Princeton, New Jersey: Princeton University Press.

———. 1999. The Uses of Complicity in the Changing Mise-en-Scene of Anthropological Fieldwork. In S. Ortner (ed.), *The Fate of 'Culture' Geertz and Beyond*. Berkeley, Los Angeles, California, and London: University of California Press.

Marcus, George and Michael Fisher. 1986. *Anthropology as Cultural Critique*. Chicago, Illinois: University of Chicago Press.

Maybury-Lewis, David. 1965. *The Savage and the Innocent*. Boston, Massachusetts: Beacon Press.

Mayer, Adrian C. 1989. Anthropological Memories. *Man* (N.S.), 24(2): 203–218.

Mead, M. 1977. *Letters from the Field: 1925–1975*. New York: Harper.

Moeran, Brian. 2006. *Ethnography at Work*. Oxford: Berg.

———. 2007. *Creativity at Work: From Participant Observation to Observant Participation: Anthropology, Fieldwork and Organizational Ethnography*. Creative Encounters Working Papers No. 2, pp. 1–25. Frederiksberg: Samfundslitteratur.

———. 2009. From Participant Observation to Observant Participation: Anthropology, Fieldwork and Organizational Ethnography. In F. Kamsteeg and H. Wels (eds), *Organizational Ethnography*, pp. 139–156. London: SAGE.

Newbury, D. 2001. Diaries and Fieldnotes in the Research Process. *Research Issues in Art Design and Media* [online], (1). http://www.biad.uce.ac.uk/research/riadm/issueOne/printerFriendly.asp (Accessed on 12 November 2002).

Okely, Judith. 2007. Fieldwork Embodied. *The Sociological Review*, 55(Suppl. 1): 65–79.

Pelto, Pertti J. and Gretel H. Pelto. 1978. *Anthropological Research: The Structure of Inquiry*. Cambridge: Cambridge University Press.

Powdermaker, H. 1966. *Stranger and Friend: The Way of an Anthropologist*. New York: W.W. Norton.

———. 1967. *Stranger and Friend: The Way of an Anthropologist*. London: Secker & Warburg.

Quinn, Naomi (ed.). 2005. *Finding Culture in Talk: A Collection of Methods.* New York: Palgrave MacMillan.

Rabinow, Paul. 1977. *Reflections on Fieldwork in Morocco.* Berkeley, California, and Los Angeles, California: University of California Press.

Reed-Danahay, D. 1997. *Auto/Ethnography: Rewriting the Self and the Social.* Oxford: Berg.

Sanjek, Roger (ed.). 1990. *Fieldnotes: The Making of Anthropology.* Ithaca, New York: Cornell University Press.

———. 1996. Ethnography. In Barnard, Alan and Jonathan Spencer (eds), *Encyclopedia of Social and Cultural Anthropology,* pp. 193–198. London: Routledge.

———. 1994. The Sahara Samaj: An Effective Construct of the Sahara Polity. *Indian Museum Bulletin,* XXIX: 81–93.

Sider, G. and G. Smith (eds.) 1997. *Between History and Histories: The Making of Silences and Commemorations.* Toronto: Toronto University Press.

Soto, Hermine G. and Nora Dudwick (eds). 2000. *Fieldwork Dilemmas: Anthropologists in Post-Socialist States.* Madison, Wisconsin: University of Wisconsin Press.

Spradley, James P. 1979. *The Ethnographic Interview.* New York: Holt Rinehart and Winston.

———. 1980. *Participant Observation.* New York: Holt Rinehart and Winston.

Srinivas, Mysore N., A. Shah and E. Ramaswamy (eds). 1979. *The Fieldworker and the Field: Problems and Challenges in Sociological Investigation.* Delhi: Oxford University Press.

Stewart, Alex. 1998. *The Ethnographer's Method. Qualitative Research Methods Series 46.* Newbury Park, California: SAGE.

Sundar Nandini, Satish Deshpande and Patricia Uberoi. 2000. Indian Anthropology and Sociology: Towards a History. *Economic and Political Weekly,* 35(24): 1998–2002.

Vered, Amit. 2000. Introduction: Constructing the Field. In Amit Vered (ed.), *Constructing the Field: Ethnographic Fieldwork in the Contemporary World,* pp. 1–18. London and New York: Routledge.

Whittaker, E. 1992. The Birth of the Anthropological Self and its Career. *Ethos,* 20: 191–219.

Zumwalt, Rosemary Lévy and Isaac Jack Lévy. 2001. Memories of Time Past: Fieldwork among the Sephardim. *The Journal of American Folklore,* 114: 451.

13

Tales of Everyday Politics in West Bengal

Suman Nath and Bhaskar Chakrabarti

E thnography is seen as a data production technique that is suited to study politics (Soss, 1999), yet the ethnographic study of politics has hardly been a priority for researchers. While scholars of political science and sociology use secondary materials, formal models, and statistical approaches, they do miss studying the foundations of political institutions and their associated practices (Auyero and Joseph, 2007). This results in problems in grasping political details and their day-to-day complexities (Baiocchi, 2005; Lichterman, 1998).

Following Geertz (1973a) and Ortner (2006), we can argue that ethnography is suitable for providing a thick narrative of political information. An example would be the study by Brubaker et al. (2006) in which they focus on the importance of the observation of everyday experiences. In this case an ethnographic approach is imperative. They focus on the disjuncture between intense nationalist politics and the ways in which they get embedded and expressed in everyday life. Ethnography as a method for investigating political processes focuses on the people and not on the states or the electoral process as a privileged space for political processes. The immediate attention to location (Gupta and Ferguson, 1997), lived experiences (Burdick, 1995; Edelman, 2001) and intended actions (Ortner, 1995; Wolford, 2003) enhances an ethnographer's understanding of political processes and micro dynamics of social movements.

For the last couple of years we are studying the political dynamics of West Bengal—the state which experienced the longest Communist rule in the world (Mallick, 1993). Our principal aim is to assess the impact of political environment on people's lives. We investigate people's active political choices and the nature of interactions with political personnel.

Although there are regular electoral analyses by Wallace and Roy (2003), Yadav (1997), Jaffrelot (2003), Inkinen (2003), and Pai (2002), yet there are conspicuous gaps in scholarly works regarding local upsurges. In India, political studies focus on political system, institutions, political dominance, and social movements (Chatterjee, 1997). Few scholarly discussions exist on authority relations and power dynamics at the local level. Hence, we concentrate on local level political processes to study political polarization, the decline in people's participation in local governance, and interorganizational incompatibility between line departments and local governance (Chakrabarti et al., 2011; Chattopadhyay et al., 2010). We study the oligopoly of politics in resource allocation with detailed ethnographic nuances (Nath and Chakrabarti, 2011). Our background in anthropology helps us to rely on an ethnographic approach for examining the impact of political environment on people's lives.

Fieldwork on political issues at grassroots level is challenging because of two interrelated reasons. First, because of the shift from a long regime ruled by the Communist Party of India (Marxist; henceforth CPM), and the recent change in favour of the Trinamul Congress (TMC), West Bengal, has been witnessing numerous cases of political violence (see http://www. satp.org). The second, and most important, reason is that it is difficult to extrapolate the actual phenomenon from the narratives, as villages could be polarized in terms of their support to the political parties. In this essay we present our field experience in one Village Panchayat[1] region where political change has taken place. We intend to share the essence of ethnography which helps us to overcome the challenges.

The Unfamiliar Place

The place, close to Bengal's seashore holiday destination Digha and to neighbouring state Orissa, falls in Padmapur[2] Gram Panchayat. We rented a house in the village, and started roaming in the alleys with a small bag and a camera, occasionally clicking pictures of village children and of people at work. This made many enquire about our identities. We answered that we were studying villagers and their lifestyle. We found people abandoning sea fishing, and increasingly participating in fish trade and small-scale seashell industry. We often interacted with our neighbours who visited us. Regular meetings with villagers and evening chit-chats at tea stalls paved way for familiar discussions on politics, games, and cinemas. Eventually, it smoothed the ground of communication between us and them.

There were four popular places for people to meet in the evening. We met Mr Rajen Sounda, a middle-aged man in fish business, in one such tea stall near the Gram Panchayat (GP) office. Villagers often approached him for writing applications as he had been to school. He provided us the details of GP members and of important political personnel. Rajen talked about the local grievances regarding electricity. He pointed out that land allocation had been the prime mover of political change in the region. The CPM ruled Padmapur GP till 2003 when the TMC won the election. In 2003, the CPM had popularity in West Bengal. The TMC then did not have the burning issues of land acquisition at Singur and Nandigram to fight for mass support. The fight was meant for winning the 2011 Assembly Election. Thus local issues culminated in the power shift.

Our Understanding of Local Grievances

Our ethnographic fieldwork was short-term. We stayed at Padmapur for one month, and then revisited the place twice, each for seven days. Understanding of the political process, therefore, was partially based on collecting narratives.

Based on our observations and stray interactions with people, and detailed discussion with Rajen, we found two categories of people residing in Padmapur and its adjacent area. First, the insiders who had been residing there for generations; and second, the outsiders who had settled there over the last 20 years.

We met Mr Harishwa Shounda, a 48-year-old man originally from Orissa. He had settled in the region in 1998, and is involved in fish trade. Subrata, his elder son, has a motor van. The family owns a concrete house, a dish-connected television and a refrigerator. Harishwa *babu*[3] and Subrata were busy men; the best time to talk to them was after 8:00 pm. When we went to their place, Harishwa *babu*'s wife was busy watching a Bengali film. The family gave us a warm welcome with evening snacks and tea. Harishwa *babu* used to do fishing in Orissa. During monsoon when sea fishing is extremely risky he worked as a wage labourer in one of the brick kilns. His wife Sabita pushed him for migration. Sabita *di*[4] started talking when the film was over.

He was not willing to come? The money he used to earn was insufficient for our family. I knew several people who had settled in Bengal. Job opportunity is good here. One can earn thousands simply by taking tourists to right hotels.

Employment opportunity was the primary cause for migration. The family was in contact with several others who had already migrated to Bengal. In 1991, Harishwa *babu* was contacted by a Khechor—the local name for middlemen responsible for bringing in outsiders. The Khechor helped him contact Param Mukherjee, a local CPM leader. Harishwa *babu* sold his property in Orissa, and paid Mukherjee ₹35,000 along with 10 per cent of his monthly income. His income enabled him to construct a temporary shelter on the seashore where several others were living. Harishwa *babu* said,

> It was nice. As my income had doubled, I could think of saving money for a new business. Initially, Mukherjee *babu* gave a van-rickshaw to take tourists to the hotels ... eventually I joined the fish trade. I purchase fish from fishermen and then send them to bigger markets ... In our community fishing is highly valued ... but it is not worth taking risk for such a small amount of money ... the wholesalers exploit us ... From the beginning I was thinking of joining the business ...

Finally in 1998, Harishwa *babu* got four *cottah*s of land to construct a permanent building. While Harishwa *babu*'s earning was increasing Mukherjee's party was getting more funds.

> It was not easy to be entitled for permanent settlement ... I had to pay strictly 10 per cent of my earning every month ... had to say 'yes' to whatever they decided ... but I must say this system has changed my life. My six years of hardship has ultimately paid off ... after the Assembly Election I am not paying anything to them.

Increment in income brought joy to the family. The CPM helped Harishwa *babu* venture into fish trade. However, after the party's defeat in the Assembly Election, he stopped paying the 10 per cent of his income. The chance he took yielded positive results.

However, others were not as lucky. Kalicharam Shyamal, a 53-year-old migrant, was living in a temporary shelter near the sea coast. Kalicharan *babu* was a regular customer at a nearby tea stall. He had a distinct sense of humour and was the centre of attraction in evening sessions of gossip. Having abandoned his traditional occupation of fishing, Kalicharan *babu* came to Digha in 1993, in the similar process. He did not have the cash to dispense to the local party, but he paid in instalments for his shanty. He kept paying in instalments for years, participated in CPM rallies, supported the party, and prepared and pasted posters during elections. Yet, he was not given a place to settle down. Kalicharan *babu* reluctantly took us to his hut.

> You city people will not like the place ... it's dirty, dark, and may seem inhabitable to you ...

We went there during late afternoon to find 25 such constructions. Those were mud-floored, grass-thatched, and bamboo-supported shacks. Kalicharan's son ranted about the party's failure in allotting land to these people. The Village Panchayat constructed community latrines—as part of the Total Sanitation Programme.

> They did not have enough land to accommodate us. They promised hundreds that they will be given land for permanent settlement, but only five-*cottah* land was available. How could you feed so many from such a small cake? They [CPM party cadres] told my father not to speak about the land they'd promised. We remained silent. Later on we found out that they had made similar promises to several others.

The local party cadres' promises led all of them to support and work for the party, with the hope of getting permanent settlement. The failure to accommodate these people created unrest not only among the immigrants but also among the recent settlers. Each of the immigrants had close connection with recent settlers. In other words, the settlers played an active role in bringing more immigrants. Most often they were their relatives, friends, and neighbours.

Apart from land-related issues, several other matters too agitated the villagers. Rural electrification was the most important of them. Villagers from four villages of Padmapur GP were repeatedly requesting their members and Panchayat chief (Pradhan) for electrification. Neighbouring villages had been electrified during the 1990s. Yet, in the 2002 Gram Sabha, that is, the annual meeting of the villagers with the GP, the villagers' strong criticism of the inaction faced misconduct from the CPM-controlled GP. As told by a villager, on 3 December 2010,

> They took us for granted ... Pradhan said, 'You were happy with kerosene lamps ... be happy with what you have, and don't bother us.' On that very day we talked about the need for a change ... In Orissa, people altered government in every election ... we needed that strategy as well.

Familiarizing With the Local Politics

We spoke to several CPM and TMC party cadres and leaders to get insights into the political process. When we met Subhabrata Sounda, a 53-year-old CPM leader, he was visibly disappointed with the party's existing leaders. Subrata da[5] was one of the prominent figures who had helped several outsiders to settle.

It was difficult to discuss politics with him. Rajen had warned us about the possibility of Subrata *da* falling completely silent about political matters. Since the 2003 election he had been keeping himself away from politics, irrespective of the significant status of his past leadership. Initially Subrata *da* tried to avoid the political issues in our conversation.

Leave those matters ... nothing left for discussion ... those days are gone

His reluctance was our source of interest in meeting him occasionally. We thought that individual and face-to-face interaction with him was important. However, we would usually meet him at the tea stalls where it was difficult to conduct individual interviews.

The defeat of Subrata *da*'s party might have become a source of shame and embarrassment for him to open up in public. In any public social interaction what is at stake is the image of self. Often the self is judged in public interaction, and a defeated party worker may thus feel vanquished (Goffman, 1955). 'Stage fright' as argued by Geertz (1973b) indicates the anxieties of individuals about their 'on stage' behaviour. This often makes people avoid encounters that might lead to embarrassment (Scheff and Retzinger, 2000). In order to avoid these difficulties of talking in public, we made a visit to Subrata *da*'s home on a winter morning. We had already spoken to his wife Paramita *di* several times. When we went there she offered us tea. His brother runs a cottage trade from home. With his friends he makes different sea-shell products. We purchased several souvenirs and gift items from him. Then we started to talk to Subrata *da*. The informal atmosphere created a space for him to open up.

Subrata *da* joined the CPM in the 1980s and since then played a significant role in creating a political base in the region. Immigration started in the late 1980s. At that time, Subrata *da* arranged for shelters for these poor people. It had twin advantages. First, involving them in fish trade and local transport strengthened the party base; and second, their contribution to the party was a chief source of revenues. However, the situation began to change in the 1990s.

Several party cadres transformed themselves into middlemen ... They began to purchase lands from villagers and sold it to outsiders, especially to the hotels ... They became building material suppliers and labour contractors. They grew ties with the police, local administration and mafias. To retain power at the grassroots they started to bully people during elections.

Subrata *da* highlighted the failure of the party machinery to retain control over the village-level cadres. As leaders like Subrata *da* retreated, money was flowing in from outsiders who were willing to invest in the rising tourism industry of the region. CPM began to lose its ground. When senior leaders pointed out to the Local Committee members and Panchayat members the possibility of an election defeat, the latter were reluctant to accept the fact.

Later on Subrata *da* took us to two other senior CPM party workers who bore similar grudges to the party for its inability to control money-hungry cadres. One of them, Sangram Jana, pointed at the basic human nature of reaping dividends from a common pool in order to satisfy self-interest.

It is quite natural. Once a person sees easy money he loses his ideology ... and you know ideological training has stopped for quite long. Party leaders no longer take classes, read books, or think of an equal society.

When the ideological crisis became apparent, institutional mechanism could not regulate the activities of its cadres.

Narratives of grievances and failure of the CPM party machinery to discipline its cadres justify people's disgust with the party. However, understanding the TMC's strategy is as important to explain the changeover.

Political division was invisible, as the TMC and the CPM participated in the evening gossip at the tea stalls, and played cards together. However, village-level polarization became manifest when we tried to talk to the TMC people individually. A young party worker, Sudeb Shyamal, told us unambiguously that we were one-sided. We believed each and everything we listened from them [CPM people]. Our response was the serious assertion, with a smile, that we were there to listen to both. His reaction was prompt.

You want to listen? You know our family has given everything for CPM. My father paid a good part of his earning for years ... they did nothing. In the 2003 Panchayat Election, they tried to capture the booth, we have witnessed bomb explosions, and one of the villagers died ... you city people will never know ... the media did not care!

We found Sudeb interesting. He had an athletic figure; he spoke straight, fearless words. He took us to Bar, who is a strong TMC leader of the region. Sudeb was insistent, and we were interested; so Bar agreed to give us an appointment for the evening at the local fish centre. It was our first visit to a fish warehouse. Hundreds of trawlers brought tonnes of marine fish. Thousands of people were involved in packing, freezing, and exporting. We were asked to seat in the now-TMC-controlled fish traders' association office. After the Parliamentary Election in 2009 the association transformed its political identity from CPM to TMC. Over cups of tea and fish odour, we began to talk.

Bar, along with the others, spoke of the accumulated disgust of local men over the CPM's strategy. We could not probe deeper as they kept harping on the CPM's failure in understanding people's pulse, the party's involvement in money making game, and the peoples' trust on the TMC supreme, the present chief minister of Bengal, Mamata Banerjee.

On our return we decided to talk to Bar personally, and to speak with other TMC workers and leaders. Next day during our evening tea session with Sudeb and many other TMC workers, we met Debaprashad Jana, another well-known TMC leader of the region. He held local grievances responsible for the change in the region. The TMC's mass rally and their increased communication with common people had also contributed to their victory. While coming back from the tea stall, we decided to have intensive discussions with Sudeb and others who were key players at the grassroots level.

We talked to Sudeb often about the new party, and change in the political compositions. Sudeb's concise replies were restricted to his admiration of the local leaders. With a smile Sudeb projected himself as a rule obeying worker under Bar. Sudeb was a footballer. Bar used to be a good player. He organized many matches, cultural programmes, and trained many including Sudeb. So whenever Bar asked for something, it ought to be for good, and Sudeb was for good things.

A few days later Sudeb took us to the local *akahra*—a place where he and his friends did physical exercises. We found several young people training there. They were weight lifters, runners, and footballers. We sponsored the evening snacks: puffed rice and fries. We discussed the World Cup victory and how our Sports Ministry undermined the value of sports other than cricket. We called Bar to join us for the evening get together. He came and we started to discuss issues over tea and onion fries.

> It's not that hard when you have accumulated disgust (against your rival) and grown a good network with people.

This was Bar's initial reaction as we began to discuss the TMC's strategy. Local and regional issues after 2000 added to people's disappointment with the CPM leadership in Padmapur. At that time existing Congress leaders were confused about their stance, primarily because of the United Progressive Alliance (UPA) structure at the centre where the CPM and the Congress were partners. The Congress High Command instructed them to remain modest in their reaction against the CPM. While the situation in Padmapur and adjacent region demanded a strong anti-CPM movement, the Congress senior leadership remained inactive. In early 2001, a TMC central committee member contacted Bar. He was then a disgruntled Congress worker with considerable command over young adults of the region. Bar mentions his initial confusion of whether to join or not to join the TMC. However, he made up his mind as the 'situation demanded'. The TMC was the only available option to fight against the CPM.

> You ought to sense people's pulse and then be vocal about their disgust'

Bar recalls his initial estimation of the possible ways to gain more support. He started organizing rallies against the CPM under the TMC banner. In the beginning, people like Sudeb participated. Bar was threatened by both the CPM and the Congress. However, the situation changed rapidly as the small group of young men led by Bar started to communicate with each villager of the GP.

> … Soon, I found overwhelming support from the local people … and slowly we understood we could win the 2003 Panchayat Election … while I conveyed to our district leaders my feeling about winning, I started getting more funds to better organise these movements … and when you have the funds you are able to seize powerful groups …

The coupling of support base creation and use of power groups was TMC's strategy for the election. Fund was not a constraint. Bar and his team started to stand by every man in need. They formed a team of young people who would combat and intervene in personal crises of the villagers.

> We knew we did not have power to do public works, but we could help people to meet their personal needs. For example, we helped people in medical emergency, property-related conflicts … we stood beside women in need …

They effectively utilized individual requirements to strengthen their support base in the region. In early 2002, they began to organize meetings and public rallies. They gave speeches for hours without the microphone. Several young people, not directly attached to any political party, began to discuss the CPM's mistakes openly.

In May 2002, Bar was invited to a meeting with district-level TMC leaders. Other Panchayat leaders in East Midnapore participated in it to discuss their political strategies. Bar and his fellow party worker Jana expressed their fear about possible booth capture by the CPM in Padmapur.

> One of the senior party members assured us that no matter what it took we would have to stop every illegal activity in our booth. The party was ready to provide us with adequate funds to prepare for possible action.

Accordingly, Jana and Bar tried to acquire men with 'arms and muscles' to prepare for clashes in the region. However, it was difficult to acquire men from the area where the CPM had a stronghold. District-level leaders provided external aid by sending men from outside.

> External help was not enough and we needed help from local groups to sustain our political control over the region ... you know there is nothing called ideology ... it's all about money ... and we were successful to involve some of the local power groups. They are not party workers ... but we needed them during election.

Calling in external help and involving local power groups in exchange for money indicate the prominent use of violence in the elections. Later on Jana told they were certain about winning the election, but it was necessary to ensure proper voting. The coalition with local power groups is still active in the region.

The 2003 Panchayat Election was not the only example of violence during votes in Padmapur region. We had several other contradictory versions of the phenomenon. We compared them and then tried to probe the matter. Padmapur was not declared as politically sensitive; hence, security arrangement was moderate. On the day of the election at 10:30 am a group of outsiders first started to gather around one of the booths, a school near Digha Bypass. While one group assembled near the booth, another was called in. Within minutes, a car appeared near the school and a group of armed men came out of it. Two groups started to fight. Four handheld bombs were charged and one of the villagers died on the spot. Jana was with the second group and suffered a serious head injury. He was admitted to Digha State General Hospital for nine days with thirteen stitches on his forehead. Bar's newly purchased motor bike was set on fire.

Recent Political Processes

When we asked Bar and Jana individually about the present political process, both pointed at the need for making strong grassroots organizations. However, Jana mentioned his uncertainty about the TMC's organization base.

> CPM's grassroots organization is unparalleled ... they are regimented, their party line of control is enormous ... people supported us to test the change ... but to retain power in the long run we need strong organisational base ... and we are lagging behind in that process. People are opportunists ... they support us for some purpose ... it is important to create a strong ideological stance.

Bar mentions they are instructed by the TMC State Committee to reinforce control over local markets and workers. Accordingly they formed five bazaar committees in 2004, of which three are in coalition with the Indian National Congress (INC). There were also a van drivers' union in 2008, and four hawkers' unions, one per beach in Digha. In the 2008 Panchayat Election the TMC took control of the block, which gave them administrative support. In Padmapur, the party has formed a booth level committee topped by a zonal committee. The zonal committee controls workers' unions in this area.

Jana and Bar helped us talk to several committee members. The TMC faced huge resistance from the CPM in one out of ten trade union committee formations. At first, they organized a meeting at one of the prominent road crossings in the area. The turnout was unexpectedly low. It was held in December 2004. Late in the evening, at around 7:30 pm, while they were about to wrap up the programme, a group of bikers came with iron rods. They first broke down chairs and microphones. The TMC's response was also quick. As told by Jana, in December 2010,

> We were adequately prepared ... Bar called our men and we had to go through a big fight. We came out from that place while our men continued to fight until police came. Both of the group members had to be admitted to the hospital.

Revenue earning was a challenge too. In order to meet the financial needs in late 2008, they captured the local fish market-cum-warehouse. It was easy because most of the other committees were already under TMC control. One of the local bazaar committee treasurers, Sahoo, stated that several stakeholders of the fish market were TMC supporters. The mass support for the TMC made it easier for local party members to capture power.

Conclusion

Avarice and crisis of the political ideology occupy an important position in determining the political fate of the parties. The CPM lost their ideologies as their cadres were increasingly involved in monetary pursuits. Because of the ideological crisis, the CPM lost their valuable leaders. The TMC leadership is sceptical about their organizational integrity. Political strategy in the region involves exploitation of public grievances, and use of violence and counter violence.

The above narrative shows that in order to understand the political dynamics, it is important to focus on people's interaction. Our purposeful evening visits at tea stalls gave us insights into local networks, power groups, and their operations. Participating in evening discussions empowered us with the base knowledge of the local political processes. Our further discussions with the political personnel were fruitful as we could prepare for targeted interviews.

Reviewing fieldnotes in the field is also an essential process. Several discussions could not be recorded. We took notes immediately after coming back to the field camp. On several occasions key points were recorded in the recorder immediately after the sessions. We spent time by discussing and debating on field findings, which were aided in our understanding of the 'political'.

Finally, the study shows that ethnography depends on the relationships with key actors. Finding out familiar issues, driving people towards the issue of interest through individual and public conversations is crucial to unearth the core of the issue. These require time and repeated conversations.

Notes

1. Village Panchayat is the lowest tier of the three tier local governance system which starts at the district level—Zilla Parishad, then block level—Panchayat Samiti and village level—Village Panchayat.

2   Pseudonyms have been used for persons and places.
3. *Babu* is a Bengali term used to refer to older men.
4. *Di* or *didi* means elder sister in Bengali.
5. *Da* is a term use to refer to elder brother.

References

Auyero, J. and L. Joseph. 2007. Introduction: Politics under the Ethnographic Microscope. In L. Joseph, M. Mahler and J. Auyero (eds), *New Perspectives in Political Ethnography*, pp. 1–13. New York: Springer.

Baiocchi, G. 2005. *Militants and Citizens: The Politics of Participatory Democracy in Porto Alegre*. Stanford, CA: Stanford University Press.

Brubaker, R., M. Feischmidt, J. Fox and L. Grancea. 2006. *Nationalist Politics and Everyday Ethnicity in a Transylvanian Town*. Princeton, New Jersey: Princeton University Press.

Burdick, J. 1995. Uniting Theory and Practice in the Ethnography of Social Movements: Notes Toward a Hopeful Realism. *Dialectical Anthropology*, 20: 361–385.

Chakrabarti, B., R. Chattopadhyay and S. Nath. 2011. Local Governments in Rural West Bengal, India and their Coordination with Line Departments. *Commonwealth Journal of Local Governance*, 8–9: 33–51.

Chatterjee, P. (ed.). 1997. *State and Politics in India*. New Delhi: Oxford University Press.

Chattopadhyay, R., B. Chakrabarti and S. Nath. 2010. Village Forums or Development Councils: People's Participation in Decision-making in Rural West Bengal, India. *Commonwealth Journal of Local Governance*, 5: 66–85.

Edelman, M. 2001. Social Movements: Changing Paradigms and Forms of Politics. *Annual Review of Anthropology*, 30: 285–318.

Geertz, C. (ed.). 1973a. *The Interpretation of Cultures*. New York: Basic Books.

Geertz, C. 1973b. Person, Time, and Conduct in Bali. In C. Geertz (ed.), *The Interpretation of Cultures*, pp. 360–411. New York: Basic Books.

Goffman, E. 1955. On Face-work: An Analysis of Ritual Elements in Social Interaction. *Psychiatry*, 18: 213–231.

Gupta, A. and J. Ferguson. 1997. *Anthropological Locations: Boundaries and Grounds of a Field Science*. Berkeley, California: University of California Press.

Inkinen, M. 2003. *Mobilising the Lower Castes: The Rise of the Bahujan Samaj Party in India*. Doctoral Dissertation. Department of Government, Uppsala University, Uppsala.

Jaffrelot, C. 2003. *India's Silent Revolution: The Rise of the Lower Castes in North India*. London: Hurst.

Lichterman, P. (1998). What Do Movements Mean? The Value of Participant Observation. *Qualitative Sociology*, 21: 401–418.

Mallick, R. 1993. *Development Policy of a Communist Government: West Bengal Since 1977.* Cambridge: Cambridge University Press.

Nath, S. and B. Chakrabarti. 2011. Political Economy of Cold Storages in West Bengal. *Commodity Vision,* 4(4): 36–42.

Ortner, S. 2006. *Anthropology and Social Theory.* Durham, North Carolina: Duke University Press.

Ortner, S.B. 1995. Resistance and the Problem of Ethnographic Refusal. *Comparative Studies of Society and History,* 37: 173–193.

Pai, S. 2002. *Dalit Assertion and the Unfinished Democratic Revolution: The Bahujan Samaj Party in Uttar Pradesh.* New Delhi: SAGE.

Scheff, T. and S. Retzinger. 2000. Shame as the Master Emotion of Everyday Life. *Journal of Mundane Behavior,* 1: 303–324.

Soss, J. 1999. Lessons of Welfare: Policy Design, Political Learning, and Political Action. *American Political Science Review,* 93: 363–380.

Wallace, P. and R. Roy (eds). 2003. *India's 1999 Elections and 20th Century Politics.* New Delhi: SAGE Publications.

Wolford, W. 2003. Families, Fields, and Fighting for Land: The Spatial Dynamics of Contention in Rural Brazil. *Mobilization,* 8: 201–215.

Yadav, Y. 1997. Reconfiguration in Indian Politics: State Assembly Elections, 1993–1995. In P. Chatterjee (ed.), *State and Politics in India,* pp. 177–207. Delhi: Oxford University Press.

14

Doing Fieldwork and Discovering Harijan Art in Madhubani

Neel Rekha

Mithila, also known as Videha or Tirabhukti, comprises the districts of present day North Bihar and the Terai region of Nepal. In the present times it comprises the modern day districts of Darbhanga, Bhagalpur, Saharasa, Purnea, Monghyr, and Terai region of Nepal. Famed for being the birthplace of two religions, Buddhism and Jainism, and also as a seat of Sanskrit culture and learning, the region has acquired recent fame for producing handmade reproductions of ritualistic paintings now known as Madhubani paintings. Madhubani which literally means 'forest of honey' has acquired international attention for producing these handmade paper paintings by upper caste Brahmana and Kayastha women. Villages Jitwarpur and Ranti near Madhubani town have produced celebrity artists such as Sita Devi, Baua Devi, Jagdamba Devi, Mahasundari Devi, and Ganga Devi. The past few years have also seen the emergence of new styles such as *Gobar* and *Godana* by Chamar and Dusadh castes now known as Harijan Madhubani, Harijan Mithila paintings, or Dalit paintings[1] (Rekha, 2003).

This essay is a memoir of my journey into the world of painters of Madhubani and experiences gathered during ethnographic fieldwork between 1999 and 2004.[2] It describes how my ethnographic fieldwork aimed at locating the history of Mithila paintings and understanding the mechanism of assertion of identity of upper caste women painters ultimately led to the discovery of Harijan art—a hitherto unknown aspect of Maithil culture and tradition. Recalling my interactions with noted Harijan artists such as Jamuna Devi, Shanti Devi, Chano Devi, Roudi Paswan, and Uttam Paswan, I demonstrate how their attempts to evolve a distinctive tradition of their own led to the rediscovery of their rich cultural roots. The methodologies evolved during fieldwork and continuous interactions with Mithila artists helped me not only trace the history of evolution of Harijan Mithila painting but also locate contested voices in Maithil history.

Not having an elaborate tradition of floor and wall paintings such as *aripana* (floor paintings) and *kohabar* (wall paintings),[3] women artists from the Chamar and Dusadh castes made their distinctive mark as artists by evolving their unique *gobar* and *godana* styles and projecting their own god Salhesa, an important folk God worshipped by the Dusadh caste.[4] This novel use of religious iconography initially appeared to me as an attempt to assert their identity, inspired by the current politics of Dalit assertion.[5] But extensive fieldwork slowly revealed that these new attempts had actually brought forth voices of past Maithil history. Many folk gods and goddesses were actual historical figures who made their mark in local history and sometimes even revolted against the elite. But they had not been recorded in written accounts and had passed into obscurity. However, remembrance of their exploits through oral accounts and conversion into folk gods and goddesses though ritualistic worship had preserved fragments of these past memories (Narayan, 2001). It was these aspects of the past history of the region that I attempted to discover through fieldwork.

My journey into the world of painters began in June 1999 during my visit to Jitwarpur village in connection with searching answers for my dissertation titled, *Art and Assertion of Identity: Women and Madhubani Paintings* (Rekha, 2004). Having read extensively about upper caste connections of Mithila paintings,[6] I had planned to interview upper caste Brahmana and Kayastha celebrity artists from village Jitwarpur and Ranti. I met and interviewed artists such as Sita Devi, Baua Devi, Mahasundari Devi, and Godavari Datta. However, my investigation took a very different direction during my first visit to Madhubani when one of my upper caste informants introduced me to the newly evolved Harijan *gobar* and *godana* styles. I was also intrigued to find some of the paintings of Salhesa being made in the households of upper caste artists. With a view to know more about the history of Harijan style and its relations with the upper caste *bharni* and *kachni* styles, I arranged interviews with some noted Harijan artists. Subsequent interviews revealed different oral versions of the story of Salhesa. Some of the versions revealed to me by local scholars and folklorists actually suggested that Salhesa had occupied an important place in the history of Mithila. A memoir of these interactions forms the main subject matter of this essay. The recollections reflect how a historian aiming at locating the history of Mithila could use ethnographic techniques to learn the social world of anonymous village artists, locate contested voices, and understand the mechanism of assertion of identity.

Research Context

Mithila paintings or Maithil paintings acquired unique international attention and patronage in the past few decades (Anand, 1984; Archer, 1949; Jayakar, 1969, 1971, 1975, 1989; Hart, 1995; Mathur, 1966; Szanton, 2003; Thakur, 1982). But focus on the work of upper caste Brahmana and Kayastha artists, its association with the Hindu religion as well as women's rites and rituals, have silenced the true meaning and historical significance of this artistic tradition. For centuries, women hailing from the region of Mithila in North Bihar and Terai region of Nepal have been expressing their social surroundings through the medium of paintings which received international acclaim and recognition as Madhubani paintings. But its discovery in the colonial period and later on its promotion inspired by post-independent cultural policies soon converted them as past expression of the Hindu women's rites and rituals. Ethnographic accounts of Westerners unable to understand the nuances of an Indian village and Orientalist representations soon converted them as examples of an exoticized past.

Although the problems of ethnographic representation in the case of Mithila art have been brought to notice by some scholars (Brown, 1982, 1996; Heinz, 2006), the objective of giving agency to Mithila painters remains unfulfilled. The task of reading Mithila paintings beyond its usual understanding as an expression of women's rites and rituals and showing that Mithila painters have a voice of their own still needs to be done. Very few studies have attempted to show that Mithila painting has a history of its own and that it reflects the social world of painters and the surroundings of the artists. More importantly, the objective of using ethnography as an art historian's methodological tool remains to be highlighted. Some of these problems were sought to be addressed in my PhD dissertation and ethnographic fieldwork was an important methodological tool to supplement primary and secondary historical sources. A memoir of the experiences of ethnographic fieldwork forms the main theme of this essay.

I have till now given a brief introduction and context of my study. I shall now provide a brief review of fieldwork traditions in Madhubani as a background against my own work. Recalling my own fieldwork experiences,

I shall reveal how a shared process of interaction helped me trace voices of the past. Paintings which were made as part of a livelihood initiative soon became a means of identity assertion and also a means to recover fragments of past Maithil history.

Reviewing Fieldwork Tradition in Madhubani

As described earlier, Mithila painting has been unique in the amount of elite attention and patronage that it has generated. Ever since it was brought to the notice of the outside world, a number of scholars—mostly anthropologists and folklorists—have visited the region. It was W.G. Archer (1949) who discovered these paintings for the outside world after making a survey of floor and wall paintings made in various parts of Mithila. After it was transferred to paper, the first Westerner to arrive in Mithila in 1973 was Yves Vequaud from France. He stayed here for two years and made a film and a book *Women Painters of Mithila* which brought international popularity to this art (Vequaud, 1977). The next scholar to arrive in Madhubani was Erika Moser, an anthropologist who made 14 short films on the painters (*Fourteen Short Films with a German manual and English Summaries*, 1973–1978). Another anthropologist Raymond Lee Owens conducted a 15-month cultural study of Jitwarpur and founded the Master Craftsmen's Association of Mithila (MCAM) in 1977 (*Five Painters*, 1983).

Another anthropologist who has done extensive research on Mithila paintings is Carolyn Henning Brown. Arriving in Mithila to study the *Panji*[7] system, her interest in Maithil art was generated when she came across Vequaud's book and found how women from Mithila were misrepresented. Her writings have shown the problems of ethnographic representation in Mithila art. She has in particular been interested in questioning the connections of Tantricism with Mithila paintings. Recently she has also documented the wall paintings of Madhubani (Brown, 1982, 1996; Heinz, 2006). In the last decade, the most notable scholar who has visited the region is David Szanton. A social anthropologist, he has made frequent visits to Madhubani with a view to promote the art form. He organizes exhibitions to promote this art and argues that this art has been transformed from a folk art to a fine art (Szanton, 2004, 2005, 2006; Szanton and Bakshi, 2007, 2012).

Compared to anthropologists, very few art historians have visited Madhubani. Some of them include noted art historians such as Lanius

(1988), Chavda (1990), and Jain (1997). However, extensive fieldwork has not been done by any of them. The most extensive work is by Jyotindra Jain on the life and works of Ganga Devi. However, most of the work is based on the interviews with Ganga Devi during her stay in New Delhi in the Crafts Museum. Apart from art historians, some sociologists and folklorists too have studied this painting tradition. Among the sociologists, the most notable work is by Manishekhar Singh (1999, 2000, 2004) who has examined the sociological aspects of Mithila painting tradition after it was commercialized. Many local scholars have made invaluable contributions in providing contextual information on this art (Jha, 1962, 1986, 2002; Maun, 2000; Maun and Neeraj, 2002; Mishra, 1975; Thakur, 1988; Yadav, 1981).

Interaction with Harijan Artists of Mithila

Against this background, my fieldwork was a bit different. Its aim was to recover the social world of painters through the niceties of this art as an enquiry into the historiography revealed that works on Mithila art had not attempted to locate the historical roots of this art (Rekha, 2004). An elaborate coverage of the social world of Mithila painters was warranted. Aiming to recover the history of Maithil art and examine the mechanism of assertion of identity of women, I arrived in Madhubani in June 1999 aiming to interview celebrity artists in villages Jitwarpur and Ranti. Although different villages around Madhubani have been involved, I concentrated on villages Jitwarpur and Ranti—the two most important villages known for producing Mithila paintings.[8] Situated at a distance of only 10 km, a metalled road from the district headquarters leads to these two villages.

Village Jitwarpur—now almost converted into an exhibition village—has been famous for having produced celebrity artists such as Sita Devi, Baua Devi, Jagdamba Devi, and Jamuna Devi. Inhabited by all castes, the most important caste residing in the village is the Mahapatra Brahmana community—a caste associated with performing death rites. Other upper castes residing in the village are Karna Kayasthas, Rajputs, and Bhumihars. Apart from upper castes, untouchable castes such as Chamars, Dusadhs, Doms, and Pasis also reside in this village. Village Ranti is another important village in this respect. Known as Ranti Deorhi, being the zamindari of Shrotriya Brahmanas, the most populous caste residing in the village is that of the Karna Kayasthas. Other castes include Rajputs, Bhumiharas, and lower castes such as Dusadhs. Other villages known for producing Madhubani paintings are Laheriaganj, Harinagar, Simri, and Rajnagar.

Two basic questions were to be addressed in my thesis: What was the history of the evolution of this art? What was the mechanism of assertion of identity by women? Most of these answers were to be sought from primary sources which included 14th-century texts such as Jyotirishvara's *Varnaratnakara*, Chandeshwara's *Krityaratnakara*, Vidyapati's writings[9] such as *Purushapariksha, Likhnavali*, and *Padavali* (Rekha, 2004). However, as a clue to understand the mechanism of assertion, I planned to interview artists and collect some folk songs, oral histories, and information on ritual traditions of the area. Local scholars suggested the name of Krishnakant Jha, a Mahapatra Brahmana artist, who became my local informant for the rest of my research. He became a valuable source as he had been witness to the whole process of commercialization. As a child, he had watched not only his mother and aunts evolve their unique styles but Harijan artists evolving their styles. Apart from making me aware of Harijan art, Jha also contributed to the discovery of *Geru* style of painting—a style which provided clues regarding the connections of Tantricism with Madhubani art (Rekha, 2004).[10]

Having known the upper caste styles through secondary literature[11] and my questions framed around that information, I was a bit puzzled when Krishnakant introduced me to six different styles in Madhubani—*kachni, bharni, gobar* and *godana, geru*, and *tantric* styles.[12] Even though I showed more interest in *bharni* and *kachni* styles—the two caste-based styles even talked about by Archer—he insisted that my investigation could not be completed unless I visited Harijan *tola* (settlememt)[13] of Jitwarpur. He introduced Roudi Paswan, husband of Chano Devi, to me who had incidentally landed in his house for discussing his plans to travel to a craft exhibition. The use of Roudi *Bhai* (brother) from the mouth of a Brahmin and an established painter came as a surprise to me, as caste feelings are quite strong in Mithila. Also the discussion on sharing exhibition spaces and travelling together for a craft exhibition was a revelation. My intention of meeting Harijan artists was reinforced when I found paintings of Salhesa in their households. On asking them if it was God Indra, the most important Vedic god, they answered that those were the paintings of God Salhesa.[14]

I began my investigation according to my plans meeting with the celebrity artists. The first few days were just spent listening to their recollections of the early days of commercialization. Pupul Jayakar, Upendra Maharathi, and Bhaskar Kulkarni figured in their accounts.[15] However, the most prominent figure was Bhaskar Kulkarni, the officer-in-charge of the drought relief programme. Elderly artists remembered with fascination his long beard, and the affection with which he made them evolve their individualistic styles. Quite prominent in their accounts was the description of foreign scholars who had visited Madhubani. Vequaud, Raymond, Erika, and Hasegawa[16] came up quite frequently in their accounts. On the other hand, most of the secondary literature which I had consulted before coming to Madhubani did not talk much about them.

Establishing a good rapport with the painters was the first important task before me as I was still viewed as an outsider. Crucial role played in these interactions was that of my uncle, Dr N.N. Singh 'Nirala', a local historian well respected among the artists' community. Although fluent in Maithili, I was many times unable to express myself fully. He would come to my rescue using typical Maithil words to convey my ideas to the artists. I had another advantage as I was familiar with the cultural traditions and rituals of the area. They did not require providing me with many explanations as they needed to do with other researchers. Being a woman and my capability to speak their language thus put me in advantage. I could also sense that they could relate very easily to me. They would sometimes sing songs based on folklores to explain their rituals.

While I was visiting both the villages, I had realized that my research had to include Harijan paintings of Mithila not knowing where it would fit in my thesis. Hoping to include this history in my story on the commercialization of Mithila art which I would use for linking the two important sections of the thesis, I proceeded with my plans to interview the artists. However, I was a bit hesitant as it would distract me from my original research plans. An important intervention made at this stage was by my supervisor late Prof. V.K. Thakur, who insisted that my enquiry into the mechanism of assertion of identity would remain incomplete if I ignored the recent emergence of Harijan paintings.

This objective of providing agency to Mithila artists and recovering voices of the past, Prof. Thakur felt, could only be achieved by a fuller study of Harijan paintings of Mithila. This was important as most of the texts of the region rarely talked about these castes and their culture. Unlike upper caste paintings which still found indirect reference in texts such as those of Vidyapati, there were scanty reference to lower castes and their culture. The prevalence of feudalism in the region had led to the proliferation of castes with each caste assigned its own duties. Some of the texts such as the 14th-century text Jytorishvara's *Varnaratnakara* referred to them as *manda jati*s (lower castes), but an elaborate description of their culture and tradition was warranted. Governmental initiatives to promote Dalit artists had brought some aspects of their culture to limelight but large-scale production of paintings, especially the tattoo designs and stereotyped perceptions about village artisans, had portrayed them as examples of primitive art. With a view to know more about their culture, I started my work with Chamar and Dusadh artists—the two castes involved in paintings.

The Chamars, also known as Rabidas, were by occupation makers of footwear, cultivators or labourers. Their traditional occupation was the disposal of dead animals and preparing different objects from the skin of dead animals. Despite being untouchables, they had a significant role to play in Mithila's traditional society. During *Shardiya Navaratra* (autumnal Durga Puja Festival), the Chamars used to give *Dagar* (beat the ceremonial drums) which was considered to have some Tantric significance. The services of their womenfolk known popularly as *Dagarini* were frequently requisitioned as midwives.

The Dusadhs were one of the useful castes in the area owing to their value as agricultural labourers. They reared cattle, pigs, etc., and supported themselves mostly by labour and cultivation. They also monopolized the post of village *chowkidars* (watchmen) in the district. One of the titles among the Dusadhs was *Paswan* which means a watchman or a guard (Mishra, 1975; Roy, 1964). Their women supplemented the income of the family by working as labourers. However, in the colonial accounts, the Dusadhs were enlisted among the criminal castes of the district.

My investigation started with Jamuna Devi, the pioneering artist credited to have evolved the *gobar* style of painting. Krishnakant took me to Jamuna Devi who met us with great love and affection. The first day of our interaction was spent having a look at all her certificates, awards, and medals which she showed us with pride. Our subsequent visits to her house revealed the history of evolution of *gobar* styles. Hailing from Chamar caste, she narrated how she imitated upper caste painters such as Sita Devi and Jagdamba Devi. But getting encouragement from Bhaskar Kulkarni and Upendra Maharathi, she went on to evolve her unique style of painting known as *gobar* painting. Using *gobar* (cowdung) wash, she began making scenes from day-to-day village life and caste duties assigned to the Chamars. She remembered how recognition brought her prestige in the village (Rekha, 2003).

The story of evolution of Harijan art was developed further when I visited the second important artist Shanti Devi at her home in village Laheriaganj. The growing sense of self-confidence among Harijan artists got reflected from these interactions. She narrated how she evolved her own style using double lined parallel lines filling it with dots and cowdung wash. I also recorded the history of emergence of folk gods and goddesses in Harijan Mithila art. She recalled how her father-in-law, a Dusadh priest, had inspired her to evolve stories of gods and goddesses from their caste. Gods such as Govinda, Rahu, and Salhesa[17] were deliberately projected against upper caste paintings of Krishna and Rama. An important point that emerged during my interactions with her was the importance of God Salhesa who frequently appeared in her accounts.

After visiting Jamuna Devi and Shanti Devi, I had been able to record the history of evolution of *gobar* style as well as the emergence of Salhesa. But the history of evolution of Harijan Mithila painting was still incomplete as the evolution of *godana* painting was not recorded. Krishnakant took me to Roudi Paswan, whose wife Chano Devi had evolved the *godana* style. The coming of Erika Moser, her suggestion to introduce *godana* designs after having a look at the tattoos on Chano's body was narrated to me. Roudi recalled how Erika inspired her to involve Palti devi, a *natin* for this job. The stories of its evolution from simple tattoo designs to the making of the stories of Salhesa, and the use of natural colours were narrated to me. Though Chano had evolved the style, she remained mostly silent in our conversations. Her husband Roudi was more vocal narrating most of the history.

While he was narrating the history of evolution of *godana* painting, I witnessed that he was continuously making reference to Salhesa. Primitive motifs of horses, elephants, parrots, fishes, and creepers all had a meaning for him. They were not simple motifs or designs to ornament their paintings. Most of these had taken the meaning of Salhesa stories. Many designs resembling upper caste *kohabar* motifs were explained to me as representing the garden of Salhesa in Nepal. There was constant reference to Salhesa and places related to his exploits. Men mounted on horses were Salhesa's attendants, woman on the lion was his sister Bansapti and fishes were represented to be in the pond of Salhesa. These descriptions were in total contrast to the upper caste artists who were unable to provide any contextual meaning of paintings.

The deliberate projection of Salhesa and his importance in the life of Dusadhs was slowly getting revealed to me. I kept on visiting other villages to collect further information on Harijan Mithila art. Most of the information gathered further confirmed the projection of Salhesa. The deliberate projection of Salhesa was revealed when on a chance meeting Jamuna Devi revealed that she also got a national award when she made a painting of Salhesa. A film made by Raymond lee Owens in 1984 showed that both Salhesa and Govinda were being made by Shanti Devi during that period. But in the late 1990s, the paintings of gods Govinda and Rahu had almost disappeared. It was only Salhesa who was receiving their attention. All Harijan artists such as Shanti Devi, Chano Devi, Roudi Paswan, and Rampari Devi had something different to say about him. This period of interaction thus revealed that Salhesa had a definite role to play in their cultural lives and that he was also being projected by them. It also revealed that Dusadhs had occupied an important place in the cultural history of Mithila.

After finishing my interviews with Harijan artists, I spent some time collecting versions of the story of Salhesa from the libraries. The oldest written record was a version collected by Grierson (1882) in his *Maithil Chrestomathy*.[18] I also collected some other local versions. Most of the versions were more or less similar to what had been recorded by Grierson. The many versions available revealed that Salhesa had been an important folk god of Dusadhs in Mithila. However, an interesting point to note that in all the versions, women played more important role than Salhesa. In front of them, Salhesa was a powerless hero (Jain, 1995).

My second visit to Madhubani in 2001 was determined at finding more about Salhesa, his stories and the contemporary use of his mythographies as a means of identity assertion. More importantly, I was interested in knowing if these versions could reveal traces of the history of subalterns in Mithila. This time I planned to meet local scholars and ask them their versions of the story. I also collected some publications from local literature. However there was still a curiosity which remained unsatisfied. Was Salhesa a historical figure? Had he revolted against the elite? With all these queries, I made some more visits to Madhubani. An account of Salhesa by Shankardeo Jha revealed some important facts about Dusadhs, their importance in Mithila and also about Salhesa (Jha, 2002). My subsequent interaction with a folklorist 'Maun' and a local scholar started revealing some interesting facts of Maithil history. I got information of a version in which Salhesa had saved Mithila from foreign invasion.

It was at this juncture that I had to stop my investigation as my dissertation had to be finished. The history of evolution of Harijan art and the projection of Salhesa became a chapter of my dissertation having an equally important place as the other chapters which discussed upper caste women's assertion of identity. The investigation into the stories of Salhesa inspired me to investigate the importance of another goddess Naina Jogin[19] made in Maithil Brahmana households. Not able to include the information of these deities in the main text of the thesis, I decided to put the supplementary information in the appendix. However, a large amount of fieldnotes remained uninterpreted. I could not reflect on these until I began my postdoctoral research on the emergence of Salhesa iconography in Harijan Mithila art.

In the last five years, I have continued working on Salhesa and his use as a means of identity assertion. The years of fieldwork which I spent interacting with artists in Madhubani as well as local people had given me enough evidence to continue my research. I have looked at the various reasons for the projection of Salhesa. I have argued how the projection of Salhesa is not only inspired by a quest for artistic identity but also as a means for recovering social prestige and achieve political ends. Salhesa, I have also argued, is a means for registering social protest. Salhesa lived at a point of time and revolted against the elite. As he belonged to the lower class, his revolt could not be registered (Rekha, 2003). All these arguments were only possible on the basis of information available through extensive fieldwork in Madhubani. If I had remained confined to the libraries in Kolkata, Patna, and Darbhanga where I did most of my research work, my analysis would have represented them only as folk gods and goddesses of lower castes whose history was shrouded in anonymity.

Status in Madhubani

In the last four years, I have not visited Jitwarpur and Ranti but have been in touch with the artists through my local contacts as well as telephonic conversations. More importantly, I have known them through the activities of Ethnic Arts Foundation, United States.[20] The Harijan artists now more popularly known as Dalit artists (Szanton, 2012; Szanton and Bakshi, 2007) have further elaborated their growing sense of self-pride and identity by diversifying stories of Salhesa. Recent paintings include the garden of Salhesa in tattoo paintings style (Szanton and Bakshi, 2007). All these facts suggest that Salhesa still appears to be a favourite theme.

It is interesting to note that Salhesa stories are further being used in other novel ways to project their caste identity and to invent new histories. Inspired by the *Adi Hindu* movement, they are attempting to highlight the fact that Dusadhs were the original inhabitants of Mithila. The use of tattoo paintings is further being made to claim social status for the lower castes. The projection of the epic Ramayana by upper caste painters is countered by the parallel use of Salhesa story as a means of assertion. More importantly, Salhesa stories have become a means to register social protest and recover contested voices of the past (Rekha, 2010).

In future, I want to visit the places where he actually lived.[21] I also want to initiate research into many anonymous Mithila paintings in the collections of museums, universities, and private individuals which have a history of their own. The tradition of enquiring into the history of other gods or heroes could bring into light many aspects of Maithil culture. Mithila has not only been a birthplace of religions such as Buddhism, Jainism, or a seat of Brahmanic culture and learning, it is also a land where indigenous people have lived for ages. Maithil culture and tradition has not been built only by Brahmanical traditions but by a positive interaction between high culture and subaltern culture. An enquiry into paintings as a resource for recovering these hidden voices of the past through ethnographic fieldwork could thus bring forth valuable facts about the past.

Concluding Note

This essay has examined the memories and moments of fieldwork in Madhubani between 1999 and 2004. This essay has described how my ethnographic fieldwork aimed at locating the history of Mithila paintings and understanding the mechanism of assertion of the identity of upper caste women painters ultimately led to the discovery of Harijan Mithila paintings. Continuous interactions with artists helped me locate the cultural tradition and history of marginalized groups in Mithila. However, the process of recalling and recollection was not one sided. It involved continuous innovations in my methodology and active participation on the part of various artists as well local people. The methodologies evolved during the fieldwork and continuous interactions with Mithila artists helped me locate contested voices in Maithil history.

Postcolonial art histories have given third world art a prominent place but its association with primitivism and little traditions has made them the preserve of anthropologists. Notions of anonymity attached to artists and Orientalist tendencies of exoticizing the other make it difficult to locate these traditions within a historical framework. Mithila painting tradition when brought on paper got wide international and national acclaim. But very soon, large-scale production of repetitive ritualistic paintings and *godana* designs sold in craft bazaars and emporiums converted it into examples of primitive art whose meanings were lost in anonymity. This essay has reflected how my research attempted to look beyond these stereotyped perceptions and located the voices of marginalized groups. The overall purpose of the essay has been to demonstrate the importance of ethnographic fieldwork in historical studies.

Madhubani painter Bhagvati Devi with a Geru Painting

Source: Photos by Dilip Banerjee.

Madhubani paintings in Godana Style by Chano Devi

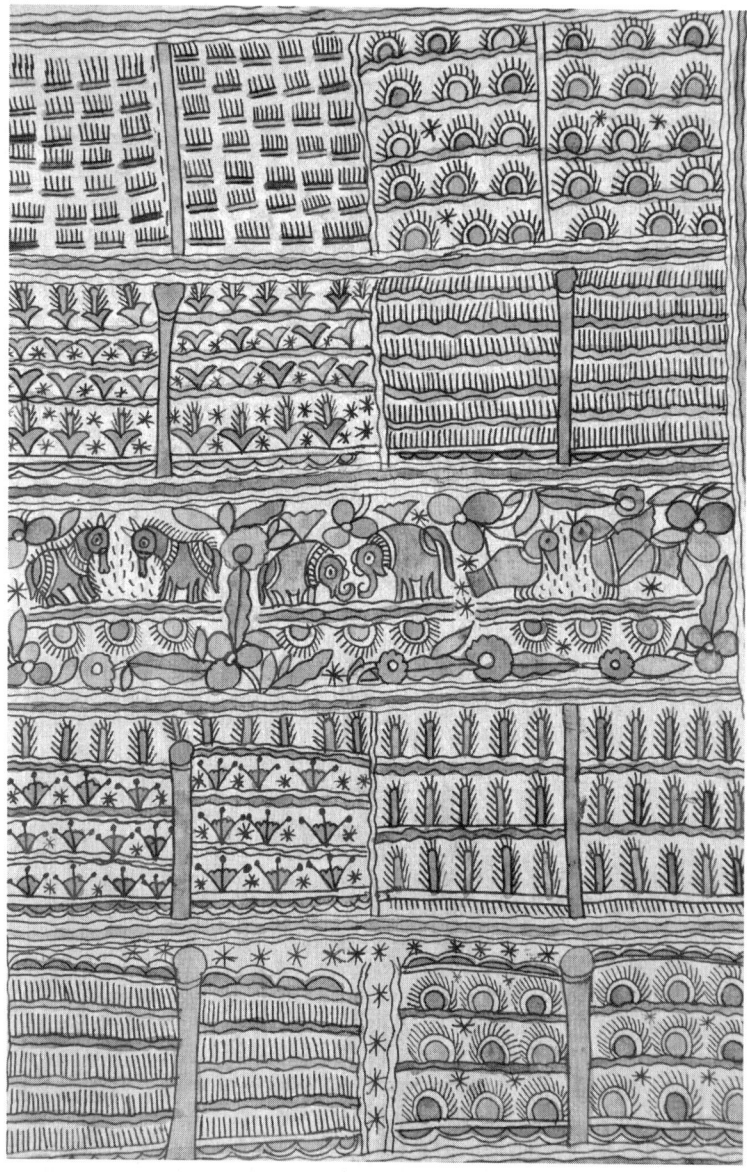

Source: Photos by Dilip Banerjee.

Notes

1. These variant names derive from the ones used by Gandhi and Ambedkar for erstwhile untouchable castes. While Gandhi called them 'Harijan' meaning sons of God, Ambedkar preferred to use the term 'Dalit' meaning oppressed. I have used the term Harijan Mithila paintings as the artists in Madhubani preferred to use this nomenclature while I was doing my fieldwork. In the past years, there has been a tradition of calling it Dalit paintings.

2. Fieldwork for this study was conducted in villages Jitwarpur, Laheriaganj, and Ranti near Madhubani town between 1999 and 2001. The information gathered during this period was further corroborated by the fieldwork conducted in 2002 and 2004.

3. There were two important traditions of painting in Mithila—*aripana* and *kohabar*. While *aripana* refers to the floor paintings that were made on ritualistic occasions in Mithila, *kohabar* is an elaborate painting done on the walls of the *kohabar ghar* (wedding chamber) where the newly weds spend their first four nights after the wedding ceremony. The central motif comprising mainly of *purain* (lotus plant) and *baans* (bamboo grove) are surrounded by different painted images: two parrots making love in the air, fish, tortoise, the sun, the moon, palanquins, grass mats, bamboo grove, and a scene of worship of Gauri (Rekha, 2006).

4. I have discussed the recent emergence of Salhesa in detail.

5. For more on the relationship between art and the politics of Dalit assertion, see Tartakov 1990.

6. It was W.G. Archer who first described Mithila paintings in terms of caste styles in his article in '*Marg*'. Mithila painting he described could be categorized into Brahmana and Kayastha styles (Archer, 1949).

7. The *Panji* or Chronicle locally known as *Panji Prabandha* of the kings of Mithila and other important people is an important document prepared in the time of Harisimhadeva, the karnata king of Mithila (C. 1303–1326 AD). *Panji Prabandha* refers to the writing down of the genealogies for all the superior castes in Mithila. Genealogists began to record each family's ancestors for six generations to avoid incest. This system became popular among the Brahmanas and Karna Kayasthas of Mithila. Along with genealogies, it also enlightens us on the socio-religious condition of the people during the period.

8. For more on the history of commercialization of Mithila paintings, see Jain (1980).

9. The celebrated Maithil poet Vidyapati (1350–1450) was a famous Vaishnava poet of Mithila. Vidyapati became immortal on account of his songs in Maithili, now commonly known as *Padavali* in which he sung praises for Radha and Krishna.

10. *Geru* style of painting was characterized by the use of *geru* colour and lack of ornamentation. It was made by artists like Bhagvati Devi and Ookha Devi from village Jitwarpur.

11. For more on upper caste Brahmana and Kayastha styles (Archer, 1949, 1977; Jayakar, 1981).

12. *Bharni* style, or the colour painting style was marked by the use of vivid colours and minimal use of lines. Considered to be the finest of all painting styles, *Kachni* or line painting style was marked by the less use of colours. The patterns were very intricate and ornately patterned and the details filled with the intricate use of line strokes. Unlike other studies which have talked only in terms of *Bharni* and *Kachni* styles, I have attempted to discuss all the styles (for more information see Chattopadhyay, 2005).

13. Harijan *tola* refers to separate settlements of untouchable castes in the villages of Mithila. The Harijan *tola* in village Jitwarpur has groups of settlements of Chamar, Dusadhs, and Pasis.

14. Indra the most important Vedic god was worshipped in the region. Artists in the 1960s and 1970s were making the paintings of Indra and his consort Indrani seated on an elephant. The same iconography has now been given the name of Salhesa and his consort Dauna Malin.

15. Pupul Jayakar was the chairperson of Handloom Handicrafts Export Corporation (HHEC) and the main force behind the commercialization of Madhubani (Maithil) Painting. Upendra Maharathi, an artist, designer and a Gandhian was involved in the promotional programme of Madhubani art. Many of the earlier paintings of 1960s and 1970s can be viewed in the Upendra Maharathi Institute for Industrial Design, Digha, Patna. Bhaskar Kulkarni was the field office in charge of the drought relief programme in Madhubani. Under his guidance women artists evolved distinctive styles such as *Geru*, Tantric, and *Gobar* and *Godana*. Bhaskar is also credited with discovering Worli paintings made by the tribals in Maharashtra.

16. The last foreigner to visit Madhubani in 1989 was Tokio Hasegawa, a Japanese who set up the Mithila Museum in Japan. This museum has concentrated totally on the acquisition, display and research of Mithila paintings.

17. Salhesa Rahu, Govinda and Salhesa are Gods worshipped by lower castes in Mithila. While Rahu and Salhesa were worshipped by Dusadhs, Govinda was worshipped by Halwais, a caste traditionally involved in making sweets. The Dusadhs worship Rahu occasionally as this worship involves a lot of money. This *puja* is observed during the Hindu month of Magh (January–February) by those who have taken a vow in his honour. The *bhagats* or the masters of the ceremony are invited along with friends and relatives. For a description of Rahu worship in Harijan Mithila paintings, see Jain (1995), Rekha (2003).

18. The version preserved in *An Introduction to the Maithili language of North Bihar* was published in 1881 in the form of a journal of Bengal Asiatic Society. Later on in the famous book *Maithili Chrestomathy*, the entire story of Salhesa was included along with other valuable literary source material. Grierson had obtained the story from a Dom, a caste traditionally involved in sweeping. The book has the English translation of the *Gatha* (story) and a brief introduction of the Dusadh caste and of Salhesa story. For a short account of his version, see Rekha (2003, 2004).

19 Naina Jogins are the four veiled women painted in four corners of the *kohabar ghar* in Mithila and are supposed to ward off the evil eye. Archer mistook them

to be brides on account of their veiled faces. Many photographs and paper drawings of Naina Jogins were taken by him and are now the property of the India Office Library records, now part of the British Library.

20. The Ethnic Arts Foundation (EAF) is a non-profit organization founded in 1980 dedicated to the continuing development of Mithila Painting. The foundation also works for expanding national and international appreciation of the painting tradition by promoting research and publications. In January 2003, the EAF established a free Mithila Art Institute in Madhubani to further the training and opportunities of talented young Maithil painters.

21. Phulbari and Manikdah Pokhara are important places in Mithila connected with the Salhesa story. In village Phulbari, the place of Salhesa's birth, fairs, and festivals are held every year and attended by Dusadhs from all over Mithila. For more on this see Jha (2002), Maun (2000).

References

Anand, Mulk Raj. 1984. *Madhubani Painting*. New Delhi: Publications Division.

Archer, Mildred. 1977. *Indian Popular Paintings in the India Office Library*. London and New Delhi: UBS Publishers.

Archer, W.G. 1949. Maithil Painting. *Marg*, 3(3): 24–33.

Brown, Carolyn Henning. 1982. Folk Art and the Art of Books: Who Speaks for the Traditional Artist? Review of 'The Art of Mithila', by Yves Vequaud. *Modern Asian Studies*, 16(3): 519–522.

———. 1996. Contested Meanings: Tantra and the Poetics of Mithila Art. *American Ethnologist*, 23(4): 717–737.

Chattopadhyay, Suhrid Shankar. 2005. Mithila's Pride. *Frontline*, 11 February, pp. 65–72.

Chavda, Jagdish. 1990. The Narrative Paintings of India's Jitwarpuri Women. *Women's Art Journal*, 11(1): 25–28.

Grierson, George Abraham. 1882. *An Introduction to Maithili Language of North Bihar Containing a Grammar, Chrestomathy and Vocabulary, Part 2*. Calcutta: Asiatic Society.

Hart, Lynn M. 1995. Three Walls: Regional Aesthetics and the International Art World. In George E. Marcus and Fred R. Myers (eds), *The Traffic in Culture: Refiguring Art and Anthropology to The Traffic in Culture*, pp. 127–150. Berkeley, California: University of California Press.

Hasegawa, Tokio. nd. *Cosmology of Prayer*. In Japanese. 42 illustrations in colour, and 43 in black and white of paintings in the collection of the Mithila Museum.

Hasegawa, Tokio. nd. Ganga Devi. With Introductions by Pupul Jayakar and Jyotindra Jain. Black and white and colour illustrations of 26 painting by Ganga Devi, plus designs of 72 kohabar and aripan motifs. Mithila Museum.

Heinz, Carolyn Brown. 2006. Documenting the Image in Mithila Art. *Visual Anthropology Review*, 22(2): 5–33.

Jain, Devaki. 1980. *Women's Quest for Power: Five Indian Case Studies.* New Delhi: Vikas.

Jain, Jyotindra. 1995. The Bridge of Vermilion: Narrative Rhythm in the Dusadh Legends of Mithila. In B.N. Goswamy and Usha Bhatia (eds), *Indian Painting: Essays in Honour of Karl J. Khandalvala*, pp. 207–222. New Delhi: Lalit Kala Akademy.

———. 1997. *Ganga Devi: Tradition and Expression in Mithila Painting.* Ahmedabad: Mapin.

———. 1998. *Other Masters: Five Contemporary Folk and Tribal Artists of India.* New Delhi: Crafts Museum and Handicrafts and Handloom Exports Corporation of India.

Jayakar, Pupul. 1969. Paintings: Forms of Gay Abandon. *Marg*, 22(4): 47.

———. 1971. Paintings of Mithila. *The Times of India*, pp. 29–37.

———. 1975. Paintings of Rural India. *The Times of India Annual*, pp. 53–62.

———. 1981. *The Earthen Drum: An Introduction to the Ritual Arts of Rural India.* New Delhi: National Museum.

———. 1989. *The Earth Mother.* New Delhi: Penguin Books.

Jha, J. 1986. *Lok Jivan O Lok Sahitya.* Laheriasarai: Mithila Research Society.

Jha, L. 1962. *Mithila Ki Sanskritika Loka Chitrakala.* Darbhanga: Sarisaba Pahi.

Jha, S. January–March 2002. Raja Salhesa. Darbhanga: Rachna.

Lanius, Mary. 1988. Mithila Painting. In Michael W. Meister (ed.), *Making Things in South Asia: The Role of Artists and Craftsmen*, pp. 135–141. Philadelphia, Pennsylvania: University of Pennsylvania.

Mathur, J.C. 1966. The Domestic Arts of Mithila. *Marg*, 20(1): 43–55.

Singh, Maun P.K. 2000. *Hamare Lok Devi Devta.* Edited by B.K. Singh. Muzaffarpur: Sameeksha Prakashan.

Maun, P.K. Singh and R.P. Neeraj. 2002. *Raja Salhesa: Sahitya Aur Sanskriti.* Muzaffarpur: Namita Prakashan.

Mishra, N. 1975. Some Aspects of the Dusadhs of Darbhanga. *Journal of Social Research*, XVIII(II): 10.

Narayan, Badri. 2001. *Documenting Dissent: Contesting Fables, Contested Memories and Dalit Political Discourse.* Shimla: IIAS.

Rekha, Neel. 2003. Harijan Paintings of Mithila. *Marg*, 54(3): 64–77.

———. 2004. *Art and Assertion of Identity: Women and Madhubani Paintings*, Unpublished PhD Dissertation, Patna University, Patna.

———. 2006. *Salhesa Iconography in Madhubani Paintings: A Case of Harijan Assertion. BASAS Conference.* London: Birkbeck College.

———. 2010. From Folk Art to Fine Art: Changing Paradigms in the Historiography of Maithil Painting. *Journal of Art Historiography*, 2: 1–20.

Roy Choudhary, P.C. 1964. *Bihar District Gazetteers*. Patna: Superintendent, Secretariat Press.

Singh, Manishekhar. 1999. *Folk Art, Identity and Performance: A Sociological Study of Maithil Painting*, PhD Dissertation. Department of Sociology. Delhi: University of Delhi.

———. 2000. A Journey into Pictorial Space: Poetics of Frame and Field in Maithil Painting. *Contributions to Indian Sociology*, (n.s.), 34(3): 409–442.

———. 2004. Journey Into Distant Land: Poetics of Mithila Painting. *Indian Folk Life*, 3(4), Serial no.17: 11–14.

Szanton, David L. March 2003. *Some Observations on the Continuing Evolution of Mithila Painting*. http://www.mithilapainting.org/MPObservation2003. html. Accessed on 13 September 2010.

———. March–April 2004. Folk Art No longer- An Essay on the transformations of Mithila Painting. Biblio: A Review of Books. *Biblio: A Review of Books*, IX (3&4). New Delhi.

Szanton, David L. 2005. Mithila Painting: The Evolution of An art Form. *Museum of Craft and Folk Art, San Francisco*, 21(1): 1–6.

———. 2006. Mithila Painting: A language of Perception, Meanings and Expression. Arts Annual, India Habitat Centre, New Delhi.

———. 2012. Mithila Painting: A Dalit Intervention. In Gary Tartakov (ed.), *Dalit Art and Visual Imagery*, pp. 219–234. New Delhi: Oxford University Press India.

Szanton, David L. and Malini Bakshi.. 2007. *Mithila Painting The Evolution of An Art Form*. California: Ethnic Arts Foundation. PinkMango.

Tartakov, Gary Michael. 1990. Art and Identity: Rise of a Buddhist Imagery. *Art Journal*, 49(4): 409–416.

Thakur, Upendra. 1982. *Madhubani Painting*. New Delhi: Abhinava Prakashan.

Thakur, Vijay K. 1988. *Madhyakalin Mithila*. Patna: Indralaya Prakashan.

Vequaud, Yves. 1977. *The Women Painters of Mithila: Ceremonial Paintings from an Ancient Kingdom*. London: Thames and Hudson.

Yadav, Motilal. 1981. *Lok Gatha Salhesak Adhyayan*. Unpublished PhD Thesis. Darbhanga: Lalit Narayan Mishra University.

Videos

Moser, E. *Fourteen Short Films with a German Manual and English Summaries 1973–1978*. Available from Mrs Elke Geilhaupt, e-mail: elke.geilhaupt@ iwf.de, Documentation department/Infotheque—IWF Wissen und Medien gGmbH Nonnenstieg 72, Göttingen.

Owens, Raymond, Ron Hess, and Cheryl Groff. 1983. *Five Painters* (video 40 minutes, colour, sound) *on the Lives of Five Mithila Painters* (Ganga Devi, Sita Devi, Krishnanand Jha, Shanti Devi, and Baua Devi). Film Guide. Available from the South Asia Film Program, University of Wisconsin.

15

Memories of My Third Visit to the Nicobar Archipelago

Vijoy S. Sahay

Memories of my second visit to the Nicobar Islands, with special reference to the Island of Chowra, was earlier published in 2007 under the title 'Experiencing Anthropology in the Nicobar Archipelago' in the journal the *Eastern Anthropologist*. In December 1974, I left for the Nicobar Islands with a batch of postgraduate students of Department of Anthropology, Ranchi University. This was my third visit to the archipelago. In the third week of January we reached Nancowry. Our team put up in the Enunga Village of Nancowry Island in a boys hostel of the only upper primary school in the central group of islands. The hostel was just below a hill. In front, there was a small playground. Across the playground was the office of the Akooji Jadwet and Company, the only firm that had the license to trade in these islands. To our right were some quarters for the school teachers and to our left were some classrooms. Other than these wooden structures, the rest were all huts of the natives.

The Rani-Hood!

Nancowry harbour is supposed to be one of the most beautiful landlocked natural harbours in the world. There are four islands in the Nancowry group, which are, Nancowry, Kamorta, Trinket, and Katchall. Though the administrative headquarter of the central group of islands is situated in Kamorta, the

Nancowry Island, particularly the Enunga village, is still supposed to be the political headquarter of the whole of the central group of islands. Historically, it was the seat of a very influential lady, namely Isolone, who was later known as Rani Isolone. After Isolone, her daughter Laxmi lived here, who was called Rani Laxmi. Now Rani Laxmi's daughter Ayesha and her son Rashid live here.

The institution of Rani-hood (queenhood) is not indigenous to these islands. Neither of the aforesaid ranis was ever coroneted either by the British or by the Government of India. During the British time, Isolone lived in the Enunga village of Nancowry. Her ancestry could be traced from Teressa Island. Still the family has lots of land in Teressa. Though matriarchy has never prevailed in these islands, but in the central group of the Nicobar Islands, women still enjoy right to property and have considerable say in decision-making in family affairs. But it is because of their relative economic independence in comparison to Car Nicobar or other smaller islands. Besides Teressa, Isolone had inherited an enormous amount of land in Nancowry, Kamorta, and Trinket. She had married several times in her life; the last one was with a *tehsildar*, a local from Port Blair. During the British time, except once or twice in a year, hardly any officer from Port Blair visited these islands. Therefore, a *tehsildar* was all powerful. Isolone must have been a clever lady, full of leadership qualities. Because of her proximity with the *tehsildar*, she learnt the art of administration and official protocol. And because of her leverage over land and proximity with the *tehsildar*, she exercised enormous influence over the natives. Her influence over the natives helped *tehsildar* also to smoothly discharge his administrative duties. In turn, Isolone witnessed and participated in all official ceremonies and seldom missed any occasion to meet visitors and outsiders, being his wife and so close to him. To the visitors, *tehsildar* introduced Isolone as a Rani (Queen) of these islands. Thus, the title of Rani (queenhood) was bestowed upon Isolone by the *tehsildar*, and not by the British or anyone else.

After the death of Isolone, her daughter Laxmi inherited the legacy of her mother and was thus called Rani Laxmi. Rani Laxmi also married more than once in her lifetime. Last, she was married to a Minicoy Muslim, who was the Captain of the small ship Safina, which was owned by Akooji Jadwet and Company. After marriage, she converted to Islam and bore several children to him, including Ayesha and Rashid. However, despite conversion, she retained her name as Rani Laxmi. Any dignitary, who visited the central group of islands, was necessarily taken to Rani, and, thus, she also exercised as much influence as her mother did. Nowadays, all the girls in the subsequent generations of this family are married to Minicoy Muslims, and the family has acquired an enormous amount of land in the neighbouring islands. As because the Minicoy Muslims, who are married to the girls of the so called

'Rani's' family, are cleverer in terms of material and economic acquisition, they are found inclined to usurp as much of the land as possible in Kamorta and other islands. An undercurrent of dislike and discontentment can be easily observed today among the family members of Rani and the local population. However, Rani's family, on account of economically being the strongest, and, thereby, exercising enormous political and administrative clout and influence, the local population has not been able to defy them openly.

In 2002, when I revisited the Islands Rashid gave me a booklet. The booklet attempted to institutionalize the queenhood by an act of bravery exhibited by Rani Isolone during the war period (the First World War or the Second World War, it has not been mentioned in the booklet); as if, the British Government, having been pleased by that act of her bravery, bestowed upon Isolone, the title of 'Rani' (a queen). The incident, as described in the booklet, has been that during the war a ship was sighted in the sea approaching the island. In those days of yore, very rarely, only once or twice in a year, any British officer from Port Blair visited these islands. Whenever their ship was sighted, the *tehsildar* used to unfurl the Union Jack at the top of the hill in Enunga that signified the British occupation in these islands. On that fateful day, when Isolone sighted the ship, and in absence of the *tehsildar* on the spot, she did not fail to unfurl the Union Jack. Incidentally, the ship that was sighted was not that of the British, but of the enemy nation. When they saw the Union Jack unfurled atop the Enunga hill, they thought that the British Army was present on the island, and they immediately fled from the waters. Later, when this fact came to the knowledge of all, Isolone must have been applauded by all, including the British; however, there is absolutely no official record whatsoever that on this account she was ever coroneted or bestowed upon the queenhood, either by the British or anyone else.

Teamwork and My Key Informant Gabriel

Teamwork in anthropology has its advantages as well as disadvantages. So was the case with me. Because of my earlier acquaintance with the Nicobar Islands and the Nicobarese culture, every member of the team wanted to consult me on his/her respective topic of research; and thus, engaged most of my time. As a result, I could not move independently. However, the advantage was that every day I moved to one of the students to collect data on his/her topic of research. This gave me the opportunity to understand various aspects of Nancowrian life and culture within a short time. In the night hours all the members of the team prepared their daily reports. Then they consulted me for verification. Thus, despite the fact that I could not move independently to collect data, huge amount of information with regard to their life cycle, belief system, economic and political organization, intra- and inter-island relationships, etc., was collected within a limited period. During this phase of fieldwork, my key informants were Reverend Fred and Gabriel Kulilong. Reverend Fred was a priest from Car Nicobar, a man of short stature, but very kind, meek, and gentle. He was in charge of the church in the Enunga village in Nancowry Island. Gabriel was a native of Nancowry.

During the entire course of my fieldwork in the Nicobar Islands, I came in closest contact with Gabriel and his family. Gabriel Kulilong was his full name and people called him Kuli. A man of very calm and simple disposition, Gabriel lived with wife and children at the top of the hill in Enunga village in Nancowry. He also had a hut down the hill in Enunga, which he provided me to live in as long as I stayed in Nancowry. I usually took my meals with his family atop the hill. Sometimes, his wife prepared meals down the hill in the hut where I lived. During my stay in Nancowry, I was not only considered as an Enunga villager but also people there considered me as a part and parcel of Gabriel's family; as if, I was a member of his family. Wherever I went for data collection, the entire family of Gabriel moved with me. Gabriel had inherited a huge amount of forested land from his mother. He commanded enormous respect in the central group of islands because of his extremely meek and simple nature, as also because of his leverage over land. Nancowrians approached him for a piece of land to make gardens. And Gabriel always obliged. He liked drinking toddy, which he called 'white stuff', and always remained boozed, but never lost his meek and gentle temperament; and always remained smiling. In 2002, when I revisited Nancowry, I learnt that he had died in 1976, only a year after I had left the island. I went to his grave and stood there in silence for a few minutes. I remembered the pleasant days I had spent with him and his family in Nancowry almost 27 years back. I felt a very painful sadness in my heart; therefore, praying for peace to the sublime soul in heaven, I turned back and left the graveyard in silence.

Annahanam: Initiation Ceremony of a Nancowrian Girl

The team stayed there for a little over 30 days. During this period, I witnessed the 'Annahanam' of the daughter of Rani Laxmi. Annahanam is a rite de passage of a Nancowrian girl. As soon as a girl attains the age of puberty this ceremony is organized. It is marked by the occurrence of her first menses. Annahanam could be called as an initiation ceremony of a Nancowrian girl. As soon as the information of the first menses of the girl is known to the family, the girl is taken care of. She is kept aloof, secluded in a dark hut. She is given food there and not allowed to come out of the hut. She is not allowed to go out even for toilet or any call of nature. All arrangements are made inside the hut itself. Some old ladies always surround her. The girl is never left alone in the hut. In the night hours, either her mother or some senior female member of the family or the neighbourhood sleeps there. As long as the period continues, the girl is kept like this.

When the menses stop, the girl is first taken to the shore for a bath. Then she takes a bath with fresh water at home. In the meantime, the room where she was confined for a couple of days is cleaned. Then the girl is taken inside the hut again and given new clothes to wear. Thereafter, all the ladies, particularly the married ones, visit the girl one by one. Every such lady carries a small stick with her. As her turn comes, she strikes the girl with her stick gently so as not to cause any injury and then gives her precious preaching, such as, 'Look, now you have become a matured girl, you are no more a child; you should behave like this and that. You should not freely mix with boys, and so on and so forth …' All such sermons are given to the girl so as to make her an ideal Nancowrian girl. She is also warned that if she doesn't follow the suggestions and violate any of the norms, she would not be beaten lightly, but severely by the same stick.

Outside the home an elaborate communal feast is organized by the male members of the family. As Rani Laxmi was the most influential lady of the entire central group of islands, besides relatives and friends, the whole population of Nancowry was invited. I witnessed that a number of guests from the neighbouring islands of Kamorta, Trinket, and Katchall also visited Rani's house. They all came with some gifts either in kind or cash, and enjoyed the feast.

Deadly Encounters during Misadventures

During this period, I remember two occasions, when I narrowly escaped deadly encounters in the harbour; first, either with a shark or a crocodile, and secondly with two crocodiles. And on both the occasions, Nishi (a teammate) was with me. Nishi had developed good rapport with an informant who lived across the Nancowry Harbour in Kamorta towards the gateway to Katchall. At the invitation of his informant, one evening, Nishi and I picked up a small canoe from the beach and started for the destination. In Nancowry I had very ably learnt rowing a canoe. Nancowry Harbour, as I have already described, is one of the most beautiful landlocked harbours in the world. It has two gateways, the eastern channel that opens towards Trinket Island, and the western channel that opens towards Katchall. Our destination was towards Katchall. As we crossed the harbour halfway, we turned left, and Enunga village disappeared from our sight. To our left was a forested hill, and across the channel was the extension of Kamorta Island. In front, we could see the opening of the channel and across that at a distance Katchall Island was visible. By the time we reached near the opening of the channel, the sun had already set, still there was some visibility. There was no sign of any life there. The loneliness of the place was scaring. Earlier, I had never witnessed such lonely surroundings. Except for the sound of splashing water that was caused as we rowed the small canoe, there was deadly silence all around. Out of fear both of us were silent. It appeared that if we spoke anything, it would perhaps reverberate in this silent atmosphere. I wanted to return, but could not utter. I didn't know what was in Nishi's mind?

Anyway, in that grim and distressing atmosphere we continued to row our canoe. Nishi pointed out across the channel. Below the forested and hilly backdrop, we sighted one or two huts along the shore. As I was rowing from the rear end I moved the direction of the canoe towards the hut across the channel by positioning the rowing blade accordingly. After some time, we reached ashore. There were only two huts surrounded by the dense forest. Behind the hut was thickly forested upland. We lifted our canoe out of the water. Light from some lamp was coming out of one of the huts. We went near it and called for someone. To our pleasant surprise, it was the hut of Nishi's informant (I do not remember his name). He greeted us and took us inside the hut. He lived with his wife and children there. The adjoining hut was that of his brother-in-law.

Inside the hut some men and women were sitting around. At the centre was a container full of toddy. A woman was serving toddy after pouring it on a half-split coconut shell. It moved round the group one by one. We were also asked to join the group. In one corner of the hut, the children were busy in eating, perhaps their supper. Unmarried girls did not join such toddy sessions of the elders. We also consumed several rounds of toddy. Baked fish was also served to us. We could not collect any precise data there, but learnt that the family-friend of Nishi's informant had come from Kakana village to invite them for some ceremony to be organized next week in Kakana. I was getting worried. It had already been dark. I wanted to leave the place as soon as possible, because I had already started to feel the kick of the toddy. From my earlier experiences, I knew that such toddy sessions of the Nicobarese would continue till late night, sometimes till next morning; at least as long as the stock of the toddy had not exhausted. At last, we took their leave. Two men, besides Nishi's informant, came down the hut to help us launch the canoe in water. They dragged the canoe from the shore and Nishi and I began our return journey, only to face the worst.

As we lighted down the hut we faced a light cool breeze. The kick of the toddy had already made us mildly inebriated. The light cool breeze on our face made the environment even more pleasant. But as we rowed our canoe a little distance, the situation changed abruptly. It was pitch-dark all around, and we rowed our canoe ahead. Below our canoe was the deep sea and above our head was the clear starry sky. In front was the glimpse of forested hilly end of Nancowry Island that appeared like a silhouette under the starry sky. All around, the place appeared to be completely desolate. There was such solitude and silence that except for the splashing sound of water that emanated from the rowing blade nothing could be heard. For a moment, I shuddered to think that if for any reason the canoe capsized or overturned then what would we do in this desolate and deep harbour. No one could come to our rescue; nor could anyone hear our shouts. All our inebriation had vanquished by this time. Nishi and I both had some premonition that something terrible would happen, therefore, we remained silent. It appeared that if we uttered anything, it would perhaps reverberate in this silent and desolate locus.

I wanted to reach the other end of the harbour as early as possible, which was though equally hilly and forested and desolate; but what was in my mind that if any mishap took place, we could easily swim a short distance and reach the shore. Moreover, I thought that the sea would also be not as deep as it was then. The very idea of the depth of the sea below our primitive type of small canoe made me uncomfortable. I wished to reach the shallow waters along the other end. And we finally reached; however, no sign of life around the place still haunted our minds. But at least we were a little more comfortable.

I planned to row the canoe along the shore until we crossed the hilly end, wherefrom village Enunga could be reached. After crossing the end, I turned the canoe to the right, and we could see about half a kilometre ahead, a faint light of a lamp emanating from a hut in village Enunga. With a view to avoid the deep sea as far as possible, I continued to row the canoe along the shallow waters. Beneath our canoe we could see the deposits of coral reef. Suddenly something hit the front end of the canoe so hard and violently that for a moment our small canoe was in the air. After having been in the air for a few seconds, it hit the water again. Luckily, it did not overturn. Nishi and I both shouted as loud as we could, knowing well that no one on earth would come to our rescue there. Fortunately, we had not dropped our rowing blades. We started to beat the water on both sides of the canoe by the blades in our hands. Then I shouted at Nishi to row as fast as he could. Soon we entered into the deep waters of the harbour, and for the next 20 minutes, I believe, we knew nothing but the need to escape for our lives. Non-stop, we continued to row until we reached the shore of Enunga. We lifted the canoe out of the water and lay down flat on the sandy beach for at least half an hour to normalize our breathlessness. Still we remained silent. After half an hour, we got up and returned to our camp. We did not tell this incident to any of our teammates.

A second encounter with the crocodiles took place near Enunga jetty. Today, the jetty there, is cemented and pucca one. Then, it was a wooden jetty. The height of the jetty was about 12–15 feet above the water. An electric bulb lighted the jetty for some time in the evening by the power supplied by the generator of the Akooji Jadwet and Company. One evening, a number of our teammates were just idly sitting on the wooden jetty and enjoying the breeze blowing across the harbour. In the meantime, as the teammates knew that I was a good swimmer, someone asked me whether I could jump into the water from that height? I said, 'Yes, I could.' And I removed my shirt and pant, and wearing the underwear I was ready to dive into the water. Nishi also followed me. First, I dived; and Nishi followed me so soon that his hands touched my legs. I have always felt uncomfortable if anything has touched me while in the water. Anyway, we swam a little distance, caught hold of the ladder, and climbed up the jetty. The teammates persuaded us to take another dive. This time I told Nishi to dive first so that he would not touch me again. After Nishi dived, I took the stance to dive again. A second before I could jump, I heard the splashing sound of water from my right side. This area was comparatively darker. I thought someone might be rowing a canoe. Though I was almost half bent to take the dive into the water, on hearing the splashing sound, I waited for a second and thought to let the canoe pass. However, my sixth sense perhaps alerted me, and within no time I saw two crocodiles with their heads above the water surface fast approaching Nishi. I shouted at my full throat at Nishi and asked him to escape as fast as he could. He did not understand and instead asked me what the matter was. I had little time to explain anything to him. On my left was Moses (a Nancowrian) with a long five-cell torch in his hand. Finding no other way to avert the situation, I snatched the torch from his hands and threw it at the crocodiles. This instant action or for that matter reaction of mine made two impacts; first, both the crocodiles turned a little away from Nishi, and, secondly, Nishi understanding the gravity of the situation swam towards the ladder as fast as he could. Thus, he was saved. Whenever I recall this event, it comes to my mind that if I had also dived into the water, what would have happened? Both of us would have become sumptuous meals for the crocodiles perhaps.

Chasing Money

After 35 days of fieldwork, on its way back to Ranchi, the team returned to Port Blair. I had plans to stay in the field for a couple of months more; however, I also came to Port Blair for two reasons. First, to see off the team and, second, I had learnt from a letter from my mother that some money had been sent to me. During the course of my fieldwork, money was sent from my home generally by bank drafts addressed to me, c/o Anthropological Survey of India (ASI), Port Blair. So, I thought that I would see the team off at Port Blair and also collect the draft from the office of the ASI. After the team left, the next day, I went to the office of the ASI, where I was told that the money was sent to Kamorta Island, c/o one Mr Mondal who was working in the ASI and doing fieldwork there. I asked the office staff why they had sent the bank draft to Kamorta. They told me that the money had been sent by telegraphic money order (TMO), instead of bank draft, and that if the money by TMO was not delivered to the addressee within 15 days, the rule was to return it to the sender. The office staff at the ASI had no information about my coming to Port Blair. They only knew that I was in Nancowry Islands. Therefore, they redirected the TMO to Kamorta, c/o one of their employees.

I was completely at a loss at this. I was also running short of money. The staff also told me that it had already been 10 days that the TMO was redirected to Kamorta. First, I wondered why the money was sent by TMO and not by bank draft. Later, it came to my mind that since I had written a letter to my mother and told her to send me some money, she might have thought that I needed it urgently, and therefore, she sent it by TMO, so that I could get it at the earliest. There was no telephone facility at my house and the telephonic facilities were not as available as they are today. Hence, I could not talk to my mother. Anyway, I rushed to the office of the Marine Department to enquire about the next ship to the Nicobar Islands.

I had earlier planned to stay for a couple of days at Port Blair, but I learnt that a ship was leaving for the southern islands the next day. I booked a ticket for Nancowry.

On the third day I reached Nancowry. I straight went to Kamorta Post Office to collect my money. There was a postmaster who told me that the TMO was redirected to Kakana village of Kamorta Island. I asked him why on earth it was sent there. He told me that since the TMO was in c/o Mr Mondal, and someone told the postmaster that Mr Mondal was at Kakana, so he sent it to Kakana Post Office. Having been disappointed again I returned to Enunga village in Nancowry. I went to Gabriel's home. Nobody was there. He had left for some other village with his family. Then I went to Reverend Fred's house. He too was absent. His wife told me that Reverend Fred had gone to some other islands to inaugurate a chapel. I was feeling hungry. There was no hotel, not even a tea stall, where I could eat or drink something. Nearby, there was a tube well. I went there and at least quenched my thirst. I had no place to stay. At last, I carried my baggage and went to the school, spread my bedding in the verandah, and slept without any food.

The next morning I got up and placed my baggage in one corner of the school verandah. After attending the call of nature along the seashore, I left for Akooji Jadwet and Company to inquire if any boat was going to Kakana. To my delight, already the engine of a boat had started, and I was told that it was going to Kakana. I boarded the ferryboat at once. It moved towards the channel of the harbour, which opened towards Trinket Island. As it passed the gateway, the current of the sea from the opposite direction was very strong. We saw four or five Nancowrians on a canoe struggling hard against the current. They shouted at us and waved their hands. Our boatman approached them. Then they threw a strong rope from the canoe, which was tied with our motorboat. Three or four of them jumped over to our boat, and thus the boat slowly began to tow the canoe. These men sat in one corner of the boat, spread a piece of cloth, and began to eat something, which I could not make out. When they saw me looking at the food they were eating, one of them offered me a piece. I asked them in Hindi what it was. One of them said 'turtle'. I hesitated for a moment because I had never consumed the flesh of a turtle. However, on the one hand, I was very hungry because I had not eaten anything since yesterday; on the other hand, the fellow repeated his offer smilingly. I didn't think twice and accepted his offer with thanks. I can't say whether I liked the taste of it or not because there was no salt mixed in it; it was only boiled perhaps. But I must admit that in that state of starvation I wanted to ask

them for more such pieces of flesh, but hesitated and resisted my tempta-
tion anyhow.

We reached Kakana. After getting down the boat, I enquired about the
post office and straight away went there. To my further disappointment,
the postmaster told me that the TMO was of course in my name, but it was
in c/o Mr Mondal. And Mr Mondal had left for Katchall a week ago, so he
had redirected it to Katchall Post Office. He advised me to go to Katchall.
I was again in a fix. I didn't know what to do next. Then I thought that at
least I could collect some information of anthropological importance as
long as the boat stayed here. But I did not know anybody in Kakana. Then
I remembered that Gabriel had told me once that one Captain Dawood,
a very old person, lived in Kakana, who once traded with the Malaysians
during the British time. I enquired about his residence. I was shown a big
hut nearby. I went there and told the man who was in front of his residence
to inform captain Dawood. After sometime, a very old man with wrinkles
all over his face, hands, and all the exposed parts of his body, clad in a half
pant and a colourful Hawaii shirt with a big felt hat on his head, climbed
down the stairs of the hut. I greeted him with a handshake and introduced
myself. He also shook hands with me warmly. Then I began asking him
about the days when he traded with Malaysians. I had to ask him very
loudly, as he was partially deaf, therefore, heard little. Someone from his
family brought a cup of black tea and two pieces of banana while I interviewed him. I asked him for a glass of water, instead he brought a coconut.
He split the coconut for me to drink its water. I told him to split it further
so that I could eat its tender kernel also. I wanted to take photographs of
the old man but I had left my camera in my suitcase. In the meantime, we
heard the whistle of the boat. The man present there asked me whether I
had come by boat. When I answered in affirmative, he said that the boat
was leaving for Enunga. Midway I stopped interviewing Captain Dawood.
I had hardly eaten the banana and finished the cup of tea. I took leave of the
Captain, and ran towards the boat. The boat had already started moving.
When the boatman saw me he slowed it down. I jumped over the boat,
and returned to Enunga. Again, I enquired about Gabriel and Reverend
Fred. Both of them were not present. That evening again I slept in the
school verandah without any food. Sometimes my stomach ached because
of hunger, but there was no alternative.

The next morning I again went to Akooji Jadwet and Company. I learnt
there that after an hour a boat would go to Katchall. I boarded the boat
and reached Katchall. The post office was about ½ km from the shore. I
went to the post office. Though all the doors of the post office were opened,

nobody was there. After I shouted several times for someone to come, a man clad in a lungi and banyan appeared from behind. He was the postmaster, I learnt. First, I introduced myself and then enquired of the TMO. He said, 'Yes, there was one TMO in somebody's name c/o Mr Mondal, but I think, I returned it to the Port Blair Office, as I was told by someone that Mr Mondal had moved to West Katchall for a fortnight.' This was the last thing I could hope for. I was so disappointed at his reply that for a moment I was left speechless. I didn't know what to ask him further. However, I told him in a few sentences how for the last three days without any proper food, I was chasing the money and the money was chasing me. Having seen me so disgusted, he said, 'Let me check it again.' He went inside the room and brought a bundle of papers tied with a string. After untying the string he began to search and suddenly announced that it was there. I can't explain how relieved I felt at his announcement. Then he asked me whether I had an identity card. 'No', I said. Then he expressed his helplessness. He could not give it to me, unless Mr Mondal was there, or if anybody could certify my identity and sign as witness, because he did not know me. Then only few mainlanders lived in Katchall. I remembered a Bengali gentleman who worked in the electricity department. He often visited Nancowry, and we had met a couple of times. I referred his name to the postmaster. He agreed and told me where he lived.

I started to return by the same way I came to meet the Bengali gentleman and seek his help. It was midday with the bright and scorching sun over one's head. I walked down the desolate metal road all alone. Dense forest and tall tropical trees stood along both sides of the road. I was dead tired and felt completely worn out but the very thought of finally locating the TMO reinvigorated me. In the meantime, I heard the bell of a cyclist from behind. I turned my head to see who it was. I saw a long bearded man on a bicycle. His hair had also grown long and was unkempt. He too looked equally tired and exhausted. For a moment, he reminded me of the character of Bengun in *Treasure Island* by Robert Louis Stevenson. He passed me, looking intently. Then at a close distance he stopped and without alighting from his bicycle turned to face me. I became a little suspicious; however, I continued to walk down the road. As I reached near him both of us looked at each other intently. Suddenly he asked me in English, 'Are you Mr Sahay from Ranchi University?' I was completely taken aback and replied, 'Yes'. I also started to think who he might be? Then I wondered who else than an anthropologist could recognize me in these far off islands. I asked him, 'Are you Mr Mondal?' To my utmost delight he was Mr Mondal. I told him the entire story of my running after the TMO without any break. I asked him how he recognized me. He told that once he had seen me at the office of ASI in Port Blair. Anyway, we immediately returned to the post office. Mondal had his identity card, so the postmaster had no difficulty in delivering the amount to me.

Lobster's Dinner

In Enunga, I again knocked the doors of Gabriel and Reverend Fred. Both were absent. I went to the school verandah, spread my bedding and lay down to relax. I still felt hungry and exhausted, but at least I had no tension to chase anything. The cool breeze was blowing from the harbour side and I didn't know when I felt asleep. Soon after dusk, after a sound sleep of a few hours, I got up and went near the tube well, washed my face and drank some water; then looked towards the village. Near Gabriel's hut down the hill there was some faint light emanating from a lamp. I thought Gabriel must have arrived. When I reached there I found him sitting with Robert on a mattress made of pandanus leaves, in the centre was a bucket, full of toddy, baked fish on a plate, and both of them were comfortably gossiping and sipping toddy. I was relieved to see him; at least I knew that I wouldn't have to starve anymore. Gabriel saw me with surprise and said that he had expected me to return after a fortnight from Port Blair. I told him in brief about my plight for the last three days. As carefree as he was, instead of uttering a few words of sympathy, he straightaway offered me toddy and baked fish. I knew his nature and temperament; he bothered little for anything. However, I knew that now onwards he would take all possible care of me without exerting any sense of obligation. So kind and gentle he was.

As my stomach was almost empty, after a few rounds of toddy with baked fish, I began to feel the kick of the brew. I was feeling so relaxed and secured that I was enjoying each moment, each sip of toddy, and each bite of the baked fish. I had absolutely forgotten about the wretched plight of the last three days. In the meantime, I heard Reverend Fred calling me from behind, 'Mr Sahay, my wife told me that you visited my house several times.' I looked at him and said, 'Yes, Reverend Fred, for the last three days I [have been] running after my money, and money was running after me.' And I told him the whole story of my plight from Kakana to Katchall. He asked me, 'Where did you spend the night?' I told him on the school verandah. Gabriel was startled and realized perhaps under what conditions I might have spent the three days in his absence. He began to offer apologies, and said why didn't I live in his hut, as it was not locked. I told him I couldn't have entered without his permission. Anyway, Reverend Fred began to scold Gabriel in Nicobarese that instead of offering me food, he was offering me toddy. And before Gabriel could speak to his wife to prepare food for me, Reverend Fred took me to his house for supper. And that was perhaps the best supper I have had in my life. Reverend Fred's wife had prepared lobster, chicken, and pork, besides rice of course. He told me that one of his disciples had presented him a big lobster before his return from the village where he had gone to inaugurate the new chapel. After a stomach full of delicious meal that evening at Reverend Fred's house, I returned to Gabriel's. Together we brought my luggage from the school verandah, and after meals, Gabriel left in his hut atop the hill with his wife and children, and I slept in his hut down the hill. Since then, for the next three months, this hut of Gabriel's remained my field camp.

The Next Three Months

The next three months that I spent in the Enunga village of Nancowry Island are one of the best periods, in terms of anthropological experiences, that I have ever had. No doubt, the previous year, I had spent three and a half months in Chowra, all alone, except Abednego, completely cut off from the outside world. But the difference between fieldwork done in Chowra and Nancowry was that despite receiving all cooperation from the Chowrians, I could not live like a Chowrian, I didn't live the life of a Chowrian; of course, because of Abednego. In between me and the Chowrians, there was Abednego, who himself was not a Chowrian, but a Car Nicobarese, and a staunch Christian. Abednego was my interpreter. I could not directly interact with the Chowrians, as I did not know their dialect; nor did the Chowrians know Hindi or English. As the Car Nicobar was the most developed and educated island in the Nicobar group, with a little over 97 per cent of the Christian population (the rest being Muslims), wherefrom Abednego belonged, he was considered 'an outsider' in Chowra. He was also the cousin of Bishop John Richardson, who was called 'Architect of Modern Nicobar', and considered 'Uncrowned King of the Nicobar Islands', therefore, the Chowrians considered Abednego to be far superior to them; in a way, they feared Abednego. This also prevented me from mixing with the ordinary Chowrians. However, despite this unseen wall in my interaction with the Chowrians, I had developed extremely good rapport with them. I remember two comments of the Chowrians that Abednego told me.

Chowra women called me *kareyava*. *Kareyava* means 'a statue'. Why they called me that because, as Abednego told me, while collecting data in the village, I usually sat cross-legged with my notebook and camera in front of me; and Abednego sitting either on my left or right. On such occasions, men and women (married only) generally sat in a circle and the host lady served toddy in a half-split coconut shell, one by one, round the circle. Such sittings have continued for hours together, sometimes for four to five hours. All through, Abednego interpreted our conversation, and I noted down in my notebook, until the kick of the toddy made me helpless to do so. As long as such sittings continued, I remained cross-legged. I got up only when I felt the call of nature; then I got up, climbed down the hut, and after a few minutes joined the group, and again sat in the same posture. So, they called me *kareyava*. Many wooden *kareyavas* could be seen inside the houses of the Nicobarese in different postures, sitting cross-legged or standing. People of all the islands of the Nicobar group, earlier, made such *kareyavas* in the memory of the deceased in the family.

Again, when I was finally leaving Chowra, Abednego told me yet another valuable comment of the Chowrians on me. After a little over three and a half months of stay in Chowra, one morning, Abednego and me were to leave Chowra by canoe for Teressa. When we reached the shore along the Elpenum bag and baggage, I believe the entire population of the island must have come to see us off; and most of them had brought one presentation or more for me. Among many other things, such as glass boya, toy canoes, mats, baskets, taluva, bunches of plantain, coconuts, Chowra pots, cross-bows, etc., I had also received nine live chickens. It was a very touching farewell which I cannot forget throughout my life. Before boarding the canoe, I also became a little emotional, and told Abednego to heartily thank them on my behalf for the help and cooperation that I had received from them during my entire period of stay there. Abednego thanked them and said, 'you know Mr Sahay, what they say of you?' I asked him, 'What do they say?' 'They tell you that you are a noble person,' said Abednego. I was absolutely moved at their comment. I asked Abednego, 'Will you write it down in my notebook on behalf of Chowra people Abed?' And Abednego did so in my notebook. For years, I had preserved that page of the notebook as a certificate of my successful fieldwork and respectable living in Chowra. But in due course, it was lost. I wish I had framed it and kept it safe.

On the contrary, the situation in Nancowry was different. Gabriel was both my key informant and interpreter. And above all, he was a Nancowrian of the grassroots level. Despite having inherited large area of land and forest, he never exerted his leverage over land, or posed as an elite. Wherever I moved with him and his family, I was considered as a member of his family, as good as any Nancowrian. This had a great advantage. People did not get shy of me. Their behaviour and activities were as natural as they would have been even in my absence. Moreover, almost all Nancowrians understood simple Hindi; some of them could even converse in it. Therefore, I could easily interact with them and establish a rapport.

However, I had maintained some reservations as long as I did fieldwork in any of these islands, which were as follows:

1. I seldom interacted with any of the mainlanders who lived in the Nicobars. The reason was that all the mainlanders, who were there, worked in one or the other Department of Andaman and Nicobar Administration, such as teachers in schools, forest department, fisheries department, block office, subdivisional officer's (SDO) or additional deputy commissioner's (ADC's) office, etc. These employees considered their postings as punishment transfer because they felt socially isolated in the islands. They were generally hated by the Nicobarese. The Nicobarese considered that all the mainlanders had only three interests in Nicobar; first, coconut oil; second, toddy; and third, Nicobarese girls and/or women. Therefore, they seldom mixed up with mainlanders, and in no case allowed them to visit their houses.

2. Then, there was fear of Bishop John Richardson. If any mainlander was found purposelessly roaming about the Nicobarese villages, it was reported to the Bishop. Bishop was politically so powerful that instead of talking to the chief commissioner or any of the higher officials at Port Blair, he would directly talk to the home minister at New Delhi on the phone, and would complain that 'such and such person was not desired in the Island'; and the alleged person would be transferred within 24 hours with a black spot in his/her service career.

3. I had also observed that the mainlanders also hated the Nicobarese equally and seldom failed to criticize the partisan attitude of the Village Captains in general, and the Bishop in particular.

Considering the above factors in my mind, I maintained as much distance as possible with the mainlanders. I thought that if the Nicobarese would find me freely mixing with the mainlanders, they would maintain equal distance with me also, which in turn, would jeopardize my research purpose. On the contrary, quite often, I did not fail to criticize the main-landers for no reason before Abednego, Reverend Fred, or Gabriel. These were the reasons that when I first landed in Car Nicobar in 1974, before meeting any Nicobarese or entering into a Nicobarese village, I first sought an appointment with the Bishop through the ADC of Car Nicobar, Miss Janak Juneja. Only after I apprised the Bishop the purpose of my visit, I began to interact with the Nicobarese in general, and village captains in particular (Sahay, 2007).

In Nancowry there were a handful of mainlanders. All of them were schoolteachers. Other side of the harbour was Kamorta Island. All the government departments were in Kamorta, where a number of mainlanders lived. Regular ferryboats plied between the two islands. One could also go by canoe to Kamorta.

My daily routine was as such: I got up very late in the morning, often around 11:00 am. Then, after getting fresh in an hour, I moved to Gabriel's house at the top of the hill. There I often ate a few pieces of banana, drank coconut water, also consumed its tender kernel. While I was talking to Gabriel and verifying a number of information collected on the previous day, Gabriel's wife was cooking food, which consisted of boiled yams, sometimes rice too, fish was inevitable, sometimes chicken or pork also. Around 2:00 pm after lunch, we all—Gabriel, his wife, his children, and I—went down the hill and entered anybody's house in the village. Generally, it was decided during the lunch. Sometimes, we chose to go to other villages of Nancowry. Gabriel was acquainted with all the Nancowrians, therefore, welcomed everywhere. Every Nancowrian also knew that I lived with Gabriel and his family, and was one of his most respected guests. So, they did not mind my presence anywhere.

Wherever we went, the first thing that the host did after formal greeting was to offer us toddy without any delay, followed by dried or baked fish. Men and women, generally adults, joined us from the neighbouring huts also. And thus, I began to collect data. Again, I sat cross-legged with Gabriel sitting either to my left or right. My camera, tape recorder, and my notebook, which I always carried in my bag, were also put in front of me. Gradually, more people joined the group. All sat in a circle. The lady of the house served toddy to all in a half-split shell of coconut. Round after round the toddy session continued, until the stock exhausted. Sometimes, more stock of toddy was brought from the neighbouring households. Such sittings continued till late evening. We dispersed only when the stock of toddy was completely finished. Thereafter, Gabriel would generally say, 'Let's go to X's house. He must have stock of toddy.' And we went to somebody else's house at some distance. There also the same business started. Mostly, one or the other hosts offered us supper. In case no one did, then Gabriel's wife would return to her hut down the hill and prepare food. But it seldom happened so. Thus, I remember that till late night, most often till 2:00 am, we roamed about the villages from one house to other, consumed inordinate amounts of toddy; and finally, I retired to my bed in the hut down the hill, and Gabriel went to his hut with his family. Under the circumstances, very obviously, I slept till late morning, only to get up around 11:00 am.

Collecting data in this manner had advantages as well disadvantages. The advantage was that within a short time, I was getting massive information of immense anthropological importance about the life and culture of the Nancowrians; and the disadvantage was that I had to consume an inordinate amount of toddy in such sessions. Sometimes, after 9:00 pm. I was unable to write in my notebook. Then often I recorded the statements of informants, which Gabriel translated for me the next day when I visited him in the morning.

Out-Sea Fishing

One episode in Nancowry during this period is worth mentioning here. It was the onset of Easter. Earlier, on several occasions, I had told Gabriel that I wanted to witness out-sea fishing in deep waters. Every day, I saw people on small canoes engaged in fishing in the harbour. I also knew that often they go to out sea, several nautical miles from the shore; they stayed there for over 12 hours, especially in the night, and returned with big catch. The Chowrians also did so, but I had never participated with them in such fishing. I wanted to have an experience of it, before I completed my fieldwork and returned to the mainland. Gabriel had assured me that one day he would organize out-sea fishing.

Thus, a day before Easter, Gabriel came to my hut with Robert around 2:00 pm and told me to get ready for out-sea fishing. I was very glad to learn it, and within minutes I put on a half-shirt and a short, and got ready to move. We came to the shore near the harbour, launched a medium-sized canoe on water, and started for out-sea towards the eastern channel that opened towards Trinket Island. Gabriel was at the front end, Robert at the rear, and I was in the centre. On the canoe, fishing hooks and lines, some spears, and DAV (iron blades) were kept; even some coconuts were taken to quench thirst during such fishing expeditions, as in the out-sea, drinking water could not be available. The fishing lines were tied in such a frame that could be rotated to loosen the line, and when inversely rotated it could be wined up. Equipped with all these tools and implements, we set out from Nancowry Harbour. Of all the implements, the presence of the sharp and pointed spears puzzled me; for I did not know why they were needed, as we were not going to a jungle to hunt for any animal, or we were not expected to confront a sea-monster.

We had just crossed the channel. In front of us was the Trinket Island; and to our left and right at some distance was the open sea. Suddenly Gabriel and Robert both began to converse briskly in their dialect; and both drew the spears lying on the canoe from each side. Their move was so quick as if a reflex. Both of them stood on each side of the boat with spears ready in their hands; Gabriel at the front end and Robert at the rear. For a moment, I thought it was my end perhaps. I got scared. I could not understand what they were talking. I too stood on the canoe out of fear, holding the pole on which the sail of the canoe was fixed. I looked at Gabriel questioningly, and asked him what the matter was. Without responding to me both of them again uttered something in their dialect, and simultaneously threw the spears in the air. Still I could not make out anything, but watched them completely bewildered. The spears were in the air for sometime, then with the sharp head-end downward, they hit the surface of the water, and then submerged. After some moment it again appeared floating on the surface of the water. They quickly rowed the canoe near the spears; and to my surprise, a number of small fishes were there on the head-end. Then I understood the whole episode. In fact, they suddenly discovered that a particular variety of fish that moved in thousands was just passing beneath the surface of the water. Gabriel told me that he could know it from the ripples on the surface water that fish were there. He shouted and told Robert to throw the spear. They threw the spears in such a way that the head-end hit the water surface, and thus a number of fish were hit and caught. I told Gabriel that it was a good augury that right in the beginning we caught some fish, upon which he said, 'No, no, we will not eat them, but use them as bait.'

Anyway, all my fears were gone, and we proceeded towards west. The sails were opened. There was mild breeze, so our canoe also moved leisurely. Within an hour, Nancowry Island was left far behind. I couldn't guess how many nautical miles we were away from the harbour. But at one place we stopped. The sails were folded; and a small anchor was dropped into the sea. Fishing hooks and lines were made ready. However, before we could drop our fishing lines into water, Gabriel and Robert again started talking in their dialect. They seemed to be a little worried. Then they began to wind up everything. The anchor was lifted and the sails were unfolded. I asked them what the matter was. Gabriel told me to look towards the western horizon. There were black clouds at the end of the horizon. From the appearance of the clouds, they could envisage that it would be followed by very strong wind, like a storm. We hurriedly started to return towards Nancowry. But within a few minutes, we were caught by a storm and heavy rain. The wind was so fast that we could not sail towards the harbour; instead we headed towards the other end of the island. The sails were opened and because of very fast wind our canoe also moved at a very fast speed. We were completely drenched. The waves were rising very high. We didn't have to row; only Robert from the rear end used his rowing blade as rudder to maintain the direction, and save the canoe from overturning due to rise and fall of the titanic waves. Anyhow, we reached the shore on the opposite side of Nancowry. The rain and storm continued to lash. We pulled out the canoe from the water, and after dragging it on sand for a distance, tied it to a tree with the help of a rope.

I didn't know what they would do next, or how we would return to Enunga. It was already evening, and because of the rain and clouds there was darkness all around. But I found Gabriel as relaxed and comfortable as ever. I asked him, 'What next?' Upon this he commented, 'Don't worry, I have friends here. We will go to them and have white stuff' (i.e., toddy). We trekked a distance along the woods and reached a village. His friends greeted him, and in no time we sat together for a 'toddy session' with baked fish and ripe jackfruit. Our host also offered us some boiled yams. Jackfruit is not indigenous to Nicobar archipelago. No one knows who brought it from the mainland; but the inhabitants are very fond of it. They do not use it as an item of vegetable, as the mainlanders do; but they relish its sweetness when it becomes ripe and treat it as an item of fruit.

After a little over two hours, we took leave of our host, and trekking the woods again, came to the shore, where we had tied our canoe with the tree. We untied the canoe and again launched it in water. I thought we would perhaps return. But lo! Our canoe again moved towards the west in the open sea. I asked Gabriel where we were heading towards. He said, 'We shall fish throughout the night. You wanted to see night fishing.' I did not reply, but I was happy that at last I would experience night-hour-fishing.

After the storm, there was lull all around. The sea was as calm as I had witnessed the previous year, when after the storm, Katharina (the ship that had dropped me one night at Chowra) had left Katchall in the night hour on our way to Chowra (for details, see Sahay, 2007). The sky had cleared. Over a quarter size of the moon also appeared in the sky in the western horizon. Very mild and cool breeze began to blow. We opened the sails of the canoe. In tune with the mild breeze, undulating but gentle and rhythmic waves also began to form. Our canoe continued to play in the open sea for a little over an hour. It was a very scintillating experience for me. The very thought that beneath our canoe, in this hour of night, was unfathomable deep water of the sea made me quiver with sensation. Again, I could not make out how far we had left the shore behind. However, at one point we stopped, unfolded the sail, and anchor was dropped into water so that the canoe did not drift far under the current. The fishing hooks and lines were ready in advance, and we put the the fish that we had caught in the afternoon as bait, and dropped the lines deep into sea water.

Initially, the task appeared to be very boring to me, as no fish was lured by our bait. But after half an hour or so, first I felt a sharp and sudden pull in my right hand by which I was holding the line. I was excited and told Gabriel that I had got one perhaps. He advised me to slowly pull the line and I did so. I could see beneath the clear water of the sea that there was one big fish—bigger than a foot, I believe. This was the first catch of my life. I lifted it on board, and Robert removed the hook from the jaw of the fish. He also placed another flesh of the fish on my hook as bait, and again I dropped the line into the deep water. Soon thereafter, Gabriel got a catch, then Robert, then again me, and then for the next three hours, I hope, it turned into a fishing-spree. One after another, all the three of us were getting a fish in our hook and line. Almost half the canoe was filled with fish. Then suddenly I got another jerk in my line. I began to pull it. While the end of my line where the hook was tied still a few fathom deep in water, I could see the white belly of a big fish caught in my hook, like a saber gliding towards the surface of the water. Then suddenly it reversed and moved towards the deep water. Its reverse move was so powerful that if I had not freed the lines off my hands, it would have either cut my palm or any of my fingers, and I would have been wounded. Again holding the line, I told Gabriel that it seemed to be a big fish. I noticed that Gabriel became alert, and he told me that it might be a shark. The very name of shark made me scared and I left the fishing line again. Then he told me not to be frightened and tried to lift the catch on board the canoe. After repeated trials and errors, finally I successfully brought the prey on board. As soon as I placed it on the canoe, Robert hit the shark repeatedly by his iron blade, until it became motionless. For fear of its sharp teeth, instead of removing the hook from its jaws, Robert cut the line itself and tied yet another hook in my line to fix bait.

The shark had dampened my spirit. I had begun to feel tired because since the previous afternoon we were on the move. In the meantime, another shark was caught on Gabriel's hook, and then in Robert's. I became apprehensive. I sensed that Gabriel was also uneasy. I told him that it seemed to be a shark infected area now. It would be better to quit this place. Upon which, Gabriel anxiously uttered, 'I also don't understand why sharks are coming.' In the meantime, Gabriel noticed that Robert had been scaling a fish by his iron blade, and intermittently dipping the scaled fish into sea water for a wash. Smell of the fish scale perhaps attracted the sharks. Gabriel cried out at Robert in exasperation and began to scold him for his foolish act that attracted the attention of sharks. He announced to wind up our lines and hooks, and we decided to return.

It must have been around 3:00 am that we started to return. The moon had already disappeared into the horizon, and all around, the surrounding was dark. First, we had to row our canoe, but soon cool eastern morning breeze started, and we opened the sails. Smoothly, our return journey began. Forgetting Gabriel's scolding, Robert was again busy in scaling fish in the same manner as earlier. However, no untoward incident took place during our return. We reached the harbour in an hour; and pulled the canoe out of the water. Robert made strings from the bark of a nearby tree and began to insert one end of the string into the nostrils of each fish; thus, in each string, a considerable number of fish was tied. All the fish were tied in four such strings. Gabriel brought two thick bamboo sticks, at least three feet each in length. A bunch of fish tied in string was hung on each end of the sticks, and thus, Gabriel and Robert both carried one such stick laden with fish on each of their shoulders.

I felt extremely tired. The time was around 4:30 am. I wanted to go to my hut at the earliest and retire to bed because since the previous noon we had been on a fishing expedition. When I told this to Gabriel, he replied, 'No, no, we shall go to the top of the hill, and my wife will prepare meal for us.' I told him that I had never taken any meal in my life at this hour of the morning. But he did not allow me to leave. We started for the hilltop. As we were passing through the hut where I lived, I told Gabriel that I had some rum with me, and asked him, 'Should I take it with me, as we felt very tired, and it will be nice if we take it before meals.' Gabriel said, 'No, no, I have some "white stuff", we will take that only.' I had no answer to his comment; however, I thought with regret that rum would have been certainly a better choice than toddy.

But I was proved wrong. We reached the top of the hill. Gabriel woke up his wife. His children also got up, and were very happy to see the bunch of big fish. Gabriel's wife soon started preparing meals for all. Robert had already scaled a number of fishes. In the meantime, Gabriel brought three small tea-glasses, and lifted down a coconut shell that was hanging on the wall in a corner of the hut. It contained his 'white stuff'. He poured some toddy in each glass and placed before us. I felt a little disenchanted to think whether such a small quantity of toddy in a tea-glass will deliver any kick at all? However, as I brought it near my lips for a sip, its smell was so strong that I got scared and put down the glass on the floor. It appeared as if it was poisonous. I asked Gabriel what kind of toddy that was. He told me that was fermented for over three weeks. I waited either for Gabriel or Robert to sip the glass first. When I saw them sipping relaxingly, I held the glass in my hand, closed my eyes, and gulped down the glassful of toddy at one go. The taste was so pungent that to avoid the bitterness in my mouth and throat, I chewed and swallowed lots of baked fish thereafter. And the punch of the brew was so strong and quick that within minutes I felt as if I was flying over the sky of Nancowry harbour.

It was just a little before dusk. The cool breeze was blowing across the harbour. We were sitting on a mat on the floor down Gabriel's hut, atop the hill, wherefrom the entire harbour was within our sight. In the meantime, Gabriel's wife brought meals for the three of us. The meals consisted of rice and a full size of boiled fish, and a paste-like preparation of a sour fruit (locally called kinyaya) mixed with chilly and salt. Gabriel plucked plantain leaves from nearby. Three such leaves were spread before us and Gabriel's wife served us meals on those plantain leaves. Needless to say that under that hungry and inebriated state, out of the punch of that extremely fermented toddy, and after having been tired throughout the night in fishing expedition, the meals proved to be a real treat of the life. It was most satiating a meal I have ever had. By the time the day broke, we finished our meals, and I returned to my hut to retire to bed.

Easter Day Embarrassment and My Escape

I woke up only after Gabriel called me from outside my hut around 1:30 pm. He told me to get ready soon to move to his friend's house, as it was the Easter Day. We first went to Robert's house. His was a big hut. He lived there with his wife and several children. After formal greetings, he invited us inside his hut. He looked very happy. He had also got a good share of last-night-fishing. We climbed the notched ladder of his hut. Already there were some men and women sitting in a circle. Toddy container was at the centre; and a lady, probably Robert's wife, was serving toddy in a half-split coconut shell to each, one after the other. We also joined the group. And thus, our Easter celebration began with a grand toddy session, supplemented with chicken, pork, fish, and a variety of local food items prepared for the occasion. I knew that the group would not disperse until the complete stock of toddy was exhausted. And Robert brought container after container of toddy, which he had preserved for the last couple of days, especially for this occasion. After a few rounds of toddy, some men and women got up and they began to sing and dance at the centre. The toddy container was removed from the centre, and kept just out of the circle from where a lady continued to serve toddy to the participants.

The dance was very unrhythmic. Under the influence of toddy, they just wobbled from one side to another; occasionally beating their foot on the floor of the hut that caused thumping sound. No music; the Nicobarese do not have any indigenous musical instrument. First, I wanted to record the songs; but it was more of a noise than any melody, so I gave up the idea of recording. In the meantime, I observed that a fair complexioned lady of a tall stature looked at me very intently. From the look of her eyes, I could guess that she might have been looking at me for sometime. I began to talk to Gabriel and diverted my attention from her. However, after sometime, our eyes met again; and for a moment, I shivered at her look. She looked at me piercingly—like a tigress looking at its prey. I felt embarrassed and again engaged myself in a conversation with Gabriel. I decided not to look at her to avoid any awkward feeling. More men and women joined the dancing group. They began to sing more loudly, and thumping sound of their beat also became louder. Ultimately, the scene became completely boisterous. Meanwhile that lady just fell on Gabriel's lap first and then on mine. Gabriel got annoyed, and said, 'Oh, this lady always creates problems,' and shoved her away from my lap. The lady stood with a stagger, and again joined the dancing group, though still fixing her piercing gaze at me. Singing loudly and thumping their feet on the floor, the dancing group at the centre, slowly moved in anti-clock direction. Thus, two circles were formed inside the hut; one of the dancing group at the centre, and the other, encircling the dancing group, the ones who did not join the chorus, but were sitting and boozing toddy. Occasionally, one or two of them also shouted, as if joining the chorus. However, all of them, those who danced as well as those who just watched them dancing, were completely inebriated. I too felt very inebriated and exhausted and wanted to escape any more food or drink, rather, even my stay over there. But without Gabriel's wishes, I did not want to move at my own. Suddenly the same lady, this time, fell in my lap, and looked at me intently. I could very well guess that it was a deliberate fall upon me. I could not withstand her mysteriously shining eyes. I looked at Gabriel, helplessly.

Gabriel began to curse her again. He also began to scold her in Nancowrian dialect, but there was hardly any impact on her. Then Gabriel again tried to shove her off my lap. She denied and stiffened her body. At last, I lowered down her frame on the floor, and moved a little distant from her. However, in this entire muddle, my sixth sense alerted me, and I thought that the sooner I leave the place the better. I realized, first, that the Nicobarese did not mix up with the mainlanders because they thought that mainlanders were mostly interested in Nicobarese girls or women; and, second, that the command and respect that I received from the Nancowrians in general and Gabriel in particular, rather my excellent rapport with both, was because of my fair and good conduct that I had always maintained during the entire course of my fieldwork. And in no case, I could afford to lose them. Therefore, I told Gabriel that I wanted to retire to my hut. As it was expected of him, he said, 'No, no, we shall go to somebody else's house; there would be plenty of white stuff (toddy). This lady is creating problems for us. Let's go somewhere else.' I knew Gabriel's nature. He would not let me leave until the stock of toddy was completely exhausted in everyone's house; or he would himself like to retire. I hit upon a plan, and said, 'Look Gabriel, if I consumed any more food or drink, I would start vomiting.' I remembered that a couple of weeks before, when the team was still in Nancowry, one evening I had consumed so much of toddy with Gabriel and Robert that ultimately I began to vomit. When Gabriel saw me vomiting, he had become so nervous that he immediately took me to our camp and offered apologies to every member of our team for my plight. He thought he was responsible for my predicament. And this worked out succinctly. Immediately he said, 'No, no, you mustn't vomit. I will take you to your hut.' And thus, I was spared any further embarrassment.

The Final Words

In the above paragraphs, I have furnished some experiences that I have had during the course of my fieldwork for my doctoral degree during my stay in Nancowry in the Central Group of Nicobar Islands. It may be questioned by conventional anthropologists whether an ethnographer or an anthropologist should include his/her personal account in the account of 'other's culture', or not? In this context I am very clear in the sense that anthropologically, I think, it is of course significant to describe what I know of the Nicobarese; nevertheless, it is equally significant to explain how I came to know about them. I believe that the success of an anthropologist does not merely depend upon the amount of data that he/she brings from the field but it also depends upon the amount of help and cooperation that he/she receives from his/her informants and the people whom he/she studies. Accordingly, it is believed that the better the rapport of an anthropologist in the field the better his/her understanding of the 'other's culture'. After all, as long as an anthropologist stays in the field for data collection, despite being an undeniable intruder, the people whom he/she studies must accept him/her as a 'social person' as long as he/she continues to live with them.

Cohen (1978) has very aptly observed, 'Ultimately, the ethnographer's success does not depend upon intellectual mastery (alone), but upon the competence with which he/she can interact socially with the members of the field studied, and on the help provided by informants.' He further observes:

> The latter (i.e., help provided by informants) is of crucial importance, for the anthropologist is a nuisance. We (i.e., the anthropologists) need help not only to negotiate the tortuous social paths of the field, but often also for our very physical well-being. We intrude upon people and require them to bear the burdens of our presence. Our intellectual task is [therefore] to represent them fairly. Our moral responsibility is to approach them with humility and integrity.

References

Cohen, A.P. 1978. Ethnographic Method in the Real Community. *Socilogica Ruralis*, 18(1): 1–22.

Sahay, Vijoy S. 2007. Experiencing Anthropology in the Nicobar Archipelago. *Eastern Anthropologist*, 60(3–4): 401–430.

16

Discovering the Self and Others in Jammu, Kashmir, and Ladakh

Abeer Gupta

The Road to Visual Anthropology

In the summer of 2002, within weeks of the riots that started from *Godhra*, I found myself in Ahmedabad. The air was dense with the dust still settling over the raging communal discourse. But that very moment was also the beginning of a new life. Living with mates from distant corners of our land and discovering practices beyond comfortable stereotypes. A couple of semesters breezed by and soon I found myself in the midst of a personal crisis: I had to research, shoot, and edit my first documentary film, for a final classroom project. For the first time the field was looming ominously—where do I begin?

Each year, a large procession of *Tazias* started from the *Jamalpur Darwaza* and ended at *Khanpur Darwaza* (within the walled city of Ahmedabad), where they were finally immersed in the Sabarmati, on the 10th day of Muharram—*Ashura*. The procession did not take place in 2002 as the period coincided with the riots, and in 2003 it was not allowed, as the state feared further violence. In 2004 the procession was conducted, under a tight security cover but with aplomb. I was drawn to the process of construction of these marvellous models, the procession had fascinating cultural overlaps, but most importantly it was the energy and the sense of community— the performance of the procession and the rituals,[1] the smaller side-shows involved, drew me to the subject. I decided, what I did not know then, was that it was the beginning of a much longer interest and engagement.

The first few days were overwhelming—while making things look good was easy, my greatest worry was to not romanticize or to make the other (Behar, 2007; Grimshaw, 2001; Rapport and Overing, 2002) look exotic, in my voyeuristic curiosity and enthusiasm. The subject, I knew little of but was very interested to explore; but completely lacked any methodology or approach. We were still learning to balance content and form—dealing with the reality around and stylistic choices of its portrayal. If filmmaking was an intervention, how much was to be enough?

As I was stumbling through my research, I realized how little the communities interacted, beyond formal business ties, and knew about each other, while the people I met from the old city of Ahmedabad—my subjects, the *Momins* (Shias), invited me to their homes and were eager to share—on the other side, with the Hindu middle class there was a strange silence—either people were clueless or did not want to comment. There was plenty of documentary work screaming about these polarities, playing on populist notions but they simply did not connect with my experience on the field. So there were complexities, and subtleties, which I could sense, but did not quite understand, and moreover did not have the capacity to interpret onto the film at the time. What did I discover was the futility of questionnaires—I realized I had to develop the power of informed observation—what I did discover was, I had to revisit the space with a larger frame of understanding.

In Bombay, assisting on a documentary film[2] on the city gave me the opportunity to develop an understanding of a master narrative of the city within which to plot a research—a direction. We were researching alternate and unheard voices from the city: characters from the underbelly of the entertainment industry and exploring the process and politics of representation within the mainstream. It was during this time that I slowly started discovering patterns, which linked the cities of Ahmedabad and Mumbai. Both cities were linked to textile trade, and while Gujarati was the language of the business elite, the underworld had equally strong ties. It was the religious ghettoization and the rise of the right wing which provided the impetuous to choose Govind Nihalani's *Dev* as the subject for my dissertation. The film was overtly based on the events of February and March 2002 in Gujarat but was set in Mumbai. I started with looking at the evolution and embodiment of dissent through the character of 'the angry young man' (Chatterjee, 2005; Kavoori and Punathambekar, 2008) in Indian cinema from the 1970s and the use of the space of the *chawl* to map how events that occurred in Gujarat in 2002 had been transposed onto Mumbai. The dissertation thus explored the notion of a national identity (Dutta et al., 2000) within contested urban spaces.

Along with that, for my diploma film,[3] I began to work with a young fisherman, from the Koli community in Versova village. This time I had a much clearer plot in my head, and we were trying to document the village in the context of the city expanding into the space of an indigenous community. There was a lot of talk then that a new Metro Railway project might completely engulf a large part of the village—used for drying fish, nets, and making of new boats. This was my first experience in an ethnographic exercise and I somehow rather unknowingly adopted a participatory observation model. So I gave *Darshan*, my main character, a video camera and the film was edited out of both of our footages—as a dialogue between his concerns and mine. The word 'subjectivity' had not yet arrived in my vocabulary or at least not with the connotation I was to discover in some time.

Bombay was a great provider, it was giving me a hectic learning curve, some money and the will to get out of there and travel. I had always wanted to explore the Himalayas and after a holiday in Bhutan, the following year I found myself volunteering to teach at a residential school, Students' Educational and Cultural Movement of Ladakh (SECMOL), in a non-descript village in Ladakh for a couple of months. Bombay never gave me the time to research my holidays, just the desperation and enough time to pack my bags, so when I arrived in Leh in February 2007, I really did not know what was in store. I spent my days teaching History and English to students preparing for their board exams, and hung out with the audio–visual unit. We went to Leh a couple of times to get some supplies, once to see *Dosmoche* at Leh Palace, drove to the *Thikse* monastery on a rickety old scooter one Sunday afternoon. A student was going home to his village, for *Matho Nagrang* I tagged along. Ka Norphel (Leh Nutrition Project) took the students and volunteers one day to show the construction of artificial glaciers under the *Chang La* and discussed the importance of water harvesting. The visit was marked though, by an incident, between the then DC, Leh, and Sonam Wangchuk[4]—who had established SECMOL and contributed remarkably to the education system.

This holiday was to be very different, as I did not really have a plan. I spent my free time sitting in the library reading about Ladakh, from Andrew Harvey (Andrew Harvey, 1984, *A Journey in Ladakh*) to Rizvi (1996). Unconsciously, I was making the transition from the romantic notion of the place to sterner stuff. I had made friends, travelled and worked with them and for some fleeting moments became a part of their lives and before

I knew it I did not feel like a tourist at all. Years later I realized that these were perhaps the most precious days of fieldwork for me, which helped me develop an insight into Ladakh and forge associations which gave me the confidence to return.

Since I finished NID, I had been harbouring a plan to study further, but was not quite sure, exactly what. When a dear friend suggested I look up the Visual Anthropology programme at Goldsmiths—it felt like a miracle. It seemed to address the issues I was grappling with and I joined the course in the autumn of 2007. There I was introduced to the works of Alfred Gell (1998), and Christopher Pinney among others, and their work with popular and religious iconography in the subcontinent, how images and objects of mechanical reproduction (Walter Benjamin, 1936/2008, *The Work of Art in the Age of Mechanical Reproduction*) were making a swift transition into the digital age, and were being processed socially. I saw the opportunity to draw from my experience in Ladakh and started working on a paper on the images of Tibetan diaspora, particularly the posterized image of the *Potala* Palace in Lhasa[5]—and how it works socially as well as politically, within the Tibetan populations in exile in India. This was the period when I finally came across the notion of subjectivity within the context of anthropology's encounter with documentary film (MacDougall, 1997). Films such as *Photowallahs*, by David MacDougall, *Forest of Bliss* by Robert Gardner clarified the possibilities of kind of documentary cinema that attracted me.

The Fork in the Road

On my return to India, in the spring of 2009 I was offered to design and teach a documentary filmmaking course in Srinagar, Jammu and Kashmir. I wanted to get back to Ladakh and knew next to nothing about Kashmir. This was an opportunity to understand the workings of the region closely. The Ladakh Autonomous Hill Development Council (LAHDC) (Martin, 1999) had been set up some years back but Ladakh continued to be administered from Srinagar in summer and Jammu in winter, that is, these were still the centres of power and decision making for the state.

The Kashmir valley had been the epicentre of poetry, philosophy, and crafts (Jaitley, 1999) with historical links to West and Central Asian cultures but in the last two decades it has been embroiled in bitter conflict with the Indian state. Every day in Srinagar was a learning experience— first getting used to the uncertainties of living in a conflict area, learning about its political history and slowly comprehending the current conflict.[6] My students and colleagues invited me to their homes, we spoke of films, photography, and art but the discussions invariably veered towards 'the Kashmir issue' (Kaul, 2011). Soon I started noticing the effects of two decades of armed conflict on the lives of ordinary citizens and subsequently the workings of the media in such a space.

Saiba Varma spent 15 months doing ethnographic fieldwork in Kashmir for her dissertation. She completed her PhD in socio-cultural anthropology from Cornell University in 2013. I an email correspondence dated 3 September 2013 she wrote:

> There are many issues that people seem to talk about a lot in the media and in human rights reports, but on the ground, they look quite different ... More than anything, I felt that formal interviews distorted the responses I would get to things (because people are so conscious of journalists, etc.) and it was more in the casual, everyday conversations that I was able to glean the 'truth' about what I was looking at (i.e. mental health, trauma and Post Traumatic Stress Disorders in Kashmir) ... it opens up new narratives which otherwise do not get told in a context that is already saturated with media stories.

In Srinagar, a project for the Directorate of Tourism initiated a research in the crafts and historical architecture,[7] which in turn introduced me to Kashmir's Sufi past. It took me to the interiors of the old city of Srinagar, *Downtown*—which bore remarkable similarities to the walled city of Ahmedabad. Parts of *Downtown* were known to be troublesome and tourists rarely ventured there. But it was where elderly master craftsmen—weavers, embroiderers, and painters—lived and practised their art and somehow effortlessly managed to preserve (something) through the testing times. They were keen to discuss colour, form, patterns, and the evolving tastes of contemporary clients. The city of Srinagar bears a continuous legacy (Hasan, 1959/2005; Sofi, 1979) of over a thousand years, during more than half of which it has been ruled by outside forces. It was in the old bazaars around *Zaina Kadal, Nowhatta, Maharajgunj,* and *Lal Chowk,* that the vestiges of past empires, artists, and mystics, lay scattered waiting to be assimilated in the eyes of a keen observer. The craft practices were the focal points to the development of trade and urban culture in Kashmir (Savasere, Winter 2010–Spring 2011) and its evolution followed that of the capital city, Srinagar. As the main political centres shifted and grew with its temples, mosques, and urban settlements so did crafts and artisans. In *Downtown, mohallas* still bear the names of craft communities such as *Qalamdaanpora, Ranger-stop, Namdagaari Mohalla,* and *Bandhukgar Mohalla.*[8]

Aditi Saraf, who has been engaged with her doctoral fieldwork for the past few years in the valley, shares my interest in trade and culture ...

... because it has repeatedly called into question taken-for-granted notions of secularism, democracy, representation, justice, foreignness, belonging, and cohabitation. In particular, I was interested in how religious morals and ethics inflect modern notions of community and citizenship. In choosing to work in a heterogeneous space like the bazaar I hope to approach these questions through everyday practices and modes of relatedness in the city (Srinagar).

Perhaps the most insightful experience I derived was the local industry around Pashmina, which had marked political treaties[9] and regional stability for centuries. Walking around the markets I also discovered a rich distribution network for Sunni Iconography in the form of textile scrolls, posters, *jaenimaz*-prayer mats, and a host of other objects.

A visit to the Amar Mahal Museum and Library, Jammu, opened up the third dimension to the grid. Historically a stronghold of the Dogra Rajputs, who put together the state of Jammu and Kashmir as it exists only in our imagination today. Jammu had been a landing ground of several hill tracts—such as Basoli, Chamba, and Kangra which constitute the Pahadi cultures to the east, Poonch and Rajouri in the west, Doda, Badarwah, and Kishtwar in the north and migrant nomadic communities of Gujjars and Bakkarwals. During the years of insurgency in Kashmir, Jammu had borne the brunt of forced migration of Kashmiri Pandits from the valley and become a preferred destination for large populations of Ladakhis for graduate studies.

Ankur Datta[10] who worked on Kashmiri Pandit refugees in Jammu says:

The dominant imagination of Jammu and Kashmir is primarily influenced by Kashmir. Jammu was and remains a city that does not figure in the imagination ... Jammu as a city is like any other city in North India. The sounds of Bhangra music blaring takes you away from imagining an exotic world, which I must admit, though, works in the Kashmir valley.

The museum was trying to rediscover itself, its role and relevance to the community—so along with building a resource centre for *Pahadi* Visual Culture, we got around creating a digital archive, of historical photographs, which would be periodically exhibited. The library also had a collection of rare historical publication, mostly 18th- and 19th-century travelogues of European explorers, actors in the great game. But the museum and library offered a great repository of material on the political history of Dogra Empire and opportunity to study the roots of the current political situation.

The scathing inter-regional relations provided a context to study its socio-cultural history,[11] and question what was keeping these seemingly incongruous regions together. Not surprising the answer lay in the historical trade routes interlinking them (Rizvi, 2001), both internally and with their neighbours. Perhaps the most notable of these is the interaction around historical movement of raw materials such as *pashmina* from the high plateaus of eastern Ladakh to the valley of Kashmir where they continue to be transformed into magnificent shawls (Rizvi and Ahmad, 2009). The drastic shift, which took place in 1947, has been affecting the processes both in material and in form and has opened up a wide area of material culture studies in the region. Especially in the context of advent of Islam to Kashmir and its spread into Baltistan and Ladakh,[12] it had influences on the local architecture and visual culture. For this was a fertile field to explore the movement of religious artefacts and iconography through urban (market) settlements such as Kargil and Leh within the context of contested borders and identity issues.

I revisited Leh in the summer of 2009 during the International Association of Ladakh Studies conference in Leh, but it was not until the next summer when I returned to conduct a workshop at Ladakh Arts and Media Organization (LAMO)[13] that these ideas started taking some shape. It was the same year that a cloud burst and flash floods hit Ladakh, and I spent several months involved with documentation of relief work. That year I found myself in the midst of many like me, who had been inexplicably drawn to Ladakh.

Quentin Devers is a PhD candidate in archaeology at the Ecole Pratique des Hautes Etudes (Paris). His researches focus on the fortified sites of Ladakh. He narrates:

> I had to choose a field for specialization for my Masters. I decided to work in Ladakh for my second year of Masters … Then, during the summer following that, I went to Ladakh with two researchers to do some work on rock art. I decided from that time onwards to work in this beautiful region … What I saw and experienced in Ladakh has been better than anything I had thought or imagined before. I don't know if I can say that it was really different, it was just a better version of everything I had read or studied about it … As for the people, I didn't have much preconceived ideas of what they would be like. For some reason, the things I imagined were the landscapes and the archaeological remains, not the people. I have to say that it was very nice to discover such warm and welcoming people.

Reading around context of inter-regional trade, and the exchange of visual and material culture, I found that little had been written about the experience of the Islamic inhabitants of Ladakh[14]—the Islamic cultures of Ladakh also pointed towards the rich plurality of Ladakhi society and how historically local culture appropriated religion—something I had been interested in since my initial strides into the field in Ahmedabad. I met with local scholars such as Abdul Ghani Sheikh (2005, 2007a, 2010) (Leh), Jigar Mohammed (Jammu), and started drawing up a list of works by Fernanda Pirie and Martijn van Beek (2008), Nicola Grist (1995, 1998), and the more recently published works of Fewkes (2008).

Ladakh has long existed in popular imagination as a quiet Buddhist retreat. The common traveller's perception is that of a land of high passes, maroon robed monks, and a remote frontier. Historically Ladakh had been a key trading post for subcontinental and central Asia and often found itself in the midst of the power struggle of eastern and central Asian forces, Tibetan, Chinese, and from Kashmir. Ladakh was thus a witness to military incursions, merchants, and missionaries on the roads, which connected the Arab world, Lahore, Delhi, and Srinagar to Tibet and China. The passage from Bon to Buddhism and the advent of Islam in the 13th century, through the travels of Shah Hamadan—in the Nubra Valley en route Yarkhand and Bulbul Shah—to Baltistan and Moravian Christians in the 19th century resulted in unique multidimensional social practices. Followers of Buddhism and Islam inhabited very close to each (Sheikh, 2007b) other for most of this time and shared, till recently, most cultural practices. Ladakhi families even today have cousins who are Buddhist, Muslim, and Christian.

Radhika Gupta (2005), an anthropologist, shares:

> In 2005, I had the opportunity to visit Kargil for the first time to participate in the IALS conference. I was struck, at first on a very superficial level, by the Islamic imagery that began to appear as one drove past Mulbekh. However, next to nothing or so little had been written about the Muslims in Ladakh, especially the Shia Muslims. I had always been interested in the anthropology of Islam since taking an elective course titled 'Southwest Asia' during my MA at the Delhi School of Economics. So when I decided to apply for a PhD (Oxford) in 2006 I thought working in Kargil would allow me to combine this interest with a general love of the mountains and Ladakh that had captured my imagination for no rational reason.

The Islamic population of Ladakh (Aabedi, 2009) belongs to Shia, Sunni, *Ahl-i-Hadith* (Khan, 2000), and *Nurbakhshi* (Basir, 2003), a sort of Sufi sect. The *Nurbakhshis* are mostly found in the region adjoining Turtuk and in the Nubra Valley. The Shias of Ladakh are mostly in the district of Kargil

(Grist, 2008) but those in Leh and in *Chuchot, Shey, Phyang,* and *Thikse* are mostly of Baltistani origin (Zubdavi, 2005). The Sunnis are either descendants of Kashmiri merchants or those who came from Yarkhand. The community of *Arghon*s came into being when these traders married local women and settled there. Leh being the district headquarters and commercial centre in the region attracts large populations of seasonal migrant labours and businessmen, such as Sunni Kashmiri businessmen who deal with handicrafts, second hand clothing, and contraband items and men from Doda (in Jammu), who for several generations have worked as masons. They are concentrated in the Old Town of Leh and some of its adjoining areas, where cheap rented accommodations have come up. This area has also become the hub of migrant workers from UP and Bihar—there are some Muslims among them.

While the spoken language is Ladakhi across the communities, the Islamic communities have over the years adopted the Urdu script. But evolving religious norms have rendered certain practices unacceptable, such as singing and dancing—which was once popular among the Islamic communities. With a growing tourism-led economy and increasing number of young Ladakhis moving to cities such as Jammu and Chandigarh for their education, complex new notions of identity are forming both at home and beyond. Sonam Chosjor (2010), in *Beyond Kashmir, Understanding Ladakh* in *Identity Politics of Jammu and Kashmir,* highlights the politics of Ladakh within the larger conflict in Kashmir, the movement of gaining Union Territory status and the alienation of Muslims of the region. Another article by Yoginder Sikand, *Buddhist–Muslim Relations in Ladakh* (May 2010), further elaborates on the communal strife in the late 1980s, the politics of the Ladakh Buddhist Association (LBA) and the inter-regional politics of Leh and Kargil. These issues along with the acceptance of contemporary forms of west Asian Islam have left deep impressions on the otherwise plural society of Ladakh.

Ladakh has had urban spaces, such as Leh and a history of cosmopolitanism. In the 16th century, King Jamyang Namgyal (1555–1610) married Yabgo Sher Ghazi's daughter, Rgyal Khatoon (Akasoy et al., 2011), as part of a peace treaty with the Baltistani kings. Queen Rgyal Khatoon continued to practise Islam and introduced musical traditions to Ladakh originating in Islamic cultures—which are practised even today. Her son, King Senge Namgyal, moved the capital from Shey to Leh around the 17th century and it developed as a trade hub, but it was probably around the time that Ladakh was under Dogra rule in the mid-19th century that some traders might have started to settle in Leh. Administrative and military officials sent by Dogra kings were stationed in Leh[15] at that time and groups of missionaries were allowed to settle and interact with the local population.

In the period between 1950 and 1970 Ladakh was a restricted area but large numbers of teachers, administrative staff from Kashmir, along with the Indian army, moved in. Since the mid-1970s when Ladakh was opened to civilians and foreign tourists a much more radical transformation has taken place. While Leh in spite of its growing Islamic population has benefitted from maintaining a Buddhist flavour, Kargil has undergone more evident Iranian Islamicization. Today a complex tourism-led economy and vast developmental projects have opened up interesting dimensions for research.

In *Ladakh, Culture at Crossroads*, Monisha Ahmed and Claire Harris speak of the 'materiality of everyday such as dress, jewellery, portable objects, articulate the complexity, and fluidity of Ladakhi life' (Ahmed and Harris, 2005). Essays in that volume further elaborate contribution of Islamic communities to architecture, the existing wood, textile, and metal crafts. They also point to the importance of examining their relation to the construction of a larger cultural process, through the confluence of Tibetan and Kashmiri styles in forms and materials. While historically Baltistani wood carvers and a Muslim architect (Sheikh, 2005) built the palace in Leh, in recent times masons from the village of Trespone,[16] near Kargil are one of the unique self-trained architects and builders who have constructed not just the elaborate new mosques of Ladakh but other significant commercial buildings, and family of Ghulam Sultan Chungkha still produce some of the most exquisite gold and turquoise jewellery unique to the region.

When the Line of Control came into being in 1947–1948, Ladakh became part of the state of Jammu and Kashmir. Baltistan, the predomi-nantly Shia part of Ladakh went under Pakistan's administration and activities at the borders with Central Asia, China, and Tibet gradually decreased. Border posts such as Daulat Beg Oldi, in Nubra, and Demchok, in Changthang, continue to be informal trading posts with activity depend-ent on diplomatic and military mood swings at the borders. Today substan-tial amount of mass-produced consumer goods imported from India and cheaper Chinese alternatives flood the various retail outlets.

My research[17] in material culture of the region focused on the evolution of movement and consumption of objects of popular visual and material culture by the Islamic communities. Ladakhi Muslims initially constructed simple vernacular structures using wooden beams, and mud bricks for reli-gious congregation to suit the local weather patterns. Some such mosques and *khanqas*[18] have been preserved in *Goma-Kargil, Aba Gurung, Baru* in Kargil, and *Shey, Chushot Gongma*, and *Tyakshi* in Leh District. These spaces are replete with a variety of Islamic iconography that travelled from west and central Asia in the hands of traders and pilgrims. My research explores the composition and the variations that have taken place in these objects in time. While the printed or framed objects such as calendars and posters provide a more contemporary engagement with visual content and styles, the textile-based objects such as carpets, prayer mats, and wall hangings display a much wider historical progression of forms. The variations in those brought back to Ladakh from pilgrimages and those developed locally point towards the evolution of a unique local Islamic aesthetic.

There is a rather endearing story, which would fascinate visual anthropologists. Haji Asgar Ali Saraf, a mason from Trespone,[19] was a self-made man who learnt the craft from assisting PWD engineers on government building projects. He made the first mosque in Ladakh (in Trespone, Kargil) with a dome and two minarets from a photograph of a west Asian mosque that was brought back from Hajj. It not until many years later, and having constructed several famous buildings, such as the *Imambara* in *Chuchot Yokma*, that he made his first trip abroad and saw for himself the grand mosques of Arabia. Before the first adequately Islamic-looking buildings in Leh the local community produced textile scrolls using chain stitch on pieces of dark velvet cloth, embroidering scenes from Karbala (Figure 16.1). These scrolls supplemented a religious landscape into the community's imagination. Today with increasing affluence, exposure to the outside world, and technologies, there is much more exchange of

Figure 16.1:
Embroidering scenes from karbala stitched on scroll

Source: Photos by Abeer Gupta.

visual expressions of Islamic culture with the centre of the Islamic world. My research explores the negotiations within visual culture of a regional cultural identity and a global discourse.

One of the most fascinating explorations for me was how certain motifs such as the *rgya-nag lcags-ri* (Ranjan and Ranjan, 2005)—the brick wall pattern inspired by the Great Wall of China, and the *yungdrung*—the interlocking swastika motif, speak of interconnectivity of these regions in the past. They also form the basis of an aesthetic inclination, which became popular and are today part of Ladakhi society across religious lines. These motifs are seen woven onto ancient carpets that travelled from Tibet, Yarkhand (Chinese Turkestan), and China, both in monasteries and in mosques. Adapted onto the *shinstag*—the characteristic multilayered carved wood panels, which the centrepieces of local architecture used for making doors and windows, of mosques and *Imambara*s as well. Notable among these are the carved doorways of the newly built *Imambara* in the Leh Bazar (Figure 16.2) and the Shia Jamia Masjid at Chuteyrantak, finally making its way to printed mediums such as calendars and posters. In fact, exploring the designs of buildings extends to the larger narrative of a community—how once a subculture defined a space for itself using local materials and techniques in an extremely economical way and how in contemporary times it represents their aspiration—which in turn points to the core of a cultural process. Andre Alexander, sums it up in my film,[20]

> Ladakh is a melting pot of cultures ... [But] it was always a distinct Ladakhi culture so they would always call it Ladakhi and have a little bit of Turkish ... Actually all cultures in the end are like that ... But here it was more multi-form. More tolerant—encompassing a wider range of ideas, because Ladakhis by their nature, have always been more tolerant, of people having different ideas, different beliefs.

The Road Ahead

Working in Ladakh is expensive, exhausting, and very unpredictable. Often baffled by the logistics, I have asked myself why I chose to work there, but somehow failed to formulate a logical answer. Clearly, it is a little more than just the love for the mountains. My friends in Leh have asked me on a couple of occasions why I chose to work with Islam? All I ever tell them is that it just happened, and things are constantly evolving and I continue to make an effort to try and keep working there.

Figure 16.2:
Carved Gateway

Source: Photos by Abeer Gupta.

As an independent (self-funded) researcher the constraints of money and time are enormous—and surprisingly the competition stiff. I began the first phase of work documenting architecture of oldest surviving mosques of Ladakh, with a grant from Tasveer Ghar and South Asia Institute, University of Heidelberg. Initially unsure, my ideas were substantiated by the material I generated and were corroborated by experts from the field.[21] In fact, I felt encouraged enough to continue and extended the project into an oral history documentation of various Islamic communities in the Leh and Kargil districts, which was supported by another grant from the TISS, Mumbai. This research included narratives of the partition of Baltistan and Ladakh, along the Line of Control; the socio-cultural upheavals between the two wars of 1947 and 1971; the negotiation of an independent identity under Kashmir; the effects of the Kashmir conflict; and the communal strife resulting from it in the late 1980s.

The year 2012 marked ten years in the field and three years of working and living in Jammu, Kashmir, and Ladakh. While a variety of design and consultative projects have sustained me, and documentary filmmaking provided a professional engagement, anthropology has lent me a way of life. I have often been questioned on ideology or politics or partisanship—but I always seek refuge in humanity and have relied on that for the narrative arcs of my work.

While discovering and working in a field where there is so much scope and so little has been done is heartening it comes with a rider of lack or limited availability of material. As oral histories have been a core of my research, building human resources, and working with multiple versions, to finally trust one's own instinct to glean the truth out of them has been the only methodology. This involves constantly returning to the field with no ready-made answers in sight.

Working in Jammu, Kashmir, and Ladakh is a linguistic nightmare, with a plethora of spoken languages and the various dialects of each of them; plus a large number of historical documents are in Persian. But in the process of my research, I have constantly attempted to go beyond the textual content of classical history writing to be able to interpret it within the context within which it is spoken. So a thorough study of the background of the field has always come in handy, as in most cases once I have been able to clearly communicate my interests, the relevant details have reached me one way or another, in time.

Sustained interaction with the field, and being involved in professional projects, provides extensive insights but has its reverse challenges; often your subject becomes your friend and confidante. A friend recently telephoned me in the middle of a tussle from Ladakh and said, 'You know how these Ladakhis are ...' the comment at once made me feel very close and frightened me. Over a period of time I have learnt to constantly balance this distance with a much higher degree of responsibility. This reminds me of a conversation with a colleague; about how much we could never report, knowing very well the implications of such public declarations—both on our own relations with the field and those on our subjects.

It is rather strange that in spite of the scores of international as well as Indian anthropologists working in the region there isn't a single faculty for anthropology in the numerous universities and colleges in the state. Perhaps the discipline needs to rediscover itself from its erstwhile perceptions into interdisciplinary possibilities it offers in its contemporary avatar. As Ankur suggests, 'Close attention to detail facilitated by long-term fieldwork subverts dominant imaginations' or as Aditi wrote to me once,

> There's something to be said even just for observing and inhabiting a place sensitively and continuously over a period of time. I'm under no illusion that it will 'change' or show a way to 'resolve' the Kashmir crisis, but the effort to understand the diverse forces that make the everyday, contemporary milieu is crucial. I also think anthropological methods are useful for tracing important intangibles like aspirations, ethics, questions of freedom and morality, and their transformations.

And Radhika added,

> Anthropology is the only discipline, which provides detailed and nuanced insights into a region, people or issue. This enables one to challenge superficial media portrayals. Contemporary anthropology also becomes a historical source for any work in the future.

Finally, the one thought that lingers constantly at the back of my mind is to not create further polarizations rampant in popular forms, rather while working with people's memory and reflection be reminded of Yeats,

> I have spread my dreams under your feet; Tread softly because you tread on my dreams.

Acknowledgements

I am indebted to contributing anthropologists—Ankur Datta working in Jammu; Aditi Saraf and Saiba Varma working in Srinagar; Radhika Gupta working in Kargil and Quentin Devers archaeologist working in Ladakh.

Notes

1. *Notes from the Backyard*, Dir, Abeer Gupta, Final project at the National Institute of Design, 2004.
2 http://majlisbombay.org/7-islands-and-a-metro. Accessed on 2 June 2014.

3. *Notes from a Neighbourhood,* Director Abeer Gupta, Diploma project at the National Institute of Design, 2005.
4. Details of the events of Spring 2007—http://www.secmol.org/humanrights/index.php. Accessed on 2 June 2014.
5. Clare Harris and Tsering Shakya, *Seeing Lhasa: British Depictions of the Tibetan Capital, 1936–1947* (exhibition … Organized by the Pitt Rivers Museum, Oxford, 7 September 2003–November 2004 and the Tenth Seminar of the International Association for Tibetan Studies, Oxford, 6–12 September 2003).
6. Insightful works and memoirs: Basharat Peer, *Curfewed Nights,* Aamir Bashir, *Harud* (fiction feature film), Rahul Pandita, *Our Moon has Blood Clots*—foreign researchers such as Adrian Levy & Cathy Scott Clark, *The Meadow.*
7. *Shehar-i-Kashmir, Cultural Resource Mapping of Srinagar City,* December 2010 (2 Vols, 1st edition). INTACH, J&K Publication.
8. *Srinagar Walks and Craft Tours,* a project researched and designed by Abeer Gupta and Renuka Savasere for the Directorate of Tourism, Jammu and Kashmir.
9. Both the *Treaty of Tingmosgang* (signed between the Mughals and the Tibetans) and the *Treaty of Amritsar* (signed between the Dogras and British) have considerable focus on the trade of *Pashm.*
10. Assistant Professor, South Asia University, New Delhi and did PhD in Social Anthropology from London School of Economics, in 2011.
11. On Kashmir—Zuthsi (2004), also Rai (2007). Balraj Puri, articles from EPW—on Jammu.
12. Abdul Ghani Sheikh. *Tradition of Sufism in Ladakh,* Rome: IALS (Part II Islam in Ladakh and Tibet).
13. Ladakh Arts and Media Organisation—water exhibition. http://www.lamo.org.in/exhibitions.html. Accessed on 2 June 2014.
14. Except Ghulam Rassul Galwan, Akasakal of Leh, who wrote *Servants of Sahibs,* with an introduction by Francis Younghusband, Cambridge W Heffer & Sons Ltd, 1923.
15. The *Tehsildar* would move between Leh, Kargil and Skardu (district head quarters of Baltistan) during the Dogra Period.
16. Tashi Morup. 2002. *Masons and Mosques,* in Ladag's Melong, Leh—subsequently I shot with the Mason's of Trespone for my film, *Old Routes, New Journeys,* Dir Abeer Gupta (2012).
17. Abeer Gupta. 2013. *Visual and Material Culture of Islam in Ladakh*—for the online initiative 'Visual Pilgrim' by the Cluster of Excellence, Asia and Europe in a Global Context at Heidelberg University. http://kjc-sv006.kjc.uni-heidelberg.de/visualpilgrim/demo/essay-detail.php?eid=10. Accessed on 2 June 2014.
18. A building designed specifically for gatherings of a Sufi brotherhood, or *tariqa,* and is a place for spiritual retreat and character reformation. In the past, and to a lesser extent nowadays, they often served as hospices for Sufi travellers and Islamic students. *Khanqahs* are very often found adjoined to *dargahs* (shrines of Sufi saints), mosques and madrasas (Islamic schools).

19. Interview of Haji sahib, in *Old Routes New journeys*, Director Abeer Gupta, 2012. http://smcs.tiss.edu/films/old-routes-new-journeys/. Accessed on 2 June 2014.
20. Interview of Andre Alexander, in *Old Routes New journeys*, Director Abeer Gupta, 2012.
21. Andre Alexander—THF/LOTI—restoration of the Tsas Soma Mosque in Chute Rantaq, Leh and the building of the Central Asian Museum.

References

Aabedi, Zain-ul-aabedin. 2009. *Emergence of Islam in Ladakh*. Delhi: Atlantic.

Ahmed, Monisha and Harris Clare (eds). 2005. *Ladakh: Culture at the Crossroads* (pp. 149–159). Mumbai: Marg.

Akasoy, Anna, Charles Burnett, and Ronit Yoeli-Tlalim (eds). 2011. *Islam and Tibet— Interactions along the Musk Routes*. UK: Ashgate Publishing.

Bashir, Shahzad. (2003). *Messianic Hopes and Mystical Visions: The Nūrbakshīya between Medieval and Modern Islam, Studies in Comparative Religion*. Columbia: University of South Carolina Press.

Behar, Ruth. 2007. *An Island Called Home: Returning to Jewish Cuba*. New Brunswick, New Jersey: Rutgers University Press.

Bejamin, Walter. 1936/2008. *The Work of Art in the Age of Mechanical Reproduction*. Penguin Adult.

Chatterjee, Gayatri. 2005. *Bollywood in Transnational perspective*. In R. Kaul and Ajay J. Sinha (eds), *Bollywood: Popular Indian Cinema through a Transnational Lens*. New Delhi: SAGE Publications.

Chosjor, Sonam. 2010. Beyond Kashmir, Understanding Ladakh. In Rekha Chowdhary (ed.), Identity Politics of Jammu and Kashmir. Delhi: Vitaasta.

Dutta Madhusree, Flavia Agnes, and Neera Adarkar (eds). 2000. *The Nation, the State and Indian Identity*. Kolkota: Stree and Samya Books.

Fewkes, Jacqueline H. 2008. *Trade and Contemporary Society along the Silk-road: An Ethno-History of Ladakh*. London and New York: Routledge.

Gell, Alfred. 1998. *Art and Agency*. Oxford: Claredon Press.

Grimshaw, Anna. 2001. *The Ethnographer's Eye: Ways of Seeing in Anthropology*. Cambridge: Cambridge University Press.

Gupta, Radhika. 2005. *Asad Ashura: An Indigenous Cultural Tradition*. Paper presented at the IALS conference, Kargil.

Hasan, Mohibul. 1959/2005. *Kashmir under the Sultans*. Delhi: Aakar Book.

Harvey, Andrew. 1984. A Journey in Ladakh. Boston, Massachusetts: Houghton Mifflin.

Jaitley, Jaya. 1999. *Crafts of Jammu, Kashmir & Ladakh*. Ahmedabad: Mapin.

Kavoori, Anandam P., Aswin Punathambekar. 2008. *Global Bollywood.* New York: New York University Press.

Khan, Bashir Ahmad. Spring 2000. The Ahl-i-Hadith: A Socio-Religious Reform Movement in Kashmir. *The Muslim World*, 90(1/2): 137–157.

MacDougall, David. 1997. The Visual in Anthropology. In Marcus Banks and Howard Morphy (eds), *Rethinking Visual Anthropology* (pp. 276–295). New Haven, Connecticut: Yale University Press.

Martin, van Beek. October–December 1999. Hill Councils, Development, and Democracy: Assumptions and Experiences from Ladakh. *Global, Local, Political*, 24(4): 435–459. http://www.leh.nic.in/pages/lahdcl.html; http://kargil.gov.in/lahdck/lahdck.html

Grist, Nicola. 2008. *Urbanisation in Kargil and Its Effects in the Suru Valley.* Leiden, the Netherlands: Brill.

———. 1995. Muslims of Western Ladakh. *The Tibet Journal*, 20 (3): 59–70.

———.1998. *Local Politics in the Suru Valley of Northern India.* PhD Thesis, Goldsmiths College, London University.

Kaul, Suvir. Spring 2011. 'An' You will Fight, Till the Death of It ...': Past and Present in the Challenge of Kashmir. *Social Research*, 78(1): 173.

Pirie, Fernanda and Martijn Van Beek. 2008. *Modern Ladakh Anthropological Perspectives on Continuity and Change Leiden.* Boston, Massachusetts: Brill.

Rai, Mridu. 2007. *Hindu Rulers, Muslim Subjects.* New Delhi: Permanent Black.

Ranjan, Aditi and M.P. Ranjan. (eds). 2005. *Handmade in India*, Chapters on Ladakh. New Delhi: Mapin.

Rapport, Nigel and Joanna Overing. 2002. *Social and Cultural Anthropology: The Key Concepts.* London: Taylor & Francis.

Rizvi, Janet. 1996. *Ladakh: Crossroads of High Asia* (pp. 209–212, 3rd edition). New Delhi: Oxford University Press.

Rizvi, Janet. 2001. *Trans-Himalayan Caravans: Merchant Princes and Peasant Traders in Ladakh.* New Delhi: Oxford University Press.

Rizvi, Janet and Monisha Ahmad. 2009. *Pashmina.* Mumbai: Marg Foundation.

Savasere, Renuka. Winter 2010–Spring 2011. Cradle of Craft. *A Tangled Web, IIC Quarterly*, 37(3 and 4): 286.

Sheikh, Abdul Ghani. 2005. Islamic Architecture in Ladakh. In Monisha Ahmed and Clare Harris (eds), *Ladakh: Culture at the Crossroads.* Mumbai: Marg.

———. 2007a. *Ladakh and its Neighbours, Past and Present.* Paper presented at IALS conference, Leh (Part III Regional Perspectives).

———. 2007b. *Transformation of Kushko Village.* Paper presented at IALS conference, Leh.

———. 2010. *Reflections on Ladakh, Tibet and Central Asia, Yasmin House, Fort Road, Leh, Ladakh.* New Delhi: Skyline Publications Pvt. Ltd.

Sofi, G.M.D. 1979. *Islamic Culture in Kashmir.* Srinagar: Light & Life Publishers.

Zubdavi, Sheikh Mohammad Jawad. 2005. *History of Balti Settlements in the Indus Valley around Leh.* Paper presented at IALS conference, Kargil.

Zuthsi, Chitralekha. 2004. *Languages of Belonging: Islam, Regional Identity, and the Making of Kashmir.* New York: Oxford University Press.

17

Dialogue on Indigenous Studies and Fieldwork in India

Daniel J. Rycroft and Ganesh Devy

Dialogue held at Oxford Brookes University on 16 June 2009 after a workshop on 'Seeking Bridges between Anthropology and Indigenous Studies'.

GD: Dan, what is your interest in the Adivasis [indigenous and tribal peoples in India]? How did you come to the Adivasis?

DR: I first had an interaction with Adivasi people in 1992, when I visited a friend of mine who lived in West Bengal and I was thinking about possible research projects for my BA undergraduate degree in history of art. I had an interaction with people who made Chho masks—Chho being one of the masked dance genres specific to Purulia District and Seraikela District in West Bengal/Jharkhand region. I thought that research on the mask makers might help me understand the interactions between Hindu artisans and the Adivasi people. Within the context of India the distinction between tribe and non-tribe, or indigenous and non-indigenous, is not clear cut in any given region. I used the opportunity to research the Chho dance to think about the history of Hinduization, to some extent, among one of the Adivasi groups in West Bengal, known as the Bhumij, meaning 'born from the soil'.

My research took me to an understanding that Adivasi culture is very plural. It is not a form of cultural practice that is often clearly distinct from mainstream Hindu society or Indian society. The historical memory is there to suggest that Chho dance is a fairly modern form of cultural practice amongst Adivasis, pertaining to maybe the mid to late 19th century, when the Hinduized Bhumij raja [ruler] wanted to Hinduize the culture of the region, so as to enact some kind of Kshatriya [high caste] identity amongst his fellow rajas. And so what we know as Chho, in West Bengal, is quite specific to Purulia, and involves Bhumij dancers as well as Hindu artisans in the making of the costumes, masks, etc. That led me into an enquiry into Adivasi aesthetics more generally, namely the wall paintings of some of the Santal, Bhumij, also Kurmi Mahato women of Purulia and adjoining districts.

GD: Did you meet Mahasweta Devi at that time?

DR: At that time I didn't meet Mahasweta Devi. I was not so aware of the relevance of Adivasi identity or Adivasi history and culture to the social fabric as it is within the context of, then late 20th century, now early 21st century India.

GD: So, did you bring the research idea back home? Did you continue to work with that?

DR: Yes. That was a very preliminary visit and I ended up doing that research—that I just described: on the wall paintings and the Chho and the Patkars, or the scroll painters, of the region—and that was published in 1996 in the *Journal of South Asian Studies*, under the title of 'Born from the Soil: The Indigenous Mural Aesthetics of Kheroals, Jharkhand'.

GD: How old were you at that time?

DR: At that time I was … well I was born in 1972 and I did the research in 1993–1994, so I was 22 and 24 when it was published, as a recent BA graduate.

GD: So, when did you get aware of the politics of the Adivasis?

DR: The awareness of the politics of the Adivasis came later. When I did that first year-long stint of research in Purulia, I was also involved in the collecting of some materials, and those masks and scroll paintings became part of the British Museum's Asia collection. Then on graduation I worked for a year at the British Museum on a project not related to Adivasis, but related to India and the British recognition of the 50th anniversary of independence and partition. That exhibition I worked on, 'The Enduring Image', took me to Delhi and it also took me to an intellectual space where I wanted to think more about histories of collecting, modes and practices of display. I enrolled in an MA course in the History of Art at the University of Sussex, under the guidance of Professor Partha Mitter. Throughout that time, namely the period when I was writing that research (it was still very early days, it was in a way quite an immature piece of academic writing). I was becoming increasingly aware of some of the contests around the representations of Adivasis and Adivasi culture, and I became aware—through my contact with Dr Pashupati Mahato, who is ...

GD: Yes

DR: ... is a cultural anthropologist

GD: Yes, yes ...

DR: ... [I]n the Anthropological Survey of India—that to engage in the representation of Adivasis or even other similar kind of folk-oriented cultural practice in Purulia is fraught with tensions. Inasmuch, to describe the tribe as a distinct group might not have brought to us an understanding of the complexities of the historical texture of colonialism, Hinduization (within the colonial period) of the Adivasi groups, and the sense of regionalism that now comes through the performance of Chho and other kinds of cultural articulation. So Pashupati Mahato gave me certain suggestions that I should also think about how Sido and Kanhu [Murmu], the leaders of the Santal rebellion, or more generally the Santal *Hul* [the rebellion itself], have become part and parcel of Adivasi self-representation through scroll paintings, and through maybe some dance genres as well.

So at that time I hadn't heard of Sido and Kanhu because the region that I was in was slightly distinct from the regions that were more closely involved in the rebellion. Nonetheless, I encountered at that time (when I started my MA studies) the central, or rather integral, significance of the Santal *Hul* and Birsa Munda's *Ulgulan*, in subaltern studies. I was quite enchanted at the time by the work of Ranajit Guha, *Elementary Aspects of Peasant Insurgency in Colonial India*, where the figure—the historical trope—of the tribal insurgent is very carefully thought through, in terms of what insurgency means within the context of an agrarian anti-colonial society, and what to write about agrarian insurgency means in the context of a postcolonial historiography.

GD: That's right.

DR: And so that allowed me, in a way, to question not only how Adivasis, and other people within some of these more marginal districts, represent the memory of the rebellion—but beyond that, because of my context within British academia, I was more interested in thinking from an art historical, or a kind of a visual cultural point of view. I researched how the rebellion became highly visible in both the colony and also the metropolis at the time that was contemporary with the suppression of the rebellion. So [I questioned] what it meant for British artists and British editors, either based in India or in London, to produce the image of the insurgent subaltern Adivasi at that time.

GD: Yes.

DR: Because subaltern historiography will often, well not even often, [it will] fully leave out the questions around visual representation. So I carried on research connected to a PhD at Sussex University on the theme of *Representing Rebellion*, and that work was produced as a monograph with Oxford University Press in 2006 [*Representing Rebellion: Visual Aspects of Counterinsurgency in Colonial India*].

GD: So when did you visit India the next time? You mentioned your second visit. When was the third one?

DR: I visited India twice when I was an undergraduate to work on the Chho dance and related Adivasi aesthetics in Purulia district, and then I went again [after the British Museum visit] to Gujarat in 2000 when I was starting out on my PhD. That is when I visited your own institute, Bhasha, with a view to conducting research at Santiniketan [in West Bengal] later on. I found that a very enabling moment in my intellectual development, and more generally for sharing ideas, because at that stage I had not really thought through the PhD project. I had not thought about the extent that this would become manifest in a monograph, because the ideas that it developed were much more formative then. I was thinking more about the tensions between nationalist modernist representations of the tribe, or as it was configured through modernist artistic discourse, you know, the Santals specifically at Santiniketan. I was also interested in thinking about the interplay between colonial anthropological ideas of tribe or aboriginal people and then how that discourse of difference was negotiated through some of the nationalist modernist thinkers and artists working before Independence in India.

So that was how the project was envisaged then and I found it very helpful to meet people such as K.K. Chakravarty [former director] at the Indira Gandhi National Museum of Mankind [Bhopal], thinking around Indian anthropological display strategies and collection strategies. I also visited Santiniketan but came down with a very bad bout of malignant malaria and couldn't stay at Santiniketan at that time. On returning to the

UK the project involving Santiniketan was put on hold and I directed my research attention towards the imperial archive. That was how the sole focus for that project came to be on the Santal rebellion and the British involvement in the construction of a Santhal identity within this region—known as the Rajmahal Hills, which is now part of Jharkhand—in the mid-19th century.

GD: So how do you keep up with the developments in India, staying here? What are the means? Is it books, or blogs and emails, or newspapers? You are very informed on issues.

DR: Thanks [laughs].

GD: Or is it your imaginative leap which helps you to transcend the distance?

DR: On completing the book I wanted to generate a new research project which was more to do with contemporary representations of the rebellion, the Santal rebellion, within Jharkhand. So I figured that I needed to change my method away from subaltern historiography, or postcolonial approaches to historiography, and slightly away from the Victorian era media analyses that I was doing, towards more of an engaged ethnographic approach. By invoking the concept, or practice, of ethnography I was interested in how those ideas of identity—being produced with reference to history, with reference to anti-colonial movements—actually became part of today's social and cultural fabric, especially within any given state, namely Jharkhand. I needed to, in a way, make my work known to people outside the historical and art historical studies type of communities: to make it accessible and relevant to people interested in these kinds of histories and also these kinds of ethnographic issues, to some extent, in India.

And so I met up with a person called Dhuni Soren, who is a diasporic Santal living in the UK, who I came to know through a web forum called 'We Santhals', as in we, 'us', Santals. And through his interest in the project he introduced me to a lot of interesting Santal activists, living in the Santal Parganas area of Jharkhand and elsewhere. And it was with his blessing and facilitation that I was then able to make my historical interpretations known to Santal intellectuals, such as those involved at the Sido Kanhu University in Dumka, in the Santal Paraganas, and not only intellectuals and academics but also those advocating Adivasi self-rule, with some reference to the Santal rebellion in their thinking.

That is how I then approached the visual ethnography and worked very closely with the Indian Confederation of Indigenous and Tribal Peoples

(ICITP), which is a New Delhi-based activist network involving Adivasi, or indigenous and tribal peoples, movements throughout South Asia. They have a wide representation across five so-called zones. And under the rubric produced by ICITP, towards an Indigenous Peoples' reclaiming of indigenous histories, we together embarked on a collaborative film project. This allowed me to take my visual research into uncharted intellectual territory, for me at least, because all I was really trying to do at the beginning of the project was to document statues commemorating the rebellion. The inclusion of this approach within the ICITP rubric was not foreseen at the beginning of the project. It came about through the interactions held in Delhi and in Jharkhand. I wanted to see where the statues were, to see who made them, to see what role they had either in the day-to-day lives of Santal Adivasis or in the festivals commemorating the rebellion: those kinds of things.

But the 'indigeneous histories' rubric allowed that interest to be much more networked within an Adivasi movement in Jharkhand, so that a kind of collaborative approach to the research could take place. And the result of that collaboration was two documentary films (*Hul Sengel: The Spirit of the Santal Revolution* [2005, dir. Rycroft and Tudu] and *Hul Johar: The Long March to Bhognadih* [2006, dir. Tudu and Rycroft]). One of them [*Hul Sengel*] was released on the 150th anniversary of the Hul itself, on the 30th June, and it covered the collective memory of the *Hul* through an extended conversation with descendents of Sido Murmu, through an extended conversation with other people in Jharkhand, and also outside, to whom the rebellion is of continued importance, in terms of how an Adivasi subjectivity may be established in today's society. And so this film was shown at the *mela*, the festival commemorating the 150th anniversary, which in itself was an interesting event and this formed the subject matter for the second documentary. Both of these documentaries I co-directed with Joy Raj Tudu, who is a Santal activist, and he was national coordinator of ICITP, and he took more responsibility as co-director in the second film. Really that had much more of his lead directing role, in terms of documenting the return of diasporic Santals to Jharkhand. For the first time, there was this international ...

GD: Confluence ...

DR: Yes, a meeting, involving a long *padayatra* [foot march] from Dumka all the way to Bhognadih in the days preceding June 30th in 2005. The first film is called *Hul Sengel*: 'sengel' literally translates as fire, and so we translated *Hul Sengel* as the spirit or the fire of the Santal rebellion. And then the second film is called *Hul Johar: The Long March to Bhognadih*. The first film had a very wide distribution through ICITP and the second film hasn't yet been translated into English, in terms of subtitles. It only exists as a Santali language film. I say only because it is meaningful in that sense. It doesn't serve an ethnographic research purpose. It is more of an activist line that is assumed in that film. But again the film-making process allows me to think through interesting representational issues that are perhaps ignored by subaltern studies. It deals with oral, performative, and visual and poetic responses and engagements with *Hul* memory. It has been very interesting as it opens up the whole question of what the limits of representation are. Because when you are working within the field of collective memory, often you may have a spiritual dimension that you can't really find in the historical archive. It is very important, I think, in the context of the multiple meanings of the rebellion in Jharkhand today, that this sense of connection—between today's Adivasis and the spirit of the rebellion—[is represented]. This informs quite a lot how current resistance against the exploitative processes within Jharkhand state [is imagined] and also informs how this notion of Adivasi self-rule actually articulates itself. It is almost in the name of Sido and Kanhu that some of these assertions of Adivasi autonomy are actually finding some signification.

GD: Are indigenous scholars and activists here [for the workshop at Oxford] able to relate to your work in India.

DR: I think within the context of the global indigenous peoples' movement, there is less of an awareness in the very entity of an Adivasi. I think it is more focused on indigeneity within the context of settler colonialism and the resultant nation-states. So, I find it interesting if I'm talking about indigenous studies, say to a group of students—because I have set up a course at the University of East Anglia, which is where I now teach, on indigenous arts and indigenous peoples—that it is about positioning the Adivasi history and the concept of indigeneity in India alongside Australia and America. So this terrain of indigeneity is very uneven across those three contexts, but nonetheless it brings into the research purview, perhaps, a more open approach to the whole concept of indigeneity if you are involving not 'minority indigeneities', because that is the wrong terminology, but [those that are] less visible within the whole indigenous studies remit.

GD: What may be the reason for these events? For although a lot of Indian scholarship is available in the English language—the number of such people who have written in English is fairly large—yet the awareness of the Indian Adivasis, their struggles, their plights, has not reached Africa, Australia, the North America, South America; yet here is the largest group, in sheer number, 87 million, officially. In real terms, it may be less or it may be more. Yet it is a very large number.

DR: I think there are a number of reasons. One might be because—at the beginning of this indigenous resurgence, say in the 1950s or the 1960s, when the International Labour Organization was first thinking about rights for indigenous peoples and how to, perhaps, instrumentalize anti-racist agendas through an international network of governments and unions, etc.—the notion that Adivasis were indigenous perhaps was not articulated. Because although the concept of Adivasi was out there, in relation to how the so-called tribal populations in India started to think of themselves as an inter-ethnic, inter-regional assembly or movement, it was not so readily recognized, I don't think, at that time by influential anthropologists or historians.

And so there was perhaps a [nationalist] denial, or a rejection, of colonial era and colonialist attempts to make the tribal people 'aboriginal'. Because within the colonial period, obviously racial processes were firmly in place—through the administration that assumed the aboriginality of the so-called tribal people—and the concept that the tribal people were somehow aboriginal, and that other Indians were non-aboriginal, could not at that time really fit with any wider national decolonization agenda.

Because within the national decolonization movement, for example, led by Congress, the 'tribals' were part of this wider sympathetic image of Indian civilization, seen through the lens of unity-in-diversity [was out there]. That was fine. But to suddenly think about the specific autonomy rights of Adivasis—towards Adivasi self-rule or any kind of self-determination or sovereignty, even within the context of the nation, not as in 'against the nation', but within a decentralized nation—this was just too much for the national elite to really contemplate. And part of that, obviously, is to do with partition.

GD: So please tell me, the Naxalite [Maoist] movement emerged in the 1960s. That was the great moment for them. Every newspaper had lead editorials on 'what is Naxalbari?', 'what is happening there?', 'the neglect of the Adivasis' ... And why did that Adivasi identity begin within an Indian consciousness, within Indian media, academic discourse, and writing?

Subaltern studies came up afterwards, but still [what about] the sharpness with which the Adivasi identity should now emerge, within the Indian thinking and, therefore, the global thinking? You are right. If it is not there in the Indian thinking, how will it be there in the thinking outside? So, what is the reason that while the Naxalite movement attracted attention, the Adivasi identity should not attract so much attention? Discrimination, landlessness, there being landless peasants, these were the main things that Indians discussed.

DR: I think ...

GD: But 'cultural identity' has a different history. Do you think that if such an outburst had happened outside the framework of a Marxist party [that the idea of Adivasi identity would be recognized as such]?

DR: I think it is a very pertinent question even today, as to how a Leftist intellectual configuration deals with indigeneity, because if we really did think about, for example, the convergence of subaltern studies approaches to resistance alongside, or meeting along the way, the indigenous studies interest in indigeneity or the indigenous movement, then we would perhaps have to think about how this meeting has occurred intellectually and in other contexts also. I think in the context of indigeneity and resistance in South America, for example, there may be a convergence between indigenous studies and subaltern studies, but I don't think there have been too many advocates of that kind of intellectual convergence in the context of South Asia. Partly this is because subaltern studies have generated their own set of methodological questions, their own rubric, their own dynamic within the academy, and their own movement away from agrarian insurgency to other kinds of subalternity.

And so if you are returning to the questions of resistance, indigeneity, subalternity, you are perhaps having to refer to the early subaltern studies, and those to some extent have been left behind now, I think, by historians even though people might find them of significance, encountering them for the first time. But the concept of Adivasi studies is something that we need to bring in, because it might allow us to somehow bridge the intellectual terrain of subaltern studies with the methodological and anthropological scope of tribal studies, and to allow perhaps shifts to take place in both camps, so that Adivasi studies can actually configure themselves as such.

And that is a process that I am starting to think more seriously about and something that I am trying to do through the volume that I am working on at the moment, *The Politics of Belonging in India: Becoming Adivasi*, where along with my co-editor Sangeeta Dasgupta we are trying to think about the intellectual and conceptual limitations of tribal studies as a particularly hegemonic academic entity. Tribal studies configure the tribe in ways that routinely marginalize issues around resistance, around being Adivasi, around collective memory, and instead [these tribal studies] focus, in a much more positivist and politically applicable way, on key concepts in

348 Daniel J. Rycroft and Ganesh Devy

tribal development and tribal welfare, etc. Part of the relevance that tribal studies had in India, through the decades since Independence, was that it allowed the idea of cultural difference to be configured. This routinely, in my view, subordinates and, therefore, subalternizes Adivasis to a very large extent. Now, I'm not generalizing completely, across the board in terms of all Adivasis, because it's a very complex picture of being indigenous in India.

GD: I think your aim is right. There is one more feature I wanted to ask you, if I may. The figure of the Adivasi comes up more in artistic terms, as a singer and a dancer, with the drums. Now whereas in reality, in historical facts, the Scheduled Castes had a major role to play in Indian music. They were the drum makers. They were the *shehnai* players. They played one-stringed instruments. They provided the temple music throughout South India. The Adivasis did not. It seems to me that India has imagined an identity for the Adivasis, and it is in terms of that identity that Adivasis are described.

DR: There is a dominant framework, or an enframing, of Adivasi culture that continues through popular representations, in the media, on TV. It also to some extent features in Adivasi self-representations of indigenousness.

GD: On January 26 National Parade, Scheduled Castes are not invited to dance, but Adivasis invariably come and dance.

DR: The iconography of 'the Adivasi'—no, it is not even that—it is the iconography of 'the tribal' that is portrayed. And it is the iconography of the tribal because it somehow calls up that image of otherness that was part and parcel of elite attempts to create an autonomous Indian national sphere before Independence. And this is why the Santiniketan school artists were so important, because they were really instrumental in focusing this idea of a 'Santal' [tribal] dance, and harnessing that idea of what they perceived to be an autonomous non-western cultural space. And they appropriated that and brought it into the modernist visual vocabulary as a way of articulating Indianness. And nationalist artists, as written about by Partha Mitter and Tapati Guha-Thakurta, had various ways of addressing Indianness, and perhaps it responds to some dominant orientalist and primitivist notions. But nonetheless the internalization of these notions and the reconfiguring of the image of the so-called oriental and the so-called primitive, through these modernist practices and vocabularies, are something which maybe inspired the national culture at the time of Independence to perpetuate that image.

Now that is just one trajectory. I think there are other trajectories as well. I think visual anthropologists also had a role to play, for example, the connection between Verrier Elwin and someone like Sunil Janah, and the photographic representation of tribal culture is relevant. And there are so many interesting subplots, if you like, to the narrative of visual anthropology in India and in relation to Elwin one of those subplots is to do with the gendering of the Adivasi and the embodiment, through costumes and gestures, of this so-called distinct tribal heritage. And when these terms of otherness and difference were allowed to be perpetuated through the museumization of the tribal, or in political terms the Scheduling of the tribal, the whole concept of tribal culture assumes a reified substance or texture that perhaps goes against the grain of Adivasi notions of being and belonging: because it is a version of Adivasi identity that can be museumized.

Yet I think that Indian anthropology has now gone away from that to some extent. It has critiqued it and it is devising new ways of documenting and engaging people with tribal heritage. But nonetheless it remains 'tribal heritage', I think, rather than Adivasi heritage: tribal in as much as [when it is presented] it seems to be located, within a particular state within India. They are seen as distinct tribes, which in itself is a problematic entity, due to the cultural convergence both between different Adivasi groups and also between Adivasis and non-Adivasis groups. And this is where your point about the Scheduled Caste culture, for want of a better word, is so interesting.

Well, I have seen one or two very interesting films about Scheduled Caste performance, 'songs of resistance', this kind of thing, through the likes of Himal Film South Asia, and this kind of outlet. I think there is a visibility towards Dalit performativity, through activist film-making, etc. But it is part of the longevity of this idea that tribal people are somehow distinct from mainstream Indian culture that allows this notion of a tribal identity to be so resonant in the museological and popular culture domains.

GD: This one thing I wanted to ask you: tribals are not seen as polluting in the Indian social thought. The Scheduled Castes 'pollute'. Even the shadow of a Scheduled Caste falling on you is a cause enough to go and have a bath once again. With the Adivasi that was not the case. At least, that was not said to be so. So within the framework of totems and taboos, sacred and the polluting, the Adivasi was 'outside'. Almost like the irrational 'other' of the Brahmin, in many ways. The shaman was allowed to survive. The Buddhist priest was finished, and Buddhist shamanism was finished. And the Jain *munis* were hunted out. They [Brahmins] kept fighting with Islamic prayer groups all the time. Claiming and declaiming temples and mosques. In relation to Christian priests, but for the British political power, there was not such a great sympathy. While the Brahmin priest class tried to ensure that all other priest classes or religious political classes (people with clout) were finished, they did not touch the Adivasi shaman. That is a mystery. And also, they kept many Adivasi communities outside this fold of pollution and non-pollution. They allow Adivasis to enter their houses and offer and share food, while the Scheduled Castes will not be allowed that privilege. I am using really wrong political language right now.

DR: I have seen …

GD: This is something that needs to be understood.

DR: I have seen a lot of discrimination against Adivasis, so that kind of accepting relationship that you were addressing [is less visible to me]. But that may be the case in some regions historically. And by discrimination, for example, I mean not allowing Adivasis to drink in certain tea shops. I mean, obviously, there needs to be an interaction, to allow exchanges of goods, at the marketplace. But in the Adivasi areas that I have been familiar with there have been a lot of inter-relations between some of the [non-Brahminical] artisan, Hindu, groups, and the so-called tribal, or Adivasi, people.

On an everyday level, for example, women from the metal-casting group (the Malhar) visit Santal families and do tattoos, or the scroll paint-ers (the Patkar) visit the family members of a deceased Santal at the time of a funerary ritual. And more generally within that marketplace culture that became prevalent within the colonial regime, it allowed Adivasis to have very close interactions with non-Adivasis on a weekly basis. So, on the theme of the relationships between Adivasis and non-Adivasis, or Adivasis and Hindus, I think that the colonial economy, or the Adivasi participa-tion in the colonial economy, was premised on the [colonial] fact that Adivasis had to be civilized through participation in the marketplace.

Colonials were very keen to harness the economic potential of Adivasis, and through de-forestation new agricultural practices could hold sway as commercial and capitalist activities. Obviously this eagerness underpinned a lot of the colonial endeavour, and this meant that certain changes in liveli-hood took place that went along with the wider economic transformations. There were also important social and cultural transformations, if you are thinking about it from an Adivasi perspective. These included shifts from perhaps a nomadic kind of existence, to one that was more settled. As you were speaking about in the Seeking Bridges conference, these shifts were especially relevant for the so-called criminal tribal community. Such groups were integral to colonial attempts to civilize, this is perhaps the wrong word, but somehow acculturate people who were seen as somewhat deviant, in cultural and political terms, etc. Maybe through making crafts they would be able to show off their cultural heritage, supposedly, in a way that might benefit them economically.

I am reading a book at the moment called *The Baiga*, by Verrier Elwin, which talks very interestingly of colonial attempts to shift Baiga cultivation from forest-based cultivation to an agrarian cultivation. Elwin talks quite subtly about the resistance amongst the Baiga Adivasi to these attempts to transform their agricultural practices in the late 19th century. But going back to the earlier question around purity and pollution, the sense of caste may operate also within Adivasi societies. Elwin, within that book, talks about the different Baiga identities where there is a 'caste system', for want of a better word, emerging between the dominant caste and the more, in his terms, authentic Baigas, who are themselves concerned with maintaining that connection to *bewar*, or shifting cultivation, and less keen on taking the plough.

But he talks very interestingly, and it is quite problematic as well, because at the time he was writing in the 1930s, he talked about the various levels of Hinduization amongst the Adivasi people. I think at that time he was not anti-Hindu in any way, but that he was more interested in generating a wider understanding of Adivasi religion and Adivasi spirituality centred, in the case of the Baiga, on the *gunia* (the magicians) and the *dewar* (the priests). And so that is, in a way, important because the 1930s were fraught with tensions around what constituted aboriginal culture, from the point of view of the colonialists, and what constituted Indian culture, from the point of view of the nationalists. And the sense that Adivasis had a distinct religion is something that was very hard to accommodate, maybe in both discourses.

And in relation to the earlier question around Hindu/Adivasi relations, I think nowadays with the rise of Hindutva, or right wing religious nationalism, there is a much keener attempt by some of the dominant castes to Hinduize Adivasis, in such a way that primordialises Indianness. And by that I mean it attaches an imagined longevity to the concept of *Rama-rajya*, the rule of Rama [the Vaishnava Hindu deity], and bringing into the fold of Rama these Adivasis who are seen from that position to be Indian, on account of their indigeneity, but not Adivasi. Because an Adivasi identity for them would mean to somehow rip the foundations from under the feet of Hindu nationalists, in terms of their claims to their indigeneity—this is the wrong word—their exclusivity to the Indian soil. And even the metaphor of soil is something that was very alive in the 1930s. Elwin was talking about constructing this terminology of Bhumijan, or 'people of the soil', for Adivasis. Obviously Gandhi was talking in terms of Harijan [people of God, for Dalits]. So, it's a kind of parallel identity.

GD: You see, the Mahabharata gives a wonderful commentary on the relationship between tribes—I mean, I am using the term tribe, I don't like it—Adivasis and the others in society. There are episodes, narratives, which have a good historical value, if not entire historical validity. A lot of the Mahabharata is a description of wars between eastern [Adivasi] people and the rest of Indians. It was an attempt to bring together all of the Adivasis and create an empire out of them. Krishna, Vasudeva himself, was a shepherd. He got the title of Vasudeva by virtue of having more than 10,000 cows. And he aspired to get that. He fought for it through great cunning. And he was starting to put together an empire, it seems. There is such a story in the Mahabharata: a Kshatriya clan was exterminated six times by a man called Parasuram. They were axed—the Kshatriya and Brahminical clans—altogether. These are myths, but these are not entirely myths. This is history, but it is not absolutely history based on archaeological evidence. But a lot of evidence is available, particularly through descriptions of constellations and evidence in rhythm, rhyme, language, diction, and so on.

DR: So, are you suggesting that Parasuram and the old idea of Adivasi are somehow matched up?

GD: There have been wars in India: big wars, between the 'cow people' and the 'horse people', between the pastoral nomads and the state-building Kshatriyas, and religion-building or philosophy-building Brahmins, and so on. Gautum Buddha actually built up all of these threads. His popularity was phenomenal. He spent 41 years talking about his ideas in tribal languages only. He did not use Sanskrit and he did not allow the coding of what he said. He said, 'Every time I say things, they will be different. Please feel free to translate what I am doing. In essence, change it.' This is because he belonged to the oral tradition.

DR: How do feel about the assimilation of Buddhist philosophy?

GD: He was born in a tribe, in the eastern area, near Nepal.

DR: But how do you feel about the incorporation of Buddhist thought?

GD: They [Buddhist ideas] have gone to Scheduled Castes now. The new Buddhists, all the Scheduled Castes, are taking the Buddha as an anti-Brahmin prophet.

DR: But someone like King Asoka was using Buddhism for building an empire.

GD: So Asoka, for very strange reasons, is the most remembered emperor in the country. There have been other empires. There was Vijayanagara Empire, which was in extent larger than Asoka's empire. It was at Hampi, it lasted a good 300 years. But the Mauryan Empire lasted for 75 years less than the Hampi Empire. In area it was only about one-third of the Hampi Empire. But in the imagination Asoka is much larger, for some reason.

DR: Do you see in the history of some of these empires an exclusion of societies or civilizations that might now be considered Adivasi or attempts to subsume them within early forms of state control?

GD: Whether they were excluded from these transactions is the first issue to be sorted out. If they are entirely excluded, then the question of subsuming them arises. In the Mahabharata period, they [tribal societies] seem to be playing at power. In the Asokan times, I think the power passed on from tribals and that was the end of the tribal power in the country historically. Then they were …

DR: But Adivasis would consider that they maintained forms of political integrity only outside of the zones of empire.

GD: They held onto this, yes. But particularly transportation was a big issue. They always provided protection for armies. They took toll tax if armies had to pass through. If armies had to cross rivers, they helped. For trade, they helped. For the rest of the time they gathered what they needed, they used land for growing what was necessary, they used the forest for what was already there.

I have seen such communities in my childhood. I was born just a little after Independence, in 1950. In the early 1950s, I used to see these people coming from the forest. I was in a very small village, as small as a small village can be. And these people were beyond that, beyond the small village. And so I have seen their way of life, in areas where roads were just not built. This was 1950, and so I imagine prior to that, the situation was more or less the same for about 2,000 or 3,000 years.

DR: In terms of a forest-based economy?

GD: The communication system was the same: because there were no roads, telephones, televisions, or newspapers. It is not possible that there existed good roads at one time and then they disappeared. So, I was seeing them at the verge of extinction, at the verge of entering a new world. And, in fact, my own desire to go to them is born out of the sights and sounds and the people I saw then.

DR: Can I ask you about the context of your museum-based engagement with Adivasi heritage? Because through the Bhasha organization and the museum/activist community project at Tejgadh [in Gujarat state], you are finding a space to bring about a greater understanding and awareness of Adivasi creativity and civilization. But in such a way that allows the concept of Indian heritage or Indian civilization to be enriched also. It is not necessarily an antagonistic situation or antagonistic relationship between the Adivasi and the non-Adivasi. It is much more harmonious. I am interested in the philosophies and histories that underline that sense of unity.

GD: You see, I got interested in them in my later years through an awareness of the disappearing languages. And in terms of my visual memory I had seen the communities. My high-school years were spent in a school built exclusively for DNTs [Denotifed and Nomadic Tribes], for the stone-crushers, and the workers. I knew their language. I picked up its nuances, I used to go to their homes, eat with them. In those years I was not aware that these people were 'denotified', I had no idea of the history, but I had first-hand knowledge of how they thought. So, I did not look at them because I had some political persuasions. I went with an open mind, as a blank slate.

Then somebody suggested to me that a museum could be created in Baroda and I found that idea very shocking, for the simple reason that building a museum in Baroda would have taken ₹30 lakh [300 thousand] or more. But to go to an Adivasi village from Baroda, getting in a bus, would have taken only ₹30. So I said, this is a sheer waste of money. Who has the right to uproot the whole leisure of a community and bring it here for commerce and for cheap entertainment? Therefore, I decided to build such a museum in the village.

The first step of retaining cultural identity is to articulate traditions. Then out of that pride, one can find the courage to present to the world the wisdom that one has, and also demand the rights that have been earned. So, it is to generate a strong sense of identity that I wanted the museum. For the museum at Tejgadh we do not have a wall on one side and a wall on the other, like the walls in this room. In the building we have only one wall. On the other side there is no wall. It is a courtyard. Children come and play in the museum. People are allowed to touch the objects, which means they are allowed to pick up things and take them away, and bring new things. Though we have a good register of what belongs there. Nobody has ever stolen anything.

But we never look at them as objects, never. When they bring their musical instruments, they bring them with prayers, they worship them. All of that is part of the museum.

DR: When you say, 'a pride in an identity', that identity is presumably quite a multifaceted one. Not just about being a member of a so-called tribal group, or any given village, or region, but does it allow for a national citizenship to be negotiated in a particular way, or an international indigeneity to be negotiated in a particular way?

GD: You know, the Indian government has turned them into beggars. The situation is so bad that if anything has to be done in a village, people now believe that it is the government's duty: that the government will come into it. Through them, nothing happens. If it is within the family or extended family, they [the Adivasis] do everything. But if there is a broken truck, lying slightly outside the village blocking the road to the village, they will not remove it. They may take away the planks and burn them as firewood, but they will not remove it. They say that the government will do it. Even if they are to do family planning, they will expect to benefit from a government scheme or something like that. This has happened to all Indian villages.

The Indian village is broken in the last 50 years. I think that is the most tragic thing to have happened in India: because India was essentially the village. Even a large city is an Indian city because it is village-like, not because it is like New York, or London, or something like that. Bombay and Calcutta are two exceptions because they were built especially to be like what they have, and fairly recently, just 300 years ago. So, I was saying that it is the broken spirit of the Indian village that is also affecting the Adivasi villages.

DR: Is the articulation of Adivasi identity and heritage, within this framework of 'village India', part of an anthropological paradigm or a political swadeshi [Gandhian self-reliance] paradigm, or both, or neither?

GD: I have not been so interested in other [non-Adivasi] villages. Of course, if a natural calamity takes place there, like earthquake, I'll definitely rush to the rescue. Or, if there is a war, I'll go and work as a volunteer, in the first aid or send dispatches and so on. I do not have hatred for other villages or societies, but I do have a special affection now for the Adivasi villages. I am convinced that the technology of one's civilization, which encourages greed without limits, is taking the world to a great ruination. And I believe that Adivasis have a model of life, ways of life, which provide a meaningful alternative.

DR: But what about those Adivasis who have become incorporated within the fabric of a global India?

GD: It is natural that this should happen. If one was to try to restrict them, or be overcritical of them, that would be something like Hindu fundamentalists being critical of people who wear short skirts. No, it is a natural process. There are always transgressors, migratory people. When this happens to a larger section of that community, it is a thing to worry about. But if there are some individuals to whom this is happening, 10 to 20 per cent or something like that, this is because they live in the 21st century. They live in Indian states, the universities are in their travelling distance, and government jobs are there. Factories have come up. If you put up 25 factories 50 km from a tribal district, why will people not go and find jobs there? It is very natural. So, many Indians have migrated from the cities to the US, the UK, Asia, and Australia. Decidedly, something similar is happening there [in relation to out migration from Adivasi districts]. But having said this there is still a substantial population of Adivasis with an understanding of their traditions. That understanding is worth preserving.

DR: Is that understanding shaped by a frame of reference, such as tribe or indigenous, or Adivasi, or is it of a particular region, or a particular locality?

GD: Adivasi. Not janajati, not tribe. These are people that traditionally, even prior to the British times, have been seen as Adivasis. Though the term is being used after the British time, and the English term 'tribe' came in and was used in the official language. In medieval and ancient literature you have a notion of Adivasi, and to any sensible Indian it does not appear as a recent term. Though its use has acquired a greater currency in recent times, in the consciousness one always knew that Adivasis lived not as part of the village, but slightly outside the village.

DR: But what about the concept of swadeshi, autonomy or self-reliance, or to some extent indigenous belonging? This is a concept favoured by Gandhi obviously. Do you think the concept is relevant in relation to Adivasi heritage?

GD: Well you know the historical context. Gandhi, and before Gandhi Aurobindo Ghosh (after Bengal was partitioned), came up with the idea of swadeshi as an economic boycott of British goods. Gandhi continued with it, in this sense. But Gandhi did not carry it forward in other areas of his thinking. He did not say that pardeshi [non-Indian] participation in the swadeshi movement was undesirable. Or about knowledge, as such, he did not have much of a problem. With technology, he did have a problem, but it was not pardeshi technology as against swadeshi technology, but destructive technology against non-destructive technology. Gandhi was a Universalist in his outlook and swadeshi—in that context of boycotting the goods—to break the back of empire. It was Gandhi's politics and not his philosophy.

But swaraj [self-rule] is part of his philosophy, and not part of his politics. Incidentally, on 15 August 1947 [national Independence Day], Aurobindo

Ghosh was alive, and so was Gandhi. Neither of these were in Delhi, neither were invited to the celebrations, nor did any newspaper in India print even a statement by Aurobindo or Gandhi on the great happening. For them, freedom was not so much of a political programme, but something way beyond that. They were thinking of larger humanity, as in the typical 19th century or universal philosophical tradition.

DR: But can I ask just one more thing about whether the concept of Adivasi swaraj or Adivasi self-rule resonates in response to the Gandhian ideal of swaraj, or whether it is a more particularist swaraj that only resonates in the context of an indigenous self-determination?

GD: The idea of swaraj was taken up by two others in India, political leaders. Incidentally, Ambedkar never took it up. Lokmani Tilok, he used the term for the first time, in a very strong political sense, during a 1907–1908 trial. He stated that 'freedom is my birth right', 'Swaraj is my birth right.' It was then that swaraj became an agenda in the country. But for Adivasi swaraj, the first thing to note is that Gandhi did not have any great engagement with the Adivasis. His contribution was that he knew Thakkar Bapa. And Thakkar Bapa and Gandhi had different philosophical trajectories, though they belonged to the same state.

Thakkar Bapa worked in the Panchmahals, north of Tejgadh. He met Gandhi and Gandhi respected him, but it was not a relationship like Gandhi and Nehru. When Elwin went and lived in Gandhi's ashram, he was kept in the front room and was not allowed much access to Gandhi's home. Elwin felt that the room was like a cage. I think Elwin has described how visitors used to stare at him, because he used to wear shorts. Gandhi asked Thakkar Bapa to guide Elwin. Thakkar Bapa had not taken that seriously. Sardar Patel had asked Elwin to meet Jamnalal Bajaj. Bajaj told him about going to Bastar. Elwin did not have anything to say about the notified communities, not once.

DR: Do you think Gandhi or Thakkar Bapa made an imprint on Elwin's perception of Adivasis, or Bhumijan, as he called them?

GD: A very deep imprint, in the sense that Elwin decided to give his life for this cause. Because he had seen Gandhi and he respected Gandhi's fight for India's independence. But Elwin was very clear that Gandhi understood nothing about Adivasis. And, in fact, he mocks at Gandhi's way of life. But about Gandhi's sacrifice and integrity, Elwin was very respectful. In fact, these are the things he carried with him through his life. But he was not a Gandhian.

DR: But what about the concept of swaraj, because to some extent Elwin was attuned to issues around—not necessarily self-determination—but some kind of political power for Adivasis?

GD: During the first settlement he was. Then he started getting worried about police persecution. Then came the issues of funding. He went through a period of lack of funds. He had to go to Bombay to seek funds. I think as he moved to the second ashram he underwent a change. He had left Bapu [Gandhi] by then. Look at his writings, and he had a good style, he was a good essayist and non-fiction writer, but he does not have any significant piece on Gandhi's assassination.

DR: Do you think Elwin inspires ...

GD: That was a very tragic moment in India's history. The entire country adopts a fast. I remember, I mean I was born just a few years afterwards, but I remember the echoes of that day in my early childhood. People used to talk about that.

Swadeshi, Elwin ... you see, when the constituent assembly was formed and the policy discussions started happening, Elwin's contribution is not known as any great contribution. It was the prince in Chhatisgarh, the rajah of Bastar, Jai Pal Singh, he was a political leader. He fought for the honour and dignity of the Adivasis, and that is how the Schedules have come up: the Fifth Schedule, the Sixth Schedule, they came up because of the prince of Bastar. Jai Pal Singh fought tooth and nail, legal battles in the constituent assembly, before the Constitution was founded. Elwin had nothing to say then. But Elwin contributed later to the administrative policy.

DR: You said Elwin had nothing to do with the participation of Adivasis in terms of the decolonization?

GD: He did not think they were colonized. He did not think they had to be decolonized. I think so. I may be wrong, but he was worried about the destruction of Adivasis at the hands of Indians, not so much the colonial government.

DR: But in relation to the Baiga he was quite attuned to the fact that there were some colonial policies that were having a negative impact on forest access.

GD: Yes. There is one thing. He did use his access to the English, the governors, and Indian Congress leaders, writers in the country, anthropologists at SOAS [School of Oriental and African Studies, University of London] to promote the—not to say welfare—well-being of Adivasis. That he did. He was an honest person. He was not pretentious. But he was not a great political thinker. He had a somewhat romantic fascination for the Adivasis.

DR: Does he inspire you, your work at all, or any of your colleagues?

GD: Inspiration is in many forms.

DR: [Laughs].

GD: You know that Mahasweta Devi has a lot to do with our work. Anand Coomaraswamy did not say anything about tribals, but said a lot about craft. I have some link with him, also with Aurobindo Ghosh who was the reason for my going to Baroda. Aurobindo used to teach at the Baroda College, 80 years before I decided to go there. From Gandhi, of all the people, I have a great sense of inspiration. Elwin is somebody who consoles me when I am very gloomy.

You see, my task has been institution-building, not of my choice, but because this work developed in the form of an institution and I had to build it. And this means fund-raising, struggling with bureaucrats, explaining to friends who are not willing to see the things the way you want them to see: but not politically, not in my attitude to folklore, attitude to health care, attitude to agriculture. But at a personal level, when I feel, 'How will I sustain myself in this work?' then I often think of someone who has come all the way from England and worked here, giving his life. Why should I not do it?

But the man who most inspired me is someone I have never met and whose writings—because he did not write anything—I have never read. He was killed in Chhattisgarh by the police in the early 1980s. He was a wonderful thinker, and he would have given a new turn to this entire generation that went to Andhra Pradesh, and created the Andhra to Nepal corridor of MCC [Maoist Coordination Committee]. His name was Shankar Niyogi-Guha [pause]. The government knew, he also knew that he was being killed. He put in a complaint, but they gave him no protection. I had read the news of his death, and somewhere in my mind, I thought somebody had to continue this work.

DR: What was his involvement?

GD: He was a splinter from the Naxalite [Maoist] movement who did not agree with violent means of changing the society. And so he went to Chhattisgarh. He encouraged the creation of Chhattisgarh [as a separate state]— of self-rule. He created many constructive projects from the protest.

Santal Hul (rebellion) memorial, Bhognadih village, Jharkhand

Source: © Courtesy of D.J. Rycroft, 2003.

Sonthal dance by moonlight

Source: Courtesy of the *Illustrated London News*, 1851.

Glossary

Adivasi	Indigenous people/tribe
Bagachas	Bangladesh Garo Students Organization
Bahariya	Servant
Bakhu/Kho	The Bhutanese national dress for the male
Barmiang	Dried fish
Betaoma	Female
Betaosa	Male
Bhai	Brother
Biraderi	Patrilineage
Bombo	Shaman
Borak	Bamboo mats tied into cylindrical silos to hold potatoes or maize cobs
Cartos	Ammunition
Charninuoh	Temporary hut designed to keep bones and ashes
Charpais	Simple string beds
Chiring	A magazine
Chormoubailukhlaimo	Death ritual
Chow mtouh	Rice beer
Chu	Garo rice beer
Daal	Lentils
Dagar	Beat the ceremonial drums
Dah	Dagger/billhook
Dewar	The priest
Dhaka	Carrying basket-loads of grain harvest
Dobashisas	Particularly agricultural demonstrators and village-level workers
Druk Gyalpo	The king of Bhutan
Dzong	Fort, from administration in run
Dzongkha	The national language of Bhutan
Gajar ka halva	A dessert made of carrots and cream

Gewa	Mourning feast
Ghutka	Betel nut
Git-im	Hamlets
Gobar	Cowdung
Godi	Livestock
Gora	White
Gunia	The magicians
Harijan	The people of God, for Dalits
Hoho	Lotha elders
Hongha-motai	Two stones
Horsni	Pollution for closed group only
Huk	Jhum or slash and burn cultivation
Hukka	A smoking apparatus
Hul	Santal rebillion
Jaenimaz	Prayer mats
Jamabaju ha	Loose garment
Jana andolan	The people's movement that forced King Birendra to restore parliamentary democracy to the country
Jawans	Soldiers
Jhum	Slash and burn cultivation
Jimidar	The chief revenue collector
Kacha	Non-black topped
Kahsmang	Funeral song
Kala	Pitcher
Kali puja	Worship of Goddess Kali
Kanorphel	Leh nutrition project
Kazis	The former Sikkimese aristocrats
Khamkhaja	Drum
Khels	Wards
Kheto	Settled cultivation
Kohabar	Wall paintings
Kothoi	Dead
Kothoiaukchai	Priest for the dead
Kotli Loharan	A village whose name meant literally 'abode of the blacksmiths'
Kshatriya	High caste (warrior caste)
Kulfi	Locally made ice-cream
Laotao	Woman believed to be a spiritual person who mediates between the deceased and the afterworld

Leng and romo	As contracted between women, or the term used for leng's wife-romo
Lhadenglubatibabelari	From the time when people spoke with gods and spirits
Lohars	Blacksmiths
Maa	Mother
Madeshi	A Tarai person descended from Indian immigrants who had arrived in the 19th and 20th centuries
Mai shya	Water buffalo
Maiyohmi	Food for the deceased
Manda jatis	Lower castes
Mandi-rang-nichiti	Garo newsletter
Mangchouh	Pyre
Me shya	Beef
Mochi	Cobbler
Momins	Shias
Motaihaia	Evil spirit
Mraa	Weeds
MrangshingPhyeeba	Swiddening
Mudalalis	Businessmen
Naga shya	Chicken
Namja	Bad
Nawba	Wind
Niamarodakbewal	Customs and culture
Niamraka	Core principles
Nishi	A teammate
Nokroms	Heirs
Nuohkhai	Basket
Nuppashimmm	WeternTamang with parodied accent
Padayatra	Foot march
Pahari	Hill people
Pala	Layer
Panga	Thread
Panji	Clan
Panji-haro	Clan structure
Paraka	Organization for publishing the Garo newsletter
Pardesi	Non-Indian
Pohla	White cloth of the height of the deceased
Pullao	Food item made of rice and meat
Raja	Ruler

Rama	The Vaishnava Hindu deity
Rangma-nawba	Human soul
Rani	Queen
Rani-hood	Queen hood
Riwasa	Bamboo stick
Rusamphi	Small plant
Sahab	Sir
Sengel	Fire
Shagirds	Apprentices
Shardiya navratra	Annual Durga *puja* festival
Shoense	Morning
Songsarek	The followers of the Garo community religion
Sufis	Muslim saints
Swadeshi	Gandhian self-reliance
Swmangnuoh	Temporary memorial hut
Talwaran Mughlan	Sword of the Mughals
Talwaran Rajputan	Sword of the Rajputs
Tamanglenglaba	Wedding temple ceremony of nepalimitlaune
Taoleing	Eagle
Taukha	Crow
Tharukalyankarinisabha	Tharu welfare association
Tilla	Hillock
Toddy	White stuff
Toi	Water
Tola	Settlement
Trangteba-tewar	Husband's younger brother
Tshongdu	National assembly, the royal legislative body
Ustaad	Expert
Wangala	A Garo harvest festival
Waphiang	Raft
Yakhli	Ladder
Yarkhand	Chinese Turkestan
Yeh gari un ki hai	This car belongs to him/her
Zameen	Land
Zamindari	A system of fief, in which over-lords grant rent-free holdings to local notables

About the Editors and Contributors

Editors

Sarit K. Chaudhuri is an anthropologist working among the tribes of North-east India for the last 23 years. During 2003–2005 he was in SOAS, United Kingdom, as a postdoctoral fellow and worked for a collaborative project with SOAS, British Museum, CCRD, and Rajiv Gandhi University, Arunachal Pradesh. He worked in An.S.I., Shillong, and for the last 18 years has been working at Rajiv Gandhi University, Arunachal Pradesh. He is currently holding the post of professor and heading the Department of Anthropology. He has published 9 books and 52 papers in journals and books.

Sucheta Sen Chaudhuri is an anthropologist and currently, as Associate Professor, heading the Centre for Indigenous Culture Studies in Central University of Jharkhand, Ranchi. She has worked in An.S.I. for seven years and posted in Dehradun as well as Shillong. During 1999–2011 she worked in the Arunachal Institute of Tribal Studies, Rajiv Gandhi University, and also worked as the Founder Director, Women Study and Research Centre in the same university. She has published three books and a good number of papers in journals and books.

Contributors

Anungla Aier is a Lecturer in Department of Anthropology, Kohima Science College, Nagaland University, Kohima. Before that he worked as a Director of the Women Studies Centre, Nagaland University. Her research interests include gender, oral traditions, and folklore; culture, ethnicity, and identity studies.

Ellen Bal is an Assistant Professor in the Department of Social and Cultural Anthropology of the Vrije Universiteit of Amsterdam. She received her PhD degree in 2000 from the Erasmus University Rotterdam along with her study of ethnogenesis and group formation processes in South Asia. Her recent book entitled *They Ask If We Eat Frogs: Social Boundaries, Ethnic Categorisation and the Garo People of Bangladesh* published in 2000. Her areas of research interest include: anthropology and history of identity formation, ethnicity, migration, transnationalism, Indigenous peoples, Indian diaspora, youth, and human security.

Gautam Kumar Bera is associated with the Anthropological Survey of India for the last two decades. He has completed his Masters Degree in Anthropology with specialization in Social-cultural Anthropology and conducted doctoral research on problems of ethnicity. He is the recipient of National Scholarship for Advance Studies, University Gold Medal, Research Fellow Gold Medal (United States), and several other prestigious awards and honours. He was elected a fellow of the Royal Anthropological Institute, London, in 1992, and advisor to the Research Board of ABI, United States, in 1996. He is credited with the authorship and editorship of 30 books and 110 research publications.

Robbins Burling is a Professor Emeritus of Anthropology and Linguistics at the *University of Michigan*. He received his PhD in Anthropology from Harvard University in 1958. Much of his work focuses on the linguistics and ethnology of tribal North-east India and Bangladesh, and of related areas further east in South-east Asia. He has been working since the 1950s (though with long interruptions) with the Garo people who are found in both North-east India and in Bangladesh. He has written extensively about both the culture of these people and their language.

Ben Campbell is a social anthropologist, and teaches at the Department of Anthropology, Durham University. He has researched the impact of development and conservation projects on subsistence farming and cultural practice in the Nepal Himalayas. Some of his books include: *Racialization, Ethnicity, Genes and the Re-invention of the Nation in Europe* (2007) and *Beyond Cultural Models of the Environment: Linking Subjectivities of Dwelling and Power* (2010).

Bhaskar Chakrabarti is an Associate Professor of Public Policy and Management at the Indian Institute of Management Calcutta. He has research expertise on decentralization and local democracy. His fieldwork experience across different states in India has focused on the ways through which people in multiple social groups, the government, and NGOs attempt to manage resources. With a core competency in evaluation of policy and institutional environment towards management for implementation of development projects, Chakrabarti synthesizes knowledge from various disciplines to foster innovation in 'people's participation' as applied to practical challenges of development governance.

Arnab Das is an Associate Professor of Anthropology at the University of Calcutta, India. Apart from postgraduate course in Anthropology he also teaches postgraduate courses in Human Rights, Museology, and Human Resource Management. In two other universities of India he is a guest faculty of anthropology and Rural Development. He has supervised 10 doctoral dissertations. He is also the member of the Academic Committee of Anthropological Section in Asiatic Society, Kolkata. Besides participating in many national and international seminars and conferences he has published nearly 50 papers in national and international journals. His co-edited and contributed book is *Human Rights and the Third World: Issues and Discourses* (2012).

Debojyoti Das has received his doctoral degree from the Department of Anthropology and Sociology, School of Oriental and African Studies (SOAS), University of London.

Erik de Maaker is a Researcher and Lecturer at the Institute for Cultural Anthropology and Development Sociology of Leiden University in the Netherlands. He studied Anthropology in Amsterdam and Leiden and wrote a PhD dissertation that takes mortuary rituals as a starting point for an analysis of social structure and community in upland north-eastern India. His current research in South Asia focuses on the material and ritual dimensions of religious practices, linked to the politicization of ethnicity. de Maaker has published several articles in academic journals and edited volumes, and is preparing a monograph on the transformation of Garo social structure. He has also produced ethnographic films, such as the award winning *Teyyam: The Annual Visit of the God Vishnumurti* (Award for Excellence, American Anthropological Society, 1998).

Ganesh Devy is the Founder Director of Bhasha Research and Publication Centre, Baroda, and the Adivasi Academy at Tejgadh and was formerly professor of English at the M.S. University of Baroda. His work combines cultural campaigns for the conservation of threatened languages and human rights activism for Adivasis and nomadic communities in India. His publications include *A Nomad Called Thief, After Amnesia, Of Many Heroes*, and *Indian Literary Criticism*.

Abeer Gupta is consulting with the National Museum Institute for their Intangible Cultural Heritage Documentation based on the UNESCO conventions in Ladakh and Jammu. He graduated from NID, Ahmedabad, and then worked as an executive producer of feature and director of documentary films. He completed his Masters in Visual Anthropology from Goldsmiths College, London, in 2008, and since then, has been working extensively in Ladakh, Jammu & Kashmir, with oral histories, material cultures, and visual archives. His project 'Material and Visual Culture of Islam in Ladakh' was awarded a fellowship on Circulation of 'Popular Images and Media in Muslim Religious Spheres' by the Cluster of Excellence—Asia and Europe in a Global Context, 2010, University of Heidelberg, Germany. Subsequently, the project was awarded the Early Career Filmmaker Fellowship, 2011, by Centre for Media and Cultural Studies, TISS, for the film to document the oral history of the community.

Arjun Guneratne is a Professor and Chair of Anthropology at Macalester College in Saint Paul, Minnesota. He received his PhD from the University of Chicago in 1994. He is the author of *Many Tongues, One People: The Making of Tharu Identity in Nepal* (2002), and editor of *Culture and the Environment in the Himalaya* (2010) and *The Tarai: History, Society, Environment* (2011). He was formerly the editor of *Himalaya: The Journal of the Association for Nepal and Himalayan Studies*. He is currently working on a reader on the culture, politics, and history of Nepal.

Ali Khan is an Associate Professor of Anthropology and Department Chair at the Department of Humanities and Social Sciences at LUMS. His research interests vary from labour issues, particularly child and bonded labour, to popular culture in Pakistan focusing particularly on cinema and sports. He has previously worked in Washington and in Islamabad for the World Bank and with the International Labour Organization. Ali Khan's book *Representing Children: Power, Policy and the Discourse on Child Labour in the Football Manufacturing Industry of Pakistan* was published in October 2007. A recent co-authored book on cricket and society in Pakistan entitled *Cricket Cauldron: The Turbulent Politics of Sport in Pakistan* has just been published. He is also the general editor for a series of books on Sociology and Anthropology in Pakistan. Ali Khan has an MPhil and a PhD in Social Anthropology from the University of Cambridge in England.

Suman Nath teaches Anthropology at Haldia Government College, West Bengal. He also delivers occasional courses and is pursuing PhD in Anthropology at the University of Calcutta. He has published articles in national and international journals on issues of water resources, local governance, and politics and development. He has been recently awarded a grant by the University Grants Commission, Government of India, to do research on politics and resource allocation.

Neel Rekha is a senior fellow with the Ministry of Culture, Government of India, working on a project titled, 'Innovation and Tradition: Changing Visual Imagery in Mithila Paintings (1960–2010)'. She is currently working as a guest faculty at the Cluster Innovation Centre, University of Delhi. She worked as a junior research fellow in the Department of History, Patna University from 1999 to 2004. She was also a visiting fellow in the Department of Theology and Religious Studies, University of Leeds, from September 2007 to January 2009. She has published her research in peer-reviewed journals and book chapters and also curated two exhibitions on Maithil art in Kolkata and Leeds.

Daniel J. Rycroft is a Senior Lecturer of the Arts and Cultures of Asia at the School of World Art Studies, University of East Anglia, Norwich. He specializes in South-Asian art and anthropological history. He took up this post in 2006, and has since co-founded the journal *World Art*. He works on numerous individual and collaborative research projects. Previously Rycroft held a Leverhulme Early Career Fellowship, focusing on *Subalternity and Visual Representation in India* at the University of Sussex from 2003 to 2005. He is an editorial board member of *Art History*, and co-founder of the South-Asian Arts Group.

Mandy Sadan is a Lecturer of the History of South-East Asia at SOAS, London University. Her main research interests relate to the ethnic conflict in Burma (Myanmar), with a particular focus on the northern Kachin region. She has also undertaken research in North-east India and Yunnan, and has been involved in research projects at Oxford University and SOAS on the material and visual cultures of Arunachal Pradesh and Tibet. Her first major monograph is *Being and Becoming Kachin: Histories Beyond the State in the Border Worlds of Burma*, published in 2013.

Vijoy S. Sahay is a Professor and Head of the Department of Anthropology, University of Allahabad. Sahay was awarded doctoral degree in Anthropology from Ranchi University, in 1979, for his fascinating research work in the Nicobar Archipelago. He is the author of 6 books and 27 articles so far. Besides participating in a number of national and international seminars and conferences, he was invited as a visiting fellow by the University of KwaZulu Natal, Durban, South Africa, in 2004. He is also the editor-in-chief of the IBSS-listed international research journal, *The Oriental Anthropologist*. He has also been the member of several research and expert committees constituted by the Ministry of Forest and Environment and Ministry of Tribal Affairs, Government of India, for the protection of environment and the Primitive Tribal Groups (PTGs) of Andaman and Nicobar Islands.

A.C. Sinha is a Professor of Sociology. He taught at North-Eastern Hill University (NEHU), Shillong, and in various universities including of India, the United Kingdom, and the United States. He has a good number of published books on Sikkim, Bhutan, North-East India, and Forest History. His major publications include: *Politics of Sikkim* (1975), *Bhutan: Ethnic Identity and Social Dilemma* (1991, 1998), *Hill Cities in Eastern Himalayas* (1993), *Historical Sociology of Eastern Himalayan Forests* (1993), *Bhutan: Tradition, Transition and Transformation* (2001 and 2004), and *The Nepalis in Northeast India* (2004).

Index